PACE YOURSELF

366 DEVOTIONS FROM THE DAILY GRIND

REBEKAH TRITTIPOE

Foreword by Virelle Kidder

Printed in the United States of America
by Lightning Source Inc.
Cover design by Dennis Davidson

Library of Congress Control Number: 2010925349
ISBN 978-1-934749-76-0

CrossHouse Publishing
PO Box 461592
Garland, TX 75046
1-877-212-0933

www.crosshousepublishing.org

Unless otherwise indicated, all Scripture taken from the Holy Bible,
New International Version, copyright 1973, 1978, 1984
by International Bible Society

Dedication

To the **one and only God**, the creator of the universe and keeper of my soul,
I pay tribute.

Without Him, I am nothing.
Without Him, the pages of my heart are empty.

Acknowledgements

This project was a labor of love—and a result of love. Daily writing for a year was a challenge not only to me but to my understanding husband. On many nights the clock clicked ever closer to midnight as the keys on my laptop did likewise. Bedtime was postponed because the empty page beckoned me to fill it. And fill it I did. Thanks, Gary, for never complaining when the normal activities of day and night had to take a backseat to my writing.

I am indebted to my three dear friends who kept me accountable and on track: Bobbie Devos, Anita Moree and Jennifer Anderson. Just knowing their inboxes awaited a daily message encouraged me to never disappoint. And when I was discouraged, one of them gave feedback that spurred me on. Without them, I'm not sure the project would have been completed.

To my mother: my cheerleader, confidante and consistent encourager. Thank you for believing in me even when others did not. Thank you for being the godly example that you are. And thank you for introducing me to the Montrose Writer's Conference, where constructive criticism alongside of heartfelt support has made this book possible.

To my family and friends of whom I write: Thank you for allowing me to share your stories, if only in part. Life is such an interesting journey!

Foreword

Several years ago, Rebekah Trittipoe and I became friends at a Christian writers' conference in Pennsylvania. She plopped down at my lunch table with a million questions and several good ideas. The following year, I stayed at her home when I spoke at her church's women's retreat. I played with her cats, ate delicious homemade bread and watched her casually handle more in one day than I could do in three.

Rebekah is like no one else. She's beyond capable, upbeat and fun, an artist in many ways, creating beauty everywhere—in her garden, in her handmade furniture, in the vivid warmth of her home. I became her fan.

But in my wildest dreams I couldn't imagine a friendship with an ultra marathon runner. While I force myself to do pathetically small amounts of daily exercise, Rebekah runs hundreds of miles at a time, something I think should be illegal. Plus, she regularly leads a pack of young women who love her enough to run endless miles through the woods with her. Why would they do that? Quite possibly because she's a magnet for those starved for a vital life of faith. Afterward, around home-cooked meals and an open Bible, Rebekah feeds the souls of these young women she loves.

So why be surprised at this monumental achievement in your hands, her first 366-day devotional? Be thrilled that you and I can spend time with Rebekah without having to sweat or nurse blisters afterward. Every day we can hang around her over coffee and hear her candid take on faith, life, loving God and loving others. Nothing matters more. You'll be glad you did.

Virelle Kidder is a conference speaker and the author of six books, including Meet Me at the Well *and* The Best Life Ain't Easy *(both Moody Publishers, 2008). She and her husband, Steve, live in Sebastian, FL.*

Preface

Pulled from the recesses of a tiny closet tucked under the stairs, the simple cardboard boxes showed their age. Each, encrusted with a deep layer of dust, held valuable treasures unfitting such a humble hiding place. Choosing one, I gently blew the surface clean and pulled open the box flaps. Not yet wanting to disturb the contents, I sat up straighter in my cross-legged position and took it in before I reached to open the remaining boxes. There before me were hundreds of letters still in their faded envelopes, most written in the mid-1940s. Each had been meticulously opened, none carelessly torn. Gingerly, I pulled one from a box and began to read.

Hours passed. My legs cramped and my hands and lap grew dirty from handling the old mail. But still, a life unfolded before me—a life I didn't know. You see, these were the letters my father had written in his college years. Long before the day of email and cell phones, he kept a steady flow of letters to his parents and chums back home. Like a ping-pong game, mail bounced in both directions. And somehow, each letter was saved and sealed into a box for safekeeping.

My dad's letters, written in that distinctive yet tiny penmanship, revealed a lot about his day-to-day life. He was a descriptive writer, sharing detail some might consider mundane. I learned about his classroom habits, I read about his play on the baseball field, I saw letters of acceptance into dental school and I viewed pictures of his pals. But more importantly, through his writing I came to understand his character. I could feel his joy and his disappointments. And, I sensed his strong and steady faith. Those boxes of letters became his life's journal. I am forever grateful.

Now sixty-some years later, I take a similar path. Though without postage, I create my own journal—a collection of stories and experiences throughout a single year. Each entry is my letter sharing real life—not life the way I wish it to be but just plain life. Some entries may seem ordinary—some extraordinary. But all are written with a singular purpose: To discipline myself to see God working every day in every way.

I invite you to journey with me as I begin to train my mind to understand that this God of the vast universe is also the God of the smallest detail. Slowly and methodically, we'll work ourselves through the good and bad, the joys and sadness, the thrills and the mundane. Too often we want a dramatic theological breakthrough but fail to see the lessons in pulling weeds or watching a simple sunrise. So take a run with me through 366 days of normal, ordinary life.

Looking Forward

New Year's Day is filled with enthusiasm for keeping freshly conceived resolutions. But I am a skeptic. I have been guilty of creating my own lists that are never fully realized. The inventory includes aspirations of consistent meditation, diligence in prayer, better training for my running, publishing goals, strategies for self-employment and . . . well, my list, if only a creation of the mind, goes on and on.

In a moment of quiet, I came across Isaiah 43:15-18: "*I am the LORD, your Holy One, Israel's Creator, your King. This is what the LORD says—he who made a way through the sea, a path through the mighty waters, who drew out the chariots and horses, the army and reinforcements together, and they lay there, never to rise again, extinguished, snuffed out like a wick. 'Forget the former things; do not dwell on the past. See, I am doing a new thing! Now it springs up; do you not perceive it? I am making a way in the desert and streams in the wasteland.'*"

The nation of Israel was reminded of God's supremacy and authority. Despite the ghastly conditions heaped on Israel during their Egyptian captivity, brought on, incidentally, by their own disobedience, God saved them as they fled their captors. "Forget about past hardships and failures," God whispered. "Look to the future and see what I will do."

Last year was far from perfect. But I don't want to dwell so heavily on the past that I am blinded to what God wants to accomplish this year. I admit it. I am shaking and quaking as I start this writing adventure. I have no idea what God has in store. What if I miss something in His message? What if I am too dense or deaf to hear His voice?

I commit to honesty as I write. I will chronicle real life, real difficulties, real solutions and real joys. Hold on tight and come with me. It's sure to be quite a ride.

Sing to the LORD a new song, for he has done marvelous things; his right hand and his holy arm have worked salvation for him. (Psalm 98:1)

Daily challenge:
Begin to write your own adventure. Journaling helps you remember.

"To-do" Lists

Yahoo! Day two of the new year and so far, I've kept my resolutions. Don't laugh! Self-made promises are hard to keep despite the most glorious intentions. I'll be happy if I can keep my promises for a good thirty days—the time they (whoever the proverbial "they" happens to be) say it takes to firmly establish a habit.

I am easily diverted by the smallest distraction. For example, I planned to run six miles the other day. It was a beautiful day with sun shining and a wind that had calmed from the overnight gusts. I was excited at the prospect. But first, I tended to other tasks. I got busy with desk work, tackled errands and since I was hungry, ate pizza for lunch. Well, my hunger was satisfied, but I realized if I tried to run then, I'd probably see that pizza again.

I involved myself in other tasks while the food digested. As the clock ticked away, dinner was calling. *Oh dear. Where did the time go?* I put supper on the table, realizing that if I ate then, I'd have to wait—again—before running. Waiting meant it would be dark and cold. I felt anything but compelled to run into the frigid night. So I devised another plan. I'll just eat and get on my Nordic Track later. After cleaning up the kitchen, I poured myself a cup of coffee, picked up my computer, checked email and lost all motivation to do anything but take a hot bath and read a magazine. Before long, my head hit the pillow. I was distraught and unfulfilled, missing the opportunity to get in those miles.

Not everyone will have frustrations over not getting out for a run. Nevertheless, I imagine most of us deal with daily failures. It takes consistent and conscious effort to stay the course. I find that I am most likely to succeed when my life is well-ordered, maintaining a clear sense of priorities: a "to-do" list helps. It defines what needs to be done and provides a sense of accomplishment each time a task is checked off.

So go ahead. Become a list person and see if you don't become more efficient.

> *For though I am absent from you in body, I am present with you in spirit and delight to see how orderly you are and how firm your faith in Christ is. (Colossians 2:5)*

Daily challenge:
Every evening, create a "to-do" list for the next day. You'll waste no time figuring out what you have to do once the sun rises.

Do As Instructed

I just read the Old Testament story about Samuel anointing Saul as the coming King (I Samuel 10). As Samuel tells Saul about the things he could expect, the text sounds like something out of a super-duper spy movie. It goes something like this:

• Leave here and take a stroll near Rachel's tomb.

• Two guys are going to say this to you: "The donkeys you set out to look for have been found . . . ."

• After that, keep walking until you get to a great big tree.

• Expect three more guys to meet you there. One will be carrying three goats, another three loaves of bread and the last, a flask of wine.

• You will be offered just two of the bread loaves.

• Go ahead and accept the bread they offer.

• After that, head on over to the Philistine outpost, Gilgal.

• As you get close, you will meet a bunch of prophets coming toward you . . . .

Wouldn't this scene fit right into "Mission Impossible"? I can hear the theme song now. But stop and listen to what happens to Saul at the end of these complicated encounters. Samuel said, *"The Spirit of the Lord will come upon you in power . . . and you will be changed into a different person. Once these signs are fulfilled, do whatever your hand finds to do, for God is with you"* (I Samuel 10:6, 7).

Is that not a phenomenal display of what happens when we precisely follow God's instructions? He changes, empowers and gives us freedom to succeed. A lot of people think that following the rules is restrictive, stymieing individualism and chaining you to an antiquated set of laws. However, consider a train. If said train decides to do its own thing and leave the tracks, just how far do you think it will get? Nowhere! It will sink into the ground and be stuck, going nowhere fast. However, if the train submits to the established boundaries of the track, it gains the freedom to follow the rails to places yet unknown.

I'm sure Saul's face distorted into one of those "You gotta be kidding!" expressions as Samuel recited the instructions. But he did as instructed—with confidence, I must add—and God changed him, giving him freedom to do whatever he desired.

> *Who among you fears the LORD and obeys the word of his servant?*
> *Let him who walks in the dark, who has no light, trust in the name*
> *of the LORD and rely on his God. (Isaiah 50:10)*

Daily challenge:
Want freedom? "Trust and obey, for there's no other way."

Three Things to Live By

I don't know about you, but the first three days of the new year have been going well. I have gotten up early, grabbed my coffee and Pop-Tart (I know . . . breakfast of champions), bounded up the steps to the office and gotten right to work. I even have a new little book where I keep a list of everything I need to do, gleefully checking off each item at the completion of the task. (I just love that part!) I have tried to be organized, careful to keep my workspace clean and clutter-free. Work on my educational websites is progressing and contacts have been made for potential consulting jobs. I have cleaned the house, prepared nice suppers for our family and gotten in my workouts. But still, my list grows larger and life seems complicated.

In a way, I think we make our spiritual lives a little too complicated. Sometimes I feel like I'm trying to become "Can-do Christian"—a hero of the faith who can enter a phone booth and emerge, big *C* emblazoned on my chest, faster than Superman can change into his blue tights and red cape. I catch myself thinking, *If I just do this and then do that, I'll be okay.*

What I forget is that God did not intend for our lives to be complex and unmanageable. Rather, He is concise in letting us know how we should live. The prophet Micah captured the simplicity of it all by his query. *"And what does the LORD require of you? To act justly and to love mercy and to walk humbly with your God"* (Micah 6:8b).

There we have it. Three simple things that will guide us in our everyday living. Acting justly controls our actions toward others. Loving mercy, on the other hand, controls our reactions, while walking humbly directs our relationship with God. It sounds straightforward, but I'm not so naïve to think that it won't take a premeditated, conscious effort to live this way. However, we are not left on our own to "get 'r done".

> *The one who calls you is faithful and he will do it. (I Thessalonians 5:24)*

Daily challenge:
Take inventory of your actions today. Did you act justly, love mercy, and walk humbly?

Bad News Bears

Ever hear of the Bad News Bears? You probably remember the story of the misfit kids who found themselves on a baseball team. There were fat kids, skinny kids, weird kids, a motorcycling punk and a girl, of all things. Their coach was a crude, rude, out-of-shape, beer-guzzling, ex-minor leaguer turned pool-cleaner who consented to coach the Little League team. After all, money was involved. Except for the punk and the girl, the lineup was devoid of talent and the team dynamics left wanting. But, as happens so often in the movies, the members mysteriously gel, discover a common goal and rising to heights unknown, knock off their arch nemesis in the championship game. Hardly realistic. But, it sure makes a good story.

Actually, as I was reading in I Samuel 22, I discovered that a very similar thing happened. Another team of misfits formed in a dark and damp cave.

David, son of Jesse, was fleeing from King Saul. With the Royal's spear sharpened in hopes of making a shish kabob of David's heart, David had to run all over the countryside hiding out from the jealous king. David relocated his hideout in Gath to holing up in a cave in Adullam. He was not alone. Interested parties showed up to check things out. However, his companions were not exactly the most stellar contributors to society. Rather, *All those who were in distress or in debt or discontented gathered around him, and he became their leader* (I Samuel 22:2). Delinquents, misfits and malcontents, four-hundred men strong.

Lo and behold, those guys became the strongest army of the day. Their success was not because they were huge, bulky men and highly trained soldiers. No. They were just guys who didn't fit. King David took that straggly bunch and conquered the world because they were willing participants in God's ordained plan.

Don't fret if you aren't perfect. Don't worry if you feel lacking compared to others. Remember, it's not you that counts. It's God working through you that produces results.

"Not by might nor by power, but by my Spirit," says the LORD Almighty. (Zechariah 4:6b)

Daily challenge:
Write down what you think is deficient in your life. Pray over it. Ask God to help you be what He wants you to be. Now, stop worrying about it.

What Now?

OK. So here we are—still in the first week of the year. We think about this and plan for that. We wonder and scheme, jotting down our grand ideas with as much enthusiasm as kids waiting for Santa a few weeks back. We are quite pleased with ourselves because our strategy seems logical, sound and perhaps even admirable. But, wait. *Oops . . . forgot something. Commit to the LORD whatever you do, and your plans will succeed* (Proverbs 16:3).

Why is stopping to consider God's will tough for us? Clearly we want to know, but sometimes we don't know how. We keep praying for a sign. Finding writing on the wall or a heavenly postcard would be convenient. But, I'm not holding my breath.

The Old Testament contains great stories; the one about David and his army is no exception (II Samuel 5 and I Chronicles 14). David had been made King and everyone knew it. Even Hiram, the King of Tyre, tried sucking up to him by sending messengers, cedar logs, carpenters and stone masons to build a palace for the new king. So without lifting a finger, David climbed atop his throne in Jerusalem. In fact, he even produced another brood of kids with more wives.

Anyway, David got word that the nasty Philistines were causing problems again. They had raided the Valley of Rephaim and were ready to fight. I guess they were still ticked off about the five little stones incident. David, not wanting them to get into the city, annihilated the enemy army outside the city limits. That should have been the end to it, right? Nope.

The Philistines regrouped and concocted another plan. They should have known better. *There is no wisdom, no insight, no plan that can succeed against the LORD* (Proverbs 21:30). David asks God what to do. *"Do not go straight up, but circle around them and attack them in front of the balsam trees. As soon as you hear the sound of marching in the tops of the balsam trees, move out to battle, because that will mean God has gone out in front of you to strike the Philistine army"* (I Chronicles 14:14b, 15). God was very specific and David obeyed. Lucky him. He had a God who told him what to do.

But, what about us? Does God tell us what to do? Sure. Granted, God is not in the business of hiring sky-writing planes. Rather, He often speaks to us in that quiet way, using His Word to guide us. My problem is that I create so much noise that I sometimes drown Him out.

Be still before the LORD and wait patiently for him. (Psalm 37:7a)

Daily challenge:
Slow down, get rid of the noise and listen.

Take It As It Comes

I'm having a hard time writing today. I want this book of devotional stories to be "real." I am certainly not the epitome of spirituality. No. I'm just a woman who struggles from day to day. Our oldest, Caleb, leaves for the next semester of college and I am bummed about that. I like having him around. Then, I am disappointed for failing to get in my running workouts a couple times last week. How am I ever going to reach my goals this year if I can't get my derriere down the road—even when the sun is shining? And, I admit my terror of writing 359 more devotionals. I hate to fail, but I'm scared of the commitment it takes to succeed.

I suspect I am not alone. Tasks can seem so overwhelming that we barely leave the runway before grounding ourselves for one reason or another. The obstacles are imposing and the required effort to reach a goal is incomprehensible, nearly invisible on the faraway horizon.

I've experienced these feelings before. In the summer of 2007, I wanted to set a speed record on West Virginia's 302-mile Allegheny Trail. I achieved my goal, but it was only because I was able to break the task up into doable parts. When I first started, I could not get my arms around running all those miles in a single week. However, I could understand running to my support vehicle parked three miles down the road. Then, I just had to run another couple miles to the next meeting point. Repeated over and over again, I found myself standing atop Peter's Mountain at the trail's terminus by week's end. Had I not broken the task into small parts, I would have given up long before I started.

It takes a conscious effort to stay focused, be able to prioritize and stay calm. Let's not get caught up in a whirlwind of worry, fretting and despondence if—no, *when*—we mess up. Take each day, each hour, each minute as it comes. Be patient. Just keep making forward progress.

> . . . *let us throw off everything that hinders and the sin that so easily entangles, and let us run with perseverance the race marked out for us. (Hebrews 12:1b)*

Daily challenge:
Make sure your goals are broken down into manageable pieces.

A Time for Everything

There is a time for everything,
and a season for every activity under heaven:
a time to be born and a time to die,
a time to plant and a time to uproot,
a time to kill and a time to heal,
a time to tear down and a time to build,
a time to weep and a time to laugh,
a time to mourn and a time to dance,
a time to scatter stones and a time to gather them,
a time to embrace and a time to refrain,
a time to search and a time to give up,
a time to keep and a time to throw away,
a time to tear and a time to mend,
a time to be silent and a time to speak,
a time to love and a time to hate,
a time for war and a time for peace.

Ecclesiastes 3:1-8 is probably the best-known section of Scripture in modern time. The song "Turn, Turn, Turn" was popularized in 1965 by a group with the more-than-odd name—The Byrds. It's ironic that a verbatim biblical song such as this gained nearly anthem status to the hippie pop culture whose mores emphasized personal freedoms to the near exclusion of personal responsibility.

However, it's hard to ignore the truth about the need for a balanced life. There is a time for everything. There is no part of our existence that is not touched by these principles. Hey, even the professional organizers so popular today can get in on the act: *a time to keep and a time to throw away!*

How should this passage challenge us? I know I need to be constantly evaluating my actions. Do I spend more time tearing people down than I do mending relationships? Am I so glum that I forget how to laugh? Am I more apt to hold a grudge than I am to reconcile?

We all may go through the day with this well-known tune bouncing around in our heads—sorry about that! But let's take advantage of that and reflect on the balance—or lack of it—in our own lives.

There is a time for everything, and a season for every activity
under heaven . . .. (Ecclesiastes 3:1)

Daily challenge:
For the next day or two, keep track of the time you spend cooking, cleaning,
working, recreating, watching TV, reading, etc. Are you balanced?

Sorry

The phone rang last evening. It was a teacher at our kids' school wanting to know if I could substitute teach. She was sick and feeling miserable. With a large project checked off my ever-present do list, I agreed to take her fifth- and sixth-graders. At least that was better than little ankle-biters. So hi-ho, hi-ho, it's off to school I go.

In all fairness, these students are good kids in a good school with mostly good parents. But that does not prevent them from being . . . well, kids. With my own kids nearly grown, I had forgotten just how noisy students can be. The girls have turned into divas, talking about guys, snickering and rolling their eyes at major offenses—like a boy saying something stupid. The guys, on the other hand, are noisy in a different way. They like guttural noises and bodily functions, having more energy than the reactors at Three Mile Island.

At several points during the day, I played mean cop. A brief lull in a lesson seemed to invite conversations, some whispered and others shouted as if on a playground. In particular, one sixth-grade girl was an incessant babbler who, when given the evil eye, would softly mutter, "Sorry." After five such apologies, I held my tongue no longer. "No, you're not sorry. If you were sorry, your behavior would change."

Most of us pull similar stunts. We likely know that our behavior is not optimal. However, we think it insignificant enough to ignore or figure that we can get away with it—at least for awhile. As a result, we go on living in the same flippant way, feeling no compulsion to change regardless of insincere apologies sent heavenward.

I'm convinced we'd be better off if a little sincerity was added to our remorseful apologies. Being sorry just isn't good enough. Repentance on any terms always requires action. *"Repent and be baptized . . . "* (Acts 2:38), *"Repent then, and turn to God . . . "* (Acts 3:19), *"Repent . . . and pray to the Lord"* (Acts 8:22), *"Repent . . . and do"* (Rev. 2:5), *"Obey it . . . and repent"* (Rev. 3:3), and *"So be earnest . . . and repent"* (Rev. 3:19).

That 70s box-office phrase, "Love means never having to say you're sorry", has been used a zillion times. But it was as wrong the first time it was whispered as the last. Love means that you know when to say you're sorry and are willing to change.

> *Remember, therefore, what you have received and heard; obey it,*
> *and repent. (Revelation 3:3a)*

Daily challenge:
Try to remember the last time you said you were sorry. Were you really?

Flexibility

I had just finished my Nordic Track workout and decided to work on core strength. I sat on the big, gushy balance ball in the comfort of my living room and started a version of sit-ups that made my stomach muscles scream after just twenty reps. Then, I laid on the ball with hands on the ground, rolling out and over the ball until my body was outstretched, ankles barely holding on. At that point, I did a push up and hoped the ball didn't slip out, sending my nose into a crushing encounter with the floor beneath. I did ten reps before moving on to flexibility.

Even as a gymnast some thirty-five years ago, I struggled with the ability to touch my toes without bending my knees. Now in my early fifties, the flexibility issue is even worse. But knowing how important a flexible body is to running health, I did some stretches and was disappointed at how badly it went. The real kicker came when I decided to try a back arch.

Nothing—absolutely nothing happened. Lying on my back I placed my hands up by my shoulders, knees bent and tried to push up into the position so easily achieved in high school. I was incredulous that I couldn't raise myself off the floor—not even a centimeter. I figured it would be hard, but I didn't count on impossible!

My failure to do a back arch can be blamed on the decrease in flexibility and strength over the years. Without a lot of stretch—no pun intended—there is a spiritual analogy in this story. It's easy to become inflexible in our approach to life, people, and circumstances. We want only to do it "my way," not unlike the Frank Sinatra song of old. Our strength and fortitude fails as well, being unwilling—or perhaps unable—to be persistent in well-doing. What results is a grumpy, unhappy person who has a hard time getting along with people.

I'm not suggesting that we give up well-founded convictions for the sake of accommodating erroneous thinking. However, I do advocate the principles of regarding others more than yourself (Romans 12:3) and letting love cover minor offenses (Proverbs 10:12, Proverbs 17:9, I Peter 4:8). A consistently strong yet flexible approach in our relationships serves the Body well.

Above all, love each other deeply, because love covers over a
multitude of sins. (I Peter 4:8)

Daily challenge:
Don't be inflexible when it comes to matters that are strictly personal preference.

Discouragement

Do you ever find yourself happy as a lark, only to be suddenly deflated by one little thing? This is exactly what happened this morning. I woke up happy, looking forward to another productive day. I grabbed my coffee and absentmindedly picked up some unopened mail. Opening the envelope of our college son's credit card, I immediately noticed an "Amount due" figure that was higher than expected. $48 worth of charges that were supposed to have been cancelled. *Grrr.* I suddenly felt anxious and annoyed.

Why do small annoyances throw us off track so easily? Certainly, no one died, our house still stood and, despite the cold rain outside, the sky will surely remain in place. Still, I felt a peculiar ache and my world turned as gloomy as the weather.

I should be able to find a Scripture verse that will suit the situation—a "feel-good" verse. Turning to the Psalms I read the words of David. I am amazed at the extremes of his emotions. At one point he is reveling in the strength and power of his God. But as quickly as that joyful chapter ends, the next reveals a woeful David despondent over his evil enemies and the oppression surrounding him.

Discouragement comes so that we can, in contrast, be buoyed by encouragement. Moses told Joshua, *"The LORD himself goes before you and will be with you; he will never leave you nor forsake you. Do not be afraid; do not be discouraged"* (Deuteronomy 31:8). God told Joshua the same thing (Joshua 8:1), so that Joshua could turn right around and tell his people likewise: *"Do not be afraid; do not be discouraged. Be strong and courageous. This is what the LORD will do . . . "* (Joshua 10:25). And since the phrase was apparently not copyrighted, David encouraged his son, Solomon, with the same sentiment: *"Be strong and courageous, and do the work. Do not be afraid or discouraged, for the LORD God, my God, is with you. He will not fail you or forsake you . . . "* (I Chronicles 28:20).

Evidently, if God told Moses and Moses told Joshua and Joshua told the twelve spies and then David told Solomon, it must be important. Discouragement is natural. But, just as discouragement comes creeping in, encouragement closely follows.

> *" . . . be strong and courageous, and do the work. Do not be afraid or discouraged, for the LORD God, my God, is with you. He will not fail you or forsake you." (I Chronicles 28:20)*

Daily challenge:
Cheer up. Encouragement is on the way.

January
12

Joy

Last night I relaxed by watching TV, my after-dinner coffee and dark chocolate in hand. I let the channel changer rest on "Man vs. Wild," a program where the consummate adventurer, Bear Grylls, will go anywhere and do anything. This time he parachuted from a hot-air balloon to the floor of the African Savannah grasslands, immediately targeting the foothills of the mountains thirty miles away.

Bear had close encounters with massive elephants, an adder with the fastest strike of any serpent in the world, a pride of hungry-looking lions, hippos and baboons. I was appalled—though not surprised—that he took his knife to a freshly killed zebra and wolfed down the raw meat, blood oozing from his mouth as a group of envious vultures looked on. He continued his trek by following a stream that turned into a roaring torrent. The water chilled him the closer he got to the headwaters, a melting glacier. After struggling up a steep and torrential waterfall, he turned to the camera, winded but unscathed and passionately exclaimed: "That was so much fun! It is so important that no matter how bad it gets, you have to find some joy. It's the only way you're going to survive and make it back alive."

Ain't that the truth? In a physical sense, I've experienced something similar. Whether suffering in the depths of the Brazilian Amazon jungle or on the Allegheny Trail or during an inordinately difficult one-hundred mile race, it sure helps to find something to smile about.

Just today, I went out for a run I did not relish. With new headphones for my iPod, I decided to fill the hours with music. Running along a country road, I did not feel inspired despite the sunshine and unusually temperate January temperature. But suddenly, a crazy beat came blasting into my ears. I smiled, my pace picked up and I think I may have danced a little. The entire run changed. I found joy in that moment and it carried me through the miles.

God did a good thing when he designed joy. Not surprising, the Scriptures associate joy with the presence of God. But joy is also allied with music, dance, happiness, obedience, blessing, victories, precepts, praise, unfailing love, consolation, prosperity, laughter, wisdom, food and wine, sunshine, conversation, good news and hope.

May the God of hope fill you with all joy and peace as you trust in him, so that you may overflow with hope by the power of the Holy Spirit. (Romans 15:13)

Daily challenge:
Look for joy. Expect joy. Embrace joy.

Think on These Things

During the warm days of spring, summer and fall, flower-filled pots fill the pool area. But as cold weather approaches, my thoughts turn to preserving the blooms. Without fail, this thought occurs precisely at 11:16 p.m. during the late news sometime in October. The weatherman mentions a hard frost and my ear antennae transmit the panic signal. I scurry into the darkness to rescue those treasured flowers. One by one, I lug the pots inside, dumping yucky water from the pot saucers down my pajama pants. Finally content that the plants have been saved from certain demise, I wash my hands and go to bed.

Now those pots look a little different than they did in July. The geraniums actually look better. On the other hand, the pots containing annual flowers don't look so hot. About half of the plants are dead and the others are on their last leg. Since there is little hope for a miraculous recovery, I grabbed my scissors and started pruning. As I did, I got to thinking about spiritual analogies. A number came to mind: the Old Testament principle of pruning for a good harvest and the John 15 passage where the act of pruning produces fruit.

However, the thought that kept banging around in my head was this: *How worthy is it to take everyday experiences and coax out a spiritual application?* I don't want to trivialize spiritual principles. Finally, I came to a conclusion.

We are told over and over again to meditate. Isaac made it a habit to meditate in the field each evening and Joshua encouraged meditation to avoid forgetting. Then, when I started looking in Psalms, meditation on the law of the Lord, His unfailing love and precepts, all His works, deeds and wonders is supposed to happen day and night (Psalm 1:2, 39:3, 48:9, 72:12, 119:15, 23, 27, 48).

Spiritual maturity is being able to view our very existence as an opportunity to better understand God, His work in our lives and our relationships with others. There is no part of life—even cutting away the dead flowers—that should be considered outside the realm of our connection with Him.

Finally, brothers, whatever is true, whatever is noble, whatever is right, whatever is pure, whatever is lovely, whatever is admirable— if anything is excellent or praiseworthy—think about such things. (Philippians 4:8)

Daily challenge:
Train your mind to see truth even in the simple things.

Appraisals

With the sun not yet peeking above the horizon and a chill in the house, I did the only reasonable thing—I sought refuge back under the covers. *Ah.* It felt so good. Before I knew it, it was 8:15 a.m. and past time to get moving. I didn't take care to properly dress myself, fix my hair or put on makeup. With coffee in hand, my unkempt self moseyed up to the office and looked at the day planner. "9:00 a.m. Appraisal." I glanced at the clock. 8:45. Shoot. How could I have forgotten?

We were refinancing the house and needed an appraisal. Promptly at 9:00 a.m., in the splendor of my grey sweatpants and amidst a messy house, I greeted the two men at the door. Charming. I know that an appraisal is not contingent on how I look or if there's a dead stink bug in the middle of the floor. Still, it's uncomfortable not having everything in tip-top shape. Things we wanted to do to the house in the past or have planned for the future don't count. What counts is the here and now.

Let me weave what happened last night into this story. I joined a room full of women in a study on Titus 2. The target was learning how to better love our husbands. Among other things, the leader encouraged us to ask our spouses for an evaluation.

Arriving at home, I popped the question. "How can I be a better wife to you?" With a chuckle and a huge grin erupting across his face, I knew exactly what he was thinking—it's a man thing. "Really, besides THAT . . . I want to know."

Essentially, I was asking Gary for an appraisal. The prophets appraised Israel and Paul appraised the early church of its works and obedience. Many of the Epistles reflect the state of affairs for the churches.

An honest appraisal will identify strengths and areas requiring improvement. We ought to be willing to enter into the appraisal process and take the necessary steps to guarantee a better assessment in the future.

I thank Christ Jesus our Lord, who has given me strength, that he considered me faithful, appointing me to his service. (I Timothy 1:12)

Daily challenge:
Ask your spouse or valued friend to help assess areas of strength and weakness.
Write them down. Set goals. Work hard to earn a strong appraisal.

Snow

I was in my office this morning catching up on email and taking care of business. The wood stove downstairs was keeping the house warm and toasty, a good thing on a cold and windy day. With coffee in hand, I hoped for a bit of inspiration. But alas, I wasn't "feeling" it.

With fingers poised on the keyboard, I stared blankly at the screen. On a whim, I turned my head and glanced out the window. Snow! Lots of it. The weatherman made no mention of this last night. My spirits soared.

We've had nothing more than a dusting and I was anxious to take that first snowy run. Grabbing the phone from its cradle, I told Gary about the falling flakes and asked for a weather report from town. Even as he reported clear skies, I noticed a slight reflection on the hood of the truck. Oh no! The sky seemed to be brightening. Did this mean an end to the snow squall? Before I hung up, the snow stopped as suddenly as it started. *Phooey.*

Why the fascination with snow? For me, a soft shower of flakes is magnificent. The world turns silent and seems to slow, as if taking a well-needed rest. As kids, we stood for hours in our living room, looking out against the brightly shining street light to see the contrast of the snow against a dark sky. What jubilation at the thought of a cancelled school day! We headed out, exuberant about creating fresh tracks in the snow. When the cold crept into our fingers and toes and snowy boots and icy gloves mounded on the kitchen floor, Mother treated us with hot chocolate and mountains of cinnamon toast. Simply wonderful!

Snow, in its pristine form, is symbolic of purity. The Psalmist entreats, *Cleanse me with hyssop, and I will be clean; wash me, and I will be whiter than snow* (Psalm 51:7). If for only a moment, the morning's snow reminded me of the cleansing blood of Jesus Christ and my purity before God.

Thank you, Lord.

Though your sins are like scarlet, they shall be as white as snow; though they are red as crimson, they shall be like wool. (Isaiah 1:18b)

Daily challenge:
What does your life look like . . . the clean, new snow
or the piles of cinder-filled and dirty snow?

Don't Be Afraid

As I climbed the steps to the office last night, I heard Gary say, "Here ya go, Babe. That movie you wanted to see is on." Sure enough, "Facing the Giants" filled the screen. We had heard a lot about this movie; Gary, the king of Google, searched it out. A Georgia church decided to produce a movie with a message. With a slim budget of $100,000, the film made it into the public sector grossing an amazing $20,000,000 at the box office.

The setting is a Christian school with a losing football team that, against all odds, wins the state football title. Through the course of the story, the coach, his wife and members of the team experience a revival of sorts, understanding what it means to give God everything. Despite its predictability, the message is clear and bold. I pulled out the box of tissues. I'm a sucker for motivational movies; with an undeniably authentic message, this one was special.

The movie had many memorable statements, but one stood out. The scene is the locker room where the pensive coach is awaiting the arrival of his players. It is the calm before the storm. Enter the coach's own boyhood coach. During the exchange of well-wishes, the facts of the ensuing battle arise. The opposing team has three times as many players and has been state champs for several years, physically powerful and enormous. They are the "giants"—the little "David"s barely nip at their heels. Fear had to be conquered if the battle was to be won. The wise coach offers, "God says in his Word, 'Do not fear' 365 times. So, go out there and play . . ." (paraphrased).

Three-hundred sixty-five times. *Wow.* It occurred to me that there is one "do not fear" for every day of the year. As always, God is sufficient for every situation, every day. In the Bible, we see people being afraid for many reasons—opposing armies, cruel captors, pestilence, death, evil people, a storm on the seas, the dark night . . . the list goes on. And yet, there is reason to be fearless even in the direst circumstances. As Jesus told the synagogue ruler, *"Don't be afraid; just believe"* (Mark 5:36).

Moses answered the people, "Do not be afraid. Stand firm and you will see the deliverance the LORD will bring you today." (Exodus 14:13)

Daily challenge:
What are you afraid of? Write it down and give it over to God.

Coincidence

Coincidence. We all use the word quite freely. The online Merriam-Webster dictionary tells us the word originated in 1605 and has a dual meaning: "1) The act or condition of coinciding : CORRESPONDENCE 2) the occurrence of events that happen at the same time by accident but seem to have some connection . . . ."

A while ago, I flew to a work assignment. When I arrived at my destination, I found that the person I just met knew a good friend of mine. Then, waiting in the airport on the return trip, I spotted an acquaintance I had not seen for years. I might be inclined to say both of these occurrences were of a coincidental nature.

The term *coincidence* is not an evil word. However, *providence* may be more accurate. We had our Ladies' Fellowship last night. My role, in part, was to arrange the music. Usually, we sing a few simple songs. As I looked over the talking points that our speaker, Marion, was going to present, I wanted to do something different. I pulled out a handful of worship CD's from the shelf and popped them in the player. I listened to a few songs, but they just didn't seem right. That is, they didn't seem right until the familiar tune of "It Is Well with My Soul" wafted from the speakers. Time froze as I listened to those memorable lyrics. Yes. That was the song and I would follow it with a less familiar rendition of "Be Still My Soul."

Pushing the play button, the melody filled the room. Marion shot a glance at me. "Did you pick that just for me?" Marion inquired as the last note faded and wet eyes dabbed. The hymn had deep, personal meaning and she shared the story with the group.

Afterward, Julie approached. She and Susan had been planning the next song for the kids' handbell choir. "I told Susan, 'It Is Well' has been on my mind so much. I think we need to do that," Julie recounted. Coincidence? No. Providence. The right song for the right time for the right people.

There is nothing in life that happens by accident. Each event, no matter how small, has been orchestrated by God Himself. Indeed, God is the God of every detail.

"Indeed, the very hairs of your head are all numbered. Don't be afraid; you are worth more than many sparrows." (Luke 12:7)

Daily challenge:
Train yourself to recognize God's hand in everyday life.

Sonshine

The sun will come out tomorrow. Bet your bottom dollar that tomorrow there'll be sun! . . .. (From *The Sun Will Come Out Tomorrow*)

Is that catchy little tune sung by a curly redhead now stuck in your head? Sorry. But as I got out of bed and walked to the bathroom, that was the first thing that popped into my head. Really. No kidding. The sunshine, bright and bold, bounced off the new snow. It nearly blinded my just-opened eyes.

Yesterday morning was quite the contrast. It was anything but sunny as the snow fell. Though the snow was beautiful, the skies were dark and gray. I loved it and eagerly went for a run in the fluffy stuff. I suppose I would even welcome several days of snowy skies. However, at some point, I would be craving the bright rays.

A phenomenon called Seasonal Affective Disorder (SAD) frequently occurs in the winter time, particularly in parts of the world that get little daylight in the long, cold months. It is seen more frequently in women than men. Feelings of sadness and lethargy, disrupted sleep patterns, depression and weight gain are common indications of the condition. Interestingly, the major treatment is to spend time in the light, often in the form of a 10,000-lumen light box. For effective treatment, it is necessary to look directly into that light to induce the chemical changes in the brain.

For the Christian, it's all about the light. We have no life until we gaze directly into the Light of the World, Jesus Christ. Living in the Light illumines our path. Conversely, when we wander away from the Light, our world gets dark and lonely; we get lost. And unfortunately, being in the dark encourages misbehavior, because we think we can get away with it. John 3:19 says, *"This is the verdict: Light has come into the world, but men loved darkness instead of light because their deeds were evil."*

Whether the sun is shining or not, we need our daily dose of the Son. No need for sunscreen here. The longer the exposure, the better.

> *When Jesus spoke again to the people, he said, "I am the light of the world. Whoever follows me will never walk in darkness, but will have the light of life." (John 8:12)*

Daily challenge:
How do you plan to get enough Sonshine today?

Freedom to Run

This morning I beat the sun up. No. I didn't actually "beat" it as in *smack, punch, kick* and *thump.* I just rose before it did. It's not that I look forward to getting up early. Too many years of early mornings at the hospital have permanently thwarted my enthusiasm for those wee hours. Nevertheless, I dutifully set the alarm, easing out from under the covers two minutes before the annoying beep-beep-beep of the alarm.

Deb and I planned an early start, running trails for about three hours. As we ran along the narrow paths, we encountered many intersections that required a decision. To the right? To the left? Straight? Since neither one of us had spent a lot of time on those trails, we opted for ones we did not know, the spirit of exploration spurring us on. Things went well until our newly cut trail came to an abrupt stop. *Hmm.* We saw the intended course ahead of us was marked by wire flags shoved into the ground. But following those markers meant weaving through the brush, climbing over downed trees and under low-lying branches. Deciding to see where the trail was going to go, we happily proceeded.

We kept thinking this trail was going to turn to the right and head for a well-known ridge. Instead, the yet-to-be-completed path continued to the east. After about thirty minutes of trekking in hopes of finding the other end, we gave up and retraced our steps.

Surely, we were not on the path described in II Samuel 22:37: *You broaden the path beneath me, so that my ankles do not turn.* We were definitely in ankle-busting territory—literally. By contrast, once we found our way back to maintained trail, our progress was rapid and the footing more predictable. Seeing directional signs and posted maps gave us confidence that we were on a trail leading us back to our cars.

It's not surprising that there are many references, particularly in Psalms and Proverbs, to God's broad and well-lit path. Safety and security result when deviation from that path is avoided. However, staying on the path requires keen attention. Even a short distraction can produce a false sense of security until you suddenly discover that you have no idea where you are or how you got there. The only way back onto the path is by the illuminating lamp of the Word. But once you're there, there's freedom to run.

I run in the path of your commands, for you have set my heart free.
(Psalm 119:32)

Daily challenge:
If your way seems rocky, it may be that you have wandered from God's path.

Feed the Fire

Boy. Is it ever cold! I guess that's why they call it *winter.* As the weather fore-casters describe it, the arctic air from the north is pushing down into the south, bringing with it frigid temperatures and gusty winds. The temperature last night was in the teens and the thermometer is supposed to hit single digits tonight.

We live in a 110-year old house, give or take a few years, that is hardly the air-tight, energy-efficient home of modern, technologically-savvy construction. The two heat pumps, installed in the 1970s, work—but not optimally. So, when a wood-burning stove was offered to us, we gladly sanded, repainted and installed the massive beast into our existing fireplace. Off to the woods went Gary and the boys, chainsaw in hand. A pile of dead-fall logs steadily grew in front of the house. Then, it was *chop, chop, chop.* The axe flew through the air and manageable chunks of wood stacked for easy access. All was in place for us to stay nice and warm . . . at least while the wood supply lasted.

Having the wood stove takes considerable effort. It's a good thing Seth is such a workhorse. He loves chopping wood. But all the work is worth the effort when we are warm, soaking in the stove's heat.

I laughed out loud when I read about another strategy for keeping warm. Apparently, Old King David could not stay warm. Perhaps poor circulation could explain his chills. Nonetheless, his servants came up with a novel idea.

When King David was old and well advanced in years, he could not keep warm even when they put covers over him. So his servants said to him, "Let us look for a young virgin to attend the king and take care of him. She can lie beside him so that our lord the king may keep warm." (I Kings 1:1, 2)

What's my point? Simply recognize that staying warm physically—and spiritual-ly—takes a conscious effort. It doesn't just happen. Just as we need to keep the fire stoked to warm the house, our spiritual stoves need filling as well. Feed the fire with Scripture and prayer. Exercise our minds to dwell on truth. Put into action what we know to be godly. Keep the fire burning!

When Jesus spoke again to the people, he said, "I am the light of the world. Whoever follows me will never walk in darkness, but will have the light of life." (John 8:12)

Daily challenge:
What will you do today to feed the fire? Pick one thing and do it.

Work, Work, Work

I have a dilemma. Last year, I became dissatisfied with my work situation. I traveled all the time. In the fall I was gone so much that I missed every one of Seth's soccer games. Sometimes I wasn't even home when Caleb had a college break. With tears rolling down my face I often packed my suitcase. Clear and simple, I didn't want to go.

I grew discontent with my life—because I felt I had no life. Even when I was home, I felt compelled to be at my desk morning, noon and night in order to prove my worth to the boss. My phone was glued to my hip, even if I was running. I finally resigned but offered to stay on through the summer—just to be "nice." I soon regretted not exercising a short thirty-day notice; the work expectations got worse.

At the moment, the consulting business I launched has not made it off the pad. One job I did nab is refusing to pay and the online education business that I simultaneously started is getting less than anticipated action. Prospects to stay in my profession are growing dim. I am frustrated.

When I resigned, I felt confident that God was going to honor our decision for me to work from home. But if "honor" meant dropping work into my lap, that has not happened. I want to have faith that God will meet our needs, but I feel as though I need to work harder to make something happen.

When I opened my email this morning, an online devotional was waiting for me. It encouraged business people to keep perspective, refraining from becoming workaholics. Relentless work, suggested the author, actually demonstrates a lack of faith, fearful that without our own extended efforts, God won't be able to get the job done.

I'm not sure how my job situation will pan out, but I guess there is only so much that I can—or should—do. I trust God to provide.

In vain you rise early and stay up late, toiling for food to eat—for He grants sleep to those He loves. (Psalms 127:2)

Daily challenge:
There is a fine line between being a hard worker and working too hard.

Decently and In Order

Riding the work wave from yesterday, I hit the beach with my sights set on a major reorganization project. It's funny how motivating it can be to know first-time visitors will soon come knocking. Yesterday, the 110-year old wood floor in the living room was looking its age. I felt compelled to put some shine to it. But as good as the floor looks now, the guest bedroom is dreadful. During the fall, Gary's hunting clothes, bows, guns, doe pee (that is not a typo), and other paraphernalia swamp the room. Mind you, hunting is not the problem. I just want my guest room back!

It took a grand effort to unload the room and transport all that stuff to Caleb's bedroom, abandoned for college and therefore open as the hub for organizational efforts. After four hours of dumping out buckets, folding clothes, sorting ammo and pairing socks and gloves, I stood back to take a look. *Hmm.* If camouflage is supposed to blend into the surroundings, how come I see piles of it all over the floor? Still, the neatly labeled bins and piles of sorted hunting equipment will remain until Gary gets home from work. I need help paring down the twenty-six hunting caps that have mysteriously reproduced over the years.

I got to thinking that it would be easy to validate the concept of organization. Imagine my shock—followed by raucous laughter—when I read the words of Isaiah to King Hezekiah: *This is what the LORD says: "Put your house in order, because you are going to die; you will not recover"* (II Kings 20:1).

It didn't get much better when I got to II Samuel 17:23. *When Ahithophel saw that his advice had not been followed, he saddled his donkey and set out for his house in his hometown. He put his house in order and then hanged himself . . ..* Wow. The guys in my house might use these as proof-texts about organization being lethal.

Doing things decently and in order (Romans 13:13) is a viable Biblical concept, albeit a little out of context if you want to apply it to a pristine closet. But being organized forces us to monitor the number of items we own and helps us take care of what God has entrusted to us.

Being organized is all about stewardship of time and resources.

> But everything should be done in a fitting and orderly way.
> (I Corinthians 14:40)

Daily challenge:
Take care of what you have. After all, it's God's.
Does it make sense to trash something that doesn't belong to you?

Got Wisdom?

James wrote to the believing Jews scattered over the Middle East, Europe, Egypt and down into Africa. In the early church many were persecuted because, just like today, Jesus was not widely accepted as Messiah. Purposing to encourage those Believers and recognizing their encountered difficulties, he penned this lesson: trials and testing should be a joyful occasion for perseverance; maturity will follow. But, and there's always a *but*, he directly follows those ideas with, *If any of you lack wisdom . . ..* I wonder about the connection between wisdom and joy.

In Psalms and Proverbs God is the undisputed source of wisdom. In the case of renowned King Solomon, the depth of that wisdom is described: *God gave Solomon wisdom and very great insight, and a breadth of understanding as measureless as the sand on the seashore* (I Kings 4:29). We also know that *the fear of the Lord is the beginning of wisdom* (Proverbs 9:10). And, there is an obvious and natural outcome of wisdom—*knowledge and understanding* (Proverbs 2:6, 10).

It's not that I don't understand the concept of wisdom, but I am still perplexed by the sequence of statements in James 1. Help me think through this. Let's assume that a wisdom deficit means that knowledge and understanding have not yet been produced. Perhaps James is saying something like this: "I know you are suffering, but you need to be able to look at these circumstances as an opportunity to mature and persevere. If you don't understand the 'why' behind what is happening, ask God. Don't be afraid to ask, because he will not fault you for not understanding—you are human, after all. But, rest assured that if you do ask for wisdom—the ability to understand all things in the context of God's plan for this life—you will be doing a good thing. Go ahead. Admit you don't understand. God will give you needed wisdom without holding it against you."

Some suggest that if you "question God", you inevitably err. To question God in the sense that He must have made a mistake is totally inappropriate. However, God fully expects us not to understand everything that happens and does not fault us for that shortcoming. Remember, omniscience was never bestowed on us just because we became Christ-followers. Incomplete comprehension is par for the course. Recognizing our deficiency and asking for wisdom is required if we are to *live by faith, not by sight* (II Corinthians 5:7).

> *If any of you lacks wisdom he should ask God, who gives generously to all without finding fault, and it will be given to him. (James 1:5)*

Daily challenge:
When you can't understand, believe anyway. God is in control.

Days of Trial

Five years ago, I could not have imagined the scenario. What transpired was devastating to the ebb and flow of our daily activities and took a dramatic toll on our resources. Countless nights of restless sleep, if any at all, and the weighty cloud of uncertainty hovered just above our heads. For us, the sun no longer shone. Now, our actions at the settlement office were an effort to bury the last vestiges of those dark days.

It was several years ago that a former boss sued Gary and me for over eight million dollars, laughable if you knew our finances. Our shoulders bore the crushing, nauseating yoke—one that left us hardly able to inhale a single life-sustaining breath. We had been falsely accused by a man driven by hate and vengeance. As the days, weeks and months slowly passed, the world ground to a halt as we watched our savings vanish and our carefully laid plans for the future disintegrate. Despite the fear and mental anguish, however, we prayed that we could remain honest and truthful. We wanted to be a testimony to God's sufficiency as we knew that our kids and others would be watching our reactions to this fiery trial.

The entire lawsuit took nearly two years to finalize. I would love to say that we prevailed in every sense and recovered the tens of thousands of dollars spent on our defense—but I can't. Two weeks before the scheduled court date, our accuser wanted to settle. As unconscionable as handing him a single penny seemed to us, we paid him a small sum, a far cry from the millions he wanted. It was the wise thing to do: the expense to get to trial would have cost another $20,000. But knowing this man would likely broadcast that he "won" made it difficult to write the check.

As we signed the papers refinancing our house, I felt like we were closing another chapter in our lives. We can now put this desert experience in perspective. Our deep thirst drove us to God, who matured, sustained and satisfied us.

Remember how the Lord your God led you all the way in the desert these forty years, to humble you and to test you in order to know what was in your heart, whether or not you would keep His commands. (Deuteronomy 8:2)

Daily challenge:
If you are in a desert place, know that God will lead you out in His own time.

Whatever Is True

Whatever is true, whatever is noble, whatever is right, whatever is pure, whatever is lovely, whatever is admirable— if anything is excellent or praiseworthy—think about such things (Philippians 4:8).

I've read that verse a gazillion times and memorized it somewhere along the line. When it crossed my path again this morning, it occurred to me that journaling my thoughts every day is helping me stay true to the instruction.

I distinctly remember many an adult telling us kids, "Garbage in. Garbage out." It was often used to dissuade us from listening to that "evil" rock music of the 60s and 70s that promoted rebellion, drug use and free love. Other times, it was a plea to limit viewing of the television, or as it was commonly known, the *Boob Tube*.

When that term originated, it implied that you would turn into a "boob"—a kumquat, a non-thinking coach potato—if you indulged the on-button too often. In the current timeframe, "Boob Tube" may more closely describe what can be seen on the screen. In either case, filling the mind with things of little value will only encourage the living out of those same wanting values.

It's not surprising that Christians are instructed to fill time by thinking about honorable things. We are to contemplate those subjects that are lovely and uncontaminated. It's like a horse with blinders. The horse's owner does this when he wants to keep the animal from being distracted by the periphery. Although we don't walk the streets with big black flaps over our eyes, we consciously control the address to where the mind wanders.

The kids' song, "Oh be careful little eyes what you see . . . ", is theologically correct. The gateway to the mind is the eye and the ear; controlling what those senses encounter directs the mind.

Our sin nature makes it difficult to bring our thoughts under submission. It takes an act of the will and the empowering of the Spirit to focus on that which is profitable. If we take the offensive to meditate on those things that are true, noble, right, pure, lovely, admirable, excellent or praiseworthy, there will be very limited time to get ourselves in trouble.

But his delight is in the law of the LORD, and on his law he meditates day and night. (Psalm 1:2)

Daily challenge:
Take note what you listen to and watch. Is it true, noble, right, pure, lovely, admirable, excellent or praiseworthy? If not, turn it off.

Patience

"Patients. I want patients and I want them NOW!" a very frustrated operating-room director screamed into the overhead PA system. All who heard—which was pretty much everyone within a city block—stopped dead in their tracks as they took in the ranting of the normally laid-back and affable director.

The efficiency of any operating room depends on the ability to accurately estimate the set-up time for each procedure, the procedure itself and the transition to the next case. Patients need to be moved from place to place at just the right moment. When it works right, it is a fluid string of actions that results in a smooth move 'em in, move 'em out flow. However, on this particular day, nothing was going right. The Director lost patience because she was not getting her patients.

The lack of patience is not foreign to me. I lost patience a lot when the kids were younger. Caleb, in particular, went through a long stage of the "why?"s: a million questions asked, answers given, followed by more "why?"s. The cycle was endless. And when the why was followed by a toddler story taking approximately thirty-seven minutes to tell . . .. Well, let's just say I was not the poster-child for longsuffering.

However, patience—or lack thereof—raised its ugly head again this morning. No, my kids did not regress and, in fact, were not even home. I was impatient all by myself. Needing to do a long run, I decided to take to country roads for twenty miles. One problem, though. I didn't want to. I put it off as long as I could and then half-heartedly started down the driveway. It was a chore and as hard as I tried, my attitude did not improve with time. I felt overwhelmingly impatient. I knew it was going to take about three hours and there were things I wanted to be doing besides smelling cow poop as I ran past farms. Thankfully, I left my phone back at the house, making it impossible for me to bale out and call Gary to come get me.

We must learn how to be patient. If we take it one step at a time, we can achieve our goals. Throw aside extra weight, look straight ahead and keep on moving.

Therefore, since we are surrounded by such a great cloud of witnesses, let us throw off everything that hinders and the sin that so easily entangles, and let us run with perseverance the race marked out for us. (Hebrews 12:1)

Daily challenge:
Be as patient with your kids as Christ is with you.

Old Becomes New

I was in one of those organizational frenzies, carrying storable stuff to the attic. With the pull-down steps situated right beside the main stairwell, I had to be especially careful. The steep aluminum ladder was precariously bent and a slip would be easy, launching me to the level below. Nevertheless, I continued to make progress moving up and down the ladder and rearranging the items in the space. My harried state worked up a sweat, making me appreciate the contrasting cold air in the non-insulated attic. I was in my glory.

Momentarily distracted, I noticed a few pieces of castaway furniture, abandoned years ago in the dark recesses of the attic. Crawling under the rafters, I first inspected an old lamp table, the kind that has two wings that can be lifted into place to make it larger. With endless possibilities and a fair amount of effort on my part, the table ended up in my kitchen for inspection. It was old and dirty, the top covered with ugly flowered contact paper. Removing the now brittle paper left a sticky residue and revealed a quote by Benjamin Franklin inartistically etched into the wood. Could this table be saved? Maybe.

Gary's grandfather had long ago built a chess set. The board was a work of art. Out came the power tools, hammers, drills and scrap wood. By the time the afternoon passed, the table was altered to accommodate the chess board, recessed flush into the surface. The table now stands ready for a friendly game.

That old table was dead; hidden away, it had lost its purpose. But, with a little imagination and just a few hours of work, the desk came to life and was turned into a useful object. How much more does Christ do? He takes us, who are as dead as doorknobs and infuses life by Spirit-breathing into our souls. Only then do we become functional to the Kingdom of God.

The process of regeneration makes us alive, but the course of a total restoration often requires a lot of sawing, sanding and chipping away at the rough edges. It's not always pleasant to be on the receiving end of construction—but it is necessary. No matter how painful or difficult a process, submission to the tools of the Master Carpenter will make us into beautiful and useful people.

Therefore if any man be in Christ, he is a new creature: old things are passed away; behold, all things are become new. (II Corinthians 5:17)

Daily challenge:
Begin to see "lost causes" as potential beauty.

Search Me

The attic was calling me again, drawing me up those rickety steps. Compelled to retrieve another table abandoned in the shadows, I wrestled it—literally—through the opening in the attic floor, nearly dropping it on my head as the accumulated dust floated into my upward-looking eyes. With battle won, I took it directly outside into the sunlight to plan my attack.

This piece looked like a dressing table of some sort. It had spindle legs, a single drawer and an ornamental backsplash with a narrow rectangular slot, perhaps to support a mirror. I took a picture of it for posterity's sake and sat in front of it, staring. Suddenly, an *Ah-ha* moment. I decided to take off the backsplash and re-purpose it as the base for a reading lamp. It was a perfect, no-cost solution to too little light in my bedroom. Then, the main piece would become a sofa table. I could re-use a shelf I had from Seth's room and suspend it from the underside of the table to fashion a floating shelf. Perfect. The well-conceived plan was in place. Now it just needed to be implemented.

I removed the backsplash and plugged in my finish sander. I initially thought that a light sanding was going to be enough to prepare the table for paint. The sander whirled into action. But I was discontent with the rate at which the top was being smoothed. With coarser-grit sandpaper, progress picked up. However, as I continued working, I realized that the sanding was revealing deeper problems that required attention. If I didn't get to the root of the problem, no amount of paint could keep the flaws hidden forever.

I think we have a tendency to gloss over our own problems. We put on a façade in an effort to disguise the defect. *No one ever has to know.* The problem is, while we may be successful at hiding a heart issue from others, it is no secret to God. What's needed is profound soul-searching, exposing and debriding the gash much like the way a physician treats an infected wound. It is only when we confront our demons with Truth that the gouges are filled in and wounds are healed to reveal a useful, functional and beautiful Christ-follower.

Search me, O God, and know my heart; test me and know my anxious thoughts. (Psalm 139:23)

Daily challenge:
What are you hiding? Confront it and allow God's grace to heal the wound.

Testing

Test. Sometimes the word is right up there with other four-letter words. It strikes terror and causes sudden increases in heart rate and blood pressure. Sweat glands open, body temperatures rise, muscles twitch and panic sets in. Sound familiar?

Last night I received a phone call from the grammar-school principal asking me to finish standardized testing. That was a novel request. I was to administer the tests to kids who had been absent the first-time around. It was my job to read the instructions, watch time limits and proctor the children as they progressed question by question. I agreed.

I felt for those students. I distinctly remember the standardized tests in my past. I loathed them and seldom did well. I was not a whiz kid; I had to work hard for everything I got. My scores were mediocre at best, regardless of how hard I concentrated or how neatly I filled in those stupid little circles with my #2 lead pencil, eraser standing guard at the opposite end of the sharpened point. Somehow, I always second-guessed myself to the detriment of my score. It's not surprising that I felt nervous as test times came rolling around from elementary school to the high school SAT's and college GRE exams.

Smiling, I used the most nurturing and maternal voice I could muster up as I read the carefully orchestrated instructions. I wanted to make them feel at ease, poised to do their best. As I watched the children choose their answers, I wished I could reach out and guide their hands to the correct answer. But alas, I could not.

I'm not comfortable with tests—and I'm not alone. Countless times God tested Israel's faith and obedience. Unfortunately, the people failed as many times as they passed. Then, in the book best known for its discourse on testing and trials, James states, *Consider it pure joy, my brothers, whenever you face trials of many kinds, because you know that the testing of your faith develops perseverance. Perseverance must finish its work so that you may be mature and complete, not lacking anything* (James 1:2-4).

Testing is not always pleasant, but it can be the catalyst for growth. Even our transient failures can point the way to repentance, recovery and restoration, ultimately guiding us to a passing grade.

> *Blessed is the man who perseveres under trial, because when he has stood the test, he will receive the crown of life that God has promised to those who love him. (James 1:12)*

Daily challenge:
Don't shy away from tests. They can produce results otherwise impossible.

The Right Tools

Grrr. My frustration mounted as I wrestled the wire cable. This was supposed to be a simple, five-minute job. Instead, it turned into a fiasco that left my fingers pin-pricked and bleeding. All I wanted to do was hang a shelf below a sofa table, suspended with thin metal cable. At the Tractor Supply store, a down-home kind of store where barn doors, gun safes and chicken feed are sold under one roof, I selected the cable I wanted. The clerk effortlessly cut a length of twelve feet with his cable-cutting machine. It looked so easy—and it was. I didn't even think about asking him to cut four equal pieces.

When I got home, I fetched the tin snips from the garage and started cutting the cable. Well, not quite. I was unsuccessful. Cable half the diameter of a pencil did not submit to the blades. Rather, the cable just got "smooshed." I ran out to the garage again, cable in tow and went through three different tool boxes trying to find some other implement of destruction. It was useless. A few tools severed a fiber or two, but that only created sharp points. I was fast losing patience—and blood.

Finally, I spied an axe over by the wood pile. *Ah-ha. I'll show that cable who's boss.* I grabbed a piece of solid oak and spread the cable across the board, just as a butcher places the chicken's neck on the block. I let the axe descend, striking the cable with a firm blow. Not much happened. With each strike the cable radically twisted, as if in protest and trying to escape. Finally, after many maniacal blows, the cable began to give way. I triumphantly held the two ends in the air. I still had to tame the finger-mincing frayed ends, but at least the cable was cut.

With the right tools, cutting that cable would not have been a problem. Instead, the job was a nightmare. Spiritually, we do the same thing. Rather than equip ourselves with the tools that are provided for a triumphant life—the helmet of salvation, a belt of truth, a breastplate of righteousness, the sword of the Spirit and our feet ready for battle—we try to get by with whatever is convenient and "easy." In reality, this only makes our tasks more difficult and frustrating.

Therefore put on the full armor of God, so that when the day of evil comes, you may be able to stand your ground . . .. (Ephesians 6:13)

Daily challenge:
Do yourself a favor: Invest in a good set of spiritual tools. It's worth the cost.

Into the World

Most evangelicals recognize the Great Commission, spoken by Jesus to the eleven remaining disciples after he had been crucified, buried and risen to life again. I distinctly remember at least 392 missionaries using the text at the end of their slide shows. Everyone within hearing distance felt compelled to start packing suitcases. But is a suitcase required to *"go into all the world"*?

This morning I was working on the tedious job of creating a database of every hospital in the country that provides cardiac-surgery services. Fortunately, I found a web source that houses all the information. It requires, however, that I follow links to each hospital, state by state, inspecting their websites for the services provided and then transferring that information to my evolving database.

That being said, I was busy clicking away when I came upon the general site for the Baptist Memorial Healthcare Corporation. From there I discovered fifteen hospitals in a handful of states that operate under this corporation's umbrella. I delighted to find the following statement on every page of each hospital's website: "In keeping with the three-fold ministry of Christ—preaching, teaching and healing—Baptist Memorial Health Care Corporation will be the leader in providing quality health care." *Wow.* In such a secular world, I was amazed to find a mission statement so forthright. With further browsing I noticed a Scripture verse on every solitary page. The verses were taken from Old Testament books such as Joshua, Psalms, Proverbs, Lamentations and Joel and New Testament samplings from Hebrews, Colossians, Philippians and I Thessalonians and more.

I was not expecting to find spiritual encouragement from hospital web sites; yet I did. None of the hospitals used the same verses, indicating that the "Daily Bread" feature did not come from a corporate office. Rather, it appears that each hospital had found a simple way to take the Gospel to the world—a world of individuals who are sick, mentally needy, rejoicing in new birth, or facing life's greatest challenges, even death.

> He said to them, *"Go into all the world and preach the good news to all creation." (Mark 16:15)*

Daily challenge:
Look for specific ways to reach your world.

Under His Wings

For weeks now, God has brought to mind a friend and her family who, following a traumatic event, moved out of state to begin again. For several weeks, we corresponded. It was a great time of encouragement for us both. Then, without explanation, the emails stopped coming, creating a void of meaningful messages in my inbox. I felt guilty for not continuing to write, but I didn't want to make her feel obligated. However, I have not been able to shake the feeling that something is wrong. *Really wrong.*

After weeks of being prompted to pray for her, I finally sat at my computer and selected an e-card. My dilemma was to know what to say. I didn't want to open mouth, insert foot. More than anything, I wanted her to feel wrapped in the Father's embrace and safe under His wings.

The beautiful imagery of protective wings is portrayed in an amazing documentary, "The March of the Penguins," shot in the frozen Antarctic wilderness. Months were spent capturing the life cycle of the emperor penguins, stalwart birds in an unforgiving environment. The playful penguins were full of whimsy as they slid effortlessly down the icy slopes or dove into the waters, swimming the eloquent sequences of an underwater ballet. But the harsh reality was not to be missed: the required inland trek of hundreds of miles, exposure to the darkest, stormiest and most frigid winter days, the risk of being eaten by hungry seals and the females' daunting task of making a return trip to the sea to bring back food for their spouses and babies, yet unborn.

In the penguin world, the eggs are laid by the females but protected by the fathers. Papa Penguin immediately takes the laid egg and cradling it on the tops of his feet, pulls it under the protection of his feathers. There it stays. If the egg rolls off onto the frozen ground for even a moment, the chick inside will freeze to death, leaving the mother to grieve on her return. The penguin chick, while in the egg or once hatched, fully depends on his father for shelter and ultimately, for his only chance of survival. That God uses the analogy of protective wings to help us understand His role in our lives is hardly surprising. Under the cover of His wings is safety and comfort.

> *He will cover you with his feathers, and under his wings you will find refuge; his faithfulness will be your shield and rampart. (Psalm 91:4)*

Daily challenge:
If you are feeling cold and exposed, retreat to the warmth of God's wings.

Love Loudly

Some days I wonder whether I have anything to write about. Today was one of those days. It's not that the day was uneventful; it was anything but. Gary and Seth drove four hours to northern Virginia to pick up a truck bought on E-bay only to return empty-handed: multiple problems undisclosed by the seller. *Hmm . . .* time wasted or busted plans for topics? *Nah.*

What about cutting corners, sanding away imperfections, hitting the nail on the head? I had played carpenter again, building a hefty dining-room table. *Nope.* Even my run, which went exceptionally well—surprisingly—failed to give me any food for fodder. I moved on to preparing dinner, hoping something would come to me. Nothing seemed quite right. So off to my bath I went.

Submersed in luxurious bubbles, I used my soaking time to read a magazine. Browsing the issue at hand, I was intrigued by a piece pertaining to the use of the words, "I love you." The author presented a case for the trivialized overuse of the word trio. During her childhood, those words were not used freely, now making her uncomfortable to use them willy-nilly. She even chooses to draw a heart rather than spelling out the words. She was stingy in her reproach to declare love, but at least it gave me something to think about.

Does saying "I love you" a hundred times a day make us better Christians? I've heard it said—I think it was my mother—that you should take every opportunity to use the phrase, because it might be your last chance. There is truth to that. My family was an "I-love-you" sort, while Gary's group was more reserved. Love abounded in both homes, but the DeLanceys were admittedly more vocal about it.

Those we love should never be wanting in hearing those words used sincerely and often. Even more, they should never be without feeling our love. There is no better reminder of what that love looks like than portions of The Love Chapter.

> *Love is patient, love is kind. It does not envy, it does not boast, it is not proud. It is not rude, it is not self-seeking, it is not easily angered, it keeps no record of wrongs. Love does not delight in evil but rejoices with the truth. It always protects, always trusts, always hopes, always perseveres. Love never fails . . . And now these three remain: faith, hope and love. But the greatest of these is love. (I Corinthians 13:4-13)*

Daily challenge:
Love often. Love loudly. Love today.

Forgiveness

On this Super Bowl Sunday I thought I would be writing about "superness." But no. Just when I thought everything was under control, I got blindsided, sending me into the doldrums of disappointment. When Dr. Dobson wrote *Parenting Isn't for Cowards*, he wasn't kidding.

A sign over our front door reads "Return with Honor." A Marine mantra, we adopted it as a reminder that we represent God and family every time we step over the threshold. Unfortunately, we learned this morning that someone in our family had betrayed our trust and lied about it to boot. The actions were not honorable; now we have to figure out where to go from here.

My first reaction was disbelief; my second, anger. How could this person have been so . . . so . . . well, stupid? There, I said it. He is not dumb, but he sure acted like it. When confronted, he offered explanations for his behavior, none of which had any particular merit. With one really bad decision, all the trust that had been built—especially over the last six months—flew the coop faster than a chicken. He knows he did wrong, is apologetic and understands consequences will follow. If only he could be like his parents . . . (heavy sigh) . . . *oops*, he is.

As I think about his error, it hit me that I'm just as bad. I lie to God. I promise to do something and don't follow through. Or I say I love God but fail to love my neighbor. I have every intention of doing right but allow circumstances to dissuade me. I have broken the trust but assume that God will, because He declared that our confessed sin is removed *as far as the east is from the west* (Psalm 103:12), continue to love and care for me.

So, what should my reaction be toward my son? How can I balance the delivery of inevitable penalties for misdoings with forgiveness and everyday interaction? Am I supposed to act mad or grumpy or dejected just so he understands how much he wounded me? Or, shall I "forgive and forget," acting as though nothing happened?

The Apostle Paul writes this to the Corinthians: *Now instead, you ought to forgive and comfort him, so that he will not be overwhelmed by excessive sorrow* (II Corinthians 2:7). Ah. I'm beginning to understand. It is my role to extend love, forgiveness and encouragement. I must emulate my Father's way of dealing with my own sin—with delightful mercy.

> *Who is a God like you, who pardons sin and forgives the transgression of the remnant of his inheritance? You do not stay angry forever but delight to show mercy. (Micah 7:18)*

Daily challenge:
Constant reminders of past sin disprove forgiveness.

Limits

I made a fresh pot of coffee to kick start my sixteen-year-old's brain. I don't always rise to see Seth off to school, but after yesterday, I wanted to encourage him in the new day—a new start.

Once he left, I painted more polyurethane onto my new table, contemplating the concept of sin, sorrow, repentance and forgiveness. My bedside talk with Seth last night, made in the cover of darkness before he dropped off to sleep, brought a sense of restoration to both of us. He seemed truly sorry for his deceit and was wrestling with the question that plagues many of us after a bonehead move: "How could I be that stupid?"

But what will happen when he asks to do something and we say "no" based on his recent behavior? Is that fair? Is that "no" paramount to unforgiveness on our part? What does God do after we sin? *Hmm . . . .*

In fact, why does God dictate behavior in the first place? He tells us not to have other gods, do not steal, do not murder, do not lie, do not commit adultery and more. Now, follow this hypothetical conversation between God and human:

> Human: "Hey God. I want to go out with my friends tonight. That OK with you?"
> God: "What will you do? Where are you going?"
> Human: "What? You don't trust me. That's not fair. You make me so mad!"
> God: "You're right. I don't trust you. Sin natures cannot be trusted. If you were intrinsically trustworthy, no boundaries would ever need to be set."
> Human: "That's dumb and I have rights. You're just still mad about the other weekend."
> God: "No. You asked for forgiveness and I extended that to you. I am trying to protect you from yourself. I know that given the chance, your old nature can surface."

Get the idea? Limits are set because we broke the trust. In fact, in and of ourselves we are incapable of keeping the trust. But God forgives and loves us all the same. As parents, we have a responsibility to forgive and love when trust snaps. And, just as God sets parameters by which we should live, we have a responsibility to set limits for those we love. Setting standards is truly God-like.

From their callous hearts comes iniquity; the evil conceits of their minds know no limits. (Psalm 73:7)

Daily challenge:
Set limits bound by love and mercy, not contempt.

I Run

I'm rushing. There is a house to tidy, painting supplies to put away, firewood to stack, errands to run. Then, at 2:00 p.m., I get to run with young women in a running class at Liberty University. I enjoy gathering the girl power into one big running herd, heading for the hills.

Although Professor Horton usually manages to embarrass me by telling stories, he also asks pointed questions. One of the questions I can count on, asked after he describes the numerous injuries I sustained over the years, is this: "Why do you run?"

"Because I can" is my standard answer. While that is true, today I'm going to answer it differently.

I have always approached athletics—as a participant and coach—as a way to spiritually mature. Sports teach so many lessons about steadfastness, staying the course, perseverance and wholeheartedness. We equate the toils of training as opportunities to *press on* (Philippians 3:12-14) and run the race *with perseverance* (Hebrews 12:1).

There is certainly nothing wrong with using athletic analogies. The authors of Scripture used this parallelism to make the concept more understandable. However, when thinking about God's sovereignty, I realized that His purpose was to make me athletic. It was His purpose to make me a runner. It was not something that just happened.

Why is that? Is it so I can set records? Is it so I can be in great shape? While those things might happen, I suggest those are not reason enough. The reason that God made me a runner was to equip me to ultimately reflect His character.

I have to look at my athletic endeavors as a means to an end, not a means unto itself. If I can run to present Christ to people, then I will run. If I can set trail records so that it gives me a platform to write a book about God's faithfulness, then I will go to the woods.

Run on, friend. Run on.

There are different kinds of gifts, but the same Spirit. There are different kinds of service, but the same Lord. There are different kinds of working, but the same God works all of them in all men. All these are the work of one and the same Spirit, and he gives them to each one, just as he determines. (I Corinthians 12:4-6, 11)

Daily challenge:
Your talents are not yours to keep. Share them to share God.

Consider the Sun

The flu can be a terrible thing. Just ask the teacher who called me to substitute. From his first *hello*, I could tell he was more than a little out of sorts. The plague had overtaken him and he succumbed to his desire to escape a school day. "Are you willing to teach tomorrow? It will be a full day, but I need them to do something constructive." I jumped at the chance. Usually, I get calls to sub in the grammar school, but those little people scare me. It's not that I don't like them; it's just that I prefer students who can presumably walk and talk at the same time.

When I arrived at school, I looked over the Algebra 2 class material. We began a new section of adding, subtracting and multiplying polynomials. How fun! I had no problem teaching this section and they responded nicely.

Then it was on to 8th-grade Physical Science. The topic was Newton's Second Law. We included discussions about friction, microwelds, whether a bullet dropped and a bullet shot horizontally would simultaneously reach the ground and other perplexing relationships. We ventured into the world of gravitational pull, size of objects and the distance between said objects. This led to musings about what happens to weight when one is standing on a scale inside an elevator that is falling on the moon, Mars and Jupiter. Fascinating albeit random contemplations.

The textbook gave a scientific explanation of why the earth maintains its orbit instead of being flung into deep space. While the facts were valid, the details lacked a certain element—God's design. God set the sun in place and hung the stars. He designed a magnificent set of physical laws that keeps the planets aligned, lights the day and keeps the oceans in their place. None of this splendor happened by accident. God spoke the world into existence and by His word, maintains it.

> *When I consider your heavens, the work of your fingers, the moon and the stars, which you have set in place, what is man that you are mindful of him, the son of man that you care for him? (Psalm 8:3, 4)*

Daily challenge:
See the sun. Remember the Son.

Dirty

I was delighted to be in the classroom again. Algebra 2 provided a healthy dose of amusement as I pitted one team against another in problem-solving at the board. Then, it was on to 8th-grade Science, a classroom full of adolescents who demanded a firm hand and clear instructions to realize any academic gain. With a major chapter test looming, we spent the class period in review. I hit every term associated with Newton's first law and happily jotted important concepts on the board, hastily erasing them to make room to calculate velocity, distance and acceleration. Over and over the process was repeated. It was exciting to see them suddenly exclaim, "I got it!"

When the bell rang marking the end of class, I walked back to the home room, greeting teachers and students along the way. One teacher was so sweet to ask, "Are you okay today?" How nice for someone to care. I dropped off my books and making my way to the lunch room, intercepted Gary, who also works at the school.

"Ah . . . Have you looked in a mirror lately?"

Oh my. What is he talking about? I scurried into the bathroom and lost my appetite. Imagine someone working in a coal mine, only the whites of their eyes showing against a black, coal-encrusted face. I knew I didn't leave the house looking like that. What happened? I had used a new makeup foundation that supposedly adjusts to my complexion. Still, I seriously doubted that it could turn me into a person of color.

Then it hit me. Long gone were the green chalkboards of yesteryear. White boards, black markers and ink-trapped erasers were used throughout the building. With all the writing and erasing I had been doing, the black on my hands must have been transferred to my face when brushing my hair back or unwittingly touching my skin. And those kids never told me!

Scrubbing the black blotches from my face, I thought about how I can become oblivious to the blotches of sin in my life. I simply proceed "as is," never looking in the mirror of my soul. Unless someone tells me of my blemish, the ugly fact escapes my conscience.

Search me, O God and know my heart; test me and know my anxious thoughts. See if there is any offensive way in me, and lead me in the way of understanding. (Psalm 139:23, 24)

Daily challenge:
Each time you look in the mirror, inspect your heart as well.

Forgiveness Again

Some thoughts hold on tighter than a kid on Mr. Toad's Wild Ride. Lately, I'm stuck on sin and forgiveness. I'm learning to forgive without raising ugly walls fabricated by grudges. God is revealing practical ways for me to extend forgiveness even within my own family. However, as I read in Psalms, I rediscovered a chapter that presents the issue from a totally different perspective—that of the sinner himself.

There have been a couple things in my life that I deeply regret. If I could roll back time and have a do-over, I would. I have repented, the one who was offended has offered forgiveness and yet, sometimes I don't "feel" very forgiven. The guilt monster crawls out from under my bed and in the spooky darkness, makes me afraid—afraid of my own shortcomings and afraid that my sin will be remembered and held against me—by God and others—despite assurances to the contrary.

Guilt can be cancer-like, eating away at your very existence. I find past actions so reprehensible that I can not imagine how I ever stooped so low. How could I have been so stupid? How could I have been so vile? There are "bad" people who wouldn't think of doing what I did—and I'm a Christian! The sharp barbs of my own accusations cut to my soul's core, rendering me sorrowful and sad. I tell myself that I am forgiven but find it hard to accept. Rather, I carry the misery and guilt on my shoulders as if in penance. But, is this how it should be? Not according to Psalm 32.

> *Blessed is he whose transgressions are forgiven, whose sins are covered. Blessed is the man whose sin the LORD does not count against him and in whose spirit is no deceit. When I kept silent, my bones wasted away through my groaning all day long. For day and night your hand was heavy upon me; my strength was sapped as in the heat of summer. Selah. Then I acknowledged my sin to you and did not cover up my iniquity. I said, "I will confess my transgressions to the LORD"— and you forgave the guilt of my sin. Selah. (vs. 1-5)*

Notice that the writer says not only were his sins forgiven, but the guilt of his sin was removed as well. He no longer needed to be crushed under its weight. And, what was David's response once freed from the guilt's shackles? He rejoiced.

> *Rejoice in the LORD and be glad, you righteous; sing, all you who are upright in heart! (Psalm 31:11)*

Daily challenge:
Though sin bears consequences, chronic guilt after forgiveness is not one of them.
Let it go. God covered that, too.

Through His Eyes

John Satore is a fabulous photographer. Though a bit eccentric, he is the consummate example of an artist in motion. With cameras in hand and loaded with lenses nearly as long as his arm, he travels the world looking for the perfect shot—the perfect moment. Whether in the Bolivian rainforest or the frozen wilderness of Alaska, he works countless hours capturing scenes that tell a story. The images freeze moments in time. The spectator can experience what he sees through the viewfinder.

I sat in the living room with Seth watching the documentary on this world-renowned photojournalist. *What is he thinking?* I pondered, watching my son's expressions. Seth has shown strong talent as a photographer. He is serious about his genre of art, even selling his cherished motocross bike to buy his first camera. Now, after being hired to shoot weddings and family portraits, he purchased a camera capable of capturing the drama and lightning-paced action of sports. He has shifted gears in school and has become focused, no pun intended, in his work.

"Seth, does this motivate and inspire you?" I anticipated a resounding "yes" but it never came. Instead, Seth commiserated.

"No, Mom. It discourages me." I was shocked. "I have never shot one photo that is anywhere close to the quality of his work." Though I beg to differ, Seth isn't really interested in what I think. He is comparing his work against someone with years of experience, the best equipment and the most intriguing locations.

Perhaps without realizing it, Seth has made clear a spiritual truth. Without the advantage of looking through the lens of God's eyes, seeing all things perfectly, our perspectives can run amok. What might appear to our eyes as "good" may, upon closer inspection, be fuzzy and out of focus. If only we could see through His eyes . . ..

If we could see
through His eyes
Then we could dare to love
the way God loves . . .
Then we would understand
the way God understands
For His eyes see through the
surface right down to our needs
Far beyond where we are
to where we can be . . ..
(Chorus, *Through His Eyes* by For Him)

Daily challenge:
The Scripture is God's viewfinder. Look through it and find focus.

Stupid Children

John 3:16 is oft read on end-zone signs waved by shirtless dudes donning multi-colored clown wigs. You've seen them. Although the truth abides, it is hardly a fair representation of the message. That God's love can be so deep, so selfless, is utterly amazing.

None of us will ever realize the angst we brought our parents in our growing-up days. If you happen to be one of the few perfect children ever born—or have hatched one—you need read no further. However, given the fact that the clear majority of us have brought offenses to our mamas and papas, you might want to read on.

Parenting gets tougher as kids get older. Trust me on this one. At one point, a wooden spoon flapped in the air elicited an appropriate response. When matters of discipline occur on that level, there is seldom any mental anguish that lasts more than a few moments. I can't remember anytime I lost sleep over toys not being put away. But as the kids grow older and independent thinking becomes highly esteemed, it has become much harder to find rest at night.

It's difficult to watch kids make bad decisions despite counsel to the contrary. I feel like I'm turning blue, out of breath from talking. I use sound Biblical concepts. I use logic. I make sure they understand the impending consequences should they ignore or defy us. I try being silent. I try speaking my mind. I feel helpless to elicit a mindset and behavior change, though I pray for them constantly. My heart feels damaged. I ache for them to grow up and make wise decisions. Our friends speak about how they were twenty-five before getting their acts together. I find no particular solace in that. I wonder if I can last that long.

I asked my husband what we did wrong. "Nothing. The boys have to accept responsibility for their actions and attitudes." But all the same, I wish I could make them act perfectly. Then I think about this. How much more do I grieve my Father? He wants only the best for us, yet we somehow don't get the message. We resist the instructions that He so freely gives. Somehow, we think that we know better than He is. Shame on us.

His heart must infinitely ache for His children who are stubborn and stupid. And yet, the Father remains faithful.

> *For God so loved the world that he gave his one and only Son, that whoever believes in him shall not perish but have eternal life. (John 3:16)*

Daily challenge:
We can train our children, but only God can change them.

Who Am I?

Even in my fifties, I struggle with who I am and what I'm supposed to become. The latest chapter in this saga recently came to a head. With a big race looming, I knew I needed to run long. Joining a girlfriend for the run, our conversation quickly turned to plans for the coming year. She had just decided to accept a sponsorship offer from a shoe company. I, on the other hand, had just gotten dumped after a lengthy sponsorship. I was wounded but decided it might be okay. No contracts holding me to do "x" number of races. No pressure to turn in good results. But what do I do? I commit to a tough race schedule anyway.

It wouldn't be so bad except that I have come to dread training. I am less than enthusiastic to go out in the cold or give up six or seven hours on a Saturday. I don't really even like racing, probably because of the diminishing returns I get from year to year. But, The BEAST series, three spring races (35, 26 and 31 miles) and three fall races (100, 54 and 67 miles) beckons. I want to do it, but at the same time, I don't.

On top of that, I can't even figure out what I want to be when I grow up. After a twenty-some-year career as a perfusionist, leaving the clinic and launching a consulting business is not going well. I love building things and organizing closets, but how do I make that a business? Or maybe I'll be a motivational speaker or go back to teaching. All the while, I substitute teach for peanuts, trying to fill the income hole created when I quit a "real" job five months back.

Who am I? I'm really not a perfusionist anymore. If I quit racing, I lose the distinction of being a competitor. I am a wife, but I'm not sure if I'm a good one. And, my role as a mother—well, I feel less than adequate.

Intellectually, I know that I am God's and my true identity is in Him. But practically, I'm not sure who I should be right now. I'm searching and doubt that an answer will come in the next two lines. However, I can be confident that God does have a plan. Stay tuned . . ..

> *I run in the path of your commands, for you have set my heart free.*
> *Direct me in the path of your commands, for there I find delight.*
> *(Psalm 119:32, 35)*

Daily challenge:
Let uncertainty be the portal to God's perfect plan.

Restore to Me the Joy

In Psalm 51, the prophet Nathan had just confronted King David of his sin with Bathsheba, jerking David's heart back toward God. The reader feels the depth of emotion as David pleads with God to have mercy, blot out sins, wash away iniquity and cleanse him. The sin had made the king miserable, even to the point of "crushing his bones." And yet, as he cries out in remorse, the desperation gives way to the sweetness of God's forgiveness. *Restore to me the joy . . ..*

The joy I previously found in training is gone. Sometimes I catch a little glimpse of it on a particularly beautiful day when my legs feel fresh and the air crisp and clean. However, many days the thought of venturing down the road is a chore that only keeps me from doing other things. Maybe I should take a break from racing and the mandatory training. But if I do, I forfeit goals and dreams.

Now I am conflicted about whether or not I should run a race this Saturday. To the non-athlete, this may seem like a small matter—hardly one to interrupt sleep or plague my every waking moment. And yet it's important to me, because this decision impacts my goals for the entire year. No race . . . No Beast. It's now or never.

I don't like living under a dark cloud. It paints everything the same color of gray. Given the uncertainty with my job situation, I know to be careful about transferring my less-than-optimal feelings to everything else, including this decision. While I don't want to be subject to emotional bondage to train, I don't want to abandon a challenge.

It would be easy to go to the race this weekend to have fun from the sidelines. But that would be the easy way out. I don't want to be a quitter based on what may be transient emotions. So I have finally decided to ask God to *restore to me the joy*—even in the cold, predawn hours and when my legs and lungs are screaming for mercy.

Create in me a pure heart, O God, and renew a steadfast spirit within me. Do not cast me from your presence or take your Holy Spirit from me. Restore to me the joy of your salvation and grant me a willing spirit, to sustain me. (Psalm 51:10-12)

Daily challenge:
Restored joy trumps unpredictable emotion.

Classical Learning

Today I stand guard in the school's lobby, monitoring those who come and go. After figuring out the phone system and greeting the occasional visitor, I sit in this less-than-stimulating environment without much to do. Well, I should probably do some writing. But what shall I write? Then, a stream of consciousness rushes in—school . . . teach . . . teaching . . . classical education. I wonder if I can identify what things are to be taught –and how—from a Biblical perspective?

Classical education is based on the Trivium: grammar, which emphasizes foundational concepts and facts and the dialectic that builds on core knowledge and logical reasoning. Then the rhetoric component builds on prior knowledge and asks the student to creatively and effectively espouse and defend his positions.

Doing a quick electronic rummage of *teach,* I found no less than 349 occurrences in the Bible. Admonishments to teach the laws and decrees fit the grammar element, since this is rudimentary. Instructions are also given to teach music, language, literature, truth, the fear of God and what is right—all necessary for a productive and vital life.

Principles of the dialectic stage of learning were also abundant. In this stage, the student is asked to apply reasoning to his foundation of facts. The Bible instructs us to pursue wisdom, understand precepts and use knowledge to exercise good judgment—all critical in the process of logical thought. In dialectic schooling, the use of a question/answer interchange is an essential tool to accomplish the goal. There are many examples of this in Scripture, the technique being used by Christ Himself as He taught in the synagogues.

And finally, can we identify elements of Rhetoric education? I Corinthians 11 speaks of analyzing cultural norms. Other passages ask the student to use *true and reliable words* so that sound answers can be given. We are also to distinguish messages that have true authority and discern what is holy and common, true or false doctrine. Questions prompting introspective thinking were even used by the Pharisees, a group priding themselves in their education, religiosity and piety.

The search confirmed my preference for classical education. But the process is not confined to a school building. We should learn the facts of Scripture (grammar), identify how they apply to us (dialectic), and then articulate, demonstrate and defend them (rhetoric).

But grow in the grace and knowledge of our Lord and Savior Jesus Christ. To him be glory both now and forever! Amen. (II Peter 3:18)

Daily challenge:
If you never move beyond the facts of Scripture, your education is incomplete.

Be My Valentine

Valentine's Day. Oh what memories. In my grade-school years, Mother took me to the store to select just the right package of the corny cards, often allowing me to buy heart-shaped candies to give to my friends. With list of classmates in hand, I carefully selected just the right card and candy for each student, sealing the envelope with my sticky slobber. A shoebox was decorated with pink construction paper, heart-shaped paper doilies, cupid stickers and a slit cut into the top of my "mailbox." I was thrilled to have Bobby drop in a card and a candy reading "kiss me."

But, the real buzz was to produce the world's largest Valentine card for my teacher. I gathered all the construction paper I had, laid it out on the floor and after taping it together, cut out a very strange-looking creature. With a huge "I love you" written on the paper, I nearly burst with pride as my teacher unfolded the gigantic greeting, eight or ten feet in length and exclaimed, "Oh my . . .." Of course, I took that as a compliment!

I heard on the news that the average sum a man spends on Valentine's Day is about $175. It's unfortunate that some women come to view such as an entitlement. Or, they somehow equate the amount of money spent on the level of offered love. While it is easy to be self-righteous in not holding high expectations, we can be equally at fault if we play the "it's the thought that counts" card. Now, I am not suggesting that something has to be purchased for love to be expressed. However, if the "it's the thought that counts" phrase translates to no action taken, it might border on a lousy excuse.

Just as faith without works is dead, love without action is equally lifeless. Love is the action of being patient. Love is the action of being kind. Love is the action of not being rude or selfish. Love is the action of forgiveness. Love is the action of hope and protection. Love is the action of perseverance.

Although we should act out love every day, Valentine's Day gives us a special opportunity. Whether the action of loving includes the purchase of something is up for grabs. However, to come up with a creative way to demonstrate our love is a very good thing. It may take some thought and effort, but we will be obedient to love by doing.

And now these three remain: faith, hope and love. But the greatest
of these is love. (I Corinthians 13:13)

Daily challenge:
Find a way to show your love by an act of kindness.

Choosing to Suffer

Tomorrow I will run a thirty-five mile race and I know what's coming. For the first two miles I will be forced to run faster than I want, pulled by those in front and pushed by those behind. Then, when the trail gives way to an old grassy road that climbs a hill, I will reduce to a brisk walk, catching my breath. I will try not to be frustrated by those running full speed ahead. I shall tell myself to be patient and enjoy the day.

My legs will be getting tired by the turn-around point. I'll think that the five miles back to the aid station on this reverse loop course is never-ending. Once there, I will begin to count down the miles. On a narrow and rocky trail around the lake, I will likely trip multiple times, hoping to avoid chilly plunge. I will see the finish line across the inlet, run another mile and finally cross the line. Exhausted and back hurting, even the steps up into the bath house will seem monumental.

So, if I know I'm going to suffer, why do I voluntarily choose to do so? I chose this path because it will be worth it in the end.

Think about those who chose to suffer for reasons much more substantive than mine. Paul and Barnabas traveled together, preaching and teaching in Iconium. Though many Jews believed, those not convinced of the Gospel rallied the Gentiles against the two missionaries. A plot to kill the men rose but undeterred, they simply left to preach in nearby Lystra. Healing a lame man, the crowd misunderstood their healing power. Thinking they were actually the gods Zeus and Hermes, they bowed the knee, pagan priests bringing sacrifice. Of course, Paul and Barnabas protested, proclaiming they were of the true God. But unbelieving Jews from Antioch and Iconium, looking to entrap the men, rallied the crowd. Paul was dragged from the city, horrifically stoned and left for dead.

Most people—if they survived—would take that as a sign never to return. Not Paul. He ventured back into the city, bruised and bleeding. The next day Paul and Barnabas traveled to Derbe to preach but soon returned to Lystra, the place of his suffering.

Suffering can be tolerated only if there is hope for things to come.

Then they returned to Lystra, Iconium and Antioch, strengthening the disciples and encouraging them to remain true to the faith. "We must go through many hardships to enter the kingdom of God," they said. (Acts 14:21b, 22)

Daily challenge:
Look beyond your suffering to the prize.

The Run

Shortly after the starting gun sounded, I watched the new day dawn. With calm winds, the thirty-degree temperature felt comfortable. I was running relaxed and surprised that I was not feeling the anticipated angst of running a pace other than my own. Will the day be better than I thought?

I wrote yesterday about suffering during the race, fully resigning myself to the inevitable. But as I visited with friends last night at the pre-race briefing, I felt an unfamiliar calm. Chatting easily, I realized opportunities to share my recent prayer for joy to be restored. The comments came naturally, not contrived. As I finally laid my head on the pillow, I was thankful God allowed me to represent Him in such a unique environment.

Running with my iPod plugged into my ears, I consciously tried to be content with my position and merely do what I was supposed to be doing: run smooth and efficient, eat before I'm hungry and drink before I'm thirsty. I felt surprisingly strong, happy I was running.

The music seemed perfectly choreographed during the race. Perhaps the best example was about one mile from the end. As the first notes of the bold introduction wafted through my earpieces, my steps become lighter and easier, pace swifter. It was just what I needed to carry me through the remaining miles. The Twila Paris song entitled "Runner" had worked itself into my heart years ago. It inspired me then and was God-sent in the late stages of the race when fatigue set in.

God was so faithful to make my suffering bearable, buoying me and allowing me to set my sites on future challenges. It was worth it all.

"Runner when the road is long
Feel like giving in but you're hanging on
Oh runner, when the race is won
You will run into His arms." (chorus)

Daily challenge:
Sometimes faith requires action despite our trepidation.

Worth It All

I can get stuck thinking about one thing for several days running, no pun intended. In this case, I've had this idea of suffering drifting through the back hallways of my mind. I anticipated suffering in the race. And sure enough, the race and recovery afterwards offered an element of suffering. But that suffering was nothing.

Years ago, while I lived in Ohio, our church hosted a group from the Shepherds Ministry in Union Grove, Wisconsin. This ministry began in a local church to assist one family with a special-needs child. Wanting to provide an appropriate Sunday School environment, other mentally-challenged children were included and the class grew. Finally, in 1964, the Shepherds Home & School was founded as a residential facility for thirty-six children. Built out of love and service, the ministry grew along with the kids, many with Down Syndrome. An additional but necessary focus was placed on vocational training. To this day, the home provides a nurturing environment for full and part-time residential living as well as assisted independent living.

Living out acts of service, teams from Shepherds traveled to churches and schools, providing inspiring handbell, choral or Gospel presentations. These children and young adults spoke and sang with genuine purity. They demonstrated the simplicity of God's unconditional love. Despite challenges that much of society deemed severe enough to render them worthless, that group glowed with Christ's love.

Surely they had experienced enough suffering to last a lifetime. They had not asked to be handed such challenges. Yet, by God's grace, they embraced their weaknesses so that God was honored. They were happy, delightful and passionate people. And, at the conclusion of their program, a song by Esther Kerr Rusthoi was offered in benediction. Somehow in those moments, the world became much simpler and our own problems insignificant.

Oft times the day seems long, our trials hard to bear,
We're tempted to complain, to murmur and despair;
But Christ will soon appear to catch His Bride away,
All tears forever over in God's eternal day.
Refrain
It will be worth it all when we see Jesus,
Life's trials will seem so small when we see Christ;
One glimpse of His dear face all sorrow will erase,
So bravely run the race till we see Christ.
When We See Christ.
(*It Will Be Worth It All*, Words and music by Esther Kerr Rusthoi)

Daily challenge:
When you think you have it bad, look around and be grateful.

Learn to Learn

Yippee! I found out that my submitted abstract was accepted for presentation at an international perfusion meeting.

So that you know, perfusionists maintain a patient's life when the heart is stopped during surgery and blood no longer courses through the heart and lungs. Training is critically important, including study in anatomy and physiology, extracorporeal technologies, pharmacology, coagulation and hemostasis, myocardial preservation, acid-base balance and other subjects. The perfusionist must make split-second decisions and communicate well with other team members lest an unfortunate mistake be made, resulting in patient death or permanent injury. It's no wonder that not all are drawn to a profession that carries such risk and responsibility.

My research into the way perfusionists learn revealed a preference for kinesthetic learning and a secondary preference for aural learning. Two additional learning styles, visual and a read/write, were not particularly prevalent in the perfusion population. In other words, perfusionists like to do and hear. *Forget the manual. Get out of my way. Here I come.*

Depending on the situation, the perfusionists' inclination to jump in with two feet may or may not produce positive results. However, there is a Biblical principle that does hold true and relates to learning.

Proverbs 16:20 says, *Whoever gives heed to instruction prospers, and blessed is he who trusts in the LORD. The instruction must first be heard and then action must follow.* Likewise, Psalm 107:43 states that *Whoever is wise, let him heed these things and consider the great love of the LORD.* Again, the idea is to hear—then heed. Simply hearing does not qualify as true learning.

Also critical to the learning process is "observe to do." *I applied my heart to what I observed and learned a lesson from what I saw . . .* (Proverbs 24:32). Once you observe what is true and you do it (apply your heart), it is only then that true understanding is gained (learn a lesson).

No matter if you prefer to hear, see, or read, the truth is that God requires action.

> *". . . observe all these commands I am giving you to follow—to love the LORD your God, to walk in all his ways and to hold fast to him . . .." (Deuteronomy 11:22)*

Daily challenge:
Don't keep knowledge to yourself. Share it. Do it.

More Birthdays

February is a big birthday month. I have a niece born on the 16th and another on the 24th. My sister-in-law is the 20th, my twin brothers on the 21st, Gary is the 27th, I'm on the 28th and my Dad was one of those Leap Year babies. Unfortunately, I'm not good with snail-mail cards. Thankfully, e-cards give me an easy out.

There are certainly plenty of options. I went to my favorite card sites and began the arduous task of searching. I prefer animated cards with sound or music, but some were childish and others just stupid. Then, there were the cards that were "nice," some with Scripture. Finally, I found ones I liked, scripted my personal greetings and set the delivery dates. Hitting the "send" button, I was pleased to cross this off my list.

A common thread across the sent cards contained light jesting about getting old. My brothers will be 47 and my sister-in-law hits the big 5-0. Personally, I liked the ring of "a half-century" when I reached that landmark.

Although my running times reflect the accumulating years, I don't really feel that old. Sure, my skin isn't very elastic, my face is getting baggy and my body is repositioning itself. Still, I have a hard time thinking of myself as an "older" lady. I tried hard not to be forty, fat and frumpy in the last decade and don't want to be caught in the common misfortunes of the fifties. I see the fifties as an opportunity to be fit and fabulous.

Regardless of our age or how great we feel, we will surely die at some point unless Christ returns in our lifetime. We count on having another twenty or thirty years to live. And yet, we may not see the next sunrise if the Lord so ordains.

Surely, the time we have on earth is just a speck along the timeline of forevermore. We cannot afford to squander it. The hymn writer, Avis B. Christianson, penned these words in the early 1900s and the truth lives on.

. . . Only this hour is mine, Lord—
May it be used for Thee;
May ev'ry passing moment
Count for eternity . . ..

Daily challenge:
Keep track of today's wasted time. Then make a plan
to use those minutes more wisely.

Morning

I rose before the sun. Heading for the bathroom, I glanced out the sunroom windows facing east and spied an orange glow cast low on the horizon. *Ah, the promise of a pretty morning,* I thought as I planned my attack on getting my face and hair ready for the adoring public. (I jest about the adoring public.)

While I drove into work, the sky unfolded its full glory in an array of yellow, gold and orange. The light played off the clouds, creating iridescent pillows floating across the morning firmament. Like the drifting clouds, songs ascribing attributes of the morning floated through my mind. "In the morning when I wake . . . give me Jesus" sings Fernando Ortega. Or, "When morning gilds the sky, my heart awaking cries, may Jesus Christ be praised," the words penned into the German hymnal, Katholisches Gesangbuch (Würzburg, Germany, circa 1744) and set to the familiar tune in 1868 by Joseph Barnby. And how could I not think of "Morning has broken like the first morning," made popular in 1971 by Cat Stevens (though the poem was originally inked as a children's hymn in 1922 by Eleanor Farjeon)?

Later on, I came across an unfamiliar hymn. The words were written by Thomas Ken in 1674 for the *Manual of Prayers for the Use of the Scholars of Winchester College.* At the time, many considered any song not taken directly from Scripture as sacrilege. Nonetheless, Ken wrote the hymn, laden with theology, for the college men, instructing them to sing it only in the privacy of their bedrooms. How ironic that the last verse of this very long hymn, 11 stanzas long, has become the most well known melody in the church today.

Awake, my soul, and with the sun
Thy daily stage of duty run;
Shake off dull sloth, and joyful rise,
To pay thy morning sacrifice . . .
Praise God, from Whom all blessings flow;
Praise Him, all creatures here below;
Praise Him above, ye heavenly host;
Praise Father, Son, and Holy Ghost.

Daily challenge:
When I awake, I will be satisfied with seeing Your likeness. (Psalm 17:15)

For complete lyrics: http://happywonderer.wordpress.com/2007/04/15/the-doxology-awake-my-soul-and-with-the-sun/

Instructions, Please

The school is fully engaged in preparations for the annual Recitatio, a program showcasing classical education. Small children not much larger than puppies reciting two hundred major historical events, complete with motions, and second-graders verbally diagramming sentences produce gasps of wonder from the audience. Throw in Latin recitation and literature translation—in the original Greek —and you get a room full of captivated spectators. Hence, it was very bad timing for one of the key teachers to fall ill.

A few days ago, I was left with instructions on how to prepare this class for their role in the program. They were to recite three pages of Latin Catechism—grammar rules of the language. Then, each student had to write from memory each of these rules for a test grade. The problem was that they had never seen a third of the material. *Oh dear.*

I created a fill-in-the blank exercise with supplemental transparencies. I tried hard to give them novel study techniques, seeking to calm their fears. I emphasized that their test was an exact duplicate of what we were doing in class. No surprises. No tricks. They all seemed content as they left the classroom.

Enter the class today. One child announced that her mom called the ill teacher and was told they didn't have to test over the new part. All of a sudden, the entire class was revolting about taking this test, an immensely easier version than the one the teacher had left. My only recourse was to relate that I was operating on the instructions I was given; we would proceed as planned, leaving the regular teacher to sort out the details.

The problem evolved because everyone had lost contact with the source of information—the teacher. Those left holding the fort had to rely on handwritten notes, memory of prior comments and surmising about an ill-defined goal.

Isn't this the reason we get into so much trouble in our Christian life? We lose contact with the authoritative source. We rely on circumstances, feeling and emotions. We factor in what others are doing. And sometimes, we purposely avoid going to the instruction book. The result is confusion and spiritual failure. The solution, however, is to turn back to the Source of knowledge.

> *For from him and through him and to him are all things. To him be the glory forever! Amen. (Romans 11:36)*

Daily challenge:
Where do you turn for instructions? People, books—or the Bible?

A Simple Screening

For weeks, I've been trying to schedule a TB test at the health department. With a mere four hours per week when the clinic does the testing, my eyes shifted to the clock. Forty minutes remained. There was no time for procrastination.

I entered the building and approached the woman sitting behind the massive glass wall. Unceremoniously she shoved a clipboard through the opening in the glass window. "Sign in," she uttered matter-of-factly. Looking around, I noted I was alone in the cavernous waiting room. But, okay. If she wanted me to sign, I would sign. Passing the clipboard back through the opening, she took one look at my name, checked it off and with obvious satisfaction at following the procedure, immediately picked up a black marker and obliterated my name. I worked hard not to look around for cameras, sure they were hidden to capture my response to a ridiculous situation.

As I stood there, the woman spent substantial time typing information into her computer. At last, I took my seat in the empty waiting room. The nurse poked her head through the doorway. "Rebekah!" she shouted with gusto, as if wanting to be heard above a crowd's din. Alone in the room, I giggled and looked again for those cameras.

The nurse was pleasant enough. I handed her a copy of my last TB test and signed a paper allowing her to ask me "random questions"—her words. At the end of the inquisition, she determined I didn't need a TB test after all. Apparently, I was not high risk for being a TB carrier. She handed me a paper confirming I had been properly screened. "That will be $25, please." The nurse knew the questions to ask, saving me from the testing. Perhaps if there was a screening process for Christians, we could avoid exposure to things that make us sick and needing treatment.

- Have you ever had a transfusion, being saved by the blood of Christ?
- Do you have a persistent pattern of behavior, coughing up unseemly gunk from the depth of your soul?
- Have you experienced any loss of character or good works in your life?
- Have you ever had a reaction to an exposure to sin?
- What was your reaction to sin?
- Have you been visiting places that increase your exposure to sin?

Consider the blameless, observe the upright . . . Whoever is wise, let him heed these things and consider the great love of the LORD. I have considered my ways and have turned my steps to your statutes . . .. (Psalm 37:37, 107:43, 119:59)

Daily challenge:
A preemptive inspection may stave off full-blown testing.

A Firm Foundation

"I know what they'll be playing at your wedding," my dad teased with a twinkle in his eye. "'How Firm a Foundation' followed by 'Sound the Battle Cry'!" I can see him now. No matter how many times he told his little joke, something inside his head tickled him like an invisible feather. Dad erupted into laughter, coaxing tears from his eyes. I guess he thought I was puppy-like—feet too big for the body. That's where the "firm foundation" idea spawned. I think the second hymn just struck his funny bone. But as a young girl, I didn't really care. I was grateful for a dad who liked me enough to joke around.

Every time I dig a foundation, I think of my Dad. He's been with the Lord for over two decades, but he is never far from my mind. I was digging the holes for a new structure by the pool and his teasing came flashing back. I smiled as I continued to dig the holes for the massive posts intended to support three hammock chairs. I wanted to make sure they were deep and wide enough to provide structural stability. It certainly would not be good form to have our guests look forward to a restful sit, only to end up on their backs, feet pointing skyward.

On an architectural level, the building—and rebuilding—of Solomon's temple was impressive. Several chapters in I Kings speak of the foundation stones being massive in size, some as large as ten by eight cubits. (A cubit is about 18 inches.) Certainly, a lot of building can rise from a foundation of that girth.

The idea of needing a firm foundation resounds from one end of the Bible to the other. Psalm 104:5 states that *He set the earth on its foundations; it can never be moved.* I Samuel 2:8b concurs. *The foundations of the earth are the LORD's; upon them he has set the world.* And, *Righteousness and justice are the foundation of your throne; love and faithfulness go before you* (Psalm 89:14).

No structure, no organization, no faith can stand against the assault of a storm without a proper foundation. *Nevertheless, God's solid foundation stands firm . . .* (II Timothy 2:19).

> *For no one can lay any foundation other than the one already laid, which is Jesus Christ. (I Corinthians 3:11)*

Daily challenge:
Can the foundation of your life hold up to the building inspector's scrutiny?

Keeping Up with the Joneses

"Keeping up with the Joneses." We all know what that means. If one neighbor builds an addition to the house, the other neighbor follows suit. Or perhaps a new sports car arrives in the garage of 101 Jealousy Lane and soon, an equally impressive car pulls into 102.

According to *The Encyclopedia of Word and Phrase Origins* by Robert Hendrickson, the phrase was first used as a comic strip title originating in 1913. "Keeping up with the Joneses" referred to the main character's neighbors, mentioned but never seen. Speculation has it that the cartoonist's Jones family was actually a reference to North Carolina railroad tycoon Pembroke Jones, socially elite and lavish in the party and possession categories.

Now, I'm not jealous of our neighbor's possessions: cows, tractors or barns. But I find myself jealous over cooking. No joke. Here's what happened.

Seth has taken an interest in cooking. He seems to enjoy the process as well as the results. Me? I'm not a fancy cook but like to believe that my family has been well-fed over the years, even if meals have their humble beginnings inside a cardboard box.

My friend Robin, however, is the quintessential cook. She invites young women to her kitchen to teach skills, enjoying the time of preparation and consumption. Enter Seth. Robin is now hosting my sixteen-year-old as well. Afterward, her cooking is extolled. Mine rebuffed.

I admit it. I'm jealous thinking that Seth prefers Robin to me. In reality, there's plenty of room for improvement in my kitchen. I've been trying hard to find new recipes and cook more from scratch, stepping out of my comfort zone. Thankfully, the results have generally been well-received. We are eating better at my house not because I want to "keep up with the Joneses"—or in this case, Robin—but because I've been motivated by her culinary example.

Though Robin may not be aware of her impact, I am grateful for the encouragement to better serve my family.

> And let us consider how we may spur one another on toward love
> and good deeds. (Hebrews 10:24)

Daily challenge:
Encourage one another to use God-given talents in very practical ways.

A Career Shift

I couldn't sleep at all last night. My mind refused to turn off as I played conversation reruns over and over. I felt my heart race as the possibilities exploded in my mind.

I've been doing my share of mental gymnastics trying to figure out what I'm supposed to do with the rest of my life. This struggle has been growing more intense as my previous passion for perfusion has been melting into a puddle and steadily evaporating. There are so many other things I want to do.

Prompted by a recent project of mine a friend wrote: "An answer to prayer; I have been praying the Lord would show you what you would love to do . . . I will continue to pray that the Lord will give you clarity in a new job pursuit . . . You have been blessed, too, with an incredible creative streak. I love seeing the image of God in people! His work in us is somewhat of a picture of the work you do with your junk, old and salvaged items. I can only wonder what heaven will be like . . .." I tucked away her note for safekeeping. She put in writing what was in my heart.

Another friend called last night to see if I was interested in going into business. Mike is already the consummate businessman. He is well equipped, having earned an MBA in e-business. Now, he calls me to partner with him in capitalizing on the development and marketing of e-information. It is a complex plan, but the possibilities become clear as I lie in bed.

All of a sudden, I was struck with the idea that God may have just dropped an answer into my lap. I think the room lit up, pushing away the darkness. I know it may seem too good to be true, but should I be surprised that God appears to be answering the prayer of my heart? Perhaps this is the way I can develop my creative passions, sharing them with others while I remain at home to serve my family. Needless to say, I am excited to explore the possibilities.

In his heart a man plans his course, but the LORD determines his
steps. (Proverbs 16:9)

Daily challenge:
God gave you talents for an express purpose. Don't be afraid to use them.

Icons

It was five o'clock and time for Oprah. Although she and her guests are sometimes a little spiritualistic in a secular sense—how's that for an oxymoron?—her topics normally have some redeeming value. Today the stage was offered to famous folks deemed to be American icons. I happened to catch the segment with Henry Winkler of "Happy Days" fame.

The "Fonz," as he was known, was a motorcycle tough guy with a soft and sensitive inside. Every week for ten years, millions tuned in to see the interaction between Fonzie and Richie Cunningham, the All-American good kid, his parents and an assortment of characters. Such was the impact of the show that when an episode aired showing him getting a library card (because a library was a good place to pick up "chicks"), library-card issuance in the US went up 500%. The leather jacket which became part and parcel of Fonzie's character is now immortalized in the Smithsonian Museum in Washington DC. And incidentally, the girls in the school where Gary taught in 1976 swooned over him because of his strong resemblance to The Fonz—dark hair swept back, long sideburns, a motorcycle and a flashing smile.

As I watched Oprah chat with her guests, I began to wonder if there were—or should be—Biblical icons. Indeed, there are men and women of the Scriptures whose deeds and character are well known. If I mention Noah, who comes to mind? The guy with the big boat. What about Jonah? I see a huge fish swallowing a guy flailing away in the waves. And how about Peter? Peter is the man with the short fuse, sharp sword and wet feet from walking on water.

Perhaps the most iconic chapter in all of Scripture is Hebrews 11. A phrase recurs: *by faith Abel . . . by faith Enoch . . . by faith Noah . . . by faith Abraham . . . by faith Isaac . . . by faith Jacob . . . by faith Joseph . . . by faith Moses's parents . . . by faith Moses . . . by faith the people . . . by faith the walls of Jericho fell . . . by faith Rahab . . . .*

Finally, the author writes: *And what more shall I say? I do not have time to tell about Gideon, Barak, Samson, Jephthah, David, Samuel and the prophets, who through faith conquered kingdoms, administered justice, and gained what was promised; who shut the mouths of lions, quenched the fury of the flames, and escaped the edge of the sword; whose weakness was turned to strength; and who became powerful in battle and routed foreign armies . . .* (Hebrews 11:32-24).

We should be ashamed if our children know only the biggest names in pop culture.

These were all commended for their faith . . . . (Hebrews 11:39a)

Daily challenge:
Study the life of a Biblical icon.

The Bird

Thud. Kurplunk. The sudden noise against a sunroom window startled me enough to make me jump. I had just entered the room to clean the windows. With the noise, I looked up just in time to see pillow-worthy feathers drifting through the air as the wind blew them this way and that. I laughed out loud at the sight before tiptoeing to the window. (I'm not sure I can explain the tiptoeing, as I was hardly sneaking up on anything.) Surprisingly, I found no evidence of a dead bird. *Hmm.* I guess the collision sounded worse than it really was.

Putting the incident aside, I stepped outside to continue cleaning the glass. Approaching a window four feet away from where the collision occurred, I jumped for the second time. A big fat robin stood on its wiry legs in the narrow flower bed beneath the window. It was very much alive. No wings hung crooked and its beak remained intact. Nevertheless, it didn't fly away. I cringed at the sight. My mother was always grossed out by birds hitting the picture window at home. Maybe I got that from her. I decided to leave the dirty window in front of the birdie for another day. I didn't like the way he was looking at me.

From the beginning of time birds have held an esteemed place in creation. God created them to fill the skies, deliver the "all-clear" message to Noah and company and were important components in the process of blood sacrifices to God. There was a distinction between clean and unclean birds, and yet God used His care for the winged creatures to emphasize His greater concern for people.

Luke penned *"Indeed, the very hairs of your head are all numbered. Don't be afraid; you are worth more than many sparrows. Consider the ravens: They do not sow or reap, they have no storeroom or barn; yet God feeds them. And how much more valuable you are than birds!"* (Luke 12:7, 24)

We probably waste a lot of time worrying about all sorts of things—money, bills, our future retirement. However, the God of the birds is the God of our family. He promises and proves to be faithful in every way.

> *"Look at the birds of the air; they do not sow or reap or store away in barns, and yet your heavenly Father feeds them. Are you not much more valuable than they?"* (Matthew 6:26)

Daily challenge:
Trust God. He knows what's going on and will take care of you.

More Stupid People

"Never underestimate the power of stupid people in large groups." I laugh at Seth's t-shirt every time I see it. It's true. But, stupid people also act alone.

Earlier today, I made a major purchase and intended to pay for it with my business credit card. I handed my card to the cashier after my first attempt to swipe the card in the machine failed. He smiled, taking the card from me and said, "It's OK. I'll do it on the register. Sometimes the customer card reader doesn't work." Not so. "There must be some problem with the card." Embarrassed but sure there was no outstanding debt, I smiled meekly, gave him another card and completed the transaction. Off to other errands.

At the office store I stood at the counter waiting for one of two employees to acknowledge me. Time crawled by. Finally a young girl approached. I had commissioned two printing jobs. When the business cards came in, the printing was crooked, hardly a good omen for my business containing the word *quality*. Those had to be reprinted. But now, half of the letterhead sheets were smudged with ink. Again, a re-do was in order. She was not happy. I was amazed at how careless, apathetic, or "stupid" these people were to do such poor work so consistently.

Then my focus turned back to the denied credit card. I called the 800 number and after following the unending monotone directions, found my credit card had been blocked "just because." They arbitrarily decided that a purchase at Best Buy was fraudulent.

I shook my head and was reminded about our study in Philippians last night. One of the girls mentioned her struggle with pervasive negative thoughts about a "stupid" person at work. She came to understand that it was a conscious decision to dwell on the positive rather than the all-too-obvious negatives.

If we can discipline ourselves to find the noble, the true, the right, the pure, the lovely, the admirable, it will be difficult—if not impossible—for antithetical thoughts to co-exist. If Christ is able to take what is ugly (us) and transform us into something beautiful, I think we can cut "stupid" people a break. Look past the shortcomings and let love cover.

Finally, brothers, whatever is true, whatever is noble, whatever is right, whatever is pure, whatever is lovely, whatever is admirable— if anything is excellent or praiseworthy—think about such things. (Philippians 4:8)

Daily challenge:
When you are tempted to criticize, look in the mirror and take inventory.

Leap Year

My dad was a Leap Year baby. When I turned twelve, he was only eleven. That was cool. But why a Leap Year?

Leap Year came about because of inconsistencies in man's time tracking. There are approximately 365.2522 days, known as a tropical year, between two vernal equinoxes—or is it equinoxi? Anyway . . . a vernal equinox is when the sun is directly over the equator, moving from the southern to the northern hemisphere. As a result, approximately six hours go missing from every 365-day calendar year. If not account-ed for, the lost time amounts to twenty-four days every hundred years. Hence, to keep the seasons juxtaposed with the associated dates, an extra day is sometimes added to February of a 365-day calendar—a calendar evolved from the AD 1582 Gregorian cal-endar. Other rules apply if you happen to be using the Julian or lunar calendar system.

Since most of the world currently uses the Gregorian calendar, there are three rules to use when determining a Leap Year: 1) Every year that is divisible by four is a leap year 2) but of those years, if it can be divided by one-hundred, it is NOT a leap year, unless, of course 3) the year is divisible by four-hundred. Actually, there was an eight-year gap between Leap years from 1896 to 1904. The next eight-year gap will occur from 2096 to 2104.

And I thought the only criteria was for a year to be divisible by four. But, no. That rule was only for the calendar endorsed by Julius Caesar in BC 46 which was based on popular Roman calendar. Don't you feel better for knowing this?

Calendars are man-made inventions. All creatures whether man or animal, estab-lish habits, routines and life cycles based on day and night. Even the plant kingdom is guided by light and darkness. However, God is not subject to time, nor does He oper-ate in a time dimension. He simply is. He had no beginning. He has an end.

I have a hard time getting my arms around that. Perhaps that is why He created time when He spoke the world into existence. Our finite minds need an anchor—a point of reference. And for that, God handed us days and nights, seasons, months and years. Should we squander them or try to hoard them? I don't think so. Time has been given as a gift from the Creator. As the writer of Ecclesiastes proclaimed, there is a time for every purpose under heaven.

Before the mountains were born or you brought forth the earth and the world, from everlasting to everlasting you are God. (Psalm 90:2)

Daily challenge:
Be careful how you use your time. God can always cut it short.

Hidden Problems

"What you see is what you get." Well, not really—especially when it comes to cars. In our family, cars come and go with the wind. And at the moment, it's downright blustery.

The burst of recent car-related activity had a purpose: to decrease the amount of money sitting on a rubber base (which was already slim), and to find a car with great gas mileage. After considerable consternation over innumerable possibilities, Gary bought a 1968 Mustang to appease his desire for a non-embarrassing car (i.e., not a piece of trash) and a 1985 Diesel Jetta. A Jeep was sold in the process.

Gary and Seth made the three-hour drive to fetch the Mustang. The car looked nice, but a few details escaped the eBay description. Plus, they never made it back that night. An hour down the road the car sputtered and spit and not wanting to leave the classic on the shoulder, they limped into Gary's sister's driveway about ten-miles away. Finally, the car now sits torn apart in our garage, the guys working to fix the undisclosed problems.

In the case of the little Jetta, just getting it started was a problem. The glow plugs needed to be changed as did the cracked windshield, a fact the seller "forgot" to mention. Still, we hope it will be a good car once the kinks are worked out.

It's not difficult to see a parallel between these cars and the way we live our lives. On the outside, we give an impression that all is well when, in fact, we are simply hiding our flaws. Years come and go and no one is wiser to our less-than-admirable failings. Certainly, no one likes to air dirty laundry, but continuing to cover up the problem is a lie—a lie to self, to others and to God. The only solution is to understand the extent of the problem and turn to the One who can fix it.

> *The heart is deceitful above all things and beyond cure. Who can understand it? I the LORD search the heart and examine the mind, to reward a man according to his conduct, according to what his deeds deserve. (Jeremiah 17:9, 10)*

Daily challenge:
Hiding a problem will eat away at you the way rust eats fenders.
Face it and fix it now.

Push or Pull?

With temperatures predicted to be in the high fifties and sun shining bright, I eagerly accepted an invite for a run in the mountains. But as word spread among friends, I ended up chauffeuring four young woman, barely in their twenties, to the trail head. *Hmm.* I was more than twice their age and older than their mothers. This might prove interesting.

The run we planned was just thirteen miles, but a lot was packed into the distance. We had to run up one mountain, shift over to a higher peak, shimmy through a crevice in a rock face and run a huge descent over rock-strewn, ankle-wrenching trails before we traversed around the base of the mountain. Pleased to feel strong and bold, my goal for the day was to encourage and motivate the group. I felt an obligation not to run ahead and discourage those in the rear. However, I had no desire to make it so obvious that I was waiting on anyone, making them feel patronized. I have been the recipient of both practices and didn't like it one little bit.

Toward the end of the run, my thoughts turned to my own children and the challenges of parenting. I was trying to take the "don't push 'em too hard, but don't let 'em slack" approach with the girls and have tried to split those hairs with my own kids. I fear driving them too hard but cringe at the thought of letting them sink into the muck of inaction.

On one hand, Scripture speaks to the need to train up a child so that when he is old, he will not depart from it (Proverbs 22:6). That training includes the administration of discipline along with instruction, teaching and leading by example. On the other hand, a line drawn in the sand that is harsh and administered without love is likely to alienate the child, limiting his or her receptiveness to anything else we say.

Even as my children grow into young adulthood, we still struggle knowing how and when to demand behavior and when to allow independent decision-making. It's way harder than sitting a four-year old on the naughty step.

> *Fathers, do not exasperate your children; instead, bring them up in the training and instruction of the Lord. (Ephesians 6:4)*

Daily challenge:
No one ever said parenting was easy. Hang in there.
They'll grow up . . . some day.

In the Dark

Spelunking is a silly word. But to those who love the underground, it rings true. I'm just not sure it's my bell to ring.

Some years ago, I spelunked somewhere in West Virginia—I'm not even sure where. All the excitement I needed waited for us below. No one in our group had been through the labyrinth more than once. Furthermore, no one had a map. But with headlights attached to not-so-fashionable hardhats, we climbed the trail leading to the entrance. One by one we dropped into a hole, squeezed through the narrow entrance and navigated a ten-foot drop. Without incident, save a few expletives, our gang of a dozen people started the journey.

Belly-crawling between massive slabs of rock for one hundred fifty yards was not for the claustrophobic. Because there was so little room, we turned our heads sideways, ear to ground, and inched along. Once past that obstacle we weaved our way up, over and around boulders, our hardhats saving us from otherwise inevitable concussions. But suddenly, we arrived in a massive room with innumerable passages radiating outward. Appointed scouts dispersed to find the way while the rest of us waited. With water dripping from the ceiling and a small creek running along the floor, the subterranean air was chilly and ominous. Then we turned off our lights.

Suddenly, I understood the meaning of darkness. There was no amount of squinting that brought things into focus. I literally could not even see my hand. A feeling of hopelessness and crushing darkness overcame me. I forced myself to remain calm. In due course we found our way, but it was a difficult and scary journey. A pinpoint of light at the end a sixteen-inch-wide, water-filled tunnel gave hope that we would escape, though cold, wet and muddy.

In I John I read of another darkness. I'm intrigued that hating your brother is likened to darkness. If I get up in the middle of the night, it is sort of dark. Yet my eyes adjust to a sliver of moonlight or the glow from the clock's LCD display. But, the darkness that John speaks of is like the darkness in the cave—a total void. There is no freedom of movement. No light. No hope. All sense of direction is lost. And all this because we harbor hate.

> *But whoever hates his brother is in the darkness and walks around in the darkness; he does not know where he is going, because the darkness has blinded him. (I John 2:11)*

Daily challenge:
Don't panic. The Light will guide you back into love.

God Listens

Why am I astonished, even flabbergasted, when I pray hard and God dumps an answer in my lap?

Our oldest son came home for spring break a few days ago. I love it! But in the last eighteen months we have questioned some of his behavior (or lack thereof). And like ninety-nine percent of parents of college-aged kids, we have thought, "What was he thinking?"

He is not a horrible kid, carousing all night and involved in sordid behavior. But still, the thought of ringing his neck has occurred to us. It is obvious he is not living up to his potential in athletics or academics. Our hopes for a smooth and successful college career have been replaced by frustration.

Financially, we don't have the ability to keep him at a private college with scholarships taken off the table. At Christmas, we talked about a transfer but have not seen any activity on his part to make it happen. His lackadaisical attitude bothers us. I prayed my heart out for weeks.

In the meantime, we spoke with a friend whose sons had suddenly decided to join the National Guard. He told us about eradicated college debt, huge sign-on bonuses and a paycheck, to boot. Our heads started spinning with possibilities. But Caleb has never, ever shown any interest in the military. He is not keen on screaming drill sergeants and getting up before dawn.

As he and I worked on an outdoor project, I asked him about next year's plans. "You know. What we talked about before. I'll go to Virginia Tech."

"How will you pay for it?" I asked. He shrugged. I playfully dangled the carrot: "How would you like to get paid to go to college and come out debt-free?"

Our conversation blew me over more than the gusty winds. He embraced the idea and called an Army Reserve recruiter. We can't believe he is willing to consider this radical change. But he is. I don't know if this is a done deal, but he is happy, pleasant and upbeat. Am I surprised? Yes. Should I be? No. God was faithful to answer my bodacious request made in the wee hours when sleep was evasive and my faith was small.

"Therefore I tell you, whatever you ask for in prayer, believe that you have received it, and it will be yours." (Mark 11:24)

Daily challenge:
Don't give up. Just keep praying.

When They Are Old

I've had a day to think about this Army thing, and I'm getting nervous. Basic training will put Caleb smack-dab in the middle of it. There will be guys of varying aptitudes, social situations and cultural backgrounds. Some of these kids will be there because they can't do anything else. Others will be there because they, like Caleb, need to pay for their education. And yet others will be there out of an overwhelming sense of patriotism.

I imagine a "Boys gone wild" scenario in the barracks: lewdness, horrible language, lots of alcohol, wild women and sexual conquests. Caleb has never been a follower, influenced by peer pressure. But the thought of him in that environment makes my liver quiver.

In times like these, it makes me wonder if we have parented well. In reality, once a kid leaves home, there isn't a lot more we can do. We are totally dependent on two things: 1) *Train a child in the way he should go, and when he is old he will not turn from it* (Proverbs 22:6) and 2) enough faith to believe that God will keep His promise.

Why do we have a hard time trusting God with the children He lent us? Part of the problem is that none of us are perfect parents. Even Inspector Clouseau could figure out that imperfect parents produce imperfect offspring. And yet, God still promised that a kid will turn out okay if he is trained properly, albeit imperfectly.

But how old is *old*? How long do we have to wait for our children to come back to their roots? For a parent, this period seems like an eternity. Sleepless nights, thoughts that refuse to be quieted and a general feeling of angst settle in. We pray constantly that something in the kid will click, bringing him to his spiritual senses. Being in this waiting room is never pleasant.

I'm not concerned that our son will participate in mayhem—he's not that kind. However, he may not be inclined to seek out Christian fellowship. Am I to worry about this? If I trust in what God promises, the answer should be "no." My responsibility is to pray for protection and watch God bring glory to Himself through my son.

> *"These commandments that I give you today are to be upon your hearts. Impress them on your children. Talk about them when you sit at home and when you walk along the road, when you lie down and when you get up." (Deuteronomy 6:6-7)*

Daily challenge:
God is sovereign—even over those pig-headed, stubborn children.

Contentment

Are you content? If you said *yes*, what do you mean? Which of the following definitions fits your mindset: A, B, C, or D?

A) From *dictionary.com* (unabridged):

1. The state of being contented; satisfaction; ease of mind

2. Archaic. The act of making contentedly satisfied

B) From *The American Heritage Dictionary*:

1. The state of being contented; satisfaction

2. A source of satisfaction: the contentments of a comfortable retirement

C) From *WordNet* (Princeton University):

1. Happiness with one's situation in life

D) From *Easton's 1897 Bible Dictionary*:

1. A state of mind in which one's desires are confined to his lot whatever it may be (1 Tim. 6:6; 2 Cor. 9:8). It is opposed to envy (James 3:16), avarice (Heb. 13:5), ambition (Prov. 13:10), anxiety (Matt. 6:25, 34), and repining (1 Cor. 10:10). It arises from the inward disposition and is the offspring of humility and of an intelligent consideration of the rectitude and benignity of divine providence (Ps. 96:1, 2; 145), the greatness of the divine promises (2 Pet. 1:4), and our own unworthiness (Gen. 32:10); as well as from the view the gospel opens up to us of rest and peace hereafter (Rom. 5:2).

Whoa. There seems to be a big difference in the secular definition of *contentment* and a Biblical perspective. In the first, the emphasis appears to be based on that ever-fleeting emotion of "happiness." If something doesn't make you happy, then you don't have to be content. However, if you look at the Easton's dictionary, "happiness" is nowhere to be found. It has nothing to do with possessions, position in life, or comfort in everyday living. It has everything to do with "an intelligent consideration of the rectitude and benignity of divine providence."

What an incredible thought that we can be content regardless of circumstances and based solely on our knowledge that God is indeed sovereign. Nothing else really matters.

> *I am not saying this because I am in need, for I have learned to be content whatever the circumstances. I know what it is to be in need, and I know what it is to have plenty. I have learned the secret of being content in any and every situation, whether well fed or hungry, whether living in plenty or in want. I can do everything through him who gives me strength. (Philippians 4:11, 12)*

Daily challenge:
Contentment brings needed rest.

The Body Beautiful

The body of Christ is a beautiful thing. Love put in motion is founded on the realization that every part of the Body is essential for optimal function. Therefore, if one part suffers, it is partial suicide to ignore that part. However, the support of the Body is not limited to those within easy reach. We are globally joined with fellow Believers across the continents.

Nearly a week ago, tragedy struck my friend Danelle's sister's family. Their two-year old son walked himself out the door and into the path of his dad's pickup truck. The collision of the rear bumper and the child's head caused massive damage. Helicopter flights to hospitals for the traumatized toddler began a week of ups and downs, touch and goes. Living in far away Nebraska, none of us here in our Virginia church knew the family except by proxy. In their great wisdom, our elders decided to pay the family's mortgage. The dad is self-employed and out of work as he stands vigilant inside hospital walls. The family is thrilled for the practical help we offer, but our church, having the funds available, would be remiss not to take action.

What a contrast. Subbing for a history teacher today, we watched a movie covering the social, economic and political environment of the 1880s and '90s. We conversed about how social Darwinism brought about change. We spoke of the rise of labor unions, feelings of entitlement, crisp criticism of successful entrepreneurs such as Carnegie and Rockefeller, deficit spending and a desire for government to fulfill each individual's needs.

Playing the devil's advocate, I asked them to compare and contrast the idea of modern socialism with the "socialism" found in the early church. After an invigorating exchange, one student astutely noted that secular socialism counts on the government doing and deciding for the people—a selfish way of living as personal responsibility is diminished. In many cases, an individual manipulates the system to his own benefit.

By contrast, communal living and sharing of goods in the New Testament was a selfless act performed for others' benefit. All too often, the church has relegated its responsibility to the government. Too bad. The Body loses out; Christ is not glorified.

All the believers were together and had everything in common.
Selling their possessions and goods, they gave to anyone as he had
need . . . They broke bread in their homes and ate together with
glad and sincere hearts, praising God and enjoying the favor of all
the people. (Acts 2:44-47)

Daily challenge:
Commit to support the Body, near and far, by whatever means are necessary.

God Understands

"You just don't understand!" screams a teenage girl at her frazzled parents. "You have no idea what I am going through. You don't have a clue!" This scene—or something like it—happens all the time.

Have you ever gone to a funeral and said, "I'm sorry. I know how you feel" when in reality you have never lost a loved one? Or maybe a friend is struggling to lose weight and you, at a constant 110 pounds regardless of what you eat, find it easy to give her advice about what she is doing wrong. Not the way to win friends and influence people.

My mind turns to Danelle's sister's family of whom I wrote yesterday. How can I possibly minister to them beyond common courtesies? I don't know what its like to have tragedy strike my child. But perhaps I should look at my own hardships as an opportunity to encourage those in similar circumstances.

My father died following heart surgery. Because of my experience as a perfusionist, my family asked me to be integrally involved in the decision to remove him from life support. I "turned off" my own father. It was horrible. And yet throughout my career, I've done likewise to someone else's father, turning off the machine and watching life's last remnants leave the body. I could offer a hug with tears in my eyes and say, "I know how you feel"—because I did. I ministered to them in a way that none of my colleagues could ever hope to. They hadn't been there. They didn't know what it was like.

Likewise, I think of the lawsuit that we endured several years ago. There were tremendous stresses, financial hardships, emotional roller-coasters and problems sorting out issues like anger, revenge and worry. But am I better equipped to counsel somebody facing a similar demon? Of course.

Even our past sin can serve to assist others. The process of guilt recognition, repentance and restoration can be shared from a personal perspective, encouraging the other to follow suit with hope and expectancy.

God ministers to us so that we can minister to others. While we certainly don't need to experience everything, our personal experiences provide divinely appointed ministry opportunities that only we can carry out.

Praise be to the God and Father of our Lord Jesus Christ, the Father of compassion and the God of all comfort, who comforts us in all our troubles, so that we can comfort those in any trouble with the comfort we ourselves have received from God. (II Corinthians 1:3-4)

Daily challenge:
Your difficult past can lead to someone's bright future.

Hidden Identity

I enjoy looking around every time I stand at the starting line of an ultramarathon. Some competitors are long and lean, picture-perfect svelte running machines. There are also compact frames standing next to Clydesdale-types. These young and old, fat and thin, stout and skeletal, males and females all share the common goal of starting and finishing the race. I've been shocked by some who achieve the finish line on their own two feet. Had I seen them in a grocery store, I would never have guessed they could run one-hundred miles at a time, their ultra identities hidden under the guise of normalcy.

There are times when your true identity should be a mystery—like if you are a secret agent. But other than that, I can't really think of an instance when it is admirable to be anonymous in character and substance. However, what would be even worse is if we Christians are deemed anti-Christ based on words and actions.

Like it or not, people are watching our every move round the clock. Will they see an obvious Believer or someone hiding under the cover of darkness? You know what the old Karen Carpenter song said: "The night has a thousand eyes . . .."

I've often wondered how long it takes someone to figure out I'm a Christian. When I go to a consulting job, will I leave an impression of Christ behind? What will my response reveal when I deal with an extraordinarily frustrating sales clerk? When colleagues start trash-talking a fellow worker, will I join in and mar any resemblance to my Savior? When my kids see my reaction to a huge disappointment, what example will I set for them?

In I John, the author points out that the reason why Believers were not understood was that the culture really never knew Christ. What happens if we take that thought one step further? Do those with whom we come in daily contact know Christ because they know us? They should. If not, something is wrong.

How great is the love the Father has lavished on us, that we should be called children of God! And that is what we are! The reason the world does not know us is that it did not know him. (I John 3:1)

Daily challenge:
Our lips don't have to scream Christ if our lives reveal Him.

Just Like You

I sure enjoyed my day. This was the beginning of multiple paint, design and wood-working projects. Friends Kathryn and Derik agreed to let me loose in the house they just purchased. I arrived around noon and got busy with the prep work before opening the first can of paint. I was content.

Another friend, Bobbie, wanted in on the action. We got right to work but not before she filmed me giving some project tips. I was relieved that she didn't laugh as she held the camera to capture my HGTV wanna-be narrations. But once the film stopped rolling, we chatted easily about this and that until she commented, "I bet we have similar backgrounds." She proceeded to mention all the ways in which we are alike—creative, go-getters, disciplined, goal-oriented and adventurous.

Hmm, I mused. "I wonder if we're alike because we had similar mothers."

We came to the conclusion that our mothers must have been separated at birth. The similarities were amazing. Both have been terrific role models: godly women, mentors, independent, capable, multi-talented, full of energy and always looking to serve others. If I take after my mother in any way, I feel like I'm a better woman for it.

"If you want to know what a girl will be like in twenty years, just look at her mother." My husband gives these words of advice to the boys. To a certain degree, I think he's right. We tend to emulate the examples that are in front of us. In this case, I am like my mom. The older I get, the more similarities I see. I walk like Mom. I clean my kitchen like Mom. I organize like Mom. I use the same expressions. I am even thinking like Mom. I am becoming her.

I know I don't have any daughters; I've been blessed with sons instead. But still, now it's my turn. I desire to have characteristics worthy of emulation for the glory of God.

Lord, I want to be just like You
'Cause he wants to be just like me
I want to be a holy example
For his innocent eyes to see
Help me be a living Bible, Lord
That my little boy can read
I want to be just like You
'Cause he wants to be like me (Refrain)
(I Want to Be Just Like You by Phillips, Craig, and Dean)

Daily challenge:
Are you comfortable with what your children will become
if they become mini-me's?

Hard Head

Well, it finally happened. After years of expectation, today I ended up in the hospital emergency room with Seth. From the time he was as big as a small toad, he has been a no-fear kind of kid. He acts before thinking about the consequences.

At four years of age, he was riding his motorcycle as fast as he could through the woods while he stood on the seat. He jumped from heights unknown. Once, we spotted him at the tippy-top of a huge tree where squirrels refuse to climb. With each year, the stunts got more daring and the potential for injury escalated. But much to our grateful surprise, he never got destroyed. Yes, there were spills and thrills but no broken bones or hemorrhagic catastrophes.

Sunday afternoon Seth scored a free lift ticket at a nearby ski resort. So off he went for an afternoon of fun with Andrea—a girl, not surprisingly—and her family. Strapped onto his snowboard, he approached a jump and let it fly—literally. Unbeknownst to him, the jump had been reworked, sending him like a missile into the air. Unfortunately, launched missiles have to come down. Seth rocketed past the landing zone and crashed hard. He isn't quite sure what hit first, because he doesn't remember. What he does recall, however, are a few moments of sheer terror. Those who saw the crash were stunned he walked away.

When he got home, we all had a good laugh at his unique story-telling. He was sore for a couple days, not able to raise his head off the pillow without using his hands to help it along. But when the school called saying he was lightheaded, neck swollen and his vision blurry, it was time for action. Hence, the hospital visit.

Though Seth's CT scan was negative, he was diagnosed with a concussion. His spirits picked up, embracing the injury like a prize fighter. The doctor warned he might have a problem concentrating and maintaining focus, suffer headaches and have some fuzzy vision for about a week. What great news! It was a perfect excuse for drifting off during Brit Lit at school.

I'm grateful that though rattled like a baby's toy, Seth's hard head will fare just fine with a little rest. But we never know what a day will bring. I think again of Danelle's nephew, who has a life-threatening head injury. Our consolation is that God has numbered our days—and the days of our children. We can rest in that knowledge and trust our kids' lives to a merciful and loving God.

Man's days are determined; you have decreed the number of his months and have set limits he cannot exceed. (Job 14:5)

Daily challenge:
God cares for our kids more than we do. Trust them to Him.

Super Mouse

Super Mouse. He calls our house his home and roams freely in the silent stillness of the night. But on occasion, he darts around the corner, shooting us a sideways smirk as if to say, "Catch me if you can." He is some kind of mouse.

Not too long ago, I heard a distinctive rustling in my kitchen cabinets. Curious, I tiptoed over and opened the door. My eyes rose to the third shelf and met the creature's beady stare. He was not the least bit fazed, standing his ground atop a mousetrap from which he had already nabbed the peanut butter. Conceding the victory for this round, I closed the door and asked Gary to reset the trap.

A day or two passed when I reached for an energy bar on the same shelf. No wonder it was an unstoppable mouse. There in the basket were the remains—yea, even mere crumbs—from over a dozen of the high calorie, nutritionally-rich bars. How could he still get in and out of the teenie-weenie hole in the cupboard corner? At least he didn't get into the packets of energy gel.

Guess what? He got into the gels. As I grabbed a gel for today's run, I reached my hand into the basket and pulled out a pile of half-eaten packets. Mouse poo was stuck to the gooey mess. Gross. I threw out twenty defiled gels and washed the rest in hot soapy water. If only I could see him after all that caffeine.

My mouse must be a direct descendant of one that lived in my mother's house. She always laid out her vitamins and supplements on the dresser in her second floor bedroom, only to have them mysteriously disappear. Living alone, there was no reasonable explanation. No explanation, that is, until she had a dishwasher installed in her kitchen downstairs. As the cabinet was removed, the mouse's stockpile was found stashed in the far back corner.

Why is it that a mouse can be so persistent? Surely, there were no billboards announcing "Energy gels, top left cupboard" or "Want a softer, shinier coat? Get your vitamins in Margaret's bedroom." And yet, these mighty mice seem to have a relentless pursuit of what will make them stronger.

If rodents have enough sense to seek out treasures, why are we not equally relentless in seeking out a rich cache? Perhaps we should make like a mouse and be more determined to find and enjoy spiritual treasures that are waiting for us in Christ.

. . . that they may have the full riches of complete understanding, in order that they may know the mystery of God, namely, Christ, in whom are hidden all the treasures of wisdom and knowledge. (Colossians 2:2-4)

Daily challenge:
If you can't remember when you last sought after God's treasures, start today.

Hard Pressed

What did I get myself into this time? I plopped down on the big pile of dirt, exhausted. Since putting up the pool fence, I've wanted to create a versatile outdoor room. I was well on my way by constructing two hammock trellises and a brick fire pit with benches. A large dining table and chairs was next on the schedule.

Having to clear the grass for planting borders and the table area, I rented a sod cutter to make things easier. After a quick lesson, I followed Gary's instructions and began to guide the monster. In short time I cut strips of sod two feet wide. *Wow.* That machine was the ticket.

The problem, however, shifted from cutting the sod to disposing of it. I tried rolling the strips like they were giant Tootsie Rolls. Within a couple revolutions, the wad was so heavy, I was stretched out along the ground, straining with all my might, shoulder to the task. Before long, I gave up thinking I could get all the sod rolled and decided to work in doable six-foot sections. The task was still enormous. But at that point, I had no choice but to approach this mission one shovelful at a time. There was no easy way out and no turning back. My only hope was to stay focused on what I knew would be an outstanding result.

All too often, we get distracted by present difficulties. Whether it be a bad patch in a long race, a tough time in our relationships, challenges in our jobs or something as simple as removing dirt and grass, we get bogged down by what is in our field of vision. It's as though we are completely blind to what lays ahead.

The pot of gold at the end of the rainbow? The silver lining in the cloud? Neither can compare to the promises God gives us for the future. We need to get out those binoculars so that we can focus on what awaits us. For once we see the future for what it is, we can have hope for what is now.

> *But we have this treasure in jars of clay to show that this all-surpassing power is from God and not from us. We are hard pressed on every side, but not crushed; perplexed, but not in despair; persecuted, but not abandoned; struck down, but not destroyed.*
> *(II Corinthians 4:7-9)*

Daily challenge:
When you can't get to the end of the day, look to the end
of the next five minutes. Repeat over and over.

Love Connections

"Toe bone connected to the foot bone. Foot bone connected to the leg bone. Leg bone connected to the knee bone. O hear the word of the Lord . . . . "

Sound familiar? The traditional spiritual, "Dem Dry Bones", is an elementary anatomy lesson taken from a wise, old prophet (Ezekiel 37:1-14). Multiple stanzas string together the major bones to show the connections between them. Without one, the next bone is rendered ineffective.

When I read the passage from Peter (below), I envisioned a pyramid with interlocking levels, all of which are dependent on the other. Initial faith is the foundation of the structure. Once faith is established, goodness is the natural outgrowth of faith. Subsequently, goodness is a precipitator of knowledge and because of knowledge, self-control is attained. The pyramid rises higher as perseverance is added on top of self-control and is augmented by godliness, which leads to brotherly kindness that ultimately culminates in love. Same idea as connecting all 'dem bones.

Isn't it interesting that love is actually at the far end of interconnected nouns? Love is a term used easily and often in our society. "Oh, I just *love* him," referring to an acquaintance we may have met just once or twice—or perhaps not at all if he is a favorite actor. However, love doesn't just happen despite what we see in the movies. Love is a conscious decision that results from a specific sequence.

Even if we start with faith but skip some of the in-between elements, the connections between the "bones" break and love is not—nor can it ever be—complete and mature. The order of the elements is not haphazard. It is, in fact, mandatory.

Our running group has a saying, "There is no shortcut to fitness." Similarly, there is no shortcut to love. Want to love more fully? Want to love more deeply? Then we need to connect the bones from faith to goodness to knowledge to self control to perseverance to godliness and to brotherly kindness. Only then will we arrive on love's threshold.

For this very reason, make every effort to add to your faith goodness; and to goodness, knowledge; and to knowledge, self-control; and to self-control, perseverance; and to perseverance, godliness; and to godliness, brotherly kindness; and to brotherly kindness, love. For if you possess these qualities in increasing measure, they will keep you from being ineffective and unproductive in your knowledge of our Lord Jesus Christ. (II Peter 1:5-8)

Daily challenge:
Daily practice faith, goodness, knowledge, self-control, perseverance, godliness, and kindness. You will then love fully.

Praise Him Still

When the morning falls on the farthest hill,
I will sing His Name,
I will praise Him still.
When dark trials come and my heart is filled,
With the waves of doubt,
I will praise Him still.
Chorus: For the Lord our God,
He is strong to save,
From the arms of death,
From the deepest grave.
And He gave us life in His perfect will,
And by His good grace I will praise Him still.

Running the rolling hills of green pastured farms and contented cattle, this song by Fernando Ortega played on my iPod. The melody had been a constant companion when our family faced "dark trials" and my heart cried out for relief. Sometimes the pain was so great, I was sure I would never again feel normal. Nevertheless, as I listened again to the words, I realized just how difficult it was to *praise Him still* despite the fact that intellectually, I was confident in God's sovereignty.

As the miles ticked off, praising Him was easy as birds sang and the sun's gentle rays caressed my face. The stress of the unfounded lawsuit had left my radar—a feeling I couldn't fathom while in the midst of the legal wranglings. However, I began to think of others pummeled by difficulty: Danelle's critically injured nephew, a girlfriend going through a nasty divorce, another in the aftermath, a family trying to reach a rebellious son. I wondered if they praised Him still.

No matter how spiritually mature, I'm not sure that *praise Him still* is an automatic response. It's natural to cry out for relief. But is that praising God? I don't think so. To *praise Him still* takes a conscious, concerted effort. Despite our feelings of hopelessness, darkness and even depression, praising God requires that we acknowledge God for all that He is regardless of our emotions. That, my friend, is a very tall order.

Consider the words of King David who learned to *praise Him still.*

How long, O LORD? Will you forget me forever? How long will you hide your face from me? . . . But I trust in your unfailing love; my heart rejoices in your salvation. I will sing to the LORD, for he has been good to me. (Psalm 13)

Daily challenge:
Praise Him still no matter what.

Will Not Return Empty

On this Palm Sunday, we traveled two-hundred miles to meet up with family. Gary's mother turns eighty tomorrow and we wanted to celebrate with her. She is in the late stages of Alzheimer's. None of the kids wanted to chance missing one more family gathering. Throughout the day Mom's mind was seldom in the same county as everyone else's, but the rest of us enjoyed swapping stories and experiences.

Working in a small, rural bank, Joy, Gary's sister, gets to know her customers. For some time, a Hispanic farm worker had been coming to her window every Friday. Before long, he began sharing details of his life, including his newfound love of running. Seeing the opportunity, Joy brought with her a copy of my previous book, *Under an Equatorial Sky,* a description of my race through the Amazon jungle.

Sure enough, when Friday rolled around, Joy handed him the book, though she suspected he may not read English. Surprised but pleased, he took it. The next week, he reported he had started reading. After several more Fridays, he proudly proclaimed, "I am up to chapter three." He was ecstatic by the time he conquered chapter eight. He even brought in his bib number from a 5K race, asking Joy to share his "stats" with me. "But I didn't know she was so religious," he admitted, giving the ubiquitous thumbs-down gesture to convey his disapproval. Despite that, he finished the book and returned it to Joy. Who knew that a migrant worker would read my testimony?

I am reminded of two important concepts. 1) God's Word will never return void; and 2) Though we don't know what kind of ground the seed falls upon, our responsibility is to sow it.

Found in Matthew, Mark and Luke, The Parable of the Sower is told by Christ as He teaches from a boat, his offshore pulpit. Although deep in theological implications, Jesus talks of the seed falling on various surfaces: rocky paths, thorny places and good soil. When the seed is sown in fertile places, it flourishes. This is in contrast to seed that falls into environments less hospitable. But we know that God's Word will never return void, because the Spirit opens eyes and ears to the truth of the Gospel.

> *"So is my word that goes out from my mouth: It will not return to me empty, but will accomplish what I desire and achieve the purpose for which I sent it." (Isaiah 55:11)*

Daily challenge:
Sow the seed. Let God gather the harvest.

Deo Valente

As I remember it, my mother never backed out of the garage until she bowed her head, prayed for a safe trip and tagged the request with, "If it's Your will." When asked the plans she had for vacation, the coming week or even the music her choirs would sing on Sunday, she was quick to state, "Lord willing." And when she signed off her many hand-written notes with "Looking forward to see you," she penned "D.V.," meaning in Latin, "If the Lord wills." Her comments, though routine, did not go unnoticed by her impressionable young daughter.

With our recent attention turned on my mother-in-law's eightieth birthday, it was easy to focus on the relevance of what James wrote. Last fall, none of us believed she would live to see another birthday. When Gary's dad came to hunt at our house, he quite literally dragged Mom into the house in a wheelchair. She could not stand, walk or feed herself, had no control over her bladder and bowels and would sit slumped over, as if in a deep, unresponsive coma all day long. Even when food was spooned into her mouth, she refused to eat, growing weaker by the day. None thought she would live beyond Christmas, mentally preparing for the funeral and aftermath of Dad becoming a widower. But we were wrong. Yesterday proved the fallacy of our presumptions about "tomorrow." Although her mind is as confused as ever, she has gained strength and is able to walk short distances and talk incessantly—even if to herself—for hours on end.

My own mother's example pricks my conscience every time I hear myself say I am going to do this, that, or the other thing. We must live our lives in the context of understanding that God has numbered our days, leaving us unable to change that even for a moment. Yes, it is appropriate to plan, approaching life with gusto and enthusiasm—but only if we understand that we have no guarantees. We simply are not in charge.

Well, I need to get busy as I have many plans for the day . . . *Deo valente.*

> *Now listen, you who say, "Today or tomorrow we will go to this or that city, spend a year there, carry on business and make money." Why, you do not even know what will happen tomorrow. What is your life? You are a mist that appears for a little while and then vanishes. Instead, you ought to say, "If it is the Lord's will, we will live and do this or that." (James 4:13-16)*

Daily challenge:
Live today as if you have no tomorrow.

Worms

Big, fat, juicy worms. Long skinny worms. Short and stubby worms. Today I've seen them all. In the midst of a massive landscaping project, the work, back-breaking at best, is one I do not shun. I love riding around on our four-wheeler, hauling bricks and moving dirt. Working all day long, I had plenty of time to think and those omnipresent worms provided food for fodder.

With the first worm-sighting, I recalled a conversation with a young boy. I was at a soccer game when we chatted. Knowing it was his birthday, I asked if his Mom baked him a cake. Answering with his quirky little speech impediment, he responded, "No. My mom is giving me 'dert' and 'whurms.'"

"What did you say?" I inquisitively asked. I'm sure my face betrayed my astonishment. He repeated his answer once again, this time drawing in a few other moms. Even after more repetition, it was still difficult for any of us to understand. Nevertheless, the mystery was finally solved. He was referring to the chocolate pudding, Oreo cookies, Cool Whip and gummy worm dessert that so many kids fancy. We enjoyed a hearty laugh.

I chuckled at the recollection of the story before I pondered the life of a worm. Worms certainly do not live a glamorous lifestyle. No red carpet and diamond earrings. Though there are over one million types of worms, the most common (the earthworm of *Phylum Annelida*) spend their lives shimmying through the dirt, mouths wide open. They are like miniature steam shovels. Whatever gets in their way goes through the mouth and exits out the back end, extracting nutrients along the way. Their tunnels aerate the soil; the ability to decompose dead plants and animals make them essential to the ecosystem.

However, not everyone applauds these slithering, slimy, fish-bait creatures for their contributions. There is a down side. Worms feast on the dead. *The womb forgets them, the worm feasts on them* . . . (Job 24:20a). And in periods of depression over our sin, we can feel very worm-like (Psalm 22:6).

However, no matter how low we fall, how depraved we get, God loves rescuing worms from the dirt pile.

"Do not be afraid, O worm Jacob, O little Israel, for I myself will help you," declares the LORD, your Redeemer, the Holy One of Israel. (Isaiah 41:14)

Daily challenge:
There is no worm so lowly that God cannot save it.

Gifts

My friend whose two-year-old nephew was severely injured a few weeks back just returned from visiting her family. Little Owen is stable, but the impact on his overall health has been brutal: massive stroke, nerve damage and seizures. Financial pressures are mounting as temporary relocation closer to the hospital is preventing his dad from working. Living in a cramped room with two other children far removed from the comforts of home is difficult. I imagine those parents might say as David did, *Oh, that I had the wings of a dove! I would fly away and be at rest* (Psalm 55:6).

We heard the news that Owen is being transferred to a rehab center in Minnesota. The trip by ambulance is priced steeply at $5,000, an amount the insurance company refuses to pay. Nevertheless, the Lord brought to mind an organization my brother-in-law works with. "Pilots for Christ" offers flight assistance—free of charge—to those in need. Volunteers use their own planes to transport sick and injured patients to required destinations. Medical personnel also donate their time to assist in the transport. I placed the call to Skip, who helped me understand the process. Now Owen's dad is working with the director on the details.

Curious to learn more about "Pilots for Christ," I flew to their website, pun intended. The mission statement said, " . . . In gratitude to Almighty God for the gift of flight, we endeavor to use our interest in aviation to promote His Gospel throughout the international aviation community, in particular, and the world in general, through service."

I guess I never thought of flight as a gift from God. But one of the wonderful things about God is how he equipped His Creation to explore and discover, investigate and invent, conceive and create. The Wright Brothers are credited with the first flight, but God should be credited for giving them the intellectual capacity to believe that a heavy plane could overcome gravity, gaining the freedom of the skies only previously known by birds.

It is admirable for these Christian pilots to recognize flight as a gift to be offered. I wonder, howbeit rhetorically, if we should also use the gifts of food, carpentry, art, music, the theatre, athletics and an array of other "gifts" to benefit others and reflect the character of the ultimate gift giver, Jesus Christ.

Each of you must bring a gift in proportion to the way the LORD your God has blessed you. (Deuteronomy 16:17)

Daily challenge:
How will you use your gift to help others?

Written Words

Someday I hope to have my mom's Bible. Ever since I was a little girl, I remember her, pen in hand, taking notes along the edge of the page. Over the last thirty years when I have been seated next to her in church, she inevitably taps my leg and points to something written in the margins. I smile as I read her notation, the entry always dated.

I value her efforts and know that the jottings reflect her heart. It's not unlike a written letter. Despite her relentless purging of belongings as she moved from her home of fifty years, my father's letters written during their courting remain. I encouraged her to keep them—partly out of selfishness. My dad died over twenty-one years ago and sometimes it's hard to remember. I have fond memories but lack information about what he was like before we kids came along. Sometime I want to read what he wrote, for in doing so, I will better understand my father's character. I will see him intimately. I will appreciate his thoughts, beliefs and behavior. I will come to know my father in a way never before realized.

As I picked up my own Bible this evening, the pages opened to Psalm 31. In the margins was a note that read: "My prayer—10/27/06."

October 2007 was difficult. We were nearly a year into that lawsuit. Our accuser was untruthful and full of contempt. It's as though the Psalmist had written the passage specifically for us. Gary and I prayed to remain truthful and therefore, unable to be shamed. Now, as I read that short notation, I specifically remember my fear and emotion. I also remember offering that prayer as my own, stopping short of voicing the imprecatory supplication for his mortal life to end.

I find it comforting to know that despite the agonizing time of litigation, God was faithful to encourage me with His words.

But I trust in you, O Lord; I say, "You are my God." My times are in your hands; deliver me from those who pursue me. Let your face shine on your servant; save me in your unfailing love. Let me not be put to shame, O Lord, for I have cried out to you; but let the wicked be put to shame and lie silent in the grave. Let their lying lips be silenced, for with pride and contempt they speak arrogantly against the righteous. (Psalm 31:14-18)

Daily challenge:
Record your thoughts and then expectantly look back and recall what God has done.

I Miss My Time with You

A landscaping project has occupied me for nearly a week, putting in eight or nine hours of daily hard labor. Sometimes I merely take in my surroundings: how the wind seems nearly visible as it comes through the trees, the distant drone of big machinery digging out cedar trees, or wondering when a dangling piece of soffit will rip completely off the house. But this morning my thoughts were of a weightier nature. I was longing for my college son.

It's hard to explain my emotions, for I'm not sure I understand them completely. Nonetheless, I am unsettled. He has not returned my calls or acknowledged text messages. Easter break started at noon yesterday. Last I heard he had no plans. What if he went somewhere but never made it? What if he went nowhere and was sitting alone? I yearned to hear his voice. I wanted to know what he was doing. I craved an opportunity to "mother."

I reached for my cell pone and sent a text: "Where are you? I'm worried. I am a mom." No reply. My level of anxiety increased. But after an hour or two, my phone finally lit up with his text.

"I'm alive :) Still at school. Might go to Columbus tomorrow." *Whew.* I felt instant relief despite the fact he was alone in an empty dorm. As a mom, you never want your kid to be left out. But, at least I knew where he was.

There was a Christian song sometime back titled "I Miss My Time with You." The song speaks of God's heartbreak when His child fails to meet Him daily for communion, guidance, praise and worship. From time's beginning it was God's heart, God's passion, for fellowship. The analogy to what I was feeling became obvious.

On a very small scale, I understand God's angst at our inattention to Him. I want to be a part of my son's life, but as he grows older, that doesn't always happen. I don't think this is intentional or mean-spirited; it's just not a priority to stay tied to his mother's apron strings.

Although my son may be in the process of outgrowing my role as a mother, we can never, ever outgrow our need for God. How we must wound Him when we fail to maintain up-close and personal contact.

> *But Jesus called the children to him and said, "Let the little children come to me, and do not hinder them, for the kingdom of God belongs to such as these." (Luke 18:16)*

Daily challenge:
Have you talked with Father God today?

Consequences

The word *consequence* usually has a negative connotation. The consequence of a little kid sassing his mom might be a slap on the bottom. Not studying could mean failing an exam. And a consequence of sitting on the couch can result in a potato-like stature. However, there are actually good things that can be termed as *consequences.* An obedient and respectful child may earn extra privileges and an honest effort in test preparation can yield an exceptional grade.

As I was reading Psalm 19, I noticed no less than six consequences of God's Word, commands and laws. In each case, the subject of the sentence is followed by a descriptive adjective. Then, the consequence of properly acknowledging the subject is given. It's really not that complicated once you see the pattern.

Verse 7a—*The law of the LORD is perfect, reviving the soul.*
  Subject: *The law of the Lord* Adjective: *Perfect*
  Consequence: Revives the soul
Verse 7b—*The statutes of the LORD are trustworthy, making wise the simple.*
  Subject: *The statutes of the Lord* Adjective: *Trustworthy*
  Consequence: Makes the simple wise
Verse 8a—*The precepts of the LORD are right, giving joy to the heart.*
  Subject: *The precepts of the Lord* Adjective: *Right*
  Consequence: Gives joy
Verse 8b—*The commands of the LORD are radiant, giving light to the eyes.*
  Subject: The Lord's commands Adjective: *Radiant* (Bright/healthy)
  Consequence: The ability to see clearly
Verse 9a—*The fear of the LORD is pure, enduring forever.*
  Subject: *The fear of the Lord* Adjective: *Pure*
  Consequence: Endures forever
Verse 9b—*The ordinances of the LORD are sure and altogether righteous.*
  Subject: The Lord's judgments Adjective: Sure and pure
  Consequence: Righteousness
Verse 10 and 11—*They are more precious than gold, than much pure gold; they are sweeter than honey, than honey from the comb. By them is your servant warned; in keeping them there is great reward.*
  Subject: Keeping God's commands and laws Adjective: Precious and sweet
  Consequence: Great reward

Daily challenge:
If we aren't experiencing consequences, perhaps we aren't fully appreciating God's laws.

Easter

Easter Sunday dawned chilly and overcast, an inconvenience to those planning a sunrise service. We were not concerned. Our fellowship was going to meet as usual in our routine gathering place—a school gymnasium. But I felt an unusual anticipation of the service. Walking into the gym I viewed what I mentally predicted—little girls in frilly dresses, new white shoes and a much higher percentage of men in coats and ties, including two teenaged boys who sat in front of us. It tickled me that the level of refinement always steps up on Easter Sunday.

The harmony in song echoed with a heightened level of enthusiasm. After all, we were celebrating a pretty magnificent event. It's not every day that the certifiable Son of God is raised to life after three days of being dead. As Tim, the elder, stood behind the rickety music stand-turned-pulpit, he led the congregation through the final hours of Christ's life. Remembering the details was sobering. Most striking to me was that Christ suffered, the physical pain beyond description. But having God the Father darken the sky and turn His back must have produced unfathomable loneliness and anguish for the Son. Jesus faced bearing all the sin in the world—past, present and future—while completely removed from the Father's presence. However, it was Friday and Sunday was coming.

Tony Campolo, a dynamic preacher, passionately recalled a message he once heard. The old black preacher was describing the events leading up to the crucifixion and ended every statement the same way: "It's Friday, but Sunday's coming!" As the sermon continued, each phrase became more and more passionate. The congregation joined in. Louder and louder, "It's Friday, but Sunday's coming" reverberated throughout the church. By the time the sermon ended, the crowd was whipped into frenzy and nary a soul left the sanctuary not knowing that something good was going to happen on Sunday.

Buddha lived and died. Mohammed lived and died. Joseph Smith lived and died. Numerous other religious leaders have lived and died. Jesus Christ lived and died. But—and this is the ultimate *but*—Friday happened, Sunday came and Christ rose to live again. We have reason to hope, reason to live because He lives even now.

If only for this life we have hope in Christ, we are to be pitied more than all men. But Christ has indeed been raised from the dead, the firstfruits of those who have fallen asleep. (I Corinthians 15:19-20)

Daily challenge:
What happened on the first Easter Sunday should impact every day of our lives.

Fingerprints

I can see the fingerprints of God
When I look at you
I can see the fingerprints of God
And I know its true
You're a masterpiece
That all creation quietly applauds
And you're covered with the fingerprints of God
(Lyrics by Steven Curtis Chapman)

I had about seven and a half hours of "me" time today. With Mother's eightieth birthday approaching, I wanted to surprise her by showing up on her doorstep. I putzed along at fifty-seven miles per hour in hopes of pushing the mileage of our old VW Diesel Jetta to fifty mpg. Flipping through the radio channels, an unfamiliar song played. The song spoke of a father seeing his newborn daughter for the first time and crooned, "I saw God today. His fingerprints are everywhere." My stream of consciousness took me to Steven Curtis Chapman's song and from there to . . . well, hallway walls.

The hallway walls, the refrigerator, the windows, the mirrors, the coffee table. When the boys were young, slimy, gooey fingerprints were everywhere. It didn't matter how often I cleaned or how many times I had them wash their hands. It seemed inevitable that the surfaces were forever marred with the telltale signs of dirty young hooligans.

However, as I listened to that country song, I was reminded that those fingerprints represented something very good. Yes, my house would be cleaner if God had not given me those boys. But the fact that fingerprints existed meant that our house was filled with healthy, energetic, wonderful children.

It can take some effort to embrace the fingerprints. We have to be able to look past the imprint to appreciate the imprinter.

> O LORD, our Lord, how majestic is your name in all the earth! You have set your glory above the heavens. When I consider your heavens, the work of your fingers, the moon and the stars, which you have set in place, what is man that you are mindful of him, the son of man that you care for him? (Psalm 8:1, 3, 4)

Daily challenge:
When you wipe off the smudges, thank God for your little "fingerprinters."

Keeping Up with Mother

I am exhausted. My eyes droop and all I want to do is lie down and sleep. I've been trying to keep up with my eighty-year old mother.

I surprised Mother for her birthday. I told her she was to do her normal routine and I would tag along. And tag along I did. First we attended a writer's group. After that, it was on to the dining room for lunch, where we were seated with a bright couple in their nineties. Then, off to visit friends in the nursing part of the community, another man who used to be a neighbor, before picking up her mail. Back at the apartment she entertained a neighbor who dropped by, after which she made check-up calls to people in her cancer support group. She reported that she was on her 512th phone call of the year. Really.

It was 5:30 p.m. as we headed out on errands. Those errands ended with an impromptu visit to Mother's friends, finally arriving back at her place at 10:45 p.m. *Whew*. But, the day wasn't quite over. She was compelled to answer phone messages despite the late hour. With the clock hands approaching the bewitching hour, I am finally sitting down to write.

As I think back over the day, it's no wonder why Scripture is so clear in instructing older women to be examples. For several days, I've been surrounded by individuals in the latter decades of life. Today, I met a lady who worked as a Ph.D. scientist on the Manhattan Project. I spent time with "Aunt Ruth", who is recovering from a stroke. I heard a woman in her mid-90s give testimony that God was more real to her than ever before. And, I have watched my mother go through her normal paces of ministry.

I'm thankful for mature godly women. I believe that Christian retirement communities and nursing homes may hold the highest concentration per capita of wisdom. Instead of allowing these folks to fade into the sunset of their golden years, we should encourage them to share with us their valuable insights.

> *Likewise, teach the older women to be reverent in the way they live, not to be slanderers or addicted to much wine, but to teach what is good. Then they can train the younger woman to love their husbands and children to be self-controlled and pure, to be busy at home, to be kind, and to be subject to their husbands so that no one will malign the word of God . . . In everything set them an example by doing what is good. (Titus 2:3-7)*

Daily challenge:
Be inspired. Visit a retirement center.

The Recipe

I've been doing on-line consultant training for a company that provides in-home cooking shows. I decided this business could be fun and provide a means of supplementing our family income.

One of the lessons I completed used an acronym to communicate basic principles of customer care. The word CHEF was used as a recipe: connect, helpfulness, expand and finish. This sequence will undoubtedly be beneficial in establishing a business foundation. However, I think it could be a tool for any of us to use in establishing genuine and caring relationships with others.

Let's take *connect*, for example. The whole of idea of being connected with someone involves understanding where they are and what they're thinking. It's beyond a cursory "hello." Do we take the time to look them in the eye as we speak, or are we distracted by multitasking? Is our tone curt or welcoming? Would anyone really want to trust us with something personal? Do we *rejoice with those who rejoice; mourn with those who mourn* (Romans 12:15)?

Secondly, how willing are we to go out of our way to help? It's easy to be helpful when it's convenient but not so much when helping takes extra effort. In most cases, the underlying problem is selfishness. We hold our own needs and wants above all else. And, helpfulness and humility go hand-in-hand. *Finally, all of you, live in harmony with one another; be sympathetic, love as brothers, be compassionate and humble* (I Peter 3:8).

How can we expand possibilities? Corporately, the goal is to lead people to see the possibilities—to guide the customer to a greater involvement in the process. Likewise, we have the responsibility to hold each other accountable and to stir one another to good works. Titus 2 uses verbs such as *instruct, teach, rebuke* and *encourage*. It's an active—not passive—relationship.

But what about finish? In a discourse written to the Corinthian church, Paul's comments help us understand.

> *And here is my advice about what is best for you in this matter: Last year you were the first not only to give but also to have the desire to do so. Now finish the work, so that your eager willingness to do it may be matched by your completion of it, according to your means. For if the willingness is there, the gift is acceptable according to what one has, not according to what he does not have.* (II Corinthians 8:10-12)

Daily challenge:
Connect. Help. Expand. Finish. Not a bad way to live.

Angels

Angels are all the rage. Everywhere I look, I see them: angel lapel pins, angels dangling from necklaces and bracelets, angel note cards, angel stickers, angel figurines, angel cartoons, angels in TV shows and angels in trite phrases such as, "You're my little angel." Even angel-food cake proves the obsession.

While I'm not attempting a treatise on the theological status of angels, my mind focused on angels when I was driving home from my mother's house. Based on Exodus 23:20, both my brother and mother have made a habit of praying, "May the angels go before, behind and beside you as you travel." The verse actually reads, *"See, I am sending an angel ahead of you to guard you along the way and to bring you to the place I have prepared."* I like the idea that angels are guarding my path.

One of the songs popularized by a young Amy Grant speculated on the role angels play in our lives. Consider some of the lyrics:

> *God only knows the times my life was threatened just today.*
> *A reckless car ran out of gas before it ran my way.*
> *Near misses all around me, accidents unknown,*
> *Though I never see with human eyes the hands that lead me home.*
> *But I know they're all around me all day and through the night.*
> *When the enemy is closing in, I know sometimes they fight*
> *To keep my fight from falling, I'll never turn away.*
> *If you're asking what's protecting me then you're gonna hear me say:*
> *Got his angels watching over me, every move I make,*
> *Angels watching over me!*
> *Angels watching over me, every step I take,*
> *Angels watching over me . . ..*

The lyrics and music make for a snappy and memorable tune, one that I hummed as I drove along. Those lyrics are based on the promise God made long ago. We are being watched over and cared for like the children of a doting father. But it's not just a nice thought—it's a reality.

> *If you make the Most High your dwelling—even the LORD, who is my refuge—then no harm will befall you, no disaster will come near your tent. For he will command his angels concerning you to guard you in all your ways; they will lift you up in their hands, so that you will not strike your foot against a stone. (Psalm 91:9-12)*

Daily challenge:
Be courageous. You are never alone.

The Healer

Clicking open my email program can be frightening, but I've become a slave to it. Most days, I probably check it at least ten times, hoping to find a personal note or job inquiry. Then, there are always those spam emails that get through no matter what filter is used. So I delete most of what I get, respond to some and save even fewer. But today, I got an email that was special.

Remember when I wrote about a friend's nephew being run over by his dad's truck? That happened three or four weeks ago. At times, the two-year-old was not expected to live. A major stroke and nerve damage rendered the child unable to move and breathe on his own, let alone communicate. As the hours turned into days, even a tiny eye flicker was met with elation.

Slowly, Owen began to improve, had his breathing tube removed and received nutrition via a feeding tube. A transfer was arranged from the Nebraska hospital to a children's rehab facility in Minnesota. Again, doctors and staff have been amazed at his progress. Here is what Aunt Danelle wrote in that email. I think I felt the earth move as she jumped for joy.

"What a merciful God we have!! I got to TALK to Owen this morning on the phone!! He told me 'Hi', and what his name was, which he calls himself O-we O-we, and told me what the cow, dog and cat all say, along with his brother's name, and 'I love you.' Sarah said the report from the neurologist was so encouraging. He was predicting that Owen will be able to live a "normal" life, have a job, get married, have kids. He did say that there would have to be a restriction on playing football and hockey. The doctors at the hospital are amazed at the progress that has happened over the last week. He is sitting up and feeding himself, where even 4-days ago, that was not happening. His speech and hearing are all normal, his vision is still progressing. His depth perception and ability to judge where things are can be difficult for him to get. He still has a lazy eye, but they are hopeful that with time, it has only been 26 days, they will correct on their own. If not, there is stuff they can do for him. His right arm is still not mobile, but there is hope for that as well . . . Praise be to the Great Healer!"

The Creator of the entire universe is at work mending the innermost parts of a little boy. How's that for love and personal attention?

" . . . for I am the LORD, who heals you." (Exodus 15:26)

Daily challenge:
Nothing is impossible with God.

In Its Time

I've been living in a post-epiphany condition since February. I had come close to giving up on my long-distance running. I constantly begrudged the time I "had to" spend training, wanting to do a million things instead. But somewhere along the line, I decided to "do" races rather than "race" races. There's a huge difference. It leaves me time to do other things that interest me: faux painting, carpentry projects and landscaping.

As I approached the race this morning, a tough thirty-miler through the mountains, I was exceptionally calm. I had no expectations other than to start and then sometime later, finish. When the big brass gong sounded, I happily took the first of many steps.

Throughout the day, I ran downhills and marched uphills. I played cat and mouse with a college girl, shifting between second and third place multiple times. I knew the field wasn't exceptionally strong, but still, it was peculiar to again be in the hunt. All the while, I had my iPod plugged in and was inspired by the Brooklyn Tabernacle Choir, selections from Handel's *Messiah*, various other praise and worship selection and OK, I'll admit it, a little Hans Zimmer, Rascal Flatts, Chicago and some of "Seth's music." At one point, a younger woman went blasting past, downshifting me to fourth place. I presumed I had little chance of catching her. And I was okay with it. Nevertheless, I didn't give up.

As so often happens, things turn quickly. With about nine miles remaining, I climbed up the backside of Terrapin Mountain. By the time I reached the summit, I passed the woman and was only twenty seconds from catching the college runner. *Ah. Maybe I can catch her.* My competitive spirit surfaced, but I still felt content. Even when both calves unexpectedly cramped up, I didn't get upset that it relegated me to a third-place finish. I crossed the line, grateful to have spent the day challenging myself and pleased that I am learning to keep my running in perspective.

> *He has made everything beautiful in its time. He has also set eternity in the hearts of men; yet they cannot fathom what God has done from beginning to end. I know that there is nothing better for men than to be happy and do good while they live. That everyone may eat and drink, and find satisfaction in all his toil—this is the gift of God. (Ecclesiastes 3:11-13)*

Daily challenge:
No matter what your passion is, keep life in balance.

Move that Bus!

"Move that bus! Move that bus!"

For anyone not living in a box, that phrase will be recognized as the expression shouted out by the mega crowds at the end of ABC's "Extreme Home Makeover". With an excited family having just returned from a show-sponsored vacation, the only thing standing between them and a brand new amazing house is a big ol' bus.

"Bus driver. Move that bus!" The family jumps, screams and cries as they view for the first time a house created especially for them. Sometimes they are so overcome with emotion that they fall to the ground, unable to speak. Everything is new, inside and out. All the tools for starting a new life have been put in place.

Watching the program this evening, I thought about the family's new life. It was obvious that materially, the recipients of the new home with all the furnishings, technology and stocked closets and refrigerators had entered a novel phase of life. However, I wondered if the essence of their lives had been changed as much as their physical surroundings.

"Newness" is a Biblical concept. There are new songs to be sung, new wine to enjoy, new owners of property, new grain, new clay for pottery and a new heaven and earth predicted for the future. However, the most significant changes seem not to be in substance but in heart.

The prophet Ezekiel spoke the words of God when he declared, "*I will give you a new heart and put a new spirit in you; I will remove from you your heart of stone and give you a heart of flesh*" (Ezekiel 36:26). Notice that newness is given, not conjured up. Likewise, Peter declares, *Praise be to the God and Father of our Lord Jesus Christ! In his great mercy he has given us new birth into a living hope through the resurrection of Jesus Christ from the dead* (I Peter 1:3). Again, new birth, new life, is a gift from God and not something that was or ever could be earned. *Therefore, if anyone is in Christ, he is a new creation; the old has gone, the new has come!* (II Corinthians 5:17).

Being once dead in sin but made newly alive in Christ produces changes that should be obvious. If we still look like our old selves, maybe Christ hasn't made us new.

> *You were taught, with regard to your former way of life, to put off your old self, which is being corrupted by its deceitful desires; to be made new in the attitude of your minds; and to put on the new self, created to be like God in true righteousness and holiness. (Ephesians 4:22-24)*

Daily challenge:
What is standing between you and a new spiritual relationship?
Move that bus!

The Bride and the Groom

I sat in my kitchen, laptop on the counter and pictures loaded. Seth had just returned from photographing a wedding. I was anxious to view what he saw through the lens. The bride and groom were classmates of Caleb's a short two years ago. It was hard to believe that time had turned high school seniors into lovers standing together at the altar. I knew I was the same age when I got married—twenty—but somehow, looking into the faces of those "kids" stirred something deep inside. Click by click, picture after picture, tears streamed down my face. I don't know why. All I knew was that it was an emotional experience that far transcended the obvious beauty of the setting and the uniqueness of the photography.

From the beginning of time, God intended man and woman to become a couple—to create one identity distinct from each individual, to complement and help one another.

> *But for Adam no suitable helper was found. So the LORD God caused the man to fall into a deep sleep; and while he was sleeping, he took one of the man's ribs and closed up the place with flesh. Then the LORD God made a woman from the rib he had taken out of the man, and he brought her to the man. The man said, "This is now bone of my bones and flesh of my flesh; she shall be called 'woman,' for she was taken out of man." For this reason a man will leave his father and mother and be united to his wife, and they will become one flesh. (Genesis 2:20-24)*

It was no accident that God ordained marriage. It was a social relationship to which all of mankind could relate. It was a perfect opportunity for God the Father to paint the picture of the bridegroom's love for the bride. Surely, if man could feel, could understand what it was like to be the bridegroom or the bride, then people might be able to understand the perfect union between heaven and earth.

> *Hallelujah! For our Lord God Almighty reigns. Let us rejoice and be glad and give him glory! For the wedding of the Lamb has come, and his bride has made herself ready. (Revelation 19:6, 7)*

Daily challenge:
Does your marriage create a picture of love and sacrifice?

April Fool

April Fools Day. Who in the world came up with that?

In fact, the origin of this day marked by pranks is somewhat in dispute. Some believe that its origin began in conjunction with common festivals taking place on the vernal equinox, from March 25 to April 2. Chaucer, circa 1400, wrote the Nun's Priests Tales, a story about two fools which took place on April 1.

But during the 1500s, Charles IX, King of France, declared New Year's Day to be changed from the traditional April 1 to January 1. They made sport of fooling the uninformed—remember, this was pre-internet days—by sending gifts or faking celebrations on April 1. Those who were duped were called *poisson d'avril* (April fish). Soon, it became customary to place dead fish on the backs of those who had been duped. Later, bakeries and candy makers produced fish-shaped treats for the holiday and school children made game of trying to slip cut-out paper fish onto the shirt backs of their school mates. In the 18th century, Scotland's version included the "hunting the gowk" (cuckoo), which was a sign of contempt.

You can probably think of pranks that you experienced—or performed—on April 1. Some jokes are hilarious and inventive. Other times, cruel. Ill-advised jokes played by radio and TV stations have resulted in public mayhem and at times, outrage. But still, there is something amusing in pulling off a trick and saying, "Gotcha. April Fools"!

Despite the levity, there is actually nothing very funny about being a fool. The wise kings David and Solomon spoke often about the characteristics of a fool. The list is not exhaustive, but it is a telling inventory of what NOT to be. Foolish people . . .

- are corrupt, vile, do no good,
  and deny there is a God   Psalm 14:1
- revile God's name   Psalm 74:18
- mock God   Psalm 74:22
- do not understand   Psalm 92:6
- are rebellious   Psalm 107:17
- despise wisdom   Proverbs 1:7
- are complacent   Proverbs 1:32
- are shameful   Proverbs 3:35
- grieve their moms   Proverbs 10:1
- are malicious   Proverbs 10:10
- lie and slander   Proverbs 10:18
- lack judgment   Proverbs 10:21

- find joy in evil   Proverbs 10:23
- are easily annoyed   Proverbs 12:16
- say stupid things   Proverbs 12:23
- bring trouble   Proverbs 13:20
- deceive   Proverbs 14:8
- never apologize   Proverbs 14:9
- are hot-headed   Proverbs 14:1
- disregard rebuke   Proverbs 15:5
- bring strife   Proverbs 18:6
- are quick to argue   Proverbs 20:3
- repeat mistakes   Proverbs 26:11
- angrily explode   Proverbs 29:11

Daily challenge:
Work hard to "get the fool out."

Pray Hard

Our family sponsors a child through Compassion International—a sixteen-year old girl from India. We wanted to give Lavanya a boost in the difficult life she lives. We recently received a package that included several new pictures as well as bookmarks and a reminder to "Pray that she will know the Lord and grow strong in Him." The photo bookmark is now in my Bible.

This morning I was reading in Ephesians and noticed that Paul was constantly praying. In this instance, he was praying on behalf of other Believers. His example gives us some great prayer pointers.

The first characteristic of Paul's praying is that it was constant and in a spirit of thankfulness. Ephesians 1:15 and 16 reads, *For this reason, ever since I heard about your faith in the Lord Jesus and your love for all the saints, I have not stopped giving thanks for you, remembering you in my prayers.* All too often, we focus our prayer on difficult circumstances or get into a pattern of the "give-me"s.

Reading on, Paul prays specifically that . . . *the God of our Lord Jesus Christ, the glorious Father, may give you the Spirit of wisdom and revelation, so that you may know him better* (1:17). To be honest, I periodically pray that my sons will have wisdom, but I have not been very consistent. I wonder what would happen if I regularly prayed for our friends and family and they did the same. It's likely the Body of Christ would mature exponentially.

Paul continues by saying, *I pray also that the eyes of your heart may be enlightened in order that you may know the hope to which he has called you, the riches of his glorious inheritance in the saints, and his incomparably great power for us who believe.* And why does he pray thusly? Because

> . . . *that power is like the working of his mighty strength, which he exerted in Christ when he raised him from the dead and seated him at his right hand in the heavenly realms, far above all rule and authority, power and dominion, and every title that can be given, not only in the present age but also in the one to come. (Ephesians 1:19-21)*

Daily challenge:
Prayer is a powerful tool. Pray hard.

Act Justly, Love Mercy, Walk Humbly

On came the Oprah Winfrey Show. The story unfolded quickly and snatched my attention with such force that dinner-making was considerably slowed. It was a story of two college girls, one horrific accident and a funeral.

The blonde coeds rode together in a college van when the accident occurred. Five earthly lives ended that day, including one of the fair-haired girls. The other girl, disfigured beyond recognition, spent the next four or five weeks unaware of what had happened, tethered to equipment that sustained her life. As the family kept vigil by her bedside, the other family experienced a heart-wrenching funeral and the empty days that followed. Then, as the blonde in the hospital began to regain speech, suspicions grew into reality that this was not the daughter of the ones giving constant watch.

As the details unraveled, the coroner had mistakenly informed the wrong family that their daughter was dead. No positive identification was ever made, since no one wanted to have that horrific image as their last memory of a girl so full of life a day earlier. Ironically, one family's mourning turned to joy. The other sank to depths of sadness. They didn't even have the chance to say goodbye and lay their baby in the ground.

As the families told their stories, it was immediately evident that both were deeply committed to the Lord. The sweet spirit, the lack of bitterness, the love they had one for another could not be denied. Despite the turnabout of human emotion, they were open and honest about God's faithfulness. Many people who have sat on that stage—including Ms. Winfrey—speak often with an air of spirituality. But this was clearly different. The families drawn together in unspeakable crisis stood united in purpose—letting the world know that they were being held under the wing and in the shadow of the Almighty. They did not place blame. They even denied the bold approaches of lawyers desiring to capitalize on the situation. They extended grace, forgiveness and mercy to the coroner who made the grave error.

The host and audience sat captivated by their sincerity. No one questioned the genuineness of their message, nor could they ignore the uncanny peace and contentment despite the unfathomable circumstances. Perhaps the most poignant message of the hour was when the dead girl's father, with a demeanor uncommon for a grieving parent, looked Oprah in the eye and gave witness to his purpose for living. He said,

And what does the LORD require of you? To act justly and to love
mercy and to walk humbly with your God. (Micah 6:8)

Daily challenge:
It's a simple set of instructions. There are no exceptions, no exclusions.

Practice Makes Perfect

Practice makes perfect. If I had a nickel for every time I heard that statement . . . well, you know the rest. I would have money in the bank and be living the life of a millionaire. Nevertheless, it's true. It's impossible to become a good piano player without practicing. A gymnast doesn't perfect a routine without hours in the gym. And a tennis pro doesn't expect tournament officials to hand over big checks if he can't whack the cover off the ball. No, few people are blessed to be naturally gifted; even those cannot attain excellence without some effort.

The Online Merriam-Webster dictionary is a wonderful thing. *Practice* can be a noun or a verb and the key definitions are as follows:

As a transitive verb: 1a. carryout, preach b: to do or perform often, customarily, or habitually c: to be professionally engaged in 2 a: to perform or work at repeatedly so as to become proficient b: to train by repeated exercises

As an intransitive verb: 1. to do repeated exercises for proficiency 2. to pursue a profession actively 3. archaic: INTIGUE 4. to do something customarily 5. to take advantage of someone

In the fourth chapter of Philippians, Paul writes instructions to the church. You may be familiar with those directives: *Rejoice in the Lord always. I will say it again: Rejoice! Let your gentleness be evident to all . . . Do not be anxious about anything, but in everything, by prayer and petition, with thanksgiving, present your requests to God . . . Finally, brothers, whatever is true, whatever is noble, whatever is right, whatever is pure, whatever is lovely, whatever is admirable—if anything is excellent or praiseworthy—think about such things* (4:4-8).

Do you think Paul would have written those instructions if everyone came by them naturally? I don't believe so. What I do know is that Paul realized Christians will always have to work at putting to death the old nature and concentrate on developing those characteristics penned in his letter.

So let's paraphrase the message using modern definitions. "You need to be engaged in rejoicing. It needs to be habitual. Don't worry about anything but customarily pray and repeatedly be thankful in your requests to God. Train yourself to become proficient in thinking rightly, purely, admirably and always in an excellent and praiseworthy manner."

Whatever you have learned or received or heard from me, or seen in me—put it into practice. (Philippians 4:9)

Daily challenge:
Practice is absolutely necessary to make the unnatural natural, habitual, and customary.

The Accident

Gary rushed to my car door as I pulled up to the house. I knew something was wrong. "Is he dead?" I'm not sure I actually voiced those words, but I know they were screaming inside my head.

"It's Seth," Gary blurted out.

Following his instructions, I turned the ignition back on and sped away to where Seth was laying by the side of the road. Gary followed in the truck to load up Seth's motorcycle. In route to the scene, I spoke to Seth on his cell phone. He sounded oddly chipper. With his adrenaline levels sky high, he was unable to process what happened. My heart raced as I approached the scene. The road was blocked by a caravan of emergency vehicles, their lights eerily flashing. The firefighters at the blockade refused to let me go through. I hastily parked on a parallel road and fought my way through a wooded ravine, arriving at my son's side bloody from the work of the briars.

In my car just twenty minutes earlier, I specifically remember the spot on the road where a heart dart had been hurled to pray for Seth's safety. I knew it was about the time he should be on the way home from a friend's house and it had just started to rain. I did pray and believe that my prayer was answered. Otherwise, we might be planning a funeral. Not one, but two different cars narrowly missed smashing into or running over Seth once he was down. God is good.

An ambulance ride to a small hospital, a complicated elbow fracture, a broken pinky finger and a few other abrasions resulted. However, since the hospital had no orthopedic services and a second hospital's surgeon refused to tackle the procedure, we ended up in the trauma center of a larger hospital. More evaluations, x-rays, consults and finally surgery filled the long and lonely night.

To see your child on a gurney is not pleasant. However, Providence intervened. The caregivers were wonderful. The anesthesiologist was a partner with a doctor I used to work with. A Believer, we instantly bonded. Then, when he established that Seth's surgeon was the finest, it confirmed that God's hand had orchestrated the events surrounding the accident.

Seth is being held for another night to flood him with intravenous antibiotics. But I am forever grateful that we will be able to return home as a family.

But let all who take refuge in you be glad; let them ever sing for joy.
Spread your protection over them, that those who love your name
may rejoice in you. (Psalm 5:11)

Daily challenge:
When the Spirit says "pray," you better pray.

God Is in Control

A single second can be felt in time far removed. Gary made that observation as we were packing up our things from the hospital room that had been our home since the wee hours of Saturday morning. None of us anticipated that Seth would have his motorcycle slide out from under him on Friday night. We did not consider the impact on pain levels, recuperation, showering with a cast, decreased opportunities to work and the challenges of holding his heavy but treasured camera. And there is now the issue of a ticket that was issued for reckless driving by "failing to control a vehicle"—despite the fact he was driving within the speed limit and no one directly observed the accident. The ripple effect, should the charge stick, could be great.

Now that Seth is home and resting, we must face adjusting to a different type of life—at least for a period of time. I realize that in the scheme of things, Seth's injuries are fairly benign. It's not like he's a soldier returning from war with one leg instead of two. Nor is he suddenly a quadriplegic after a fated dive into shallow water. Nevertheless, he will eat differently, type differently, sleep differently, bathe differently and yes, be a rider rather than a driver.

There are a couple things to remember about a pivotal event. 1) Nothing is ever an accident; 2) The event does not occur in a vacuum and 3) God gives the grace to deal with whatever number one is.

As the events unfolded, we saw the hand of God directing each step in the process. I suppose we will never know "why." Perhaps the accident made an impression on Seth that will save him from future harm. Or perhaps, our borders may have expanded to bring others, previously unknown, into our lives. Maybe someone will think about Seth's brush with death and understand we have no guarantee for another day. But without a doubt, our faith has been strengthened by seeing God work definitively and dramatically.

> *"For I know the plans I have for you," declares the LORD, "plans to prosper you and not to harm you, plans to give you hope and a future." (Jeremiah 29:11)*

Daily challenge:
God is in control even when you feel out of control.

Selling

Sell. Sell. Sell. That is the down and dirty goal of any business. On my very first cooking show outing this evening, I intended to inspire a lot of buying. Let's face it. I want to make money and have some fun while I'm at it. But the "sell" cannot be bold and obnoxious, pushy and presumptive.

What goes into a successful sale? People need to recognize what they lack. And I need to demonstrate that their lives could be better if they had a tool to accomplish a task. But just as importantly, they need convinced that the tool's quality is exceptional. The benefit must outweigh the cost.

If I simply tell my clients these things, they may not believe. Nevertheless, if they see a demonstration, hear genuine testimonials and experience the tools for themselves, there is a pretty good chance of a sale. But my message can't be so loud and overpowering that it turns them away.

As I was thinking about the show, it made me wonder how we "sell" our faith. Most everyone has been turned off by a loud-mouthed Christian who lives a life of contradictions. I cringe when an unbeliever makes disparaging remarks about someone who claims Christ—and is right! But I'm equally concerned when a Believer feels compelled to beat someone with "do's and don'ts," as if the legalistic approach to life has super-spiritual powers.

So "How then should we live?" to quote the theologian and philosopher, Francis Schaeffer? Paul writes, *For I am not ashamed of the Gospel of Christ . . .* (Romans 1:16). Paul preached Christ boldly. He was imprisoned, stoned, and left for dead. He implored Timothy to *not be ashamed to testify about our Lord, or ashamed of me his prisoner. Yet I am not ashamed, because I know whom I have believed, and am convinced that he is able to guard what I have entrusted to him for that day* (II Timothy 1:8, 12). Boldness was required. But so was the sweet fruit of the Spirit.

Are we "selling" Christ by demonstrating Christlikeness? Are we appropriately bold or obviously obnoxious? Can people see a better life as a Believer? Is there a testimony of excellence and integrity? Can they see that this spiritual investment will be worth it?

> *But the fruit of the Spirit is love, joy, peace, patience, kindness, goodness, faithfulness, gentleness and self-control. (Galatians 5:22)*

Daily challenge:
If people see only hot air and unsubstantiated claims,
we should be ashamed—not of Christ—but of ourselves.

Fear and Dreams

After two days of subbing in a public high school I needed a release. One kid just returned from a three-day suspension for fighting, another wore a parole bracelet, no one achieved a test score higher than 42%, the kids looked like orphaned ragamuffins, and many tried leaving the classroom at will. The point is, I couldn't wait to get out of there and lace up my running shoes.

I headed out on a familiar six-mile route. The afternoon gave way to rays of sun, a welcome break from cold drizzle. I felt smooth and efficient—free to run, think and pray. I listened to a Josh Groban song, "Let me fall," becoming acutely aware of a phrase I'm not sure I ever noticed before: "Let me fall, Let me climb. There is a moment when fear and dreams must collide."

There is a moment when fear and dreams collide. What a phenomenal statement. I think back to when I headed to the Amazon race. I had full reservoirs of both fear and dreams. And today, the hair on the back of my neck rose at the mere thought of what it will take to finish the Grindstone 100 Miler in October—sacrifice, endurance, pain and suffering.

We sometimes experience these same feelings in the way we minister. It's easy to contemplate an encounter with a stranger, sharing our faith in stirring fashion, only to be stymied by fear that prevents us from uttering the first word. We have the best of intentions, but sometimes it just doesn't work out the way we want. How can we face the fear and realize the dream?

Moses, at the ripe old age of 120, realized he was no longer able to guide Israel. He addressed the nation before turning over the leadership to Joshua, preparing them to enter the Promised Land and conquer the mighty inhabitants. In this address, it's the perfect example of fear and courage colliding.

> *"Be strong and courageous. Do not be afraid or terrified because of them, for the LORD your God goes with you; he will never leave you nor forsake you." Then Moses summoned Joshua and said to him in the presence of all Israel, "Be strong and courageous, for you must go with this people into the land that the LORD swore to their fore-fathers to give them, and you must divide it among them as their inheritance. The LORD himself goes before you and will be with you; he will never leave you nor forsake you. Do not be afraid; do not be discouraged." (Deuteronomy 6:6-8)*

Daily challenge:
Fear is no excuse for abandoning the dream.

Remember When

"Ah, look. There's Mickey," the six-year-old screeched. No, she wasn't at Disney World. She was getting on a transport shuttle at the Orlando airport. The shrill scream came only at the sight of a Mickey Mouse poster. The rest of us chuckled as we pulled away on the transport bus. The first stop was hers: The Nickelodeon Hotel. The high-pitched uttering started up again as she took in her first view of the storybook-like hotel. Multi-colored and oddly shaped, it looked like something straight out of the comics. "There's Sponge Bob!" She nearly tumbled out of the van, her grandmother trying desperately to keep up. Still seated in the vehicle, I could see her little head bob along the window as she jumped, twirled and turned, fueled by an ecstatic enthusiasm. Her last words we heard as she bounced like a little rubber ball into the lobby were, "This is the very, very best place ever."

From my own hotel I took a run along the hotel-lined streets and into Downtown Disney. It was difficult weaving my way between strollers, families negotiating the walkways and seniors wandering about at turtles' pace. But excitement was palpable as kids took in the scenes and parents reveled in family fun. I thought about the times our family went on vacation together, feeling a pang of jealousy as I contemplated those yesteryear memories.

As parents, we have the opportunity to "make memories" with our kids. The memories don't have to be made at a theme park or on an exotic island. Some of the best memories of my dad were when we played ping-pong hockey on the living room floor. We emptied two waxy milk cartons, cutting a hole in the side to fashion a goal. Then, we rolled newspapers or magazines into tight bundles to fashion our sticks. We dropped to the floor, whacking at the ball to drive it into the opponent's goal. It was a brutal game, rug-burned knees and all. But I can still hear my dad's raucous laugh, tears rolling down his face, as he laid on the ball to shield it. My brothers and I all piled on top of him to force the ball from hiding. The result? Dad laughed all the harder before giving it up. We continued the game until everyone was pooped out, hot and sweaty. Ah . . . memories.

I'm not giving up on making more memories with the boys. But I'm interested to know if I've done enough. Will they have anything to tell their kids?

"I remember when . . . ."

Why, you do not even know what will happen tomorrow. What is your life? You are a mist that appears for a little while and then vanishes. (James 4:14)

Daily challenge:
Make memories now. Life is short.

Money: A Tool for Service

I've been to a lot of medical meetings and have been very attentive to attend each and every session. For years, I was responsible for putting the meetings together and orchestrating the ebb and flow of the events. This time, however, it was different. It had been two years since attending this particular meeting and I had no responsibility other than making one research presentation. My interest was not fully engaged since I had left clinical practice. In fact, I wasn't even very excited about attending. Maybe it was because I paid my way with money we didn't have. Nevertheless, I came because I saw this as a last-ditch effort to drum up business.

If nothing else, I've been learning that God is faithful. At every turn and despite much trepidation, God has arranged the details of our lives. In the thirty-six hours since I arrived in Florida, He continues to place people in my path who encourage me.

I ran into a good friend and when asked, explained that my consulting business was dismal. Shortly thereafter, I saw another friend and was presented the possibility of doing consulting for a large company. After that, an afternoon poolside discussion resulted in two different fellows asking for my card. And to top it off, I found a message on my phone from a company who wants me to write online education for them.

God is being faithful to encourage me with these prospects. But I dare not forget that it's not just about the money. Paul instructed the Corinthians to sow generously in order to meet physical and spiritual needs. I never want to be so focused on a dollar amount that I lose sight of the bigger goal:

> *This service that you perform is not only supplying the needs of God's people but is also overflowing in many expressions of thanks to God. Because of the service by which you have proved yourselves, men will praise God for the obedience that accompanies your confession of the gospel of Christ, and for your generosity in sharing with them and with everyone else. (II Corinthians 9:12-13)*

Daily challenge:
Money is not the goal. Money is merely a tool for service.

Provision

This was my last full day at the meeting and I fully experienced the Lord's mercy. I rose early to do a last-minute review of my paper. The presentation went off without a hitch. But I was eager for the session to end so that I could visit the exhibit hall and "network." Immediately, a wagging finger beckoned me. Out of the clear blue, the director of education for a company asked me if I would be interested in developing online education modules for them. *Are you kidding?* Of course I was interested!

Moving on through the hall, I arrived at another booth and continued a conversation that had started by email in January. My proposal to work with this company was received with enthusiasm. The more we talked, the more both of us realized the potential gains for both parties. They assured work was on its way.

It was also amazing how the Lord opened up conversations with friends I had not seen in a long time, giving me opportunity to rehearse God's faithfulness to our family. These conversations were with Believers and unbelievers alike. However, the fellowship and encouragement brought by the hand of other Christians ministered richly to me.

I've been asking the Lord to show mercy in our financial situation. I love what James 1:21 has to say. *Keep yourselves in God's love as you wait for the mercy of our Lord Jesus Christ to bring you to eternal life.* It's not that we have ever gone hungry or set up life under a bridge. But still, the money just hasn't been there. Now, perhaps God has made provision for substantial work. I am excited at the prospect and thank God for His faithfulness.

I cannot close this day without offering this doxology:

> *To him who is able to keep you from falling and to present you before his glorious presence without fault and with great joy—to the only God our Savior be glory, majesty, power and authority, through Jesus Christ our Lord, before all ages, now and forevermore! Amen. (Jude 1:24, 25)*

Daily challenge:
The process of waiting for the Lord is just as important as the provisions He makes in the aftermath.

The Missed Flight

Getting up at 3:15 a.m. to get on an airplane is not my idea of fun. I set the alarm clock in the hotel and on my cell phone and also arranged for a wakeup call. Everything went off as planned, giving me ten minutes to spare as I waited for the shuttle. Once at the airport, I made it through security hoping to find coffee on the other side. I was disappointed. At 4:45 a.m., the snack stands weren't even open. I occupied myself by watching airport TV news before deciding to sneak a few winks before boarding the 6:45 a.m. flight.

I sat up refreshed but curiously, the same news story was playing again. There was still no activity at the appointed gate. Was I in a scene from "Groundhog Day"? I pulled my phone out to check the time and did a double-take. 7:00. What?! There's no way I could have slept that long. I pulled out my glasses to double check. Perhaps I read the time wrong. Nope. My plane had come and gone and I wasn't on it. Big groan.

My body and mind are too often weak and this morning was no exception. I have good intentions. I want to do the right things. I want to be productive. I want to be steadfast. But alas, I succumb. Sometimes it's a willful act, being fully cognizant of a poor decision. However, just like me snoozing in the chair, my failures can sneak up on me. It sort of "just happens." I intended to rest just a little but instead fell into a sleep deep enough that I became oblivious to everything around me.

Be vigilant and wary enough to avoid being lulled into fruitless sleep.

"Watch and pray so that you will not fall into temptation. The spirit is willing, but the body is weak." (Matthew 26:41)

Daily challenge:
Vigilance leads to victory.

Accountability

Accountability: "the quality or state of being accountable; especially: an obligation or willingness to accept responsibility or to account for one's actions" (Source: *Merriam-Websteronline.com*)

Early on in this daily writing project, I realized there was a much greater chance of being successful if I was accountable to something other than my conscience; the latter is too easily dissuaded. Thus, I asked three friends if I could email my story each day. They didn't have to commit to anything other than an open mailbox. They did not have to react, respond or edit. I simply needed them to receive the file. No. Expect the file. Expectation is the essence of accountability and I did not want to disappoint.

The word *account* or *accountable* occurs eighty-nine times throughout the Bible, give or take a few. Often, a certain person or group of people had to give account for their possessions or actions. Sometimes the accountability was to another person, but more often than not, the accountability recipient was none other than God. Job said *"what will I do when God confronts me? What will I answer when called to account?"* (Job 31:14). I don't know about you, but I find that terrifying.

As parents, we ask our children to be accountable for their actions. Coaches expect their athletes to be accountable in training and commitment. Bosses hold employees accountable for work. Patients hold doctors accountable for their care and clients hold lawyers accountable for their defense.

Truly, being accountable is a powerful stimulus. But consider how serious it is to be accountable to the Creator of the universe—which we are. If we really understood this, I am fairly certain we would think and behave differently.

> *Now we know that whatever the law says, it says to those who are under the law, so that every mouth may be silenced and the whole world held accountable to God . . . So then, each of us will give an account of himself to God. (Romans 3:19 and 14:12)*

Daily challenge:
Trouble making good on commitments? Find a friend to report to every week.

Little Problem, Big Problem

The hands on the clock moved so slowly, I thought the time-keeper must be broken. Would the day ever end? For the last seven hours, I wrangled a bunch of kids who were not eager to study Biology. I tried my best to keep them engaged in the learning process, but the jury is still out on that one. Besides, I really didn't want to be substituting. There were a million things I needed to do. I was looking forward to my run on a favorite mountain trail.

After the last bell rang, I pointed the car toward the mountain. Looking up at the jagged peak covered in clouds I wondered if I would get wet. The temperature was chilly for mid-April—forty-five degrees, and I didn't relish a good soaking. Regardless, it was good to breathe in the fresh air and shake out the cobwebs with the first of many steps.

Making my way up the long and steep mountain trail, I noticed a slight rubbing in my shoe. Bells started going off. *High alert. Potential problem. Take care of it now!* I had learned my lesson before and did not wish to review it today.

I once did a race when a tiny little cinder made its way into my shoe. I obsessed about that cinder for miles on end. Don't ask me why I didn't stop immediately and take care of the problem. I guess I was too concerned about losing time. But how dumb was that? That little speck worked its way to a critical pressure point and brought on an ugly blister and a lot of pain. Had I just taken care of it at the first sign of trouble, I could have avoided all that.

Isn't that true in our relationships? We choose to let a small problem turn into a big one. We get so selfish and unrelenting that we refuse to let go of our stronghold. We get angry at the cap left off the toothpaste or socks that lie on the floor next to (not in) the hamper. Or, we get miffed if someone eats the last piece of cake. When that someone is your spouse, is it any wonder that we don't want to be warm and snuggly in bed?

Nip a problem in the bud. Don't let it control you. Don't be stupid and ignore it. Take care of it immediately, repenting and asking forgiveness when necessary.

In your anger do not sin: Do not let the sun go down while you are still angry, and do not give the devil a foothold. (Ephesians 4:26, 27)

Daily challenge:
At the first sign of trouble, deal with it.

You Are What You Eat

I'm subbing again at an area high school, sitting at my desk before the first students arrive. In this time of reflection, I'm not really surprised at the actions and attitudes of some of the students. But, I am astonished at their level of disrespect. None politely pause their conversations during intercom announcements nor do they honor the moment of silence or participate in the Pledge of Allegiance. Their choice is to simply continue on as if nothing else mattered.

Then there's the issue of not complying with directives. Rather, they either argue or ignore the entreaty. Some come to class with a surly, "Just try to make me learn" attitude, not bothering to bring a pencil, notebook, or backpack. Others put their head on the desk to check out for the duration. Signs all over the school outlawing electronic devices go unheeded. iPods and phones are pulled out from pockets during class. And obvious infractions of the Honor Code posted on the wall happen daily.

I'm not disregarding those kids that are polite, respectful and caring. But there is an underlying reason for the differences between the two types of students. Clearly, the rules and standards of the school apply to all but all do not apply the standards to themselves. There is a disconnect between the standards and recognizing the authority of those who wrote them.

"To establish a quality learning environment where dignity, respect and teamwork prevail." Nice mission statement. However, it didn't take long for me to understand which students bought into the vision and which did not. The clear marker of acceptance was whether they had become a reflection of the standard itself. After all, "you are what you eat."

If we truly regard God's standards, we will become a reflection of the same. We will be perfect (mature), trustworthy, right, radiant, pure and righteous.

The law of the Lord is perfect, reviving the soul. The statutes of the Lord are trustworthy, making wise the simple. The precepts of the Lord are right, giving joy to the heart. The commands of the Lord are radiant, giving light to the eyes. The fear of the Lord is pure, enduring forever. The ordinances of the Lord are sure and altogether righteous. (Psalm 19:7-9)

Daily challenge:
What are you eating? What are you becoming?

Slimy Slugs

Our Wednesday-night study group met tonight in our home. A young married couple and several college kids are faithful attendees. The three nursing students, Joy, Sarah and Elizabeth, are committed, dedicated, fun-loving and personable. I would be happy to have my sons bring home any girl like these. With fresh perspectives, they keep things lively.

Tonight's discussion focused on practical Proverbs relating to work, diligence, money, priorities and debt. The verses of particular interest compared those who are diligent and those who are not. The word *sluggard* kept popping up. That word is actually a 14th-century Middle English word meaning "a habitually lazy person." Personally, the soft-bodied mollusks commonly known as *ground slugs*, slippery and slimy, come to mind. To me, they are perfect examples of slow-moving, ineffective and completely useless entities. And, they are anything but resilient. When we were kids, a little salt shaken on the slugs provided a certain level of morbid entertainment. The slugs curled up and "melted." At least that's how I remember it.

Ancient King Solomon must have known plenty of slugs, because he wrote about them so often. He compared the lazy person with the ambitious ant when he wrote, *Go to the ant, you sluggard; consider its ways and be wise! It has no commander, no overseer or ruler, yet it stores its provisions in summer and gathers its food at harvest. How long will you lie there, you sluggard? When will you get up from your sleep? A little sleep, a little slumber, a little folding of the hands to rest—and poverty will come on you like a bandit and scarcity like an armed man* (Proverbs 6:6-11).

Don't be a slug. Be an ant.

I applied my heart to what I observed and learned a lesson from what I saw. (Proverbs 24:32)

Daily challenge:
Have you learned the lesson—or are you still enrolled in Slug 101?

Water Works

Spring has sprung. With blue skies, a light breeze rustling through the trees and the sun quickly warming the air, I was glad to work outside. Happily gathering my tools to begin the project, I turned on the garden hose and set the timer for one hour, running the water into the pool.

Our very shallow well is the same one used back when the house was built more than a century ago. We learned the hard way that using a lot of water will run the well dry. When a toilet leaked all night long, we awoke to pipes that groaned and spit. There was nothing to do but wait for the well to refill. Hence, we are careful to top off the pool in small increments.

But this year, Gary, my McGyver-like husband, decided to cut down our reliance on well water. He dammed up a little stream running through our property and retrofitted a spigot to a 55-gallon drum. The drum was secured to the trailer that was pulled by the four-wheeler after reinforcing the trailer's metal grating. Taking his gasoline-powered pump, off he went to the stream. A short time later he returned, trailer in tow and water sloshing from the drum. A quick hookup, a turn of the spigot and *presto-chango*—the water splashed merrily into the man-made swimming hole. Off he went again and again, returning each time with more wet stuff. We watched as the pool level rose quicker than expected; we were delighted with the results.

Even if filling a pool might be considered a luxury, water is crucial to our lives. Without it we cannot survive. And with just a little water, we fail to thrive. We must have a never-ending supply of cool, refreshing water if we expect to stay hydrated and healthy.

Thankfully, getting water in a spiritual sense isn't as complicated as getting water to fill our pool. Jesus, the Living Water provides *streams of living water* (John 7:38) that will never run dry.

Come drink and quench your thirst.

> *"Everyone who drinks this water will be thirsty again, but whoever drinks the water I give him will never thirst. Indeed, the water I give him will become in him a spring of water welling up to eternal life."* (John 4:13, 14)

Daily challenge:
If you are feeling thirsty, head to the Well.

Stiffness

Two weeks have passed since Seth's motorcycle accident and it was time to get the stitches removed, take new x-rays and have a new cast cemented to his arm. Seth barely refrained from laughing out loud at his nurse's winged and starched cap. I have to admit, I can't remember the last time I saw a nurse wear such a corny looking thing, perched on the back of the head and attached with bobby pins.

As the capped nurse in her matching crisp white uniform and spotless white stockings and shoes gathered supplies, she instructed Seth not to bend his arm once she removed the bandages. But Seth could not resist when she turned her back. For two weeks, it had been kept immobile and angled. I could tell he was trying, but the arm did not straighten more than about an inch. As the nurse turned back around, Seth played innocent.

The physician assistant came in and started wrapping the cast. While Seth had a little mobility in his first cast, this one offered no such luxury. As the nurse pulled his fingers painfully backward and the PA applied the hot pink cast Seth had chosen, he kept erupting in laughter, tickled by recalling a comedy skit about a guy with casts on both arms. The more he tried to stifle it, the more I laughed. I couldn't help it.

The laughter continued on the way home every time I glanced over at the florescent monstrosity. But what was not funny was the realization that his arm would be beyond stiff when the cast was removed in another month. Seth will need strength, determination and a lot of hard work to gradually work out the stiffness and have a properly functioning arm.

Just for grins, I searched to see if and when the word stiff was used in Scripture. Sure enough, nineteen times various people or groups were called stiff-necked. Does that mean they all needed chiropractors? Hardly. It was a derogatory description of proud, arrogant and stubborn people.

Just as the stiffness in Seth's arm is a detriment to his well-being, a stiff-necked person is no good to the Body. We must submit to rehabilitation directed by the Holy Spirit to resolve our stiffness and restore the Body's healthy frame.

> *A man who remains stiff-necked after many rebukes will suddenly be destroyed—without remedy. (Proverbs 29:1)*

Daily challenge:
Work out your stiffness by soaking in the warmth of His Word.

Friends

The day dawned with a touch of chill but the promise of a warm and sunny morning. My friend, Deb, arrived at my house early so that we could tackle fifteen miles of country road running, saving the rest of the day for other things. The temperature was perfect, the birds fully awake and filled with song. From the first step, we talked non-stop. We conversed easily about everyday things and upcoming events, silly things, mutual friends and running goals. But Deb also listened attentively when I voiced my concerns that few others knew.

"What's said on the trail, stays on the trail." That's what we ultrarunners cherish—a camaraderie that kicks in as soon as a group run starts. A diverse group of people are brought together by a singular purpose: to traverse X number of miles over hill and dale. No matter what the educational level, social status or experience, each runner relates on some level to the others. Stories fly as fast as the feet and laughter comes easily. But just as quickly as the next bend in the trail, the chatter often turns to deeper thoughts and issues of the heart. Concerns are shared without fear that the conversation will find its way to the streets. The trail and those who run it are bonded together.

Friendship is to be coveted because it comes from God. The Lord is said to have spoken with Moses *as a man speaks with his friend* (Exodus 33:11). Stop and think about that for a second. Can you imagine that? But we are also aware of many other human friendships: Jonathan had David, Ammon had Jonadab, David had Hushai, to name a few.

Friends bring peace. Friends stick closer than a brother. A friend has a pure heart and gives earnest counsel. A friend picks you up when you fall. Friends are constant. Friends are faithful. Friends are entwined together.

"My command is this: Love each other as I have loved you. Greater love has no one than this, that he lay down his life for his friends. You are my friends if you do what I command. I no longer call you servants, because a servant does not know his master's business. Instead, I have called you friends, for everything that I learned from my Father I have made known to you. You did not choose me, but I chose you . . .." (John 15:12-15)

Daily challenge:
Do something special for a friend.

Practice Makes Perfect

It's all about the "P."

At least that's what my devotion to the ladies seemed to promote. We were finishing up a series on spiritual stability, based on Philippians 4:2-9. Previously, we covered six of the principles for living strong: promote harmony, possess a spirit of joy, accept less than you are due, rest on a confident faith, react to problems with thankful prayer and focus on godly values. Tonight, my appointed task was to continue with John MacArthur's outline. The verse at the center of the discussion? *Whatever you have learned or received or heard from me, or seen in me—put it into practice. And the God of peace will be with you* (Philippians 4:9).

The core concept was *practice*—like "practice makes perfect" and "perfect practice leads to perfect performance." Paul's treatise was this: In order to rejoice, be gentle, don't worry, pray and petition, be thankful and do what is *true, noble, right, pure, lovely, admirable, excellent,* and *praiseworthy* (all mentioned in the preceding verses), one has to practice to establish a pattern of conduct.

Ah-ha! It occurred to me that the story of Nehemiah, my favorite Old Testament book, related to this very thing. A lesson I gave some time ago followed the same lines of living an orderly, spiritually stable life. So after arriving home from church, I eagerly got out my pencil and scissors and cut out cardstock "P"s to give to the ladies.

I suggested they write any "P" words we used from the story of Nehemiah onto their cut-out "P." Although it bordered on ridiculous every time one was mentioned, I think they got the point. The steps Nehemiah took to an ordered life were to define his pressures, begin praying, identify his purpose, define his priorities, plan strategy, persevere and persist and finally appreciate the payoff of peace.

We are wise to practice those "P's" as well.

> *Finally, brothers, whatever is true, whatever is noble, whatever is right, whatever is pure, whatever is lovely, whatever is admirable— if anything is excellent or praiseworthy—think about such things. Whatever you have learned or received or heard from me, or seen in me—put it into practice. And the God of peace will be with you. (Philippians 4:8-10)*

Daily challenge:
Practice brings stability.

Well Done

Can you remember a time when you were waiting for a judgment to be handed down? Perhaps it was something weighty like a court decision. Or maybe it was whether or not you won a valued job. For the student, the heart pounds in fear and trepidation as the teacher approaches, graded exam in hand. Regardless of the circumstance, some level of apprehension exists as you anticipate the verdict.

I thank God for some recent consulting work. I jumped on the assignments with great enthusiasm, working desperately to deliver a product my client would consider valuable. Taking care to be exact in my time keeping and refraining from anything that might offer a distraction—like television or radio—I gave superlative effort with undivided attention.

I completed the first project a few days ago and slept on it until this morning. I believe the work I did is solid, but there is always an element of doubt about how it will be regarded. A poor performance would do little to encourage a continued relationship. Now, composing the email, I attached the file, re-read the note and pointed my mouse at the "send" button. *Click. Here goes nothing . . ..*

Just before leaving my desk for the day, I took a last glance at my email. There it was. A response. My pulse quickened and I decided to leave it for later. I jest. I couldn't have opened it faster. I scanned the words before rereading them more slowly. "Thank you for the work. It was just what we wanted. Very well done." *Whew!* What a relief.

Well done. Those two little words, a mere eight letters in total, are profound. The parable of the *talents* (ancient coins) describes three individuals who were given five, two and a single talent. Each was asked to tend to the master's money. Although the servant entrusted with the single talent was called out for being too lazy to invest it, the others reported doubling their funds. The master delivered words for which they longed. *"'Well done, good and faithful servant! You have been faithful with a few things; I will put you in charge of many things. Come and share your master's happiness'"* (Matthew 25:21).

Those words are important. Use them at home, in school, on the field . . . wherever!

A man finds joy in giving an apt reply—and how good is a timely word! (Proverbs 15:23)

Daily challenge:
Never pass up a chance to say, "Well done!"

Excuses, Excuses, Excuses

Excuses. Excuses. Excuses.

Some people have an excuse for everything. A soccer player, after playing poorly, comes off the field and states, "Man, these new shoes are terrible. Besides, the refs were horrible. That's why we lost."

Or, a girl facing punishment blames it on "stupid rules." She never considers that she actually transgressed. No, there is blame to place in trying to offset some of the heat. It's actually a natural reaction. But being natural is no excuse either.

Consider the following parable found in Luke 14.

Jesus replied: "A certain man was preparing a great banquet and invited many guests. At the time of the banquet he sent his servant to tell those who had been invited, 'Come, for everything is now ready.' But they all alike began to make excuses. The first said, 'I have just bought a field, and I must go and see it. Please excuse me.' Another said, 'I have just bought five yoke of oxen, and I'm on my way to try them out. Please excuse me.' Still another said, 'I just got married, so I can't come.' The servant came back and reported this to his master. Then the owner of the house became angry and ordered his servant, 'Go out quickly into the streets and alleys of the town and bring in the poor, the crippled, the blind and the lame.' 'Sir,' the servant said, 'what you ordered has been done, but there is still room.' Then the master told his servant, 'Go out to the roads and country lanes and make them come in, so that my house will be full. I tell you, not one of those men who were invited will get a taste of my banquet.'"

The bottom line is this: making excuses might give momentary escape, but in the end, it cuts you off from everything that is good. Like the men who declined the invite, they not only were left out, they were replaced! A moment of excuse-making resulted in exclusion from the banquet.

Be very careful about making excuses—even in the small things. We only fool ourselves and set a bad example.

You, therefore, have no excuse, you who pass judgment on someone else, for at whatever point you judge the other, you are condemning yourself, because you who pass judgment do the same things. (Romans 2:1)

Daily challenge:
No excuses, no regrets.

I Can Fly

My feet barely touched the ground. Even our driveway hill, which normally spikes my breathing and heart rate, went unnoticed. The grass looked greener than ever and the sky was a perfect shade of blue. The clouds were at maximum fluffiness. The singing birds were aloft and newborn calves frolicked in the field. It was a perfect day and a perfect run. I felt like I could fly.

My blissful jaunt down country roads was in sharp contrast to earlier today. At 11:00 a.m. there was to be a meeting concerning one of my sons. A monumental decision—potentially life-altering—was to be made. I learned about this meeting last night and was so disconcerted I nearly hurled. I knew that his life was in God's hands, but realistically, I was having a hard time giving him over. My evening was spent praying non-stop. Upon waking, I was so focused on the eleventh hour that not even landscaping could distract me. Finally, as the little hand pointed to the eleven, I stopped what I was doing and bathed the meeting in earnest prayer. I wasn't quite sure how to pray but was confident that Christ, the great intercessor, could interpret my confused words to the Father. At 11:25 my phone rang. Grace and mercy was extended to my son. I wept.

With that load lifted from my shoulders, I began to decipher health insurance issues. The bills from Seth's mishaps had started to arrive. With a high deductible, I expected out-of-pocket expenses to be around $10,000. *Ugh.* After we had just gotten our finances rearranged, reeling from the lawsuit, this was going to be a huge blow.

I picked up the phone and called the insurance rep. She reminded me of our gap insurance—a rider for accidents and serious illness—that had been forgotten in the fray. This secondary policy would cover the entire out-of-pocket expenses, including that high deductible for each of Seth's two accidents. In reality, the two accidents should cost about $200. God is so good.

Running, the double load gone like the wind, I felt like an eagle in flight. These words from Isaiah rang clear in my head, carrying me down the road and back again.

But those who hope in the LORD will renew their strength. They will soar on wings like eagles; they will run and not grow weary, they will walk and not be faint. (Isaiah 40:31)

Daily challenge:
God invented flight and can teach you to fly.

Rocks and Mulch

It was a gorgeous day and I needed to make progress on my outdoor projects. Yesterday I made a stop at the stone and gravel store. Eagerly eyeing the variety of rocks, I made my choice. White pea gravel it was. This rock was going to be placed in the fire-pit area, around the hammock swings and under the table. "Load it up," I said.

And load they did. I watched as the truck bed sank all the way down to the tires. "Maybe we ought to reconsider the load capacity." Gravel guy agreed. He hand-shoveled rock off the back until the truck could handle the weight. But I was curious. "How is pea gravel made anyway?"

"Nothing has to be done. It's simply scooped off river bottoms. The water does the work to break, grind and smooth the stone into small, rounded rock." *Hmm. Interesting.* Skip to today.

With pitchfork ready, I kept busy awaiting Gary and Seth to bring me my load of mulch. When they drove up, I dove in. Wheelbarrow after wheelbarrow, I felt the warmth against my skin as I knelt to spread out the piles. From the mound still in the bed of truck the steam continued to rise. Decomposing wood and bark—that's all mulch is. Plain and simple.

When the truck was empty and the sun began to sink, I stepped back to look at my work. *Ah. How nice.* I wandered around, taking in the mulched beds and the stone between the brick borders. It looked so fine. But then it hit me. The elements making the biggest impact were tumbled rocks and smoldering dead stuff. Who would have thought that such outcasts of the natural world could become the centerpiece of a landscape creation?

Isn't that what God does with us? He breathes life into us when we are dead and ugly in our sin. But He doesn't just resuscitate us and leave us on our own. Rather, all our experiences—all the smoldering, all the jostling about—are used to refine us. He knocks off our rough edges, making us suited for beautiful service.

> *He has made everything beautiful in its time. He has also set eternity in the hearts of men; yet they cannot fathom what God has done from beginning to end. (Ecclesiastes 3:11)*

Daily challenge:
No matter how beat up and ugly we get, God makes us beautiful.

Crooked or Straight?

There is something terribly unsettling about crooked things. It drives me bonkers to look at a wall as wavy as the sea. And although there is aesthetic value in having shelf items arranged artistically, sometimes it's better to line them up like tiny soldiers in formation.

Today I needed to finish setting the posts for seating around my outdoor dining table. I got out my trusty tent stakes and hot pink string, carefully stretching it across the holes. It was crucial to get all the posts lined up the first time, since undoing a hole full of concrete is not easy.

Here's what I did: dump small rocks in the bottom, plunk in the post, check to see if the height was level with its neighbor, adjust if necessary, dump in a half bag of concrete mix, add water, stir, check the upright level both ways, adjust and then add more concrete and water. Before I moved on to the next hole, I gave each post one more look-see, making sure they stood tall, straight and plumb.

Stepping back from the project, I was pleased with the final result. It took some work to get everything lined up. A couple of times, I had to dig out one side of a hole to place the post in the center, surrounding it with the holding power of the concrete. It would have been easy to think "Why bother?", but a crooked bench is not the look I wanted.

Apparently, God must equate straightness with something good. Proverbs 4:11 says, *I guide you in the way of wisdom and lead you along straight paths.*

Truly, it is all too easy to divert from the straight path when we lose focus or decide to take an alternate route. But training our eyes on a fixed point, much like a farmer looks to a tree on the far side of the field to guide him in making straight furrows, can keep us pointed in the right direction. So, check your bearings often. Be sure you are in the straight and narrow.

> *In all your ways acknowledge him, and he will make your paths straight. (Proverbs 3:6)*

Daily challenge:
If you keep in line with Scripture, your path will remain true and straight.

Relax . . . by Faith

With the race beginning at 5:30 a.m. this morning, I chose to spend the night at the start, camping with two-hundred of my closest friends. The Promise Land 50K race, run through the Blue Ridge Mountains, is a great social event. The pizza supper the night before, race briefing, bonfire and camping in the big field create a festive atmosphere.

What was supposed to be an occasional drizzle turned out to be a torrential downpour for most of the evening and into the wee hours. Looking out from the simple pavilion where we gathered, I was having second thoughts about spending the night in my Hennesey hammock. Perhaps the bench seat of the Ford F150 truck was a better choice. I knew I would be more comfortable in the fabric cocoon, able to stretch out and assume any number of sleeping positions. However, with the rain pouring down, I wondered if choosing the hammock was wise.

My hammock has a rain fly, but to look at it, a betting man would never put a dime on its ability to keep me dry. It is thin and flimsy and to the eye does not look waterproof. However, since the top part of the hammock is mesh, I had to rely on its ability to keep out the wet.

During a slight break in the raindrops, I scurried to string the hammock beneath the boughs of two huge cedar trees. When night fell I climbed in, albeit tentatively. As I grew more confident in the soundness of my knots and dry conditions inside, I relaxed in the protection despite the storm. Soon, the rhythmic sound of the rain became comforting, lulling me into a wonderful and deep sleep.

It's difficult to trust something that doesn't look the way we think it should. I believe a rain fly should "feel" waterproof and be made of some sort of plasticized material. But my notion is of little significance if it is not based on truth.

I may think that God's protection should look or feel a certain way, but that isn't necessarily the case either. Faith is like that. Just as I had to have faith that lying in that hammock all night would not lead to a drenching, there are times when I proceed spiritually because I have faith in what I know to be true. Ironically, once we are able to act on that faith, our comfort and confidence skyrockets.

We live by faith, not by sight. (II Corinthians 5:7)

Daily challenge:
Though the first step in faith-walking is hard, keep walking.

Light into Darkness

Most understand that *Extreme Home Makeover,* aired on ABC, highlights a team of designers and builders who construct a fabulous house for a deserving family. In most cases, the families have been through the ringer: someone is deathly ill, injured or has died. Other times, the family has made extraordinary sacrifices for the sake of others. That was the case tonight.

As I padded over to the refrigerator, Seth informed me that a Christian pastor and his family were the honorees. Moving into a rough-and-tumble neighborhood, it was a dangerous place to live; shootings, drugs and crime occurred nightly. Most people would move their family as far away as they could. But not this one. They moved there to make a difference.

They decided to enter harm's way to minister to a community with great physical and spiritual needs. Impoverished themselves, they still fed the poor on Sundays and offered their own home to anyone with no place to sleep. At times, up to seventeen extra people found shelter under their leaking roof. Why? All because they put their money where their mouth was.

The result? No longer is the neighborhood known for crime. Now it is a safe haven where love is known and shown in practical ways.

I wonder what would happen if we seriously understood commitment to bring light to a dark world and salt to an unseasoned culture. I wonder what would happen if we could lay aside our selfishness and focus instead on our neighbors in need. I am inclined to think that our neighborhoods would look completely different if we trusted God to make us into the "good neighbor." It worked for this family just as it did the prophet Isaiah:

> *"Then you will call, and the LORD will answer; you will cry for help, and he will say: Here am I. 'If you do away with the yoke of oppression, with the pointing finger and malicious talk, and if you spend yourselves in behalf of the hungry and satisfy the needs of the oppressed, then your light will rise in the darkness, and your night will become like the noonday.'" (Isaiah 58:9, 10)*

Daily challenge:
Shining your light where there is light wastes energy.
Take your light to the darkness.

The Cover of Love

I love poignant quotes. In fact, I collect them. Just give me one of those inspirational desk calendars and I'm in hog heaven. Some time ago—perhaps two or three years past—I cut out several quips that seemed important at the time. Gluing them onto magnets, they now reside on the front of my file cabinet. For some reason, one of them caught my attention a few moments ago. The author was Sir William Osler. Who was this guy?

Well, that's the beauty of the internet. A quick Google search told me that Sir William was a well-known physician born in Canada in 1849. Living until 1919 he became known as the Father of Modern Medicine. He felt strongly that doctors should learn not only from books but should practice bedside medicine to learn both the science and the art. It was Osler who invented the idea of residency programs for doctors and earned wide esteem for his work as Physician-in-Chief at Johns Hopkins in Baltimore and at the University of Pennsylvania in Philadelphia.

But as well-known as he was in medicine, he was equally well known for his wit, his essays and writings, public speaking and his love of books, particularly those related to medicine. His collections are the center of McGill University's Osler Library of the History of Medicine which opened in 1929 and now house the ashes of this man and his wife.

There are entire books devoted to some of the things Osler said throughout his lifetime. Some of these quotes are pithy, some serious and relating to the instruction of student doctors and some are just candid observations. However, the quote that caught my eye is not that original—but it is sage advice. "Learn to accept in silence minor aggravations."

I wondered if perhaps he had heard his pastor-father read from the Scripture.

> *Hatred stirs up dissension, but love covers over all wrongs. He who covers over an offense promotes love, but whoever repeats the matter separates close friends . . . Above all, love each other deeply, because love covers over a multitude of sins. (Proverbs 10:12 and 17:9 and I Peter 4:8)*

Daily challenge:
Don't let the toothpaste, dirty socks or the toys strewn over the floor
railroad your love.

Inspection Day

After another horrendous travel experience, I met up with other members of an assessment team. This team was coordinated on behalf of the American Association of Blood Banks, which provides accreditation to hospitals and blood centers. My role was to evaluate the peri-operative blood management services.

This whole process of accreditation is interesting on a number of fronts. First of all, the process is voluntary. On top of that, the organizations seeking accreditation pay money to do so. Why would they choose to invite strangers into their "house," turn over all their records, disclose their secrets and reveal their weaknesses? Does this make a lot of sense? On first blush, the answer is "No!"

I suppose that one of the reasons they do this is to have bragging rights to both the public and their competitors. Everyone enjoys the opportunity to flaunt "We are better than you are!" Or, maybe they truly desire to optimize the patient care they provide, using outside eyes to identify areas for improvement. But whatever the reason, the process is long and difficult and is not entered into lightly. Mountains of work rise up in the process. Everyone involved must embrace the course, constantly figuring out how they can best meet the standards they have chosen to adopt.

Although Old Testament Joshua did not have to worry about complying with a set of hospital regulations, he did know something about conforming to God's standards. First of all, God's book of instructions must be read and time given to meditation. Why? So that you know what to do and how to act.

And what happens if you do these things? Success will be the natural end. Getting back to our accreditation example, if the hospital defines in words what they are to do, knows them inside and out and actually does what they said they would do, they pass the inspection. Likewise, if we make it a habit to know the Word and behave accordingly, we will be "accredited" before God.

But just as these hospitals never get a perfect report, it is unlikely that our spiritual assessment will be flawless. Knowing what the shortcomings are, however, allows for reassessing our position and doing a better job of complying with the standards.

"Do not let this Book of the Law depart from your mouth; meditate on it day and night, so that you may be careful to do everything written in it. Then you will be prosperous and successful." (Joshua 1:8)

Daily challenge:
Do you know God's standards? Are you complying?

Exquisite Fragrance

I'm trying to decide what plants and shrubs I should use to fill my newly created gardens. There is such an array of shrubs, annuals and perennials that it makes the selection difficult. What colors should I use? Do I want a formal or country cottage look? And of course, I have to be careful to select the plants that will do best in various sun conditions.

I suppose that my focus on horticulture made me pay particular notice to Ephesians 4:15: . . . *speaking the truth in love, we will in all things grow up into him who is the Head, that is, Christ.* Isn't it interesting that Paul did not write "grow along side him" or "grow down from him." Instead he chose the words *grow up into him.*

I immediately pictured a tiny, dormant seed planted in the ground. On a warm spring day, the rain comes down, the seed germinates and the first little sprout pokes its head up through the earth, reaching toward the sun.

But the process of germination and the production of those first cotyledons is only the beginning. The full beauty is only recognized once the plant matures, yielding flowers or fruit.

We as Believers go through a similar process. We were once dead and buried in our sin. Had it not been for the rain of the Spirit, we would still be covered by our dirt. But praise God, just like that plant, our germination is only the beginning. We grow up into him in order to fulfill our role in the body of Christ. However, just as a single flower, though beautiful in itself, cannot bring full glory to the garden, just imagine a community full of mature Believers. What an exquisite fragrance that would create!

And we pray this in order that you may live a life worthy of the Lord
and may please him in every way: bearing fruit in every good work,
growing in the knowledge of God. (Colossians 1:10)

Daily challenge:
Become a fragrant bloom in God's garden.

Be Careful

I saw tragedy strike today right before my eyes. It was dreadful. I may have nightmares about it. With no deviation to the right or to the left, he walked straight toward the edge. He went purposely as if on a mission. He did not hesitate nor did he slow his steady pace. And then, it was over as quickly as it had begun. He disappeared into thin air and fell to his death.

So just what was that caterpillar thinking? With all his little legs in full gear he plummeted into the pool, flailing just a bit before taking his last little bug breath. As I peered over the edge to see his floating body, he wasn't alone. There on the surface of the water were thousands of drowned caterpillars. It was morbidly hilarious. The caterpillar nation must not have an early warning system to warn of imminent danger.

Then I noticed that much of the ground was moving. The hairy creatures were so ubiquitous that one had crawled up to my thigh on the inside of my jeans. Not realizing what it was, I scratched the "itch," smooshing its guts all over my leg. *Yuk.* It died alone. But incredibly, one after the other, multitudes plunged to their deaths. Maybe caterpillars are blind. Nothing else makes sense.

Despite the high casualty rate today, I expect the death toll to rise overnight. You know what they say: "Never underestimate the power of stupid people [or caterpillars] in large groups." The mob mentality will leave me no recourse but to scoop them out and throw their remains unceremoniously over the fence.

As funny as this may seem, I can act just as unwisely as those caterpillars when I a) ignore my surroundings and b) follow the crowd. I must be more vigilant about what I think and how I behave.

Be very careful, then, how you live—not as unwise but as wise.
(Ephesians 5:15)

Daily challenge:
Let's be careful where we are, what we do and who we do it with.

Home Again

"But while he was still a long way off, his father saw him and was filled with compassion for him; he ran to his son, threw his arms around him and kissed him" (Luke 15:20b).

Remember the story? One family. Two sons. The one son was a steady worker, ever helpful to his father. The sibling, wanting to experience the world, left home and lived a low-life existence. However, debauchery growing old, he decided to tuck his tail, hang his head and head for home. The father seeing him in the distance dashed to his son and rejoiced, following suit with a big party. Of course, the story isn't complete without noting the jealousy of the brother for whom no celebration had ever been awarded. Nevertheless, the father rebuked Mr. Goody-Two Shoes with the fact that he should be rejoicing; his lost brother had repented and come home.

I've always loved this story, even though I sympathize with the jealousy of the well-behaved brother. It's the old "squeaky wheel gets the oil" routine and I don't fully understand it. Nevertheless, I do understand the part about a parent welcoming home a child, prodigal or not.

Caleb, our oldest, is finishing up his last final today and will be heading home. I can barely concentrate as I anticipate his return. I know that he's nearly twenty-one years old and has moved into manhood. Still, I never lose my desire for fellowship with him.

When I was his age, I was eager to move on. In fact, I was already married. So I recognize that Caleb's contentment with living at home is probably short-lived. Despite that, Caleb will be with us for the summer. As a mom, I love that. Shortly, he will be much more a visitor than a resident. For now, I will never tire of looking out the window for his approaching headlights, bolting for his car door before he has even turned off the engine.

As the kids approach adulthood way faster than I ever imagined, I can better appreciate the choice God made when He patterned our earthly relationships after His own. God understands the pain of watching a Son leave home on a suicide mission. How He must have rejoiced when Christ's work was done and that Son returned home.

The parent-child relationship is a beautiful picture of oneness, love, protection and security. It's a relationship that should be cultivated and savored, not disregarded or taken lightly.

They broke bread in their homes and ate together with glad and sincere hearts, praising God . . .. (Acts 2:46)

Daily challenge:
Purpose to make every second count.

No Water

Seth and I went to a school play last night, a delightful respite from my hard work in the garden. Of course, we knew all the kids and seeing them on stage added to the comedy. We laughed and laughed—and then promptly stopped laughing upon our arrival home. Going to the kitchen sink to turn on the faucet, I was faced with the unfortunate reality of no water. Gary rolled his eyes, muttered something under his breath and then dutifully found a headlight to shine the way into the dark cellar. I called Seth down from his room to help, kicked off my high-heeled shoes, rolled up my too-long jeans and followed Gary into the dankness.

Our well has been the object of concern more than once. On at least two occasions, the old, shallow well has run dry. A leaking toilet was the culprit one time and a drippy outdoor faucet the other. When the pump loses its prime, it takes some ingenuity to get it going again. So, out came the little pump and a bunch of hose, pulling water from the pool, into the outside spigot and backward through the system. This has worked before and we had every expectation that flipping the breaker back on would solve the problem. But no. Didn't work.

Next, we got another hose and pumped more pool water directly into the well housing. It would have been helpful if the pressure gauge worked, but it was nonfunctioning. After an hour of messing around in the grungy cellar, the kind that requires a scary descent down old, stone steps from the outside, we gave up. It was both odd and inconvenient to use my own spit to brush my teeth.

This morning, a trip into town produced a new pressure gauge and renewed interest in making the fix. My McGyver-like husband came through and water flowed through the pipes. The rest of the day proceeded normally, but I found myself once again taking the water for granted.

I think we take the Living Water for granted as well. Our "woe-is-me" mentality puts us in the middle of a spiritual draught. We attempt to fix it ourselves, but alas, we find only more dissatisfaction. If we could only remember that Christ's living water is not drawn from a shallow well. Rather, it is ever-flowing, deep and able to quench the most unfathomable thirst. Even as an underground spring may be hidden from view, it runs silent and deep for a time, bursting through the surface in a refreshing pool of water. We need only to drink from the wellspring to be satisfied.

But whoever drinks the water I give him will never thirst. Indeed, the water I give him will become in him a spring of water welling up to eternal life. (John 4:14)

Daily challenge:
Drink deep. Be refreshed.

No Fear in Love

I flipped open I John on my way to Jude, wanting to refresh the reading we had this morning in church. My eyes fell on the phrase *there is no fear in love.* I paused before backing up to verse 16. *Hmm . . ..*

Picture this. A man and woman are sitting on the beach, looking out at the windswept waves. The sun is setting, the mood pensive. You can tell there's a connection between these individuals, but something is a bit unsettled. Slowly, the nervous man reaches into his pocket and pulls out a box. Her pulse quickens, knowing she will be expected to give an answer to an obvious question. The guy blurts it out, but the girl stammers, "I don't know if I can. Do I really love you?" Before the sun lowers beyond the horizon, the poor guy is left sitting alone in the damp sand, unopened box clutched in his sweaty palm. The girl walks off into the sunset. The melancholic music plays on.

Get the picture? I've often wondered what guy in his right mind would ask that all important question if he wasn't sure of the answer. Talk about setting yourself up for a big disappointment. It would be the equivalent to saying, "Hey, I have no idea how you feel, but just for grins, wanna get married and see if it'll work out?" Doesn't it make more sense to ask the question only when you are confident in the answer? No wonder the guy on the beach was nervous. He had no confidence in her love and was fearful of a painful rejection.

The reason there is no fear in love is because confidence in the source of love supplants the fear. When we live large in the love of God, we are confident in loving others fully. We no longer need fear rejection, because perfect love drives out fear.

Perfect love without fear is reciprocal. God's love for us has drawn our hearts toward His. It is a love without hesitation or condition. And because of that, we can learn to love as God loves without the fear of disappointment.

> *God is love. Whoever lives in love lives in God, and God in him. In this way, love is made complete among us so that we will have confidence on the day of judgement . . . There is no fear in love. But perfect love drives out fear because fear has to do with punishment . . . We love because he first loved us. (I John 4:16b-19a)*

Daily challenge:
Have no fear. Love on.

Giant-Killer

Some giants were killed today, stomped to the ground and laid to rest. It came somewhat unexpectedly but victory went to the little guy . . . uh, girl, that is.

Remember the story of the Israelites right before they went into the Promised Land? Twelve guys went on a reconnaissance mission—one brave soul from each tribe. Over the border they went, starry-eyed and amazed. The land was bountiful, grape clusters so huge two men had to bind them to poles carried between their shoulders. And this was no overnight camp out. They explored the territory for forty days before reporting back. I can just imagine them standing before Moses so filled with images of what they had seen that their mouths ran on ahead of their brains.

Truly, the land was glorious but—and this was a big *but*—the people were ginormous, so much so that by comparison, the Jewish men looked like little grasshoppers. Ten men said, and I paraphrase, "You gotta be kidding. I'm not going in there! We'll get creamed, annihilated, squashed like bugs!" So convinced were they of their inevitable demise, they stirred the entire nation into a frenzy, threatening to stone Caleb and Joshua. However, Caleb and Joshua had other ideas.

The distinct minority argued that the task was large, but God was bigger. Caleb and Joshua dared to see beyond the obvious, beyond the obstacles, beyond the normal course of logic to see the possibilities. They stepped over the line to trust God's promise to give them that land. Their faith was rewarded. They were the only men over the age of twenty to ever again enter the land flowing with milk and honey.

Another line was crossed today. Bobbie, my mother-of-seven friend, came over. She has been faithful to complete the running program I assigned to her. Now, she submitted to running with me. "Don't ask how far or how long. Trust me." I said.

"When I was driving over here today, I realized I had crossed over the line," she said several miles into the run. She dared to do something she never thought possible—something out her comfort zone. On and on we ran, talking the whole while. When we finished the run, I told her that she had run double her best—nearly nine miles. "Really? I thought running that long would feel . . . well, awful. But it wasn't. I feel good."

Even if into the realm of the unknown, we must proceed by faith, gather up our courage and follow wholeheartedly. We will begin making forward progress. Then suddenly, we'll understand the reality of the incomprehensible becoming achievable.

> . . . *not one except Caleb son of Jephunneh the Kenizzite and Joshua son of Nun, for they followed the LORD wholeheartedly. (Numbers 32:12)*

Daily challenge:
God is the God of possibilities. Be brave. Be bold.

Fluff Balls

New life came to our house today in the form of four little fluff balls called *kittens.* My sister-in-law is going on vacation and didn't want to leave the six-week-olds to fend for themselves. When she called last week to see if her brother would disown her with the request to kitty-sit for ten days, I was doubtful we could pull it off. Just a day prior, Caleb was talking about wanting a kitten and Gary did not respond favorably. It's not that Gary doesn't like kittens; he just knows they will inevitably grow into cats. Nevertheless and with his reluctant approval, Joy and Skip showed up with the four cats and the excitement began.

They really are cute—gray and white, soft and fluffy. As soon as they came in the house, they started exploring. Within minutes, one of them managed to get behind the upright freezer. We could hear him squall and figured if he got in, he could get out. We waited and waited. Nothing happened. With much effort, I squeezed my head between the wall and freezer and was shocked to see no kitty. *Where did he go?* I hoped I had not squashed him while moving the freezer an inch or two. That would be a horrible start to cat-sitting. On a whim, I knelt to the floor, pulling off the plastic vent cover at the bottom. Peering underneath, sure enough, there was Mr. Kitty looking quite pleased.

Before night fell, we all took great delight in their kitty capers. Each has a distinct personality. The one named Isis is the adventurous one of the bunch. One of the girls is more timid and the remaining two, near-identical twins, seem joined at the hip. They tumble and roll before collapsing in a heap, as if someone suddenly took out their batteries. Ironically, moments ago I found the twins both nestled deeply into Gary's lap, sound asleep and being gently stroked. *Ah ha!* Mr. Tough Guy lost his heart pretty quickly.

Having these tiny cats come today is a simple reminder of the wonder of God's creation. I think God smiled when He stepped back and looked at all the creatures designed by His hand. Each animal, even a "lowly" amoeba, is a testament to God's order and complexity.

But ask the animals, and they will teach you, or the birds of the air, and they will tell you. (Job 12:7)

Daily challenge:
Enjoy all of nature and be a good steward of it.

Dead or Alive

I spied a few leafy twigs next to the house. Delighted, I exclaimed out loud, "Ah, I forgot all about them." Last summer as I was helping my Mother move out of her home of fifty years, I took a sampling of plants from her gardens thinking it would be nostalgic to have them in my garden as well. I dug out, among others, some small Rose of Sharon shrubs. But once back home, the immature plants, perhaps only eighteen-inches tall, got plopped unceremoniously into a vacant spot of ground near the house. Seeing the fresh spring leaves, it occurred to me it was time for a transplant.

Since then, I have been careful to drag the hose across the yard to give the plants a good soaking. Yesterday I noticed some of the shrubs had wilted. In fact, a few of the branches looked pitiful. So, out came the hose again; I hoped that an extra drink would revive the droopy leaves. I just hope that after all the trouble to bring these plants from Pennsylvania, they won't die a slow death.

Watching the water flow from the hose, I thought about how ridiculous it would be to water a plant that was truly dead. Although a wilted plant can make a miraculous recovery after being watered, a dead plant will be just as dead no matter how wet the soil. The trouble is, we can't always tell if something is dead, dormant or just in need of a little loving care. The only responsible thing to do is to proceed with the greatest of expectations.

I would be a fool to withhold water from a plant if I didn't know its status. Likewise, I would be a fool if I did not give testimony of God's Word, whether or not I know a person to be dead or alive in Christ. If the person is "dead", but I fulfill my responsibility, I am not accountable to God for his response. And when I present the Word to a Believer, the promise is that it will not return void.

We can be confident that God's word will be effective. There is no promise that we'll see immediate results. Just like a dormant plant, a period of time must pass until the plant shows signs of life. But nonetheless, God's purpose will be accomplished in His own time.

> *"So is my word that goes out from my mouth: It will not return to me empty, but will accomplish what I desire and achieve the purpose for which I sent it." (Isaiah 55:11)*

Daily challenge:
Don't withhold the water of the Word just because you think it will do no good.

Old Women, Young Women

Last fall I sat around a table with other ladies from church. We were meeting to plan the activities for the women's ministry. As we bantered ideas back and forth, I specifically remember verbalizing my desire to establish meaningful relationships with college kids. Tonight, I came to understand that God was faithful.

Joy, Sarah and Elizabeth are three young ladies who have become very dear to me. Each one of these nursing students from Liberty University decided to come to the Wednesday-night small group that meets in our home. No matter what the weather or other responsibilities they had in their busy college lives, they were never deterred from walking through our door, cheerful and happy. I was astounded on many occasions when one mentioned a ten-page paper or big project that was due the next morning. If that had been me, I would never have gone out until I had the assignment completed. But not these girls. The three honor students prioritized fellowship, choosing instead to spend long nights afterward completing their exceptional, A-level work.

As I have gotten to know the girls, I cherish what I've learned about them. Joy is from Laos and keeps us laughing with her storytelling. Elizabeth is a lab assistant who plans to apply to medical school. Sarah, a runner, was raised as a third-generation missionary in the Peruvian jungle. But more than these facts, I have seen their hearts and know them to be pointed True North.

While I am the older, supposedly more mature woman, I benefit in ways not anticipated. The trio has provided me untold encouragement, friendship, laughter and joy. They have taught me about steadfastness and commitment, love and dedication. I will deeply miss them as they graduate in a few days and leave their lives in Lynchburg behind.

> . . . the older women to be reverent in the way they live, not to be slanderers or addicted to much wine, but to teach what is good. Then they can train the younger women to love their husbands and children, to be self-controlled and pure, to be busy at home, to be kind, and to be subject to their husbands, so that no one will malign the word of God. (Titus 2:3)

Daily challenge:
Engage in the lives of other women.

Memories

Memory is a curious thing. Have you ever caught the slightest whiff of a scent that sends you back in time and place? Or perhaps it's a song that resurfaces emotions long-ago forgotten. But whatever the situation, the remembrance that comes flooding back is as crystal clear as an alpine lake. I distinctly recall conversations at a precise point on a mountain trail, years after having run there with friends. It's so weird. The recollection isn't always significant or weighty. And yet, the details are summoned back.

The same happens when a myriad of senses combine to elicit a recollection. A warm summer evening, a Wednesday, to be specific, and the smell of freshly cut grass takes me back to the leisurely convertible rides home from church with my Dad, the sound of a Phillies' baseball game wafting from the radio and into the night air. Just thinking about that time convinces me that I can smell that grass.

Riding the lawn mower today, the sun played a lengthy game of hide-and-seek with the clouds. When the sun hid, the clouds took on a very gray appearance, the wind seemed to pick up and I half expected the clouds to open their doors and pour down rain. My arms played host to tiny goose bumps as the atmosphere was preparing for the assault. There was a fragrance in the air that "smelled" like rain. But, the coupling of the clouds, the grayness and the smell sent me back to the Allegheny Trail last summer, somewhere in the middle of my 300-mile run.

I can picture the part of the trail now. I was suffering that day in the hot sun, tired and discouraged. As I left an exposed road section and traded it for a trail along the river, I welcomed the canopy of the trees. But my pleasure was short-lived as the trail was difficult, washed out in places and rising steeply above the river with treacherous footing. Once the trail fell again to the river bed, the sky darkened and the woods became very dark despite the noon-time hour. It was that same feeling as I had today. All the emotion of last summer's adventure came rushing back and I yearned for another chance at some other quest.

Memory is a gift. Cherish it.

So I will always remind you of these things, even though you know them and are firmly established in the truth you now have. I think it is right to refresh your memory . . . And I will make every effort to see that after my departure you will always be able to remember these things. (II Peter 1:12-15)

Daily challenge:
Repent. Rejoice. Remember.

Eagles and Vultures

He mounted the cherubim and flew; he soared on the wings of the wind
(Psalm 18:10).

When David penned these words, they were a song sung to the Lord. God Almighty was described as a great defender of the afflicted, figuratively swooping down from His throne to defeat the enemy. I envision a spirit lighting on the winged angel and taking flight together across the sky. Perhaps I've seen too many pictures of the mythological Apollo's chariot. Nevertheless, the picture painted by the Psalmist is one of power and strength.

I was not far into my run today when, glancing to the left, a movement caught my eye. The pasture sloped downward toward a creek and a herd of cows grazed contentedly. The sky was a brilliant blue and the clouds, fluffy and white, floated effortlessly across the sky, a stout breeze coaxing them on their way. And then I saw it—a beautiful demonstration of soaring on the wings of the wind.

A huge vulture, not generally regarded as handsome, spread his wings and took off. A flap or two made him rise to catch an invisible air current, launching him even higher into the sky. There he glided, adjusting the position of his wings ever so slightly to turn this way or that. He looked so free, so powerful. I wondered what it felt like to experience flight unencumbered by the trappings of an airplane. I was so intrigued by watching this giant bird I nearly ran off the road.

Regaining my bearings, I got to thinking about the inspirational *wings like eagles* verse found in Isaiah 40:31. It's not hard to imagine a creature as majestic as an eagle soaring on the wind. Eagles are beautiful and commanding, swift and regal. Soaring is what they are supposed to do. But turkey vultures with their big ugly red heads and whose lives consist of eating rotting road kill . . .. Well, it just doesn't seem right that they could soar just as well as their cousins.

To me, the lesson became clear. Truth is, we may not be *eagles*. We have imperfections and flaws that some might say disqualify us from flying with the beautiful crowd. And yet, we have been equally equipped to soar high and often.

> *. . . but those who hope in the LORD will renew their strength. They will soar on wings like eagles; they will run and not grow weary, they will walk and not be faint. (Isaiah 40:31)*

Daily challenge:
Let God carry you to new heights.

Hospitality

It's been a whirlwind around here. I had guests on Tuesday when Gary's sister and husband brought us the four kitties for safe keeping. Dinner number one. Then, three graduating college girls came on Thursday night for dinner number two. Friday was a major cleaning day. Saturday morning was filled with a run, chores and then the pinning ceremony for the young nursing graduates. Later that night, I prepared a dinner for our houseguests. Dinner number three. A French toast, sausage and strawberries breakfast this morning rounded out the special meals before we headed for church. Meal number four. I loved every minute of this, but on the ride in to church, I fought to stay awake. I guess I'm not getting any younger.

"Get whatever you want" lunch strategy allowed me to take to the sofa sooner than later. As the family dispersed to the far corners of the house, I grabbed some coffee and a magazine and settled in for some "me" time. Not many pages turned before my eyes closed in delicious sleep. I couldn't remember the last time I spent an afternoon napping, tucked under my blanket and content to doze as a cool rain fell outside. I was as snug as a bug in the proverbial rug, exhausted but pleased with the busy week.

I love being able to use our home to entertain and I learned this from my mother. I can't count the number of times we had guests, but there is a bookshelf full of autographed guest books to prove it. Some came for dinner and others for a week. Missionaries, friends from the past, visiting preachers, family . . . whoever. Everyone felt welcomed and everyone was.

There's no doubt that Mother had—and still exhibits –the gift of hospitality. She was following the New Testament example. Paul, understanding Gaius' hospitality, told Believers to *Share with God's people who are in need. Practice hospitality* (Romans 12:13). Widows cared for by the Church must have been hospitable themselves (I Timothy 5:10). And Peter also exhorts the Saints to *Offer hospitality to one another without grumbling* (I Peter 4:9).

So reach out and open your door. Let Christ's love be shown in your home.

We ought therefore to show hospitality to such men so that we may work together for the truth. (III John 1:8)

Daily challenge:
The biggest impediment to hospitality is selfishness.

Crash and Burn

Crash and burn. That's what happened to my computer today. I actually saw it coming but hoped, unreasonably so, that it would somehow fix itself. For the last four or five days, I've been getting the "blue screen of death," as Caleb calls it. The text on the screen informed me that there was some "stop error" and listed a long string of numbers. But it never actually told me what file was at fault for the malfunction. I groaned each time, called my computer-geek son to come look and then dutifully turned the machine off to reboot. My flash drive stayed busy backing up my latest documents in case the next time was acutely fatal.

Sometimes and for no good reason, my browser closed unexpectedly, leaving me stranded on the shoulder of the internet road. So, when my work this morning was rudely interrupted twice in forty-five minutes, I asked Caleb to divert from his outside chores to reinstall my operating system. That was at about 10 o'clock this morning and it is now almost seven o'clock in the evening. It has been a chore to get programs and files put back in place. The day was pretty much a wash.

I don't know about you, but these kinds of things frustrate me to no end. I had a long list of tasks to tackle but never even got in the game. Instead, I spent countless minutes gazing at the screen and drinking too much coffee as the completion indicator bar crept slowly across the display. But I had no choice. I had to sit there to click the "next" or "yes" or "no" buttons when prompted.

Unfortunately, "stupid people" are much like these "stupid computers." In most cases, there are warning signs of impending failure, but somehow, some way, we choose to ignore the ominous indicator light flashing a warning as we think, "Ah, I can get away with it a little bit longer. No worries."

So instead of taking inventory on the state of affairs, not even taking time to back-up and protect important items, we continue on our merry way hoping that a remedy will miraculously correct our ills. Guess what? It never gets better in these situations. Rather, it gets exponentially worse. There is a ripple effect and by the time the problem is full-blown, it hits us like a tsunami.

The solution? It's really pretty simple.

"If my people, who are called by my name, will humble themselves and pray and seek my face and turn from their wicked ways, then will I hear from heaven and will forgive their sin and will heal our land." (II Chronicles 7:14)

Daily challenge:
Never ignore an early warning signal. Take to your knees at the first sign of trouble.

Grass Grows

Our internet was crawling slower than a newborn baby. Yesterday I had to reinstall Windows and download all the required service packs and updates. Hence, we exceeded the 24-hour bandwidth allowed with our satellite internet plan. After slogging through my email I gave up, went for a run and then climbed aboard our beat-up lawnmower. With all the rain we've had, it was high time to give the grass a whack.

Our riding mover is an interesting piece of machinery. We bought it seventeen years ago and it has lived a hard life. Grass still falls in its path but the blades, even being replaced and sharpened frequently, are anything but pristine—too many rock encounters. We have to dump in half a quart of oil with each use, the grass shoot is cattywampus and the deck is bent. And embarrassingly, we use a screw driver in the key slot to bring life to the old engine. The vinyl seat is split in several places, with the edges rubbing uncomfortably on bare legs. But, I guess I shouldn't complain. It beats cutting several acres with a push mower.

I don't mind riding the mower. I love to look back at the lines in the grass, looking so tidy in contrast to the uneven grass and weeds yet uncut. Gary and the boys do most of the cutting, but they don't love it; they do it because they have to. I welcome the opportunity to bounce around the yard. My love for working outside comes from my parents, I'm sure. Though time-consuming, it's relaxing. And this year, there's no shortage of mowing opportunities around here.

Come August, however, it will likely be a different story. Grass without rain is a terrible combination. Before long, the grass turns an ugly brown, no longer feeling soft and squishy on bare feet. With last summer's drought, weeks went by when no mowing was necessary. The ground was brown and dusty, the life sucked out of the blades of grass.

Though grass is fragile and short lived, there is something that will stand forever— the Word of God. No drought or blazing sun can kill the Word. It lives on, strong in truth and perfect in directing our lives.

The grass withers and the flowers fall, but the word of our God stands forever. (Isaiah 40:8)

Daily challenge:
Our lives should be green and lush when watered by the Word.

Heart Darts

I ran today. As an ultrarunner, I am required by the demanding sport to prepare sufficiently for each race lest I perish. So, I run to prepare. But I also run for overall fitness, a physical release, a mental break and a time to think and pray.

I'm not nearly as consistent as I used to be. When I was running fast and furious, my training was fanatical. Although my life was chock-full with family and a demanding job, I thought of little else. My running became a god. My marriage was not ruined, but it was not a period of growth—for which I take full blame. I'm glad to be beyond those years.

There's a fine line between obsession and commitment. Back then I was totally obsessed. Now, my goal is to reclaim commitment without obsession. It's way too easy for me to come up with an excuse not to run. The days are busy, spring races behind me and the next race far off in October: a missed day doesn't have much negative impact. That is, no impact other than that small little voice that tells me, with a wagging and accusing finger, that I messed up. My conscience accuses me, and rightly so.

I'm reminded of the work that the Holy Spirit does in our lives. He pricks us when we do wrong, much like a mother who snaps her fingers at a disobedient child. But just like that child who ignores her at the grocery, begging the silently pious reproach of others who think they could do better, we continue our mischief. We ignore what we know to be right.

Romans 8 speaks to what a Believer's life is like when it is played out in the Spirit. Not only does the Spirit bring life, the Spirit whispers how we should conduct ourselves. My pastor back in Ohio in the late 70s said that He threw darts at our hearts to get our attention. Sometimes the dart was a reminder to pray specifically. Other times, the dart made obvious a sinful thought or action. Or the piercing may tell us to offer help to another.

Pay attention—and act—when the Spirit lands a dart in the center of your heart.

> *Therefore, there is no condemnation for those who are in Christ Jesus . . . who do not live by the sinful nature but according to the Spirit . . . those who live according to the Spirit have their minds set on what the Spirit desires . . . the mind controlled by the Spirit is life and peace . . . your spirit is alive. (Romans 8:1, 5, 8)*

Daily challenge:
Ignoring God's "heart dart" of conscience is equivalent to sin.

Always Prepared

Everyone knows the Scouting motto, "Be prepared." But did you know that this motto dates back to 1907? Nearly all the Scouting organizations world-wide embrace the maxim. The following, according to the wonderful world of Wikipedia, is how a scout is to prepare.

"The Scout Motto is: BE PREPARED which means you are always in a state of readiness in mind and body to do your DUTY.
Be Prepared in Mind by having disciplined yourself to be obedient to every order, and also by having thought out beforehand any accident or situation that might occur, so that you know the right thing to do at the right moment, and are willing to do it.
Be Prepared in Body by making yourself strong and active and able to do the right thing at the right moment, and do it."

Although I have never been a Girl Scout, I felt like one today. As soon as I got out of bed, I dressed myself in running clothes. I knew I would have fewer excuses if I was ready to go from the very top of the morning. I went about my chores and desk work fully prepared to head out the door at moment's notice, my shoes tied just so in double knots. And it worked. I dropped everything at an opportune moment and took the first step. I was prepared.

The "heart dart" pastor taught me another important lesson about preparation. We are to "pray without ceasing," but what does that mean and how is that possible? Does that mean we walk around with hands folded and eyes closed, just like the Precious Moments figurines kneeling by a bedside? I don't think so. Rather, we are in a constant state of preparedness to offer up a prayer when the Spirit prompts.

Pastor Brock encouraged us to never say *amen* to a prayer. The final *amen* is so . . . well, final. It tells our brain that we can check off prayer from our do-list. Done. Finished. However, if we leave it with "talk to you soon"—just like we would with a friend—we leave the conversation open. When the Spirit throws one of those darts, I'm more likely to pray if I remember the conversation has already begun.

And pray in the Spirit on all occasions with all kinds of prayers and requests. With this in mind, be alert and always keep on praying for all the saints. (Ephesians 6:18)

Daily challenge:
Prepare to pray.

At Risk

Seth had gone to work, leaving three of us for supper. Warmed-up venison stew with cinnamon toast wasn't much of a formal affair, especially since the TV was on. (Shameful, I know.) Soon, we got caught up with a show where two ex-thieves broke into a home to demonstrate the state of security. They made off with about $100,000 worth of stuff in fifteen minutes. This particular house was on a golf course in a gated community and equipped with an expensive alarm system. Following the owners' shock in finding they had been robbed blind, the rehabilitated thieves showed the owners how to make their home more secure.

These people already had an alarm system in place. Trouble was, they had never become accustomed to using it. Little good that did! They also had hefty locks on the doors and windows but failed to engage the mechanisms. Even the anti-theft measures in the garage could not prevent the prized BMW from driving away, since none of those measures were actually used.

This show reminded me that we often put ourselves at risk by not using the protective mechanisms that God has put in place. Rather, we take our chances that we'll be strong enough in our own right not to violate a law—or be violated ourselves. Let's take a quick look at some of these things—actions we can take to protect ourselves.

The Bible warns us to:

Flee from sexual immorality (I Corinthians 6:18). *Flee from idolatry* (I Corinthians 10:14). *Flee the evil desires of youth* (II Timothy 2:22). *Submit . . . to God. Resist the devil* (James 4:7). *Flee from the pursuit of money* (I Timothy 6:10). *Pursue righteousness, godliness, faith, love, endurance, and gentleness* (I Timothy 6:11). *Guard your heart* (Proverbs 4:23). *Be strong in the Lord . . . put on the full armor of God* (Ephesians 6:10a, 11). *Stand firm* (Ephesians 6:14).

God offers us impenetrable protection, but it won't happen on its own. Just like those homeowners who were either 1) ignorant 2) lazy or 3) just plain stupid, we need to take appropriate action.

> *Therefore put on the full armor of God . . . stand firm then . . ..*
> *(Ephesians 6:13, 14)*

Daily challenge:
Be proactive—not reactive.

Lonely

I'm always amazed at how different songs strike me. Today it was just one phrase from an unlikely artist singing an unlikely song. It was Whitney Houston singing "Jesus Loves Me." Really. I'm not joking. I think it was from the *Body Guard* sound track. It's actually not a bad rendition, though she departs from the traditional tune and lyrics somewhere along the way. But one phrase in the midst of all that was this: "lonely but never alone."

At the moment, I am not in a lonely place. Thank God. That's not to say I haven't felt that way. There have been long stretches when oppressive circumstances had me feeling like I was dying alone in the desert. Sleepless nights didn't help. The darkness had a way of creating an envelope of solitude. Nevertheless, that one phrase coming through my headphones today made me stop and think about the difference between being alone and being lonely.

Old King David seemed to have no shortage of lonely slumps. He wrote often of anguish, trouble and sorrow. In fact, he wrote in Psalm 116 that he was *overcome* by his predicament. Sounds to me like he was feeling pretty isolated. He was a common name on thugs' hit lists. That has to make you want to withdraw. But despite those "feelings," he was not in this by himself because, as he wrote, *The Lord is with me; I will not be afraid. What can man do to me? The Lord is with me; he is my helper* (Psalm 118:6, 7a).

Christ himself knew loneliness. Consider the forty days Christ spent alone in the wilderness. Reflect on the time alone in the garden. Think of the Father turning His back and the agony of loneliness that must have pierced His soul more than the swords in his side. But what did He tell the disciples in John 16:32? *"You will leave me all alone. Yet I am not alone, for my Father is with me."*

The beautiful truth is that when we feel alone, we are not. The Father is always with us.

> *"I have told you these things, so that in me you may have peace. In this world you will have trouble. But take heart! I have overcome the world." (John 16:33)*

Daily challenge:
"Feeling" lonely is an unfortunate choice, since we are never really alone.

Old Versus New

Steve and Robin's kitchen is, well . . . ugly. When the family moved into the house, wallpaper filled with kittens climbing from clay pots adorned the walls and carpet, dirty and beyond worn, covered the floor. They had every intention of making big changes, but when their house in Ohio stayed put on the dead-housing market, double house payments put remodeling plans on hold. Unfortunately, the only thing they managed to do was take off the wallpaper, leaving behind grungy walls and bland woodwork. Now, with the Ohio house sold, kitchen do-over plans surfaced and I ended up in the middle of it all.

Robin likes a French Country style. Me? Not so much. Yet, I get to try novel painting techniques, hoping they turn out as well in reality as they do in my head. Blue goes on first before covering it all with white paint. Then with sander in hand, I grind off some of the white to expose the peek-a-boo blue beneath. Ironically, we'll be successful if the new look makes those cabinets look old. Weird, huh?

In some cases, however, there should be no question that something old has become new. When Christ redeems us, we become brand new. The change should be obvious because only God can take something that is old and dead and make it live again.

Of course, we may not live perfectly. There is a constant battle between what comes naturally and what happens as a result of our awakened souls. It's like those cabinets I'm painting. When pressure is applied, sometimes our rough edges get sanded off, exposing our imperfections for all to see. Thank God, however, that His grace is sufficient to cover our flaws and make us beautiful and new in His sight.

> *Therefore if any man be in Christ, he is a new creature: old things are passed away; behold, all things are become new. (II Corinthians 5:17)*

Daily challenge:
Seal in your old nature with the protective coating of the Holy Spirit.

The Gift: Message to an Expectant Mom

Parenting is such a huge task, multi-faceted at every turn. I keep thinking of the phrase: "Children are a gift from God." To be honest, that's disturbing. Not because it isn't true, mind you. However, I've heard that phrase piously pronounced so many times by prim and proper women to whom I don't relate that the truth gets lost on me.

So let's approach this from a different perspective, if not a bit irreverent to the grand state of motherhood. Think back to Christmas past when you opened a box, beautifully wrapped, having high expectations for the gift. Your sense of excitement grows with each strip of broken tape. You fold back the perfectly creased tissue paper and gasp. Instead of the wonderful gift you envisioned, you find the most hideous sweater imaginable—a gaudy, heavy garment adorned with tacky glitter, gems and sledding Santas. How disappointing. You had anticipated this moment for such a long time only to find an awkward, ugly "thing" inside the box. Now, you think only of how quickly you can return it and rid yourself of the burden.

Here is the slightly irreverent part of my message. Don't be surprised if that tiny new kid isn't perfect and you feel like returning it to the baby store. He just didn't turn out like you thought he would. He might be downright ugly. He might pluck every last nerve you have when he refuses to sleep through the night until age two. He might poop on the way to church. He might not say "Yes, Ma'am" and "No, Sir" on command. Your vision of him becoming a great artist or athlete or visionary just doesn't happen. He is "average" rather than exceptional.

But—and that's a bigger but than the one we get when we are with child—there is hope for that little "gift from God." Unlike poor gift choices that we receive along the way, God does not make bad selections. Despite what our expectations may be, the kid we are handed is exactly the one God personally picked out. Let there be no doubt. If we are disappointed that we somehow got cheated or ripped off, the problem is ours—not God's. His ways are perfect.

Love that child through thick and thin, good and bad. Love him unconditionally even when you would rather strangle his scrawny little neck. Remember what kind of child you were. God must have a great sense of humor to give us the same kind of "gift" that our parents got.

Every good and perfect gift is from above, coming down from the Father of the heavenly lights, who does not change like shifting shadows. (James 1:7)

Daily challenge:
Love your children as God loves you.

Decisions

Gross and slimy, I walked through the door. I had just come in from running home from a friend's house after an afternoon of painting. I looked around the house and found the boys battling each other in cyberspace. Gary was outstanding in his field—oh, make that out standing in his field—and everyone was hungry. Once I cleaned up and started cooking, the aroma drew the kids to the kitchen. Sherlock Seth commented, "So, you ran to Robin's and home again?" That was a pretty obvious conclusion, since the cars stayed parked all day. "Well, that was sort of dumb. It's a long way." Maybe so.

The run to and fro is very hilly. It went better than expected, attacking the inclines with more energy than I've had in a long time. Except for short sections of the very steep hills, I ran them all, something I seldom can do. When I chose to walk a few steps and take a drink, what I told Bobbie during our run several weeks ago echoed in my head. "See that pole halfway up the hill? We're going to run to that point. It's a mental decision." So before I allowed myself a sip, I made a similar decision. It drew me further up the hill than I would have gone had it not been for the decisive moment.

Many circumstances demand a decision and commitment to move beyond our comfort zone. That can really be hard, because we don't know what it will feel like. Will we be able to stay on our feet? How bad will the pain be? Will the extra energy expenditure contribute to failure further down the road? And yet, if we don't push ourselves at key moments, we never have the chance for increased strength, growth and endurance.

This concept is applicable beyond athletic endeavors. Maybe it's a decision to sit in an unfamiliar church row even though the thought is nearly paralyzing. It could also be a decision to greet a visitor we don't know. Or, scarier yet, we could agree to take on the junior-high youth group.

The point to remember is that we must choose to extend ourselves and then commit to do it even when it is scary, intimidating, or painful. But we must also realize that doing this in our own power will likely fail. Thankfully, God has promised to fully equip us for each task.

The one who calls you is faithful and he will do it. (I Thessalonians 5:24)

Daily challenge:
Set goals that will push you beyond your own limits and into God's limitless realm.

Laugh Out Loud

Lately, our family has been laughing—a lot. Caleb was working at the school with his dad, keeping up with landscaping and outside chores. After cutting the acres of grass fed by the ample spring rain, Caleb parked the big mower and went inside for a break. Unfortunately, when he returned, the mower was gone. "Oh, I guess Dad must have needed it." Trouble is, his dad didn't drive off with it. After some heart-pounding minutes, he discovered it had rolled fifty yards down into a briar thicket. Two tow-straps later and hooked to a big truck the mower was rescued from its unlikely parking spot. Caleb got teased. We got to laugh.

Then today, Seth drove to school in one car and Gary and Caleb in another. With an appointment in Roanoke, Seth left school early. But Caleb had a dentist appointment about the same time. Seth left as planned; Caleb left as planned—but Gary did not leave as planned. Not understanding that Seth had left as well, Caleb just drove home, leaving Gary scratching his head in the parking lot, wondering what had happened to his car and eldest son.

Family life can be funny. We even had a good time at the surgeon's office. When the staff came into the cast-removal room, they found no cast in need of removal. Seth had grown weary of it and engaged his brother to help. Shreds of hot pink cast littered the floor by the time the deed was done. Snip by tedious snip, they succeeded and Seth was freed from the confining plaster. We cackled at his weenie arm and laughed today at an appointment designed to remove a non-existent cast.

Laughter is a wonderful gift from God. It lifts the soul and encourages the spirit. It even releases the tension in our facial muscles, engaging fewer muscles to laugh than to frown. A good hearty laugh is cathartic, dispelling worry and redirecting our negative focus. Years ago, Gary and I played a game of Bible Trivia with my parents. My dear old dad, who at the time was so discouraged with his health, laughed so hard his tears nearly created a flood. It was good for him . . . and for the rest of us.

As Christians, we have shunned the phrase, "If it feels good, do it." But in this case, it's probably good advice. Don't be afraid to laugh.

A happy heart makes the face cheerful . . . A cheerful look brings joy to the heart and good news gives health to the bones. (Proverbs 15:13a, 30)

Daily challenge:
Laugh often. It's better than crying.

Contrast

After a morning in the office, I was happy to continue working on Robin's kitchen overhaul. The transformation is getting better with every brush stroke. What was once a grayish, nondescript kitchen with countless flaws is morphing into a French-inspired masterpiece. With walls freshly painted blue and yellow and creamy whites adorning the cabinets, it feels fresh and bright. The sunlight dances across the room and makes even the massive stone fireplace look a little less ominous.

Trim painting was on the docket today. It wouldn't have been so bad had it not been for those five big windows in the dining room. I started off in a counterclockwise direction and worked my way through two of the windows. For some reason, I abandoned the windows and ended up working clockwise, closing in on where I had left off. Pausing to sip some ice water, I realized that the middle window stood out like a lone soldier. Sandwiched between two bright window frames on either side, the one in the middle looked dull and worn. Had you asked me what its color was beforehand, I would have replied "white." But now, my answer could not be the same.

It's an easy thing to get in a rut and not realize how much of our identity and distinctiveness we've lost. It's usually a slow thing. We don't intend to get old and worn in our spiritual growth, but we slack off a little bit one day. Then the next day, it's a tad easier to let go another smidge. Before long, all those little compromises make us look and behave like our unbelieving friends, blending in seamlessly. It's not until we pull up beside a long forgotten spiritual truth that we recognize the contrast. Whoa! We are amazed and wonder, "How in the world did this happen?"

Let's hold ourselves against the standard of Scripture to prevent a spiritual slide into complacency. The contrast will draw us back to where we need to be.

"It is the LORD your God you must follow, and him you must revere.
Keep his commands and obey him; serve him and hold fast to him."
(Deuteronomy 13:4)

Daily challenge:
Compare yourself only to a pure standard.

Remember When

All week long I looked forward to a soccer game between the alumni and the current team at the boys' school. Many of the kids from the dream team of 2005-2006 had returned from college to play. One was married, another getting married, some just graduated college and others completed their first year. But somehow, all looked different—more grown up and removed from the years of school dances, Greek lessons and thesis presentations. How did that happen? Where did the time go?

For what seemed like forever, the kids grew up together and played on the school team from the grammar years through high school. In the early days, long stretches went by without a win. The school was small and the athletic gene pool so limited that nearly all the other teams towered over our pipsqueaks. Goal after goal scored against us led to the adoption of an important concept: we were "building character."

But as the years went by, the kids grew not only in physical stature but in skill, technical ability, heart and teamwork. They became giant-killers. The tenacity learned from multiple defeats took them to championships on the league and state levels, culminating as the top team at a national tournament.

Although it is counterproductive to live in the past, there is good reason to glance backwards. The past encourages. The past produces confidence. But equally important, mistakes made in the past lead to repentance, repentance to growth and growth to maturity.

Remember the days of old; consider the generations long past. Ask your father and he will tell you, your elders, and they will explain to you. (Deuteronomy 32:7)

Daily challenge:
Don't live in the past. Learn from the past.

Sweet Fellowship

Of all the group runs with Dr. David Horton, I have never, ever started one as late as I did today. Despite frigid weather, rain or snow, high heat and humidity, we normally meet before the sun rises. But not today. We met at the respectable hour of 9:30 a.m. Horton had taken his almost four-year-old grandchild camping and needed the extra time to return.

The five of us who met him were excited about this run for in a short seven days, Horton would be trading the Virginia mountains for a record attempt on the Continental Divide Trail. Nearly three-thousand miles in length and spanning from Mexico to Canada, he planned to conquer it in a record seventy days. Horton, an emotional guy despite his loud and boisterous behavior, wanted our little group to gather on the trails one last time. We happily obliged.

Our distance was a mere twelve miles. The day was perfect—sunny but not too hot. A gentle breeze carried scents of wild flowers. But we were not the only trail-users, unlike the snowy, wintry runs when ours are the only footprints to be found. I guess Horton wanted it to last, enjoying the kidding and random comments that flowed so easily. He stopped and chatted with everyone we saw and amused himself with his new GPS unit. We admired every overlook and drank often from the clear, cool streams.

But alas, when we bid adieu, it was only for a couple of hours. The group met again for a "Westward-ho" party. We talked, ate and made s'mores around the fire pit. No one was in a hurry to leave—not even Horton who never sits still for very long. However, he, more than anyone else, seemed to be relishing the fellowship. Horton knew from experience that these extreme, unfathomably long-distance efforts reduced his life to nothing more than forward motion interrupted by a few hours of rest per day. There is no sitting around a campfire, no luxury of going out to a movie, no casualness to anything except making the mileage and surviving for the next day. Perhaps he has realized just how important fellowship can be.

> *But if we walk in the light, as he is in the light, we have fellowship with one another, and the blood of Jesus, his Son, purifies us from all sin. (I John 1:7)*

Daily challenge:
Prioritize fellowship. Don't be a loner.

It's Not About Me

The teaching at church today was magnificent. It was straightforward and simple; direct and to the point. At the conclusion, there was no question what the subject was or which directive for living was emphasized. As I looked around, everyone seemed to be paying attention—even the kids. I leaned forward in my seat with rapt attention and took in every word coming out of the speaker's mouth. I was taken by the teacher's whole being—he was handsome and well-spoken, a great communicator and good story-teller. No, I wasn't lusting after our pastor. Rather, I was looking directly at my husband, the appointed speaker for the day.

It's not about me. It's about God. That was Gary's theme. Our society is selfish and our pop culture concurs. Egocentric songs such as "I wanna talk about me," "I did it my way" and "You're so vain" demonstrate the point. But pop culture did not invent selfish behavior; that comes naturally.

The point is, the natural man watches out for Numero Uno—me, myself and I. And, we get lots of practice refining the fine art of selfishness. From the time we wanted our diaper changed or a binkie popped into our mouth, it was solely because our own interests were front and center. Though we may no longer fight over whose toy it is or worry that brother has a bigger cookie, we adults do a pretty good job of being selfish. Think about the last time you argued. More than likely, the squabble occurred because at least one person wanted his or her own way.

So be aware of our actions and attitudes today. Make sure they aren't all about us.

> *Love is patient, love is kind. It does not envy, it does not boast, it is not proud. It is not rude, it is not self-seeking, it is not easily angered, it keeps no record of wrongs. Love does not delight in evil but rejoices with the truth. It always protects, always trusts, always hopes, always perseveres. Love never fails. (I Corinthians 13:4-8)*

Daily challenge:
Unity is impossible until self is set aside and ambition is laid at another's feet.

The Mentor

Since it was Memorial Day, I gave myself permission to set aside my desk work and instead, run with a neophyte runner. Bobbie is a petite mother of seven, a couple kids still in diapers. Two weeks ago, I took her for a run double the distance she had ever gone before. She did great. Now I planned an adventure for her. The route I chose was anything but easy: multiple stream crossings, a ton of climb on rocky paths, long quad-crushing descents and a squeeze between huge rocks. But spectacular views awaited. Bobbie never asked how far, how long, how difficult—even when I pointed out the faraway mountain top where we would eventually stand.

The morning was gorgeous. Bird songs, squirrel and an occasional deer greeted us. We started the climb from the parking lot, turned left at the trail head and began the meandering journey around the base of the mountain before climbing to its peak. On the way to the summit, Bobbie asked, "Why did you want to bring a novice runner like me on a run like this?" It was not hard to answer.

I've gained a boatload of satisfaction from ultrarunning: running good races, meeting extraordinary comrades in the fight against the course, beholding beautiful scenery and earning a sense of accomplishment. However, fostering someone's interest in running is the most gratifying.

Actually, let me rephrase that. The most gratifying thing is to see someone suddenly understand that their self-imposed limits had been set too low. From that moment on, they look at life—including their running—differently. The raised bar spurs interest and motivation and allows for giant steps toward improvement. To know that I had a part in that eye-opening process is extremely rewarding.

Scripture gives instructions for older men to be examples for the younger guys and for mature women to teach the younger ladies. Traditionally, we assume the younger set to be the beneficiaries. But after verbalizing my answer to Bobbie, I have concluded that the mentors are equally benefited.

> *You must teach what is in accord with sound doctrine. Teach the older men . . . Likewise, teach the older women . . . then they can train the younger women . . . Similarly, encourage the young men to be self-controlled. In everything set them an example by doing what is good. (Titus 2:1-6)*

Daily challenge:
You don't have to be perfect to lead the way. Invest in someone's life.
Become a mentor.

Illusions

I took the sander in hand and wondered if I had flipped my paint can lid one too many times. Here I was, lining up freshly painted cabinet doors only to take a power sander to the edges. Why in the world would I mar a perfectly painted surface? Nevertheless, as the sander swirled into action, the pristine white gave way to reveal the underlying color—a pretty "blurple." By the time I finished grinding and top coating, those cabinet doors looked centuries old.

Next, the ugly brass cabinet pulls had to be addressed. A little tape to mask off the white porcelain section of the handle and a can of hammered black spray paint turned the dated hardware into quaint period pieces—a perfect match for the antique look of the cabinets.

So why go to all the trouble to make-over perfectly functional cabinets? It's because we hated the *ho-hum* kitchen enough to create an illusion. To make it into something it is not: a cottage kitchen in the pastoral French countryside. This kitchen will never be geographically relevant to France—or anywhere else European—but we want visitors to think it could be.

While it may be acceptable to create an illusion in a kitchen remodel, we church people are fairly adept at doing just that. I may be guilty myself. You know what I mean. We pray in such a way, words carefully selected, that all within earshot are left to marvel at our spiritual insight. We know what and when to proclaim a wise saying, posturing to maximize its effect. In essence, even though we speak truth, we are effectively creating an illusion. The simple fact that we calculate our words and actions to elicit a desired response reveals a selfish, egocentric motivation to be something we are not.

The prophet Isaiah knew something about illusions. The people were not interested in truth nor were they concerned with living according to God's instructions. In fact, they were so intent on ignoring the truth that they asked the prophets to give them only "feel-good" messages.

That, my friend, is no way to live.

These are rebellious people, deceitful children, children unwilling to listen to the LORD's instruction. They say to the seers, "See no more visions!" and to the prophets, "Give us no more visions of what is right! Tell us pleasant things, prophesy illusions." (Isaiah 30:9-10)

Daily challenge:
Don't create an illusion of truth. Live truth.

The Depth of Knowledge

The clock is ticking, the fleeting seconds almost audible. I'm trying desperately to finish writing an online course for perfusionists. This involves deciding on a topic, doing research, putting together a progression of lessons, writing a quiz and other learning activities and obtaining the proper recognition from the accrediting agency. Surely, perfusionists should be interested in earning essential educational credits without the expense of traveling to a meeting. At least that is my hope. June 30 marks the yearly deadline for clinicians to acquire the required number of credits. This opens a four-week window when perfusionists deficient in credits will be searching for learning opportunities. Hence, the rush.

It's always difficult to determine how much to include in a course. But as I read and write, I am continuously confronted with how much I don't know. The more I work on these courses, the greater the glare of my own ignorance. I feel stupid. How did I ever get out of perfusion school and pass my board exams?

The same thing happened when I was teaching high school. Leave it to high school students to make you feel like a complete idiot. It was only when I stood in front of a classroom full of inquisitive students that I realized how much I lacked. And now with my daily writing, that same feeling is coming back with a vengeance. I feel incredibly inadequate to be writing when I have a lot to learn and so much truth to translate into practice.

I'm reminded of the Romans doxology written by the Apostle Paul. I believe he understood the mind's finiteness. Nevertheless, when God switches on the light bulb, increased learning and understanding is endless.

Oh, the depth of the riches of the wisdom and knowledge of God! How unsearchable his judgments, and his paths beyond tracing out! (Romans 11:33)

Daily challenge:
Soak in knowledge so it can be wrung out and shared.

Praise the Lord

For twelve hours I have toiled over my work. I didn't even break to run. My mind is weary, leaving me blank on what to write. I am at a loss. So now at 11:15 p.m., I do what I probably should have done all along. I simply started reading Scripture.

I had half a mind to do the old "open-a-page-and-point" trick in finding inspiration. But alas, it's hard to do that on a computer screen. I did, however, open my browser and read the verse of the day. I had to read more. A song putting those words to music played in my mind. It's a melodic and comforting song, a favorite for some time now. Reading Psalm 103 (underlines mine) in its entirety gave me reason to pause and consider no less than twenty-seven characteristics of God's behavior. Be encouraged. The Word says it all.

Praise the LORD, O my soul; all my inmost being, praise his holy name. Praise the LORD, O my soul, and forget not all his benefits—who forgives all your sins and heals all your diseases, who redeems your life from the pit and crowns you with love and compassion, who satisfies your desires with good things so that your youth is renewed like the eagle's. The LORD works righteousness and justice for all the oppressed. He made known his ways to Moses, his deeds to the people of Israel: The LORD is compassionate and gracious, slow to anger, abounding in love. He will not always accuse, nor will he harbor his anger forever; he does not treat us as our sins deserve or repay us according to our iniquities. For as high as the heavens are above the earth, so great is his love for those who fear him; as far as the east is from the west, so far has he removed our transgressions from us. As a father has compassion on his children, so the LORD has compassion on those who fear him; for he knows how we are formed, he remembers that we are dust. As for man, his days are like grass, he flourishes like a flower of the field; the wind blows over it and it is gone, and its place remembers it no more. But from everlasting to everlasting the LORD's love is with those who fear him, and his righteousness with their children's children— with those who keep his covenant and remember to obey his precepts. The LORD has established his throne in heaven, and his kingdom rules over all. Praise the LORD, you his angels, you mighty ones who do his bidding, who obey his word. Praise the LORD, all his heavenly hosts, you his servants who do his will. Praise the LORD, all his works everywhere in his dominion. Praise the LORD, O my soul.

Daily challenge:
We have plenty of reasons to praise the Lord.

Miss D

She was larger than life at 6'1" and "big-boned." With disheveled dirty blonde curls, one sideways glance and hands on hips sent most kids into a frightened trance. "What? You forgot your locker combination?" she snarled. Woe to the one who delivered that news while trying to beat the bell to make it to the gym in time.

Miss D, as we called her, was my gym teacher and gymnastics coach in high school. She was imposing and feared. But once you got to know her . . . well, she was like that big furry bear who looked ferocious but wasn't too bad. Still, I felt dwarfed in her presence. I made sure I didn't cross her and did exactly as she instructed. Whether in gym class, playing field hockey, or breaking the all-time sit-up record, I yearned to gain her approval.

If you were on her gymnastics team, it was serious business. Holding gut-exploding leg lifts and working on flexibility that could make Gumby complain was just part of the picture. If she told you to throw a trick, you did. No questions asked. If she spotted, chances of getting dropped were slim to none; she was big and strong. We worked hard and long into the night, but we had our fun as well. Music blared from the record player—yes, we used one back then—and played "you're no good, you're no good, you're no good, baby you're no good" when a cocky rival team pushed open the door to our gym.

We kept in contact after I graduated, exchanging yearly Christmas cards. Though she always signed "Alana," I could never bring myself to call her anything but *Miss D.* I loved my coach.

My mom called me this morning to say Miss D's obituary was in the newspaper. It caught me off-guard and I felt a lump grow in my throat. She was only 61, the same age as my dad was when he died. I wonder if she was sick at Christmastime. That was the first time in thirty years that I didn't get a greeting in the mail. Oh, the memories . . . ..

Miss D's passing makes an impression that we have a responsibility to share Christ wherever, whenever and with whomever. We may not have another chance.

> *"Therefore go and make disciples of all nations, baptizing them in the name of the Father and of the Son and of the Holy Spirit."* (Matthew 28:19)

Daily challenge:
Don't ever pass up an opportunity to share your faith.

God Is with You

Running a few days ago, I felt good. Really good. Hills did not reduce me to a shuffle. I felt like "the little engine that could," powering up and over the top so that I could enjoy the downhill on the other side. Even the runs with friends have been effortless. I felt like a real runner, light-footed and floating. I love that feeling.

It hasn't always been this way. From 2001 to sometime in 2006, I struggled with a mystery condition no doctor could identify. It left me numb and tingling, a stomach painfully distended, legs that felt they had just run one-hundred miles, a hoarse and raspy voice and an inability to breathe in normally. I was exhausted all the time, becoming drenched with instantaneous hot flashes.

After much research I reached my own diagnosis—a calcium receptor abnormality. For the most part, the symptoms seemed to come and go for no good reason. One day I was fine and the next, I couldn't run a half mile. I finally struck on a logical nutritional approach and have been pretty much symptom-free. Symptom-free, that is, until yesterday.

As amazing as it seems, it's like some inexplicable switch got flipped on. Every symptom has returned. I couldn't even run six miles this morning. I feel awful. I don't understand what has happened. It's like a bad dream that this condition—whatever it is—has suddenly returned. Yes. I'll admit it. I am discouraged. I am frightened that the switch will stay on for a long time. And just when I was feeling so good.

My situation is nothing compared to Job's, and yet I feel akin to what Job's friend, Eliphaz, offers to the suffering Job. *"Think how you have instructed many, how you have strengthened feeble hands. Your words have supported those who stumbled; you have strengthened faltering knees. But now trouble comes to you, and you are discouraged; it strikes you, and you are dismayed"* (Job 4:3-6).

I've been finding great satisfaction in helping others tackle goals they never thought possible. "What good am now?" I think. And yet, I know I should be taking Joshua's advice:

> *"Have I not commanded you? Be strong and courageous. Do not be terrified; do not be discouraged, for the LORD your God will be with you wherever you go." (Joshua 1:9)*

Daily challenge:
Hold on. God is near.

Discretion

Friends invited us to join them at their lake house for a little R & R. What a treat! The combination of water, the breeze and a vacation retreat revives the soul.

With the boat stocked with a cooler full of diet cola, the world seemed to settle down. I still felt bad with the revolting return of my mystery symptoms. But, if I was going to feel bad, I might as well do it with friends on the water. I took some ibuprofen to mask the headache and hoped for the best.

The water was still a chilly seventy degrees and Gary and I had no intention of taking the plunge. Instead, we threw the boys off the back of the boat and into a two-seater, triangle-shaped contraption. Hadley, a cute, rising ninth-grader, laid in between the two stud muffins, hanging on for dear life. Jim drove the boat trying to dump the kids while the kids battled among themselves to force a tumble. All told, it made for some cheap entertainment for those of us in the boat.

As Jim made a particularly sharp turn, the tube ended up nearly even with the boat. With the rope lying limp in the water while the boat maintained speed, I braced for the inevitable: either the kids would go flying or their necks would snap in two when the rope pulled taut. Either way, it wasn't going to be pretty. Sure enough, the rope became cable-like, but the kids hung on. The force was so great that it ripped the "unrippable" cover right of the inflated rubber and bent the metal tow pole on the boat. The tow rope shot back toward the boat like a wild bungee cord. Thankfully, it didn't hit anyone. But it was a great lesson in how quickly an unexpected, yet preventable force, can be undoing.

Had we been a little more tuned in to where the tubers were in relationship to the boat, the snapped rope and shredded tube may not have become a reality. The damage could have been prevented had the boat immediately slowed down. But of course, the best way to have avoided the unfortunate incident would have been to prevent the potential problem in the first place.

The writer of Proverbs had the right idea when he gave his instructions for living. If we just remembered to use discretion, understanding and wisdom, we could avoid many—if not all—of the preventable pitfalls in our lives.

> *Discretion will protect you and understanding will guard you. Wisdom will save you . . .. (Proverbs 2:11, 12a)*

Daily challenge:
Avoid trouble. Use discretion in what you say, where you go and what you do.

Sunrise

. . . Sunrise, sunset . . .
Swiftly flow the days
Seedlings turn overnight to sunflowers
Blossoming even as we gaze...
Swiftly fly the years
One season following another
Laden with happiness and tears . . ..

Do you recognize the lines from the famous musical, *Fiddler on the Roof*? The story is one of love, family and solidarity in the face of opposition. Tevye the milkman and his wife, Golde, watch as three of their headstrong daughters select husbands while the family is under the rule of czarist Russia. In doing so, the daughters move progressively further from the ideals of family and religious tradition. Nonetheless, the parents watch and wonder how their little girls could have grown so quickly into beautiful young women standing at the altar. The song they sing is a touching tribute. Where has the time gone?

As we sat down to dinner tonight, I thought about these things. The conversation was respectful and mature as we leisurely cooked our individual pieces of venison in the fondue pot. We spoke freely of past mistakes and plans for near futures. Caleb, having finished a second year at college, has settled on the idea of living at home for the time being and transferring to a local university. Seth, a rising high-school senior, will be taking classes at the community college along with his senior course work, keen for a change and excited to begin his photography education.

In a sense, I feel like Golde. It's hard to believe that so many seasons of life have come and gone. Not all have been easy and gratifying. Some of those days past seemed like the sun would never again shine. And yet, no matter how dark the day or futile our prayers seemed to be, God was faithful to raise the sun without fail.

The rising sun should be a giant object lesson every day. It is exceedingly crucial to remember that God Himself is the force behind the sun's movement. But is He a mere observer or an inactive member of a universal audience? Nay. He is the one who spoke the sun into existence and programmed its celestial path. So, too, has He programmed the days, the months, the seasons of our lives.

The Mighty One, God, the LORD, speaks and summons the earth
from the rising of the sun to the place where it sets. (Psalm 50:1)

Daily challenge:
From the rising of the sun to the place where it sets,
the name of the LORD is to be praised. (Psalm 113:3)

Ants

Ants. Gotta love 'em. Gotta hate 'em. How is it that out of nowhere, a virtual legion can come traipsing across the countertop? They weren't there just a few minutes ago but now . . . goodness, it looks like they are on a mission to overtake the second shelf in the cereal cupboard.

But wait. Fodder for a story. I flew up the steps to my computer and typed in "Why do ants walk in a straight line?" Before long, I was reading a primer on ants: their morphology, social structure, living habitats, how to raise them and yes, why they walk in a straight line. I bemused myself by asking Seth, having returned from taking his last final, the same question. A gleeful smile broke out. In his bathroom was a column of tiny ants stretching from one side of the room to the other, the kitty food at the terminus. So started our experiment.

I found out that the lead ants lay down a certain chemical, a pheromone, which those who follow can smell with their antennae. Hence, an odiferous path is created for the string of workers to follow to the bounty and back again to the nest. But, if that path is disrupted in some way, the ants go crazy and randomly roam. Should they happen to pick up the scent again, they continue on their journey. If not . . . well, good luck. She'll probably never find her way back home. (Yes, the workers are all females. Any surprise there?)

We grabbed an eraser and rubbed it across the trail. Sure enough, the next one in line came to a screeching halt, the others barreling into her. It was miniaturized slapstick in action. Soon, the whole line went willy-nilly, each searching furiously for the familiar trail scent. We watched for a while, fascinated. But soon enough, I grabbed the ant spray and sent them into eternity.

Truly, ants have an impressive social structure where each type of ant within the colony has a specific and important job to do. There are sterile female worker ants, the royal queen ant and her offspring (princess ants in training), both male and female ants who become protective soldiers and whose progeny become workers. The male soldiers have big heads with a vicious bite. But as soon as he mates, he dies. Oh well!

It is not surprising that Solomon wrote of the ant, pointing out two characteristics worthy of emulation. 1) We should be active and busy, not lazy, and 2) We should be consistent and persevering in our work despite the enormity of the task. So next time we have an encounter with an ant line, consider the lessons they represent.

Go to the ant, you sluggard; consider its ways and be wise!
(Proverbs 6:6)

Daily challenge:
Better to be an ant than a slug.

Following

It looks like the floor itself is moving beneath the sunroom window. For days now, we have been noticing—how could we not?—hundreds, perhaps thousands of these little winged ants. Larger than their bodies, their wings seem to be of little use. Nevertheless, they wiggle around as if conjuring up the strength to take to the air. Ant spray kills them, yet more mysteriously appear every morning. After my ant research, I think these are the winged form of ants as they exit their pupa stage. Hence, I am still ant-obsessed.

As gross as these creatures can be, tiny ants teach us to work hard. I remember a cute little song sung by our elementary school chorus entitled "High Hopes," a Frank Sinatra tune promoting that can-do attitude. *Just what makes that little old ant think he'll move that rubber tree plant? Anyone knows an ant can't move a rubber tree plant . . . But he's got high hopes . . . he's got high apple pie, in the sky hopes . . ..*

But those worker ants also teach us about who, what and when to follow the guy in front of you. The Israelites followed Moses out of Egypt; that's a good thing. The Egyptians followed the Israelites into the sea of parted waters. That, too, is a good thing if you were an Israelite. Not so good if you were an Egyptian, for God pushed down those watery cliffs and wiped out the chasing army. But upon witnessing this event from the far bank, Miriam, the sister of Aaron and a prophetess, took her tambourine in hand as all the ladies followed her, proclaiming, *"Sing to the LORD . . . The horse and its rider he has hurled into the sea"* (Exodus 15:19-21). Now, that's a very good thing.

Later on in chapter 23 of Exodus, we are given this instruction: *"Do not follow the crowd in doing wrong . . . do not pervert justice by siding with the crowd."* Following the crowd because it's cool or hip or just convenient—that's a bad thing.

"You must not do as they do in Egypt, where you used to live, and you must not do as they do in the land of Canaan, where I am bringing you. Do not follow their practices" (Leviticus 18:3). Do so and . . . well, that's a bad thing.

But what are we supposed to follow? Here's a hint.

"It is the LORD your God you must follow, and him you must revere.
Keep his commands and obey him; serve him and hold fast to him."
(Deuteronomy 13:4)

Daily challenge:
Follow carefully. Follow wholeheartedly.

Weeds

Our brick walkways do not look tidy. The bricks had been laid down back in the 70s and over time have shifted and heaved from the constant thawing and freezing process. Inevitably, the gaps have widened, giving grass and weeds an open invitation to grow. But strangely enough, weeds seem to rise from the depths between bricks separated by the narrowest of margins. Hence, my project was to kill the unwanted weeds, methodically pulling them out, and then fill the gaps with sand. The plan sounded simple enough.

Simple? Yes. Easy? No. As I scooted along the pathways on the wheeled mechanics dolly confiscated from the garage, I came to realize several things. First, weeds grow anywhere. Even without good soil or fertilizer and baked by an effectual brick oven under a scorching sun, the weeds never seem to wilt, not even in a drought. Why is that? Beautiful flowers need much coddling to survive but weeds . . . why can't they be high-maintenance instead?

The second thing I've noticed is how hard it is to pull out the entire weed. Before spraying on the weed killer, it was nearly impossible to do anything but tear off a few leaves. Little good that does, since the resilient plants laugh in the face of the insult. But, if the weed is first done in by the poison, I have a chance. However, sometimes the weed has such a stranglehold that I have to use needle-nose pliers to dig down and pull out any remnants of the root system. If I fail to do so, it will grow back.

That old, annoying sin nature can act very much like the pesky weeds. Sin has a way of working its way into the cracks and taking hold. Without a proactive, calculated approach to prevent germination of sin in the first place, the transgressing behavior or thought becomes rooted. The longer it goes unattended, the harder it is to get rid of it. And, the longer it takes us to uproot the sin, the bigger the hole it leaves when it is finally removed.

I dare not be lax in killing the weeds of my life and filling in the cracks. Not with sand as I have been doing on the walkway, but with this:

> . . . *whatever is true, whatever is noble, whatever is right, whatever is pure, whatever is lovely, whatever is admirable—if anything is excellent or praiseworthy, think on these things. (Philippians 4:8)*

Daily challenge:
Do some weeding each and every day.

Filling in the Cracks

Still working on Project Brick Pathway, I threw out handfuls of sand along the cracks needing filled, dragging a fifty-pound bag behind me. With scrub brush in hand I swept, pounded and coaxed the grains into the cracks. The big cracks were easy to fill and progress was swift. However, those tiny cracks were another story. With what looked like a tiny hole—let's say one-quarter inch long—I couldn't believe how much sand it took until the void was filled. Where was it going? Though the defect was visibly small, there must have been a virtual cavern beneath to require such a volume of sand to fill it.

Just like that seemingly small hole, I think we are pretty good at disguising our flaws. Surely, no one wants to reveal a deep chasm of sin. Even though we know it's there, we much prefer to make it less obvious to others. But what is underground is what causes such damage.

Flipping channels a few weeks ago, I saw scientists descend into deep crevasses to study glacial movement. What they found was that just a trickle of melting water between the ground and the glacier was causing the massive ice cube to slide toward the sea.

Let's not ignore the little patterns of behavior and thought that undermine our Christian living. If we do, we'll create some pretty heft voids and find ourselves slowly slip-sliding away.

And I pray that you, being rooted and established in love, may have power, together with all the saints, to grasp how wide and long and high and deep is the love of Christ, and to know this love that surpasses knowledge—that you may be filled to the measure of all the fullness of God. (Ephesians 3:17b, 18, 19)

Daily challenge:
Being deeply rooted and established in love is a great strategy
for filling in the holes of our lives.

As the Deer

With highs predicted to be near one-hundred degrees and humidity to match, my run started early; 5:00 a.m. *Ugh.* The car even protested the heat by pegging the temperature gauge on the way up the mountain. I stopped and parked farther down the hill than I intended.

The sweat was soon pouring from my skin, but birds sang and squirrels played. Had it not been for the flies buzzing and mosquitoes humming, it might have been tolerable. Hours later and descending off the mountain toward my waiting car, I rounded a switchback on the wide trail. The little-used trail was overgrown, grasses and stinging nettles reaching out to touch as I passed by. Making a mental note to check for ticks, I let out a scream and jumped over an unrecognized form. There in the tall grass lay a newborn fawn, basking in the sunlight. As I skidded to a stop, she just looked at me with those big brown eyes, not looking old enough to stand. But as I reached for my camera phone, stand she did, taking a few faltering steps back into the woods. My photo op ended, I continued on my way.

Last year I saw five newborn fawns, three of them still wet from the birth. They were so precious—so innocent. One I held, his heart beating wildly as I cuddled it before putting him down to follow his mother back into the forest. I love watching deer, tiny or full grown, glide through the trees, stopping to eat or refreshing themselves at a stream. It is a picture of serenity.

Like all animals, deer have a need for water; without it they will die. They will drink from a stream or puddle, acquire water by eating browse with high water content or produce it as a byproduct of digestion. Their drive for food and water are insatiable; just ask any gardener whose plots are ransacked by the four-legged creatures. They will leap tall barriers and risk the shocks of electric fences to dine on delectable plants. Nothing can stop them when they are hungry.

Just as insatiable as the deer appetite should be our desire for God. If I'm honest, I am often more enthusiastic about a design show on HGTV. Perhaps I need to make a concerted effort to approach each day with renewed focus on that which is of eternal consequence.

As the deer pants for streams of water, so my soul pants for you, O God. (Psalm 42:1)

Daily challenge:
Desiring God above all else is sure to revolutionize our attitudes, our actions and our ministries.

Blisters

Blisters. They create an incredible amount of pain per square millimeter. I've had plenty of agonizing friction wounds that at the time, seemed to surpass the pain of childbirth. Even the smallest of blisters can distract to the point of being oblivious to everything else. Just ask Seth.

For some indescribable reason, Seth and a couple of his buddies decided to run barefoot on scorching hot tennis courts prior to their soccer game today. Why? I have no earthly idea. For Seth, however, the fun was short-lived, as the tender skin on the balls of his feet disconnected with the tissue beneath, producing half-dollar-sized blisters. He realized the consequences of his gleeful jaunt as soon as he donned his soccer cleats and took to the field. Eventually, several hundred milligrams of ibuprofen dulled the pain enough to allow him to score a hat-trick in the second half. But now, he is dealing with the reality of the situation.

He and a buddy have a hiking trip planned, starting tomorrow at noon. As a warm-up for a photography hike through Yosemite, the plan is to put in thirty miles in two days with fully loaded packs. Thus, wounded feet come at a really bad time. Miles walked on rocky trails, up and down mountains and under a full load are sure to be a constant reminder of the one minute when his brain lagged far behind his enthusiasm.

Lots of us do the same. We make instant decisions without much thought about consequences. We dive right in on a whim or a guttural response. If we had only taken time to consider the ramifications, we could have avoided much pain and agony.

Personally, I can't count the number of times I have "opened mouth, inserted foot." Don't you just hate it when you mess up and instantly know it—with no way to take it back? The damage is done.

So, recall the words of Solomon.

The wisdom of the prudent is to give thought to their ways . . ..
(Proverbs 14:8a)

Daily challenge:
Look before you leap.

The Desert

Deserts: hot, remote, inhospitable, scorching, desolate, solitary, barren, hostile. Venture into the elements unprepared, and death is sure. Venture into the elements fully prepared, and death may still threaten. Just ask David Horton.

Horton is the king of multi-day adventures with speed records on the Appalachian Trail, the Long Trail and the Pacific Crest Trail. He has run coast to coast in sixty-four days straight. So when he set out two days ago on a speed record attempt on the Continental Divide Trail, a 3,000-mile journey from Mexico to Canada, confidence was high. But yesterday the coffin was nailed shut.

What happened? The desert happened. Ill-marked trail and 108-degree temperatures under a molten sun made running impossible. There was no shade anywhere, making the plodding through the unforgiving terrain more difficult with every step. Alone on the last section for the day, the two liters of fluid every four miles could not satisfy the needs of his body; legs cramped and hands swelled, his brain went foggy. Having lost the trail and fearful that losing consciousness was next, he willed up all his strength to reach a windmill and wait for rescue. Eventually, however, he resumed his trek on a compass bearing, finally meeting up with his worried crew. But nausea, vomiting, dry heaves, bloody diarrhea and agonizing muscle cramping persisted. He quit, bruised, bloody and beaten.

Just like that barren wasteland, the desert-like periods in our lives serve an important purpose. Moses wrote, *"Remember how the LORD your God led you all the way in the desert these forty years, to humble you and to test you in order to know what was in your heart, whether or not you would keep his commands"* (Deuteronomy 8:2). They did not feel comforted when they went without water for three days and people fell dead around them. And yet, *"There you saw how the LORD your God carried you, as a father carries his son . . . God has been with you, and you have not lacked anything"* (Deuteronomy 1:31, 2:7).

Let there be no doubt; there are desert hardships. You feel like you are going to die and wish for it to be so. And yet, God is present and involved. Aaron, while speaking to the nation before their journey even began, witnessed God's very presence: *. . . they looked toward the desert, and there was the glory of the LORD . . .* (Exodus 16:10). In essence he said, "Trust God. Go to the desert. He is there and he will not be silent. There are lessons to be learned."

O God, you are my God, earnestly I seek you; my soul thirsts for
you, my body longs for you, in a dry and weary land. (Psalm 63:1)

Daily challenge:
As the difficulties of our own deserts seek to undo us, let God quench your thirst.

Cool Water

As I worked today—still—on my sidewalk project, the sun blazed. I fetched a beach umbrella and positioned it over my work area to block out the offending rays. I was still hot, but at least I wasn't in full sun. My thoughts drifted back to Horton and his desert conundrum. Perhaps had he rigged up an umbrella, his makeshift shade could have saved him. Too late now. He was no longer engaged in that struggle.

With his desert experience fresh on my mind, my next thought was of the old Sons of the Pioneers song entitled "Cool Water." As a little girl I went to bed listening to their music wafting from the console record player. The harmony was tight and beautiful; the men's voices blended like watercolors in a painting. I begged my dad to leave my door open so I could hear it before drifting off to sleep. There was romance in the idea of sleeping under a starry sky, horses grazing nearby as a campfire crackled.

The story line in this song is about a poor cowboy, dry and parched in the desert. He is on a quest to find the cool, clean waters that could be his saving grace. But alas, he sees only mirage-induced ripples. The mournful song goes like this:

All day I face the barren waste without the taste of water, Cool water . . . Keep a movin' Dan, don't you listen to him Dan, he's a devil not a man and he spreads the burnin' sand with water. Dan can't you see that big green tree where the waters runnin' free and it's waiting there for me and you. Water, cool water . . . And way up there He'll hear our prayer and show us where there's water, Cool Water . . . Dan's feet are sore he's yearning for just one thing more than water, Cool water. Like me, I guess, he'd like to rest where there's no quest for water, Cool water.

But why would you want to rest where there is no quest for water? Ah, I get it. It's because you would be in a place where water is bountiful. If you have plenty, there is no need to search. Just drink it in and be satisfied.

When we are in Christ, there is no magic formula or spiritual antic needed to gain access to His life-sustaining Water. No. Being in Christ automatically provides an endless supply that requires no further searching.

"Everyone who drinks this water will be thirsty again, but whoever drinks the water I give him will never thirst. Indeed, the water I give him will become in him a spring of water welling up to eternal life."
(John 4:13)

Daily challenge:
When you are thirsty, go to the Well.

Trail Hikers

Remember those blisters I wrote about a few days ago? I was right in predicting they would impact Seth's little hiking adventure. The first night, a bear took up residency by their tent eliciting a frenzied packing job and descent off the mountain. They stumbled into a trail shelter at one o'clock in the morning and scared the bejeebers out of those already sleeping there. The next day, with temperatures nearing one-hundred degrees and new blisters forming, tackling another twelve tough miles with forty-pound packs was interrupted by a dramatic decrease in enthusiasm and a phone call home.

"Mama, you doing anything right now? Can you come pick us up?" So much for the second night on the trail.

But the kids ended up bringing home more than themselves. The boys volunteered to pick up a twenty-year old Appalachian Trail thru-hiker, bring him back into town to resupply and return him to the trail in the morning. And guess what? He is spending the night at our house. *Yippee.*

Now, please don't get me wrong. I've brought hikers home, so I am not opposed to the idea. I just wasn't sure how the logistics would work. Happily, everything was fine and we had a marvelous time with "Low." We enjoyed watching him consume thousands of calories and relax around the house. It was obviously a needed break and after watching the movie, *The Runner*, a film depicting David Horton's record on the Pacific Crest Trail, he seemed motivated more than ever to complete what he had started.

When Seth first asked if the hiker could stay here, I thought it might be "inconvenient." But then I thought about the possibility being "salt and light" to him. Besides, if I were Low's mother, I would be grateful if a family offered help to my child.

By eight o'clock tomorrow morning, Low will be gone. I pray he leaves enriched and may God keep and protect him on his journey.

"It was the LORD our God himself who brought us and our fathers up out of Egypt, from that land of slavery, and performed those great signs before our eyes. He protected us on our entire journey and among all the nations through which we traveled." (Joshua 24:17)

Daily challenge:
Be open to helping those along their own life's trail.

More on Cracks

OK. I promise. Just one more thought about weeds, bricks and the cracks between them.

This sidewalk is going to be the death of me. It is so pea-picking tedious. For weeks, I headed outside, grabbed a big beach umbrella and sat my little self down onto the pathway to work. With needle-nose pliers in hand, the process gave me plenty of time to think. On a daily basis I observed that what looked to be perfectly filled cracks yesterday exhibited big gaps today. What's with that? I could only sigh and resign myself to grab another handful of sand and work the grains—again—into the new hole.

I suspect a couple of forces are at work. First of all, if the sand is wet, it clumps together and won't fit down into the tiny cracks. But once it does dry out, the sand slides further down, revealing the need for more sand. Other times, a small pebble gets wedged into the crack and prohibits sand from filling the void. Again, once the sand settles, the hole underneath the offending pebble is revealed.

If you recall the analogy we made relating weeds to sin, we begin to understand the need to purge the sin all the way down to the roots. And, the sooner we fill in the hole left behind, the better. However, what I did not clearly understand until today was that it takes a constant effort to keep that sidewalk—and our lives—looking good.

Am I going to have to do this over and over again? Clearly, the answer is *yes*. If I don't keep up with it, I will eventually have the very same problems. The instant a weed emerges, I need to kill it. And, as soon as the rain packs down the sand revealing the need for more, filling it to the brim will be required.

So it is with the cracks in our life: introspection is necessary, action compulsory.

Search me, O God, and know my heart; test me and know my anxious thoughts. (Psalm 139:23)

Daily challenge:
Never delay in filling a void.

It Only Takes a Spark

It only takes a spark to get a fire going,
And soon all those around can warm up in its glowing;
That's how it is with God's Love,
Once you've experienced it,
You spread the love to everyone
You want to pass it on.

Remember this song from your summer-camp days? Growing up, it was the first "contemporary Christian" song that I learned. I still recall how some adults were suspicious of this departure from the classic hymn. Perhaps the artists' long hair, frumpy jeans and strumming guitars had something to do with their suspicion. Nevertheless, I enjoyed the song and think of it still when I'm fire-gazing.

We've enjoyed gathering at our fire pit out by the pool for conversation and an almost sickening volume of s'mores—so much so that the boys have become privy to all my hiding spots for the chocolate. Seth, a natural pyromaniac since birth, particularly enjoys taking his friends out there, chopping wood and chipping off small pieces for tinder.

There's something mesmerizing about a fire. The flame, burning wildly at first, reduces itself to a bed of glowing embers, perfect for toasting marshmallows golden brown. The scent of the wood fire is calming, transporting the soul to a time when a fire was the rite of passage for end-of-the-week camps. Better yet is the snuggly feeling when the fire wards off a night chill. Cradling a cup of cocoa and gazing into the flame creates an oh-so-pleasant experience.

But with all the warm and fuzzies associated with a fire, the initial spark can initiate devastating consequences. Ask the folks in California who presently deal with wildfires that consume entire neighborhoods. I sincerely doubt many of them have a burning desire, pun intended, to conduct a pow-wow around the fire pit, singing *Kum-ba-ya* in three-part harmony. For them, the first spark signifies imminent destruction.

James understood this well. As he wrote to the first-century Believers, he conveyed the devastation an ill-placed word generates. Think how often tension is created by "open mouth, insert foot." So many problems could be avoided if we never allow the first spark of unkind and unedifying words to initiate a firestorm.

Likewise the tongue is a small part of the body, but it makes great boasts. Consider what a great forest is set on fire by a small spark. (James 3:5)

Daily challenge:
Only you can prevent word fires.

Royalty

Caleb and I just watched a movie. It was of the highest quality and socially signif-icant—a fascinating depiction of the interactions of complex personalities and their abilities to solve multiple and intertwined challenges. Of course, I speak of no other film than the grand, the extraordinary, the astonishing "The Princess Diaries".

Surprised? Well, I was too. Flipping channels, it caught my eye as Caleb mean-dered by. This meandering was predictable; he walks directly to the refrigerator, stud-ies its contents, closes the door, repeats the procedure at the snack cabinet and then returns to the refrigerator, as if the contents may have changed in those elapsed sec-onds. What was not so predictable was that my oldest son sat down to watch a teenage chick-flick.

In the movie, Mia was a dowdy tenth-grader who clung tightly to the bottom rung of the popularity ladder at a prestigious prep school. Through an awkward series of events, she came to understand that her father, recently passed, was the Prince of the fair land of Genovia. With no other blood relative in line for the throne, the rules of the nation placed the responsibility squarely on the shoulders of the fifteen-year old. The plot is not hard to follow.

The movie was a nice recess. I took pleasure in sharing laughs at the lighthearted film as our two kitties napped in our laps. However, what I found striking, despite the frivolous nature of the movie, was how the knowledge of being royal affected Mia's thoughts, intentions and behavior. After all, a true princess has to act the part, being careful not to embarrass the royal family.

Hmm. "King of kings and Lord of Lords. And he shall reign forever and ever . . . ." The familiar words penned by Handel in *The Messiah* certainly emphasize the royal nature of the Godhead. And if Christ is the Son of the King, then we who are made heirs through him are royalty as well.

We have a duty to act in a way that exalts the King, mindful not to bring embar-rassment. In the movie, the young girl acted without discretion and brought humilia-tion to the throne. However, the wrongdoings were confessed, forgiven and fellow-ship reinstated with the monarchy. It is a similar process for all of us; if we step out of line, we call upon the Throne of Grace to seek forgiveness and restoration.

Position does have its privileges. As prince and princesses, we need no invitation to approach the throne. The inner sanctuary is always open to family. Just be sure to drop the filth and uncleanness at the door.

> *. . . so that, having been justified by his grace, we might become heirs having the hope of eternal life. (Titus 3:7)*

Daily challenge:
Are you acting like a princess or a pauper?

Fathers

Today is Father's Day and unless you live on another planet, my guess is that for several weeks we all knew it was coming. With TV ads and newspaper circulars, each woos the consumer to purchase gifts. Grilling paraphernalia is touted as a good choice, because the assumption is that only men can grill. Actually, in our family, that probably is the case—but that's beside the point.

It does not go unnoticed that the entire concept of fatherhood dates back to the original creation. God is not "god the mother" or "god the sister-in-law" or "god the great aunt." No, he is God the Father whose Incarnate Son is Jesus Christ. No one throughout eternity has provided a more perfect model of a father's love than YHWEH. Christ himself patterned his love for us after the Father's love for the Son. "*As the Father has loved me, so have I loved you. Now remain in my love*" (John 15:9). John reiterates that same kind of love. "*How great is the love the Father has lavished on us, that we should be called children of God! And that is what we are!*" (I John 3:1).

But what else has the Father done out of love? Well, He placed everything in Jesus's hands (John 3:35). What responsibility! Think about what was required of Jesus: leave heaven's throne, take on an earthy body, be raised as fully human but be misunderstood for being simultaneously fully God, be perfect in word and deed, endure great suffering and bear the sins of the world.

Though no earthly son has expectations quite so high, the example rings true. Fathers do require certain things of their sons and disciplines to redirect behavior when necessary. When we were kids, my parents quoted the familiar Proverb *because the LORD disciplines those he loves . . .* right before they pulled out the spanking paddle.

"Yeah, right," we thought when Dad said, "This is going to hurt me more than it hurts you." But now as a parent, I know that he was right.

The discipline that occurs, as harsh as it may seem or as painful as it is to administer, produces obedience that honors the father. If for no other reason than pleasing the father, we should be teaching our sons and daughters to demonstrate their love by obedience. If my father was still alive today, I would thank him for his love and seek forgiveness for causing him pain when having to discipline me.

The father of a righteous man has great joy; he who has a wise son delights in him. (Proverbs 23:24)

Daily challenge:
Obedience is the greatest form of flattery.

One Day at a Time

For some odd, inexplicable reason, an old-time country song kept running through my head as I ran. Recorded by Christy Lane, *One Day at a Time* has an interesting mix of lyrics. Not that I really knew that. No. The only thing strumming on the chords in my brain was the first line of the chorus. I had to Google the song to find the rest of the lyrics. I'll save you the trouble.

I'm only human, I'm just a woman.
Help me believe in what I could be
And all that I am.
Show me the stairway, I have to climb.
Lord for my sake, teach me to take
One day at a time.
Chorus: One day at a time sweet Jesus
That's all I'm asking from you.
Just give me the strength
To do every day what I have to do.
Yesterday's gone, sweet Jesus
And tomorrow may never be mine.
Lord help me today, show me the way
One day at a time.

That "one day at a time" line leapt at me because of another "potential" consulting job—quotes used because some other promising jobs are not yet realized. Though my hopes rise, the contracts haven't materialized.

This afternoon I spoke with a perfusion program director asking me to develop a review course for its students. "Ah," I exclaimed. "Splendid!" Now the wait begins as the director is tasked to find approval and funding. So I wait, running down the road toward home, thinking about how nice the additional income would be. I often fret about the income and "outgo" of our family funds. Shame on me.

Even though the song's a little corny, I would be well-served to live one day at a time, remembering that God promised to be faithful at the supply depot. God watches over birds, numbers the hair on our heads (and in my brush) and even more so, cares and provides for His own.

And my God will meet all your needs according to his glorious riches
in Christ Jesus. (Philippians 4:19)

Daily challenge:
We waste energy trying to live tomorrow before today is over.

Salt and Light

I'm going a little crazy tonight. It's really not that surprising, but the catalyst is that I am going to school tomorrow. Yes. School. About two weeks ago, the principal of the high-school summer-school program in the local county called, asking if I would teach Biology. My initial reaction? "I don't think so!" However, without a signed contract from a promised consulting job, I figured the bird in hand might not be a bad idea. I agreed to take it on.

Keep in mind, the students I am assigned are all repeat offenders. All have flunked the course at least once, some on their second, third, or even fourth try. Self-control and discipline difficulties are not uncommon, so I'm told. There is no curriculum available to me or course syllabus to guide my teaching. All I have to do is figure out how to cram in an entire year of teaching over twenty-six days in about two-and-a-half hours per day. Hence, the crazy factor.

Despite my apprehension and frustration, I'm looking at this opportunity as a challenge—a challenge to motivate and mold the desires of these young people to rise to the occasion. I want to set an example for them. I want to inspire them to work hard. I want to challenge them to set goals and reach them. I want them to achieve in ways previously unknown to them. But even more so, I want to be salt and light.

Although I have taught high school before, it was in a Christian school where I was given the freedom to freely express my faith. I will not have that luxury this time around. So, if I cannot speak outright about my world view, how is it that I can effectively communicate the love of Christ to these kids? Consider Matthew 5:13-16.

> *"You are the salt of the earth. But if the salt loses its saltiness, how can it be made salty again? It is no longer good for anything, except to be thrown out and trampled by men. You are the light of the world. A city on a hill cannot be hidden. Neither do people light a lamp and put it under a bowl. Instead they put it on its stand, and it gives light to everyone in the house. In the same way, let your light shine before men, that they may see your good deeds and praise your Father in heaven."*

Daily challenge:
The way we live speaks louder than words.

Repetition

It was off to the races today. Not the horsey-kind but a race against time. It was zoo-like on this first day of summer school. Kids wandered the hallways not knowing where to go. I guess sign reading is not their strong suit. Some of us were still trying to make copies on a machine that refused to cooperate. I arrived early, but it didn't help. I got earmarked to be the hall monitor, so that pretty much shot completing my tasks before class. The bells were silent (big help that was), making herding kids to class on time difficult. Rosters changed throughout the morning on nearly illegible, handwritten lists. I faced fifteen kids who had all failed Biology at least once and assured them I would do everything possible to help them earn a passing grade.

My strategy is to use a variety of methods, but repetition is the cornerstone. To them, repetition must be a dirty word. They wrinkled their noses with disdain as I explained the process of filling in class notes, re-writing the information in their Biology Journals and writing out vocabulary definitions, prefixes and suffixes. On top of that, they will rehearse all the vocab and word parts every morning with the use of flashcards and follow that up by using online activities to reinforce the information. One kid dared to ask the "why" question. "Well, you've already tried to pass this class your way and it didn't work. Now we'll try it my way." For the moment, that discussion ended.

Repetition is a very effective way to learn. It's not only handy in academia, it is a critical element in raising children and is useful in our own spiritual development. Moses told the people, *"Only be careful, and watch yourselves closely so that you do not forget the things your eyes have seen or let them slip from your heart as long as you live. Teach them to your children and to their children after them"* (Deuteronomy 4:9). He realized that forgetting things was far, far easier than remembering.

Symbols, visual reminders, incessant speaking about the truth and writing things down. All of these are Moses-approved tactics for learning. We ought to try it more often.

"Fix these words of mine in your hearts and minds; tie them as symbols on your hands and bind them on your foreheads. Teach them to your children, talking about them when you sit at home and when you walk along the road, when you lie down and when you get up. Write them on the doorframes of your houses and on your gates." (Deuteronomy 11:18-20)

Daily challenge:
A little repetition never hurt anyone.

Oh Be Careful

I'm having trouble writing tonight. As I drove home from school, I thought of something I wanted to explore, but alas, I forgot what it was. Teaching may be taking more of a toll on me than I thought! Nevertheless, as I often do when I get "stuck," I turn to the books that I find to be rich in truth. Tonight it was Psalm 101. It begins,

I will sing of your love and justice; to you, O LORD, I will sing praise.
I will be careful to lead a blameless life—when will you come to me?
I will walk in my house with blameless heart. (v. 1, 2)

It's interesting that as soon as the writer focuses on the love and justice of the Lord, the proper response is identified. That is, because the Lord is just, I will be careful to lead a blameless life. To call down the justice of the Lord on your head because you have chosen not to live blamelessly is a pretty dim-witted approach to life. On a much smaller scale, it would be like robbing a bank in broad daylight when police officers are standing on the corner watching you act criminally. If you do that, you might as well write your own invitation to some slammer time.

So, having established that the Lord is just and that the reasonable thing to do is to be blameless, how do we do that? Let's rehearse what the writer suggests.

I will set before my eyes no vile thing. The deeds of faithless men I hate; they will not cling to me. Men of perverse heart shall be far from me; I will have nothing to do with evil. Whoever slanders his neighbor in secret, him will I put to silence; whoever has haughty eyes and a proud heart, him will I not endure. My eyes will be on the faithful in the land, that they may dwell with me; he whose walk is blameless will minister to me. No one who practices deceit will dwell in my house; no one who speaks falsely will stand in my presence. Every morning I will put to silence all the wicked in the land; I will cut off every evildoer from the city of the LORD. (v. 3-8)

If I can be simple about this, the well-known children's song seems to be a good paraphrase. *"Oh be careful little ears what you hear . . . Oh be careful little eyes what you see . . . Oh be careful little mouth what you say . . . Oh be careful little hands what you do . . . Oh be careful little feet where you go . . . Oh be careful little mind what you think . . . Oh be careful little heart what you love . . . For the Father up above is looking down in love, so be careful . . .. "*

Daily challenge:
Keep living that song. Your Father is watching.

171

Helping the Poor

Oh, no, I groaned. *Light. Turn green! I hate stopping right next to him.*

"Him" was a long-haired, dirty, grimy homeless-looking guy sitting in the median at the local Walmart. He was tanned a deep brown; I saw him when I was turning in to shop. He was not approaching cars and begging for money, but his intent was clear. A sign read, "Any little thing will help."

Sure enough, on my way out the light was red. I was uncomfortable. I averted my eyes, pretending not to see him when I obviously did. I didn't have the courage to look at him, fearful that our eyes would meet. After all, making eye contact, smiling and leaving him empty-handed didn't seem quite right either. Then I thought to hand him a banana. Strange, huh? But alas, the bananas were in the trunk and out of reach. I had a few dollars with me but could not bring myself to hand them over. I drove away wondering if I failed in my Christian responsibility.

I searched the word *poor* in my online concordance and found nearly two-hundred references. In Old Testament times, God made provision for the poor. Instructions were given to leave grain and produce in the fields to be gleaned by the destitute. The priests had the ability to adjust the required sacrifices for the poor and every seventh year the vineyards and olive groves were turned over to the impoverished.

Multiple verses in Proverbs warn against mocking and ignoring the poor (17:5, 21:13). Furthermore, blessing is promised for the man who shares his food (22:9) and curses for the one *who closes his eyes* (28:27). In fact, ignoring or oppressing the poor actually shows contempt for the Creator (14:31).

Unfortunately, I find myself interjecting a big *but*. But what if the poor guy is poor by his own doing? Maybe he is like the guy in Proverbs 20:13 who is lazy and loves his sleep too much. Does that change things?

Twice in Acts, Cornelius and Joppa were commended for *always doing good and helping the poor* (9:36, 10:31). We don't know if those helped were Believers or not, but back in Deuteronomy, the poor were not to be taken advantage of whether they be *brother* or *alien*. How's that for confusing the issue?

I'm still thinking about whether or not I should have assisted the Walmart beggar. WWJD?

A generous man will himself be blessed, for he shares his food with the poor. (Proverbs 22:9)

Daily challenge:
We are not relieved of our responsibility to help the poor just because we don't understand how it should work.

The Unlovely

After I wrote about the homeless man at Walmart, Anita Moree, who lives as a missionary in France, responded with some extraordinary paragraphs.

"I often take the bus here in Aix. Public transportation is easy here and everyone uses it, from the rich to the poor . . .. I often sit in the front, in a single seat where I can prevent motion sickness and sit alone.

"Last week I got on the bus and saw a new bus driver, new to our route anyway. He was probably about my age (late twenties) with sunglasses and sideburns. I could hear heavy metal music coming from his headphones. The bus ride went as usual, rounding the corners, stop, up the hill, stop, down the hill, stop. But then the doors opened and the would-be passenger hesitated. The bus driver spoke to him in a kind and gentle way, encouraging him to board. The passenger stepped on the bus and found a seat. Neil and I know this man. We call him 'the dirtiest man we have ever seen.' He walks around barefoot and has the absolute filthiest feet we have seen anywhere. He is homeless, poor and perhaps mentally ill; we don't know. We offered him some fresh fruit one day and he said *no*. We don't know his story, but we know what we see: he is dirty, poor and definitely a social outcast who apparently doesn't like bananas.

"I sat and watched the driver. He perplexed me. We came to the center of town and ten or so passengers boarded. The driver called out and motioned to a man still sitting on the bench, another homeless man. The driver made sure that the man knew he was welcome on his bus. I had seen drivers refuse to open doors . . . deny entry, but I had never, ever seen a driver invite a dirty, homeless person on. I sat there watching his kind face and his compassion. He seemed joyful, carefree even. I don't know anything about this bus driver except what I have told you. I don't know if he has a faith in Christ or just a general revelation that convicts him to 'love his neighbor.' As I sat there I was reminded of Micah 6:8: ' . . . *what does the Lord require of you? To act justly, and to love mercy and to walk humbly with your God.*'

"This bus driver acted *justly*; he allowed the homeless on the bus. After all, they have the same right as the rest of us to use public transportation. He loved *mercy*; he didn't just 'allow' the men on, he invited them on, he sought them out. And he walked *humbly*; he did not consider himself any better than the homeless men. He talked to them, welcomed them and served them. I praise God for this living example . . .. "

Daily challenge:
Act justly. Love mercy. Walk humbly with your God.

Risky Business

I'm really not a worry-wart. In fact, I am somewhat of a risk-taker myself—an adventurer even. I don't hesitate to run alone. I descend mountain trails knowing the risks should I fall. I take off on foot in cities on faraway continents and in countries where I don't speak the language. I've run through the Amazon jungle and journeyed the streets of Gaza. Roads in Germany and Belgium and Austria have been traversed and conquered—through busy streets, idyllic countryside and even within castle walls. I seldom give a second thought for my safety, because I try to anticipate potential problems. However, I am now in a different situation and as a mother, it feels very different.

Seth, a month shy of turning seventeen, left a few days ago for California. Once there, he met up with some friends of friends, none of whom we actually knew. Nevertheless, we had done our due diligence by speaking to parents and became more comfortable. But this was not a simple social expedition; that would be far too dull. What he formulated along with his new friend, "Moose," was a six-day, sixty-mile backpacking trip into the wilds of the Immigrant Wilderness. Moose, a seventeen-year old Eagle Scout veteran and photographer apprentice, had made this trip before and was versed in back-country survival. He knew to check in with the park rangers and register their itinerary. And, he had all the right equipment including a heavy-duty bear can, a metal container in which to store food and keep the wildlife from catching the scent of a snack. So, what's the problem? Everything seems to be in order.

The problem is that just like that mother grizzly who wants to protect her cubs, I want to protect mine as well. I'm not overprotective, a mother who constantly shouts out, "Be careful. Not so fast. Not so hard." Still, when Seth shoots across the yard pulling a motorcycle wheelie or flies kamikaze down a steep and rocky trail, I cringe thinking about the "what-if?"s. In fact, the older I get, the more prone I am to think about what could go wrong. I find the feeling of trepidation difficult to suppress.

I know that Seth is held in God's hand regardless of how many cliffs he scales or wild elk he encounters. I pray that he will have discretion in what he attempts, for *Discretion will protect you, and understanding will guard you* (Proverbs 2:11).

The LORD will keep [him] from all harm—he will watch over [his] life; the LORD will watch over [his] coming and going both now and forevermore. (Psalm 121:7-8)

Daily challenge:
Let God the Father do your "mothering".

Be Careful what You Say

The phone rang a few weeks ago and Gary, being the closest one, picked it up. The voice at the other end of the line stumbled over our name. Gary's tone became irritated, assuming it to be another telemarketer. But just in time, the caller uttered something that told Gary this was not an attempt to sell us a warranty on a car we did not own. Rather, it was a person returning a phone call to me who just happened to have a foreign accent and trouble with our name. I was concerned that the caller think Gary rude and unkind for the way he answered the phone. I should have known better. Today, I had to eat crow.

I was driving the standard-shift truck on narrow country roads when my cell phone rang. Fumbling to flip it open, I still answered with a cheerful "hello." But, in the next moment, my cheerfulness turned to annoyance. The voice on the other end spoke with a foreign accent and started with a faltering, "Hello, are you Re-bee-kah Treet-e- poe?" I assumed he was someone I didn't need to talk to.

"Yes, I'm Rebekah. But, I'm driving now and if this isn't an emergency, I am not going to take this call," I retorted.

"Oh, Okay. I'll have to call back later." I hung up and refocused my attention to the road.

About thirty minutes later my phone rang again. I immediately recognized the caller. It was the same man. "Are you still driving?" I wasn't. But my heart skipped a beat when I realized this was a customer of mine. *Oh, no!* I started chewing on that awful humble pie as I made my profuse apologies to him and went on to answer his questions. He was an understanding gentleman who laughed it off when I fessed up to my wrong assumption and less-then-cordial communication.

Although we can try to rationalize speaking like that when we feel justified, we can never be in the right. I was guilty! God has not instructed us to speak kindly only when we feel like it. We are expected to represent Christ in every way, every day, including how we converse with one another. I cringe to think that this fellow may turn to his co-worker and state, "Man, is she a piece of work!"

I repent and pray that God's grace—and this man's forgiveness—will cover my thoughtless action.

He who guards his mouth and his tongue keeps himself from calamity. (Proverbs 21:23)

Daily challenge:
Be careful what you say and how you say it.

Exam Time

I'm excited about teaching tomorrow. My students will take their first exam. I sense some are at least curious to be taking the test, anxious to see if they can pass. Most think of themselves as stupid; my second class told me as much just the other day. Admittedly, a few may not be the brightest tacks in the drawer but all of them are capable of passing if they do the required work. What excites me, however, is the feeling that some of these kids are primed for a taste of victory. I have put them to the task with structure, repetition and drill and they are doing well. I hope they will be encouraged when they complete the test and click the final "submit" button.

I searched the Scripture about this idea of testing. Many times throughout the Old and New Testaments, the Lord "tested" various people. Abraham, the nation of Israel, David, Job and the list is long, were all tested. The testing was to determine faithfulness, perseverance, and obedience. And testing was used as a means to measure up to a set standard. I Chronicles 29:17 says, *"I know, my God, that you test the heart and are pleased with integrity."* Then Moses wrote, *"Remember how the LORD your God led you all the way in the desert these forty years, to humble you and to test you in order to know what was in your heart, whether or not you would keep his commands"* (Deuteronomy 8:2).

But what if we turn the tables? What if my students decided they were going to put me to the test? Would it be appropriate to so question the instructor's knowledge that her position and authority were suspect? Probably not. Although the human analogy breaks down at some point, we have to consider the appropriateness of us testing God. We do it all the time, you know. "If you are really God, you'll do (blank) for me." Shame on us.

What audacity to test God! Moses tells us, *"Do not test the LORD your God"* (Deuteronomy 6:16). David identifies testing God as a sign of rebellion (Psalm 78:56). Christ himself quoted Scripture twice saying, " . . . *'Do not put the Lord your God to the test'"* (Matthew 4:7, Luke 4:12).

Testing is a one-way street; the position of tester reserved for those in authority. And you know what? We aren't that. Rather, we are the God-appointed test-takers.

" . . . do not be afraid. God has come to test you, so that the fear of God will be with you to keep you from sinning." (Exodus 20:20)

Daily challenge:
Embrace the test.

Aptly Spoken Word

Can you think back to when someone said just the right thing at the right time? Perhaps it was when you were feeling fat and ugly or stupid or depressed or just plain unappreciated. All of a sudden, an encouraging word came out of nowhere and those oppressive feelings vanished like the darkness at sun's rising. I remember well-timed encouragements from Mother before a big test or after an awkward fall from the balance beam. My dad could soothe my soul just by kissing me good night, saying "I love you" and putting on my favorite music.

Tonight I am tasked with writing progress reports for my students. These reports must be turned in tomorrow to be mailed to parents. Based on their history of failure, I imagine that progress reports have not always been a welcomed piece of mail. I want to change that.

I took great care in writing something personal on the forms. At this late hour, it would have been easy to simply pen a checkmark in the appropriate boxes. But, how would something so impersonal help them? I wrote truthful notes to the parents about their children—not only their newly passing grades but adjectives that describe their character, attitude or diligent classroom efforts. In a few cases, I had to try hard to find something positive but nevertheless, I discovered at least one thing good to say about each child.

I'm pretty sure that the kids, whether they admit it or not, will be pleased when they read the comments. And I trust that their pleasure will result in continued good efforts. But I'm hoping that their parents will be equally proud. I trust the encouragement will serve to open channels between parent and child that may have been shut down as past failures accumulated like dust bunnies under a bed.

A few days ago, we were thinking about the misuse of our tongues and the calamity we stir up by thoughtless speech. But what we are talking about now is just the opposite. A kind word, a positive remark, an encouraging expression is beneficial not only to the recipient but to the deliverer of the word. The wise King Solomon said, *A man finds joy in giving an apt reply— and how good is a timely word!* (Proverbs 15:23)

For as many "apples of gold" we give away to acquaintances, we sometimes forget to extend the same graciousness to our own family. I want my own children to look back on their years at home as a time when words were used to lift up rather than beat down, to encourage rather than deprecate, to hearten rather than disparage.

A word aptly spoken is like apples of gold in settings of silver. (Proverbs 25:11)

Daily challenge:
There are few "neutral" words. Choose those that bring joy and refreshment.

More on Words

As I handed out the adjusted grades earned on their first test, I saw amazement in their eyes. For kids who had miserably failed Biology during the regular school year, the A's, B's and solid C's they earned were far more than a novelty. Moving through the various activities of the morning, their interest seemed higher than normal.

Once we hit the computer lab, I announced that I would allow them to read what I had written on the progress reports before turning them in to be mailed. Immediately, they filed past my desk like a troop of little ants on the scent of something good. Their countenances changed as they read the words I had chosen; they stood straighter and had heads held high.

One tough country boy lingered by my desk. He had gotten straight F's during the year and proudly informed his father last night of his score. "I'm proud of you, son," was Dad's response. His eyes glistened with a hint of joyful tears as he reported this. He reread his report several times before handing it back.

Another student, a tall, slender girl who had studied hard, broke into a huge grin, thankful that her grandmother would get some good news for once. The scene was repeated over and over again.

And then came "John." He captured my attention the first day with his parole ankle bracelet. He was polite and cooperative but had obviously run into previous trouble. John had already been told he had earned the highest grade in the class and had read my report. The former failing student was very pleased. But this time, he approached bearing concerns for his mother, who had just received a diagnosis. "Is it fatal?" he asked with a deep level of concern. He seemed relieved by what I told him. Then he quietly added, "I'm going to be a father."

Oh. I shuddered and suddenly realized that God had just given me my assignment. My encouragement produced an opportunity to serve. The words opened the door; my actions will show the way.

Religion that God our Father accepts as pure and faultless is this: to look after orphans and widows in their distress and to keep oneself from being polluted by the world. (James 1:27)

Daily challenge:
Encouragement leads to service opportunities.

New Every Day

We have two cats that are in a state of perpetual amazement. It all started when we consented to kitty-sit four of them, all about six-weeks old. They were tiny little fur balls who could be held at once in folded arms. They slept in a big pile in a crevice behind Seth's bed and when they awoke, it was non-stop curious play. They ran from room to room exploring, chasing each other, tackling, wrestling and jumping in wild abandonment. It surprised us that four creatures so tiny could make such a commotion when playing upstairs; downstairs it sounded like a herd of wild ponies.

Now the kittens have grown into adolescent cats and their numbers reduced from four to two. We had only intended on keeping one, but it just didn't seem right to have one without a playmate. So, two it is. They act like part kitten and part teenager. Boy, can they sleep! But, when they awake, watch out. Run here, run there. Now up on the sofa, down the other side, under the table, up on the chairs, back to the couch and around the loop of hallway. They are a riot to watch as they literally chase their own tails and perform flying tackles.

However, the time that excites them most is the morning. By the time someone gets up, they have launched paws first into rambunctious play in the bathroom where they spend the night, leaping off the linen chest, pulling down towels and skidding around on the bath mat. Without fail, hand on doorknob and door pushed open, there they are. Quickly glancing upward, they tear off only to return moments later, much like Lassie returning to Timmy, to receive the morning greeting they think they deserve. Morning obviously excites them.

Oddly, I am reminded of Lamentations. Remember, most scholars believe the prophet Jeremiah wrote the book after he saw the Babylonians destroy Jerusalem, plundering the city and burning to the ground the fortress that had stood for four-hundred years. The year was probably somewhere between 586 and 575 B.C. and the prophet was lamenting Israel's continuous sin. Nevertheless, he kept the faith . . . and his enthusiasm for each new morning.

> *Yet this I call to mind and therefore I have hope: Because of the LORD's great love we are not consumed, for his compassions never fail. They are new every morning; great is your faithfulness. (Lamentations 3:22, 23)*

Daily challenge:
Perhaps we would be more enthusiastic as we crawl from bed
if we remembered that God's unfailing love renews each day.

Frustration

This morning a friend became so frustrated that it was almost laughable. Deb agreed to meet me for a long run on trails. I arrived at the spot surprised that she was not there. She had missed the road. Despite a flip turn, she still doubted the route. Nothing looked familiar. Eventually, she found me.

Next, she donned a new hydration pack. *Ugh.* The bite valve seemed to be defective. She commiserated about having to send it back and was irritated at the thought of having to pull the valve off the tubing in order to drink—a drink that turned out to be plain water. I had handed electrolyte powder to her, but in her state of mind, she forgot to add it to the water. Not a good thing on a day with temps heading into the 90s.

Twenty minutes into our run, both heels revolted. This was the fourth, and incidentally, the last time, she wore those shoes, hoping they would break in. Not so. Deep ugly blisters erupted on the backs of both heels. We tried using adhesive bandage strips, but they offered little comfort. To make matters worse, we got into thick patches of stinging nettle. Oh, the pain!

Once we stopped climbing, we hoped her heel pain would subside. Therefore, to avoid a five-mile climb back to the car, we decided to drop off the mountain another way. That plan was thwarted as well. Weeds chest-high made running impossible. We retraced our steps, again having to deal with the nettle. Despite her valiant effort, she could run no faster than a medium-speed tortoise. We finally made it back to the car and called it a day. To say the least, she was frustrated.

We normally see frustration as a bad thing. However, if God is the one who is doing the frustrating, it's a good thing. The story of Nehemiah and the rebuilding of Jerusalem's walls comes to mind. Key to his success was the interference play that God ran. *When our enemies heard that we were aware of their plot and that God had frustrated it, we all returned to the wall, each to his own work* (Nehemiah 4:15).

You see, God is very good at subverting the works of evil people in order that His own purpose be accomplished. There is no greater way to make people lose heart than to throw frustration their way. So, be encouraged and know that God's frustrating of individuals is for the protection of His own people.

The LORD watches over the alien and sustains the fatherless and
the widow, but he frustrates the ways of the wicked. (Psalm 146:9)

Daily challenge:
Frustration occurs when we lose sight of God's perspective.

Welcome Home

Seth is coming home tomorrow. To tell you the truth, he isn't real excited about it. Our youngest son, an ambitious, nearly seventeen-year old who knows no fear nor stranger, has been wandering around California for about two weeks. He and a pal ventured into the back country, caught fish in mountain lakes and slept in the cold, fresh mountain air at 10,000 feet. Of course, the memory cards are filled with a thousand pictures. There were also nights in the civilized world in pristine homes perched atop hills overlooking the city below. No chores, no responsibility, no work but all play. Yeah, I guess I would be hesitant to come home as well.

Though he may be dreading coming home, I, on the other had, look forward to having him back—and not just for the work he'll do. I enjoy his wit and perspective on life. I love his sense of humor and how he can make me laugh. Our family doesn't seem complete with his room left silent and place at the table empty.

Many Believers speak of being excited at the prospect of Christ's return. I intellectually know it will happen. And yet, I can't wrap my arms around that truth. It seems so foreign. I know heaven will be far better than what we have on earth, but despite that, I feel myself clinging to my life here. I love my family, my friends, the few minutes I get to spend in the pool on a summer day and runs in the mountains. I feel guilty for not "feeling" more excited about His return.

I suspect that Christ understands our inability to fully understand. Maybe that's why we have been given the emotions associated with the expectant return of our own loved ones. Maybe that's the only way we can understand God's anticipation for us to "come home."

I'm preparing for Seth's return. We'll have a decent meal tomorrow night and his bedroom will be tidied and bed turned down. Likewise, we are told in Scripture that wonderful preparations are being made for us in Heaven. We may not understand it all, but we can be thankful that the love of the Father is so great that He anticipates our homecoming.

"Do not let your hearts be troubled. Trust in God; trust also in me. In my Father's house are many rooms; if it were not so, I would have told you. I am going there to prepare a place for you. And if I go and prepare a place for you, I will come back and take you to be with me that you also may be where I am. You know the way to the place where I am going." (John 14:1-4)

Daily challenge:
Welcome home those who leave.

A Test with Answers

Every night, I find myself struggling with ideas on how to make sure the kids I'm teaching actually learn what they are supposed to know. With the second test looming, I have decided to take a slightly different approach. For the first test, they were told what would be on it. Most of the kids did well, but I think they can do better. Besides, I want to give the kids who are at the bottom of the barrel a chance for redemption.

Tomorrow I will hand them a copy of the test and the answers. However, both the questions and the answers will be randomized by the computer when they take the real test. I think this is more than fair and should reward the students who prepare.

Running down the road on my evening jaunt, I got to thinking about these kids and the choices I was making regarding testing. It really isn't far off of what God does with us. Testing is a part of life, for it encourages growth and makes us stronger. We know that temptation, persecution, ridicule, the challenge of doing what we know is right, taming the tongue and properly loving another will be a part of those tests. We have no idea when or in what order these tests will be thrust upon us. But, the beautiful part is that, just like my students, we have been given the answers ahead of time. We are well-equipped to pass the test if we just put in the effort to learn the lessons.

Our preparation to be God's test-takers is complete when we remember His promises. We know the righteous man cannot be shaken (Psalm 55:22). We are certain God is the source of all the wisdom we will ever need (James 1:5). We recognize that God is our rock, our fortress, our strength (Psalm 18:2). God promises that we will never be tempted beyond what we can bear (I Corinthians 10:13). We are convinced God provides sufficient grace in the time of need (II Corinthians 12:9). The Lord hears and delivers us from our fears (Psalm 34:4). We are persuaded that we can overcome evil with good (Roman 12:21). And we know beyond a shadow of a doubt that

> . . . *because of his great love for us, God, who is rich in mercy, made us alive with Christ even when we were dead in transgressions—it is by grace you have been saved. (Ephesians 2:4, 5)*

Daily challenge:
We may not know the order or timing of the tests, but we can be confident that the answers are found in Christ.

A Welcome Break

After just two weeks of teaching summer school, I anticipate tomorrow like a kid eagerly awaits Christmas morn. My students will take a test and I'm not introducing any new material. Instead, we'll have a light day punctuated with snacks I made to celebrate their hard work. Translation? No preparation! *Yahoo!*

When I agreed to teach, I assumed there would be a syllabus and plans for how to cram an entire year of Biology into five short weeks. I assumed wrong. There was nothing other than a big ol' teacher's edition that weighs at least ninety-two pounds. Hence, I spend every waking hour preparing for the next day—about four to five hours per night. This leaves precious little time for anything else. Many nights I am still working away at midnight, only to get up before dawn to finish up before heading off. I am exhausted, mentally and physically, with too much to do and too little time to do it.

Though my eyes are blurred with fatigue, today I felt the burden of my responsibilities fall from my shoulders—if only a transient reprieve. I took care of some desk work, put a chicken in the oven and headed out the door for a run. After supper I took on yard work, tidied up, did some wash and felt ecstatic not to have to pull out that paperweight of a textbook from my bag. I felt light and lively and almost like a "normal" person spending a relaxing evening at home.

I'm sure that everyone reading this has a life full of pressures and responsibilities. Sometimes life can get so busy, so crowded, that it makes us want to draw the curtains, crawl into bed and stay there indefinitely. But alas, we cannot. We sigh, inhale deeply and push on, feeling as though we may collapse at any moment.

Jesus understands. He knew what it was like to live life on this planet. Although sinless, He tired and grew weary as we do. He required food and water and needed time alone to pray. Yes, He knew better than anyone what it was to carry the burdens of the entire world on His sacrificial shoulders. Yet He says to us:

> *"Come to me, all you who are weary and burdened, and I will give you rest. Take my yoke upon you and learn from me, for I am gentle and humble in heart, and you will find rest for your souls. For my yoke is easy and my burden is light." (Matthew 11:28-30)*

Daily challenge:
God's yoke does not bind; it releases tension and carries the load.

An Anniversary

Thirty-one is a good number—not the "perfect" number like seven nor a nice, round number like fifty. It doesn't represent a milestone or the age one must be to become President. But it does represent the years spent with one man—my husband.

Neither of us qualifies as a "hopeless romantic." We are not that couple who gush drippy sentiments and walk hand-in-hand through the park. Neither are we overly schmaltzy about events—even the big holidays. We don't have high expectations for gifts, lavish or simple. In fact, we'll be doing chores tonight rather than eating a high-priced meal. It isn't that we love each other less than other couples who do these things. I suppose we have just gotten used to a simple, practical approach.

With that said, I pay tribute to my husband. I fell in love with him immediately. I was a college freshman when my eyes first rested on his slender build. With that dark hair and '70s sideburns, he strutted into the gym and up to the area where I was on a balance beam. I had secretly put this soccer player, affectionately named "Toes," on my "want-to-meet" list. When he asked me out for a trip to Young's dairy the Monday before Thanksgiving break, I nearly fainted. However, after just one date we decided to get married. I never expected it; that love-at-first-sight thing seemed so lame. But it was real. We were engaged that summer and married the next. I have no regrets.

Gary is a wonderful husband and father. He is a Christian man and gifted teacher. He is kind and thoughtful. When I speak, he stops what he is doing and looks at me, engaged in our conversation. He respects me and is not demanding, even in the most intimate situations. He is not harsh. He is considerate of my workload, duties and responsibilities. He is trusting and gracious. He handles the finances. He is industrious and honest and has a good reputation among his peers. He is wise, giving good counsel. He readily forgives and refuses to hold my offenses against me. He is an example to his children and models Christ in our home.

We have changed over the years. He has a little less hair; I have a lot more gray. Neither of us has the same body. We've had great moments and times more difficult than we could have ever predicted. Yet the love we had as college students is still strong. I can't imagine life without him. He is my love—the object of my affection.

> *. . . there will be heard once more the sounds of joy and gladness, the voices of bride and bridegroom, and the voices of those who bring thank offerings to the house of the LORD, saying, "Give thanks to the LORD Almighty, for the LORD is good; his love endures forever." (Jeremiah 33:12)*

Daily challenge:
Treat your spouse like you did when you first dated.

My Helper

Divide and conquer. That's what our family did today. No lollygagging or idling away the hours. The do-list was long. Gary laid claim to Seth and they went out to the "tunnel" to work on replacing a car air conditioner. The tunnel is a wide and very long, half-dome building—open at both ends. An ever-present breeze blowing from end to end makes the working conditions tolerable on a very hot and sunny day.

I was left with Caleb as my sidekick. Not that I minded; Caleb and I have always gotten along and work well together. After brainstorming another project by the pool, we headed off to the home-improvement store to purchase the necessary supplies. I wanted to make a permanent, two-tiered serving table and a pedestal to hold the insulated, five-gallon spigoted cooler. The three holes for the supports were already dug. We poured concrete, measured, cut and screwed together the pieces. At day's end, we proudly surveyed our handiwork.

While I am delighted with the result, I am just as satisfied with spending the day with my oldest son. Without him, parts of the job would have been very difficult for me on my own. And, the idea of having a helper appeals to me. Not only does it reduce the work load on each individual, it can be a very pleasant social time, chatting casually about anything and everything.

I began thinking about helpers. In human terms, we usually employ a helper when our own skills and abilities are insufficient. Or, we hire a helper simply because we do not have the time or energy to accomplish all that needs attention. But in searching the Scripture, I find that our self-sufficient God is oft referred to as a *helper. Hmm . . .* interesting. God is not the "helpee." We are the ones in need of assistance because of our own shortcomings.

I looked forward to today because I was confident that Caleb's help would make the day go faster and that we would reach our goal more efficiently. Likewise, we can be confident that with God as our Helper, nothing can overtake us.

So we say with confidence, "The Lord is my helper; I will not be afraid. What can man do to me?" (Hebrews 13:6)

Daily challenge:
How much better can it get when the Lord of the Universe
picks up the shovel beside you?

Freedom

Let freedom ring! All the morning talk shows displayed massive amounts of red, white and blue—broadcasting segments on hot-dog grilling and gleeful tips for a fun-filled holiday. Indeed the day started off like a holiday should; Gary and I slept in until 8:15 and I enjoyed a rare cream-filled donut and coffee. As I downed my breakfast treat, I watched a segment on the sole survivor from World War I. This man, now at the age of 107, spoke of duty, country and sacrifice in the name of freedom. These sentiments came honestly; his great-great-grandfather fought for freedom in the Revolutionary War. In reality, the pursuit of freedom has been the driving force behind every just war.

Many today understand freedom to be a "right" to do anything anytime. They don't seem to understand that freedom comes only when one submits to certain limitations.

Think about it like this. Personify a train. Mr. Train decides he wants to chug his way to the next city. However, he doesn't want to follow the tracks through the mountains. A river run is more scenic. So, he leaves the track, thinking all the while that his way is better and more to his liking. Problem is, once he gets off the track, he is stuck. He sinks into the ground as momentum is lost and the heavy train wheels get mired in the muck. Sure, he exerted his "right", but it took him nowhere. Had the train submitted to the "authority" of the track, he would have been free to follow the tracks anywhere.

A lot of us use *"everything is permissible"* (I Corinthians 10:23) as a license to do as we please without giving heed to the rest of the verse: . . . *but not everything is beneficial.*

Truly, we are free in Christ because the bondage of sin has been broken. But true freedom is a result of adhering to God's law—not an inalienable right to behave outside of it.

You, my brothers, were called to be free. But do not use your freedom to indulge the sinful nature; rather, serve one another in love. (Galatians 5:13)

Daily challenge:
Freedom is more about obedience and submission, loyalty and duty, than a passport to selfish ambition.

Footprints

Today I ran alone, as I most often do. I suppose to most outsiders, a woman solo in the forest may not be the smartest move in the world. However, I've been doing it for so long that even my husband seems fairly comfortable with the idea. Although he prefers I run with a buddy, he doesn't try to dissuade me from going except in the most extreme weather. He knows I have to train if I want to race. Nevertheless, with a long time by myself, I occasionally think through some "what-if?"s.

Today was no exception. I always tell Gary what my intended route will be and how long I think it will take to complete the distance. That way, if I don't show up when I'm supposed to, he can start the search. I try not to divert from the plan just in case something happens. But today I changed my course mid-run and had to put a plan into action.

Since the mountains saw rain last night, there was a lot of mud. From time to time I purposely ran through the gooey mess, noticing that my footprints were the only ones out there. With a distinct tread pattern on my shoes, it would not be difficult to follow me. At trail junctions, I used sticks to form arrows pointing in the direction I went. Again, this was all "just in case."

As I went through these simple maneuvers, I considered this whole idea of foot-steps. There is a familiar poem about "footprints in the sand" that can be found on wall plaques and greeting cards. But I was thinking of it in a different context: If some-one were to follow my daily footprints, to what or who would they lead? Surely, if we go back to my literal footprints in the mud, anyone following behind could easily see if I was still on course or if I took a wrong turn. Likewise, if someone is trying to follow my spiritual footsteps, would they be led to the feet of Jesus or become hopelessly lost along the way?

It's a big responsibility to have someone follow you. So be careful where you go.

Direct my footsteps according to your word; let no sin rule over me.
(Psalm 119:133)

Daily challenge:
Where are your footprints headed?

"P.S.: I Love You"

"There a lake formed yet?" my son queried as the movie credits rolled.
"Almost. Perhaps a small pond," I sniffled back. I was glad it was dark. I must have looked pitiful, all puffy-eyed and wearied from the emotional rollercoaster.

I hadn't cried that much in a long time. We had a family movie night watching "P.S.: I Love You." The story unfurled. Although I knew it was a "chick flick," I didn't know it was such a tear-jerker.

The premise of the story centered around a madly-in-love couple whose rough edges caused periodic problems. Their story began in Ireland, where they met and married. Back in New York, they had a mostly wonderful life, Gerry the happy-go-lucky singing Irishman and hopeless romantic. However, within five minutes of the movie's beginning, the scene cuts to a funeral. Gerry had died. *Bummer.*

Well, good ol' Gerry must have had some notice that his brain tumor was killing him. He prearranged letters to be sent to his wife long after he was in the grave. Each one spoke to her heart, guiding her transition into a new phase of living. All closed with, "P.S.: I love you." I sniffled as she struggled through the painful journey until the last letter arrived. But the last line of the last letter? "P.S.: I'll always love you." Not even death could not extinguish his love for her.

Sob. Sob. Sob. It was so bittersweet. I thought about letters that my mom wrote to my dad after he died. She said it was cathartic to pen her deepest emotions. I suppose the journals contain ordinary events alongside profound words. She wanted to hold onto every last vestige of a wonderful married life, understanding that with time, those sweet memories would fade. It was her way of saying, "P.S.: I love you."

I hear God whispering the same thing to us through every stage, every circumstance. When we sin and He hears our confession He faithfully proclaims, "P.S.: I love you." When we are weak and tired, He picks us up and carrying us in His arms utters, "P.S.: I love you." When the enemy engages us in battle, He meets us where we are and gives us courage with "P.S.: I love you." And when we draw our final breaths, He greets us at Heaven's gate. "P.S.: I have always loved you."

There simply is no greater love.

The LORD appeared to us in the past, saying: "I have loved you with an everlasting love; I have drawn you with loving-kindness." (Jeremiah 31:3)

Daily challenge:
Make "P.S.: I love you" your motto.

The Storm

A loud rumble woke me from sleep. I thought Seth, whose room is above ours, was doing a major revamp of his room, sliding his two beds across the bare wood floors. But a flash of brilliant light through the blinds alerted me that a storm had suddenly descended. For a time, the thunder was loud and rain torrential. But I don't think the storm lasted too long. I soon fell back into cherished sleep, content that we were warm, dry and cozy in our old farmhouse.

This time of year storms come out of nowhere. However, technology has done wonders in helping us be more prepared. Gary rode his motorcycle into work yesterday, ready for a long day. His plans changed, nonetheless, when he pulled up the local weather on his computer. Several strong storm cells were moving in. With the storm speed and direction posted, he headed home early to avoid getting drenched. Good thing he did. The predicted storms hit right on cue.

It's comforting to know that we can identify an approaching storm and take action. Unfortunately, we don't always have that luxury when the storms of life approach. Of course, if we willfully sail into the dark and churning seas, we have no right to complain about being buffeted; we brought that on ourselves. But sometimes a storm appears unexpectedly. In those instances, we need only to hurry, like King David did, *to my place of shelter, far from the tempest and storm* (Psalm 55:8).

A Shelter in the Time of Storm, a hymn penned in the 1880s, was a favorite among fishermen along England's north coast, bringing them comfort when at sea. But had they been in the desert rather than the sea, the song could still be sung.

God is faithful to protect—any time, any place.

Then the LORD will create over all of Mount Zion and over those who assemble there a cloud of smoke by day and a glow of flaming fire by night; over all the glory will be a canopy. It will be a shelter and shade from the heat of the day, and a refuge and hiding place from the storm and rain. (Isaiah 4:5, 6)

Daily challenge:
No matter where you are, God has you covered. Run to Him for shelter.

In the Beginning

In the beginning God . . ..
I find it amazing that I can't say these words in the public school. That wouldn't be very "scientific"—you know, too much religious tone to be politically correct in a community forum.

For the next several days, I will be presenting the chapters on evolution to my summer-school students. When I was first asked to teach, I told the principal up front that I would teach evolution but as a theory, not a fact. "Do you have a problem with that?" I bluntly asked. The startled response was somewhat hesitant, but I was told that my approach was acceptable.

The textbook we use is blatantly evolutionary. Although there are early references to evolution being a theory, repeated and frequent statements communicate no doubt about its assumed validity. Therefore, helping kids discern verifiable fact from conclusions based on a particular presuppositional bias is my new goal in life.

When I taught high school many years ago, I taught in a Christian school where I had an obvious freedom to present a Biblical creation position. However, it was important to spend the first six weeks covering all the theories pertaining to the origins of the universe and life. I wanted to equip my students with the knowledge to make sound decisions based on facts, logic and the recognition of their own bias. That, in essence, is the crux of education.

Whether an evolutionist, an ardent Creationist or a supporter of the increasingly popular Intelligent Design model, all are faith based. No one was there in the beginning to see for themselves what transpired and no model has ever been validated within laboratory walls. The same set of data will be perceived differently by each group. Objectivity is hard to come by. A former boss told his employee that I was mentally ill and should be placed in a mental hospital. Why? Simply because I did not believe in evolution.

I am challenged to present an honest and accurate picture of the various models of the "beginnings" despite my admitted bias. I trust that the students will begin to see the complexity and intricacy of life around them in light of random chance or purposeful design. Perhaps one of these kids will get a glimpse of the Creator.

For since the creation of the world God's invisible qualities—his eternal power and divine nature—have been clearly seen, being understood from what has been made, so that men are without excuse. (Romans 1:20)

Daily challenge:
Find the Creator in the Creation.

It's All in the Timing

Years ago I lectured about implementing quality systems into the clinical perfusion arena. In order to prepare myself to instruct others, I did a tremendous amount of research. Along the way, I discovered that the majority of the business world had shifted away from stockpiling to a "just-in-time" philosophy. This technique requires precise planning and exactness in purchasing and shipping and eliminates storerooms piled high with unused supplies. When it works well, everyone's happy. But if there's a bump in the road, the customer suffers and someone's head probably rolls.

I thought about this "just-in-time" idea as I was running. I often use my run time to figure out what I am going to write about. At times, the canvas is blank and I am at a loss. "God, you gotta give me something here. Teach me. Lay something—anything—on my heart." And just in time, a thought comes and God proves Himself faithful once again.

I began to wonder about how God views time. If you think about it, God is eternal and does not have to operate within a time constraint. And yet, when He created the earth complete with the rising up and going down of the sun, He also created time—days, weeks and years. This was for our benefit, not His.

From the opening pages of Genesis, times were given for peoples' benefit. Sarah was told that at that time next year she would be holding a baby boy. Designated worship times were given. Nehemiah set times for sacrifices to be brought to the temple. David told us that God will hear and answer us in the *time of his favor.* Ecclesiastes 7:14 instructs us that *When times are good, be happy; but when times are bad, consider: God has made the one as well as the other.* Likewise, we know that *He has made everything beautiful in its time. He has also set eternity in the hearts of men; yet they cannot fathom what God has done from beginning to end.* (Ecclesiastes 3:11)

Yes, there are times of repentance (Acts 3:19) and fulfilled promises (Acts 7:17). We find times of favor and times of judgment. But most importantly, God saves us in His impeccable timing.

> So also, when we were children, we were in slavery under the basic
> principles of the world. But when the time had fully come, God sent
> his Son, born of a woman, born under law, to redeem those under
> law, that we might receive the full rights of sons. (Galatians 4:4)

Daily challenge:
We only need to worry about God's timing. Ours is of little consequence.

Hair

The state of the hair boasts incredible power. A good hair day makes you feel beautiful and secure. But a bad hair day? *Whoa.* It can be worse than awful. The earth tilts off its axis, the skies darken, an eerie wind whips through the trees and you loathe the thought of leaving the bathroom, let alone the house. How can such a little thing hugely impact our attitude?

I've been contemplating a hairstyle change. At the moment, my hair is long. I love feeling my ponytail rhythmically swish as I run. But when I inspect my long face in the mirror, I see an aging face. The skin along my jaw line is getting saggy and my eyes look tired. So, what's a girl to do? Answer: Get bangs to cover it up. Problem solved.

When I think of hair, I remember my dad and laugh. He often joked, "God only made a few perfect heads—the rest he put hair on." At that, he would throw back his own mostly bald head save a few gray hairs, and heartily laugh. Then, he quoted Proverbs 16:31. *Gray hair is a crown of splendor; it is attained by a righteous life.* Good thing he told me that. I inherited the premature-gray gene from both parents, starting the process when I was seventeen years old. If it were not for a little help from Clairol, I would be looking pretty righteous by now.

As much as we joke—or obsess—about hair, there is some importance placed on it. The Levitical priests were not to cut their hair, nor were they supposed to allow it to become unkempt. Did they comply? Probably—the penalty was death (Leviticus 10:6). *Yikes!*

On the flip side, Absalom had such great hair that he had to cut it from time to time because it was too heavy to carry around. In fact, he sold the stuff. Solomon gets all gushy about his lover's hair: *How beautiful you are, my darling! Oh, how beautiful! Your eyes behind your veil are doves. Your hair is like a flock of goats descending from Mount Gilead* (Song of Solomon 4:1). I'm not sure I see the connection between beauty and a herd of stinky goats but . . . whatever. And then we have Mary who wiped the feet of Jesus with her own hair, a picture of beautiful servanthood.

No matter what kind of hair we have, rest assured God values each and every one. Use it for His glory.

"Indeed, the very hairs of your head are all numbered. Don't be afraid; you are worth more than many sparrows." (Luke 12:7)

Daily challenge:
Even our hair reminds us of God's care.

Motorbike Greetings

I planned to help a friend prepare for a big move. With the distance of thirty-five miles between our homes and gas at four-dollars a gallon, I opted to mount my two-wheeled steed and zoom right on over. On a beautiful summer day, it's hard to ignore the call of the open road.

On my motorcycle, I like to feel the breeze, sense the temperature differences and smell the wildflowers as I motor past. But I also enjoy an unspoken courtesy of motorcycle riders.

No matter what kind of bike you ride, it's always the same. As a rider approaches from the opposite direction, the person's left arm extends obliquely downward, hand open, as if to say, "Hi there. I'm cool and so are you." I like the greeting but keep forgetting the decidedly male-inspired acknowledgement. Me? I raise my left arm obliquely upward, elbow bent, and wave like a princess going to the prom. It probably isn't cool to the Harley rider. But I wave nonetheless, knowing they don't know who I am under my pink and purple helmet.

This idea of greeting members of your crowd is intriguing. Bikers have that minimalist hand wave. Surfers give the hang ten sign. Runners nod at each other and secret club kids have special handshakes, each an acknowledgment of common ground.

Greet one another with a holy kiss (Romans 16:16). Now, that's a grand way to say *hello*. Not only was this instruction given in Romans, it was repeated in four other Epistles. Is the writer trying to get everyone in trouble with their spouses? I doubt it. In context, the kissing was the cheek-to-cheek pecks of man to man and woman to woman. It was actually a selfless extension of graciousness and humility. It said, "I care about you. I am so glad to see you . . . I love ya, man."

It's easy to get so wrapped up in our hectic lives that we fail to extend simple courtesies. What would happen if we took an extra nanosecond to make eye contact and utter something meaningful to a neighbor? Would it make a difference if we spoke to those "invisible" members of society—the homeless guy on the street corner, the guy stocking the shelves at Walmart, or the girl wielding a broom at the local diner?

Jesus took time to address people. He did not rush by, ignoring them. He actively engaged them in conversation. He looked them in the eye. He cared enough to listen. Wanna be like Jesus? Do the same.

I hope to see you soon, and we will talk face to face. Peace to you. The friends here send their greetings. Greet the friends there by name. (III John 1:14)

Daily challenge:
Don't be disengaged. Engage with others.

Moving

Moving. You can look at it two ways—it's either a royal pain in the buttocks or an opportunity of a lifetime. There isn't a lot of middle ground.

This is the weekend for our friends and their brood of seven kids to move east a county or two. Bobbie has prepared well and the first day went off without a hitch. The rest will be moved this morning.

I wonder how oft-moving families handle the excitement time after time. Some military kids complain about being in nine different schools before finally graduating. Other kids seem to thrive on the frequent moving, welcoming the opportunity to experience new locales and meet new people. Perhaps it's all in the attitude.

Consider Israel. The people wandered around the desert for forty years. They could never hang a welcome sign and register their address as permanent with the local post office. Rather, they were forced to gather up all their tents, clothes and simple furnishings, kids, goats, sheep and oxen every time Moses said, "Moving day."

It was no small task. No VanLine movers back in those days. And, it wasn't as though they could just pick a favorite spot atop a scenic hill. Nope. There was a precise plan for how the camps were to be set up. Each of the twelve tribes was assigned a spot. For example, Aaron and his sons *were to camp to the east of the tabernacle, toward the sunrise, in front of the Tent of Meeting.* (Numbers 3:38)

Each tribe and family flew a banner, a distinctive flag, over the place they were assigned. Several hundred-thousand people strong, it must have been an organizational feat with each move to another sand dune.

I suspect that a few people grumbled, "just when I was getting used to this place . . . ." Others probably looked forward to a different view out the back window. Better equipped to see the big picture, some may have welcomed the move knowing it placed them one step closer to the Promised Land. And a few, wanting to meet new people, may have been disappointed that God sometimes demanded them to destroy their new neighbors.

I'm not suggesting Devos and company do likewise and wipe out their new neighbors. That sure would keep the Welcome Wagon from knocking! But, it is an exciting opportunity to establish fresh relationships and see how the Lord will open doors for ministry.

Each of us should please his neighbor for his good, to build him up.
(Romans 15:2)

Daily challenge:
Old or new, view your neighbors as an opportunity to serve.

Surprise

The incident started as a continuation of the big move my friends made over the weekend. Yesterday I planned to meet everyone at the new house and help with getting things in their proper place. However, once I arrived at the house, I was surprised to find it completely devoid of people. The only living things around were two left-over guinea hens and a couple of mangy cats. Since I found the door unlocked, it was obvious the move had occurred. What I did not know was that I missed Bobbie's call saying they had to go back to the old house to clean it. They would not be home for hours.

Initially bewildered about what to do, I scoped out each room. The sunken living room had newly arrived items strewn about. The loft was filled with furniture randomly placed. And in the master bedroom, the bed was still in pieces and big black garbage bags full of stuff were everywhere. Other rooms were just as disorganized. I planned my attack.

I searched the house for bedding, furniture pieces and decorative items, managing to sculpt a nice-looking loft and a newly assembled bedroom, bath and living room. I worked excitedly, hoping to be able to finish before getting "caught in the act." As I looked around, I anticipated what I hoped would be my friends' pleasure at returning home to find three rooms ready for living.

"Was it you?" Ron asked in church this morning.

"Only if you liked what you saw," I responded with a smile.

He told me that Bobbie joked she wished the Good Fairy would come visit once in a while. "But no, she never seems to find our house." *Au contraire!* Walking in yesterday she exclaimed, "Look! The Good Fairy did come!"

Good deeds are purposed to encourage the saints and show God's goodness to unbelievers. Doing good allows us to mirror God's goodness to us. Therefore, . . . *do good, to be rich in good deeds*, says Timothy, *so that they may take hold of the life that is truly life* (I Timothy 6:18).

Try it. You'll like it.

"In the same way, let your light shine before men, that they may see your good deeds and praise your Father in heaven." (Matthew 5:16)

Daily challenge:
Live the true life. Surprise someone today with an unexpected good deed.

Birthday Mishap

Five years ago today we were sitting in our lawn chairs at "church." At the time, our start-up fellowship was meeting in a three-car garage, worshiping without the trappings of a formal sanctuary. Our church had just suffered a split and I was preoccupied with a bad work situation. I didn't have it together.

Sitting in that hot garage, I glanced over at Seth. To my surprise, tears streamed down his face. To coin a phrase, "Oh dear, what could the matter be?" The matter was this: we had forgotten Seth's 11th birthday. The young boy was distraught. He could not be consoled regardless of heartfelt apologies. No "Happy Birthday" upon rising, no special breakfast, no unique gifts. It was just a lot of nothing.

Seth eventually got over his disappointment and to this day, it is one of our long-standing family jokes. So, as the sun set last night, I made sure to get in the first birthday greeting in anticipation of today. I certainly did not want him to think I could forget his birthday . . . again! On the way home from work, I made a stop to pick up some plaid shorts as a gift. I was relieved he liked them; he can be pretty picky. *Whew.* Another birthday without incident.

Kids are wonderful. Each has their unique personality, sense of humor, strengths and weaknesses. Seth has been "busy" since conception. In utero, he made like a chicken trying to peck his way out. As an infant he refused to sleep longer than twenty minutes at a time and was a front-runner to be a poster child for colic.

After him, no more kids for me. Maybe Leah thought the same thing after Judah's birth. Perhaps he was difficult as well. *She conceived again, and when she gave birth to a son she said, "This time I will praise the LORD"* . . . *Then she stopped having children* (Genesis 29:35).

At four, Seth rode his motorcycle through the woods as fast as he could, standing on the seat like a pipsqueak Evil Kinevil. In school, he was the center of attention. And now, as a young man of seventeen, he is an outgoing, know-no-stranger kind of guy, full of wanderlust and enthusiasm. His camera is a constant companion.

I thank God for Seth. He's a special kind of kid.

> *. . . and she gave birth to a son and named him Seth, saying, "God has granted me another child." (Genesis 4:25)*

Daily challenge:
Little kids are like kittens: cute and easy to love.
But don't be blind to the beauty in your big kids.

Hangman

"Hmm. One word. 15 letters. Is there a T? What about an A?"

This kind of thing happens every day in my classroom. To reinforce the lesson, I create on-line games to help the kids review. Hangman is a favorite. A clue comes up and the student starts picking letters. If they pick a letter contained in the word or phrase, all is well. But, if they pick a letter not included in the answer, the computer draws a head. Subsequent misses add a body, two arms and a couple of legs. Obviously, the goal is to figure out the word before getting hanged.

There appear to be two approaches. The conscientious student studies the clue and uses great thought in selecting letters. You can see their angst increase if they choose incorrectly. Sometimes, they even take time to consult their notes to avoid an untimely death. There is obvious glee when they beat the game and get the message, "You are correct. Well done." Truly, their approach enhances learning.

The less-engaged students have an entirely different strategy. As each new puzzle appears on the screen, they barely pause to read the clue. Rather, their fingers fly across the keyboard, randomly striking letters. In a matter of three seconds, the stick man is swinging from the end of the rope. "You lose." The unfortunate death doesn't even faze them. They simply move to the next puzzle. So much for learning anything.

Our spiritual lives can be played out similarly. For the dedicated Believer, there is a conscious effort to make all the right moves and answer the questions. Each decision along the way is prayerfully considered before any action transpires. To make certain that appropriate decisions are made, the Good Book is consulted for instructions. When mistakes are made, the "notes" are pulled out, mistakes repented and actions corrected. Finally, with the puzzle completed, we get the message *"Well done, good and faithful servant!"* (Matthew 25:23).

On the other hand, some go through life oblivious to the truth. In fact, there is no desire to find it. As a result, they proceed along willy-nilly, following whatever happens to catch their interest, randomly and thoughtlessly pushing whatever buttons seem right at the time. They have no clue they are on the road to destruction. For some, the "You lose" message at the end doesn't even register until it's too late.

> *. . . we pray this in order that you may live a life worthy of the Lord and may please him in every way: bearing fruit in every good work, growing in the knowledge of God. (Colossians 1:10)*

Daily challenge:
Be mindful of all you do.

Cattle on the Hillside

I stepped into the deepening dusk and looked up. There, high in the sky was a bright and shining full moon, replacing the sun that shone throughout the day. "Ah, I am going to enjoy this." With my reflective vest pulled on, I began to run. I needed to clear my head. Since returning home from teaching, I barely stopped long enough to start a roast before resuming the myriad of preparations for tomorrow's lessons. My head was spinning and I needed to get out.

Up the long and rocky driveway I went. Turning onto the hard surface road, a herd of cows stood contentedly by the fence, continuing to chew their cud as their heads turned to follow my movement. I smiled as a calf, head poked through the wire fence, took a few bewildered and clumsy steps, startled by my intrusion into her territory. Leaving those cows behind, I ran easily down one hill and up the next, around the big curve and to the dead-end. There, with more cows in a pasture, a song came to mind. It was written by John W. Peterson and goes like this:

> *He owns the cattle on a thousand hills,*
> *The wealth in every mine;*
> *He owns the rivers and the rocks and rills,*
> *The sun and stars that shine.*
> *Wonderful riches, more than tongue can tell—*
> *He is my Father so they're mine as well;*
> *He owns the cattle on a thousand hills—*
> *I know that He will care for me.*

I have generally interpreted this song to say that God is rich. Like the songwriter, I assumed that since I am an heir, everything God owns is mine by default. It left me with a sense of playground braggadocio: "My daddy owns more than your daddy." I'm not convinced this is good theology.

Truly we are heirs with Christ. However, we dare not forget that when one owns something, the owner has an intrinsic right to do with those possessions as he pleases. We never have a right to question what God does; He is the owner with privilege.

Truly, the God of the cattle and the hills can do as He pleases with what He owns. Thank God we are a valued part of His possessions, for He guards and protects that which He owns.

For every animal of the forest is mine, and the cattle on a thousand hills. (Psalm 50:10)

Daily challenge:
The Owner is in control. Be content with that.

Powerful Words

Truly, the spoken word has power. We just finished watching the film, "The Great Debaters." Based on a true story, a fiery, albeit politically radical, college professor molded young college students into extraordinary orators. The debate team from Wiley College in Marshall, TX, an all-black school, had a history of debating excellence. Under the tutelage of Mr. Melvin Tolson, the team rose to magnificent heights of accomplishments when it defeated Harvard University. The story was, despite a few instances of literary license, a beautiful example of the power held in a collection of words.

The antithesis of the well-spoken word walks in the hallways of summer school. I sauntered behind two young men as they proceeded down the corridor. I thought for a moment they spoke another language. But nay, it was not another language at all; it was simply English spoken poorly and without thought. Shortly thereafter, I caught one of my students blurting out an offensive expression. I heard another student tout her young niece's adeptness at vulgarity. She was so proud.

Words are powerful. Moses used them wisely and *was educated in all the wisdom of the Egyptians and was powerful in speech and action* (Acts 7:22). Our own words can be just as effective if we incorporate the power of the Scripture into our speech.

People's words fall short. Empty words leave one wanting and unfulfilled. And destructive words wound. But the powerful, transforming Word of God remains unmatched .

Choose your words carefully.

For the word of God is living and active. Sharper than any double-edged sword, it penetrates even to dividing soul and spirit, joints and marrow; it judges the thoughts and attitudes of the heart. (Hebrews 4:12)

Daily challenge:
How powerful and effective is your speech?

Bearing Fruit

"Whoa! Look at that!" My two watermelon plants that had started out as four-inch sticks are now growing rampant. I vaguely recalled that watermelon vines creep along the ground and spread out, but I had no idea they would completely dominate the pool's landscaping. Fact is, the vines have migrated into the yard and are at least fifteen-feet long. The azaleas are held in a stranglehold and the benches around the fire pit are in danger. However, as I stood amazed at what seemed to be an overnight growth spurt, I spied two petite melons hidden beneath the leaves. I am loving the idea of harvesting them. I'll just have to wait.

Then I got to my eggplant. A solitary plant went into the ground with hopes of getting several purple fruit. Not so. For some odd reason, that plant is not much bigger than when I placed it in the ground with its four puny leaves. The prognosis is grim. But the green, red and yellow pepper plants are doing better. Miniature peppers offer hope for a fresh salad. The grape tomatoes are doing okay and the roma cousins are loaded. One small plant has no less than twenty-five still-green orbs hanging from the branches.

So why is it that some of the plants are bearing fruit and some are not? I treated each one the same. I never watered one and not the other and all have been fertilized. I just don't understand why everything isn't healthy and full of life.

I do know, however, that John 15 is the best known parallel to this garden situation. The discourse begins with, *"I am the true vine, and my Father is the gardener . . . Remain in me, and I will remain in you. No branch can bear fruit by itself; it must remain in the vine. Neither can you bear fruit unless you remain in me"* (v. 1-4). Then, to make the relationship crystal clear, Jesus continues, *"I am the vine; you are the branches. If a man remains in me and I in him, he will bear much fruit; apart from me you can do nothing"* (v. 5).

This is an obvious cause/effect relationship. If I removed the softball-size melons from the vine, they would no longer have the potential for growth. But growth is exactly what the Gardener desires. Cling to the vine.

> *"This is to my Father's glory, that you bear much fruit, showing your-selves to be my disciples . . . You did not choose me, but I chose you and appointed you to go and bear fruit—fruit that will last." (John 15:8, 16)*

Daily challenge:
When we are in the Vine, our duty is to be fruitful.

Intentions

Intentions. We all have them—good and bad.

When I was a kid, my father played tennis at the local playground and I often tagged along. The tallest and steepest metal slide in the world towered above one edge of the playground, just beyond the row of arborvitae through which we ran and sometimes hid. Huge swings nearby served as a launching pad. A wading pool hosted a fountain in the middle and provided hours of splish-splashy fun. But, the best thing about the playground was the whirly-bird, tilt-a-whirl contraption, played on long before anyone worried about liability lawsuits.

Picture an upside-down ice-cream cone with seats around the fattest part of the rim, the tip balanced upon a huge metal pole. All of us kids took a spot around the perimeter, grasping the wooden seats. Running in a circle, we coaxed the giant into action. Just at the right moment, we flung ourselves onto the seats. If the mounting procedure was not done just right, the unfortunate child ended up face first in the dirt, often clobbered by the flailing feet of those who had made it on board.

One particular Wednesday, a girl on that ride did something that angered me; I don't remember what. But I know I had an intention to be mean. I threw a handful of dirt right in her face. It was such a vile thing to do that I even surprised myself. After a phone call from her parents to mine, I can assure you that my intention from then on was to never, ever do that again!

On a long car drive to my mother's house today, I listened to a program on the radio encouraging Believers to live intentionally in faith, relationships, work, health and finances. I listened as one caller described losing over three-hundred pounds. He was intentional in making wise health decisions. Another called in and described intentional decisions about tithing despite economic hardship. Each of the many callers described how blessed they were to have intended to and successfully done right.

Purposeful intentions yield satisfying results. Live intentionally.

Live as children of light . . . and find out what pleases the Lord . . . Be very careful, then, how you live—not as unwise but as wise, making the most of every opportunity. (Ephesians 5:8b, 10, 15, 16a)

Daily challenge:
Intend. Plan. Do.

Who Am I?

I am intrigued by the means God uses to reveal His will. God must have a sense of humor. Sitting in the opening session of a Christian writer's conference, I was drawn to a crazy, long-haired hippie freak actor/writer/motivational speaker who talked of responsibility, God-given talent and God's call. It was not only entertaining, it was filled with spiritual truth. His journey was long and convoluted as God revealed his life's plan from Florida to California to a shack in the wilds of Alaska to Tennessee and an exploding career.

Every turn, every twist in this guy's life bordered on insane. Perhaps the hilarity was a function of the presentation style, but I'm not convinced God would have chosen the same methods for me. Just as God has a unique plan for each of us, He has a unique way of delivering the message.

When my mother suggested we attend this conference, I agreed. At the time, it was months away. I nary gave it a second thought. Yesterday, exhausted from my summer-school teaching, I got in the car almost wishful I didn't have to go. But now that I am here, I am faced with the questions: *Why and what now?*

I am having some difficulty answering questions posed to me. "So, what do you do?" *Hmm.* Am I still a perfusionist? I haven't done a case in a year. Am I a consultant? Clients are few and far between. Am I an educator? Well, sort of. I am teaching summer school and I develop online medical education. Am I a runner? Yes, but that's not a job. Am I an interior designer? Not really. A carpenter? Not professionally. Am I a writer? I do write, but I'm not a best-selling author yet. The question remains. *Who am I? What am I to become at 51?*

I think God is whispering in my ear. He tells me He is Sovereign. He tells me he is purposeful. He tells me I am made to be constructive in the Kingdom. He tells me to hush and "Be still and know that I am God."

I will listen. I will trust. I will follow. Then, I will know who I am and what I will become.

Then Jesus said to Simon, "Don't be afraid; from now on you will catch men." So they pulled their boats up on shore, left everything and followed him. (Luke 5:11)

Daily challenge:
Listen. Follow. Become.

The Legacy

The morning was cool and inviting. Drawing in the air, still damp from an overnight rain, I stepped out the door for a run. In the early dawn, I had the streets of this quaint village to myself. Trees eighty-feet tall rimmed the perfectly manicured yards. Flowers cascaded over stone walls like water rushing over the falls. In the middle of town stood a granite tribute to the fallen soldiers of the Civil War, approximately one hundred-eighty names strong.

Still running, I turned onto a particularly steep street. There at the top, an old cemetery stood guard over the hillside. With the mist rising into the first rays of dawn, it was breathtaking. The straight rows summoned me to run amongst the graves. The dates on the stones indicated the long history of this town. There were simple graves marked by small, flat stones, the etchings worn and barely legible. Tall monuments stood nearby in contrast, perhaps indicating the social standing of the family. Some plots bore multiple graves—fathers, mothers, children all buried side by side.

But tucked into a corner and away from the hundreds of other graves stood three headstones. I noted one stone held a bronzed plaque with the standard information—name, military rank, date of birth and death. Oddly, the other two headstones were plain granite slabs. There were no names, no personal information, no way to connect to the past. Perhaps the tombstones were intended for those who yet lived. But I was confused. Remnants of flower arrangements and plastic bouquets surrounded the markers as if out of respect for the dead. If the remains of the deceased did share that hillside, it was not much of a legacy for either one.

Then I thought of another cemetery far away. My father died before my sons were born. They never got to know his character. They never heard him play that dented E-flat horn. They never heard him laugh or see him weep. They never got to play wiffle ball in the backyard or ice skate with him on frozen creeks. They never heard him pray or teach a lesson. They only know what they have been told and what they have read. Even so, if they visit Dad's gravesite, the legacy my Father most wanted to leave can be seen. Into his tombstone is etched, "Only a sinner saved by grace".

It is a fitting synopsis of a life fulfilled. Nothing else really counts. Nothing else really matters. Not money. Not fame. Not position. Not accomplishments. For without that work of grace in our lives, we are as stone cold as the granite marking the site.

For by grace are we saved by faith, and that not of ourselves, it is a gift of God, not of works, lest any man can boast. (Ephesians 2:8, 9)

Daily challenge:
What did you do today that will become a part of your legacy?

Truth Hurts

Sometimes the truth hurts. That's what I've felt the last two days. When you practice and practice only to find out your performance falls short, the sting lingers. It's like when I ran a personal best in an important fifty-mile race, only to come in third. Or, it feels about the same as working hard on a paper for a college English course long ago, only to receive a disappointing C. All that time in the gym spent balancing on a four-inch beam seemed for naught when I fell unceremoniously to the ground in front of the judges. And now, having the shortcomings of my writing made clear hurts like a good whack to the head.

Disappointments come in a variety of shapes and sizes and it takes courage to face each one head on. A childish response is to get mad, pick up our red playground ball and tromp off the court. Our feelings get hurt and we get discouraged. "Forget it. It's not worth the effort to try anymore." Our reactions are visceral, our responses selfish and our vision short-sided.

As I dared to share my writing with accomplished professionals at a writers' conference, I have not been handed unconditional kudos. Rather, each one has offered their perspective and suggestions. As I listen, I see their lips move, hear what they say and try with all my might to learn from them. But deep within, my heart aches and I now perceive my own work as woefully inadequate and ineffective.

I don't think I'm alone in these feelings. No matter how hard you try to make a nice dinner for your family, someone complains. Perhaps you feel frazzled by the myriad of responsibilities you have, dropping one juggling pin after another. You feel like a failure because you can't get your life—or everyone else's—under control.

There is little doubt that our feelings of disenchantment are real. I think of King David who suffered disappointment after disappointment. He cried for mercy. He pleaded for relief. He could not understand why he was so afflicted by his enemies. And yet, he never quit. He persevered despite the difficulties and his human disappointments vanished in the wake of God's encompassing embrace.

They cried to you and were saved; in you they trusted and were not
disappointed. (Psalm 22:5)

Daily challenge:
Don't let disappointments destroy. Turn disappointments
into providential opportunities.

The Rain

The alarm rang out all too soon. It was early and I was tired. Why is it that vacations are so exhausting? As I turned to glance out the window, the torrential rain and loud claps of thunder disheartened me. Any compulsion to run retreated quickly as I pulled the covers back over my head. I felt guilty, remaining for the moment warm and dry in my bed.

The persistent rain continued most of the day. Walking to the conference center, I noted the array of day lilies, tall and still brilliant in a nearby garden. They seemed grateful for the drenching. The grass glistened as droplets clung to the blades. In the treetops, songbirds lilted out their tunes, as if in celebration of the showers.

We often associate rainy days with dreariness and depression. As a child, I remember being devastated when rain ruined my day at the pool. More recently, the howling wind and blustery gusts of a hurricane descended on Cancun during a medical conference that my husband and I attended. The romantic notion of staring out across the ocean while waves gently lapped the shore blew away with the raging storm. How disappointing.

I am reminded, however, that despite the inconvenience of rain, water is vital to all living things. The plants need water to grow and the reservoirs of the earth must be kept full. Even our own bodies require water to maintain function. The lost desert wanderer can be saved by drinking in the satisfying water from a discovered pool, clear and cool.

But there is a water source more intoxicating than that desert pool. Take advantage of the spiritual rain. Frolic and dance in the showers. Rejoice. Be refreshed. Drink and have your thirst be forever quenched.

Jesus answered, "Everyone who drinks this water will be thirsty again, but whoever drinks the water I give him will never thirst. Indeed, the water I give him will become in him a spring of water welling up to eternal life." (John 4:13)

Daily challenge:
Without some rain, we could never appreciate the sun.

The Odd Ducks

Quack. Quack. Quack. The theme was obvious. All you had to do was look around the room. Not one head lacked the ridiculous hat perched on top. Yellow in color, huge painted eyes, an orange beak and a hunk of yellow fuzz in the back, the caps became a unifying element. Why would eighty reasonably mature adults risk mortal embarrassment by donning such a monstrosity?

The answer? Because collective behavior isn't all that odd if everyone is doing it. I suppose that could be good or bad, depending on your perceptive.

Watching this behavior reminds me of my high-school days. I so wanted to fit in. No *odd duck* label for me! I was athletic, a good student and had my share of friends. But there was one little problem. My parents made sure I looked and acted differently from the crowd. Back in the '70s mini skirts were all the rage. Was I allowed to wear them? Nope. Dances served as the social breeding ground for boy/girl relationships. Was I allowed to dance? Heavens, no. Bellbottoms, regarded as icons of the fashion world, were not on my list of approved apparel.

So, what did I do? I now admit (sorry, Mother) that I rolled my skirt waistband at school whenever possible. I pushed the limit on the frowned-upon jeans and tried to assimilate the flared pants into my wardrobe by progressive approximation, thinking my parents would not notice.

Indeed, it is much easier to blend in than standout. I have always wondered why Christians had to be described as a *peculiar people* (I Peter 2:9, KJV). But think about it. If light wasn't different from darkness, what good would light be? If salt was no different than pepper, what's the use in seasoning your food? If hot was the same as cold, a shower would be very uncomfortable. Sometimes being different is necessary for effectiveness.

"You are the salt of the earth . . . You are the light of the world."
(Matthew 5:13a, 14a)

Daily challenge:
Learn to be comfortable with being different.

Not By Sight

It was the last day of the conference and a good run was just what I needed. I wasn't quite sure where I was going. Though I had no map, I counted on my sense of direction. It was reliable—usually. With shoes laced up and ready to go, I set off down the street.

Running past the high school, I planned to find a road I presumed connected with another road I had been on the day before. If the road was there, it was going to be a nice run. If it wasn't there . . . well, it might get interesting. Okay. I'll keep running up the hill and around the curve. If no road turns to the left, I'll retrace my steps.

There it was. A road to the left. I made the turn and meandered along, a little uncomfortable that the road was unmarked. But, it sure was pretty in the early morning. With gravel crunching under each footfall, I took in my surroundings—rolling hills, fenced farmland and a lake below. I ran for a long time. Feeling some angst, my pace quickened. I had limited time and a jaunt down the wrong road was not going to be convenient.

Isn't that just like life? We choose a certain course and then get worried if the way is not clearly marked. It was like that when I quit my job last summer. Convinced it was the thing to do, I gladly drafted my resignation. But when the consulting work did not come rolling in, I got concerned. Buoyed every so often with projects, I relaxed for a period, only to fret again when the next task did not soon come knocking. Did that mean I was on the wrong course? Did I miss a turn somewhere or a sign post? No. It simply meant the journey was more interesting than anticipated. Not having a bird's-eye view, I could not see the whole picture at one time.

It was the right road for my run. Flagging down a four-wheeling farmer, he confirmed my course. Though I could not see around the next bend, I had to trust I was on the road leading to my destination. I was not lost. I was simply living out a simple demonstration of walking—or in this case—running by faith and not by sight.

For we walk by faith and not by sight. (II Corinthians 5:7, KJV)

Daily challenge:
When the path seems unclear, remember that God sees it all from start to finish.

That's Swell!

Splat! The water I was drinking spewed out of my mouth and landed on Mother's side of the table. "What did you say?" By this time, I was wiping my face, my nose, my chin, of the dripping water. Her comment caught me off guard, choking me mid-drink. In an instant, laughter erupted until we nearly wet our pants. As soon as one of us settled down, the other exploded in a secondary wave of laughter. The eyes of the other customers locked onto our table. They just didn't understand. We didn't either. We just knew it was funny.

We were enjoying each other's company on the last evening of my visit, content to linger over dinner at a nearby restaurant. "Can you please bring me a box for my leftovers?" my mother queried the waitress. When she returned, Mother took the box in hand and without hesitation blurted out, "Thanks. That's swell!"

Swell? Did I hear that right? I have never, ever heard my Mom say that. Hence, the jet propulsion of the water from my mouth. But just as surprised was Mother. She nearly aspirated her last bite. "Where did that come from?" We could not stop laughing.

The mouth-brain connection is a peculiar thing. As a child, I remember hearing "Garbage in, garbage out." The phrase was used most often to keep us from listening to rock music with nasty lyrics. "If you hear it, you'll think it, then say it." True enough.

My first language overload was when I ventured into cardiac operating rooms. Honestly, I had never been exposed to such lewd and vile language, innuendo and cursing. Before long, it occurred to me I was thinking in some of those terms. And once in a while, I uttered an unflattering word.

I'm in no way suggesting that *swell* is an evil uttering. But it does support the theory that a word suppressed or long-ago forgotten can come flying out for no good reason. Prudence suggests that guarding what we hear is an excellent strategy for keeping track of what we say.

"For out of the overflow of the heart the mouth speaks." (Matthew 12:34b)

Daily challenge:
Don't say anything you don't want coming out of your kids' mouths.

Follow My Example

The vegetables, washed and prepared, lay in a bowl. Key utensils stood at the ready and various graters, choppers, slicers and dicers lined the countertop as if waiting for battle. Ready to receive the pan, the preheated oven was primed for action. The guests filed in and the show began. Step by step, the instructor led the group in the use of the kitchen tools and preparation of two dishes. Everyone left the gathering with satisfied stomachs and receipts confirming the purchase of kitchen tools that they just had to have.

In-home marketing can be very successful. No matter if the products are pots and pans, a jewelry show, plastic goods or makeup makeovers, all have one thing in common—the guests are to follow suit with what they see. Follow the recipe, line the eyes, coordinate accessories or organize cupboards.

The idea of following suit is something to which all relate. In grammar-school gym class we had to do whatever the teacher demonstrated. It was like follow the leader. Mr. Stranges cued up the old exercise record called "Chicken Fat" on the LP player, singing along as we did the calisthenics. I wanted to do exactly as instructed and worked hard to conform. I wanted to be just like my cool teacher.

I imagine all of us can think of our efforts as teenagers to conform to the norm. I know I tried to wear jeans that were "in," shirts that were "cool" and skirts that were much shorter than what my parents preferred. Conforming meant not being noticed for being too weird. Conforming was easy; being different could result in social suicide.

But sometimes conforming to a standard is the right thing to do rather than an easy way out. The Apostle Paul compels us to be like him who was striving to be like Christ. That's a pretty bold move on Paul's part. But in this case, conforming to the ultimate example is what we are called to do.

Follow my example, as I follow the example of Christ. (I Corinthians 11:1)

Daily challenge:
Conform to Christ. Be different from the world.

The Watermelon Patch

I was away for only a week. When I returned, I could hardly believe my eyes. My watermelons must have been doing steroids. No shrub, plant or garden structure was spared from the rambling vines. The adventurous extensions of those once-tiny plants had completely covered about fifteen feet of ground lengthwise and six feet in width. But more exciting than the mere volume was what lay beneath the gigantic leaves— watermelons. Lots of them. I forced my family to gaze upon the fruit that seemed to be growing by the minute. I sighed, not understanding their lack of enthusiasm.

As of late, I've been feeling much like a watermelon. No. I haven't gotten big and rotund in a physical sense. But I have been experiencing periods of exponential spiritual growth. The writer's conference last week was like living under the power of a convex lens. The Son's light hit the lens of my heart and concentrated His warmth, direction, and love. It was a spiritual growth spurt, just like those watermelons. With proper nurturing, there is no reason for the maturation process not to continue.

But we all know about the bonfire experience on the last night at camp. Those feelings of spiritual resolve often disappear by the break of day when suitcases are packed and campers head home. I don't think it has to be that way. Certainly, we dare not measure our spiritual maturity against an emotional yardstick. Rather, God directs and enables conscious decisions to be obedient in our daily living, with or without an overtly emotional experience.

Like the watermelon, we may have periods of fast and furious growth. Other times, growth may be slow but steady. Each type of growth is appropriate for different seasons. The fact remains, however, that growth of any sort indicates life and growth supported by proper conditions and nutrition yields fruit.

"Remain in me, and I will remain in you. No branch can bear fruit by itself; it must remain in the vine. Neither can you bear fruit unless you remain in me. I am the vine; you are the branches. If a man remains in me and I in him, he will bear much fruit; apart from me you can do nothing." (John 15:4, 5)

Daily challenge:
Keep growing, keep producing. Let the Son do its job.

Never Forget

Never forget. There are some things that are hard to forget even if we want to—a traumatic childhood experience, a parent's death or grievous personal failure. Sometimes we rehearse the event over and over, keeping it at the pinnacle of our memory banks. Despite our best efforts, there are other times when forgetting is all too easy. We can barely remember the simplest things—anniversaries or birthdays.

We have watched the memory of my mother-in-law slip-slide away. It has not been easy for her or for us. At first it seemed like the typical forgetfulness associated with aging. But then came the diagnosis: Alzheimers. She sobbed when she felt like she was going crazy and had no power to make it better. Now, in what looks like to be her final days, she lies in her hospital bed in the living room of her home, oblivious to everything and everyone.

Memory is a gift from God. As a student, I often prayed that God would help me remember. As a teacher, I prayed that my students would be rewarded with good memory on the basis of the effort spent in preparation. (There is a difference, you know.) Now, I am more concerned about remembering someone's name or recalling what I was supposed to pick up at the grocery store.

As frustrating as memory can be, I'm not sure we understand the potential power our memories hold. Nevertheless, I do know that God expects us to recall key elements: God's covenant, our past, His protection, provision and faithfulness and His love and mercy. Is the reason for remembering simply academic? I don't think so. Remembering helps us to appreciate where we've been and where we are going. It keeps us focused and alive. As the Psalmist so eloquently states, *I will never forget your precepts, for by them you have preserved my life* (Psalm 119:93).

Praise the LORD, O my soul, and forget not all his benefits. (Psalm 103:2)

Daily challenge:
Recall five specific times that God directly worked in your life.
Write them down. Tell someone. Give thanks.

Rain, Please

The grass, crinkling under foot, screamed for moisture. The plants around the pool and in the field hung limp. The ground was hard like concrete, evidence of the current drought. The newscast earlier in the day predicted temperatures above ninety-five degrees for the next week with little hope of rain. It was a bleak forecast.

As we sat down for dinner, Gary prayed for rain to water the earth. Within a few minutes of his resounding "amen," we heard the wonderful pitter-patter. I looked out at the pool and saw the surface being pelted by big, fat, juicy raindrops. Wow. Gary's prayer must have made an impression!

Did it rain as a direct result of Gary's prayer? It's hard to tell. I'm sure that a lot of other people have been requesting rain as well—especially the farmers. And, we know that God is the God of the universe, capable of doing whatever He pleases. That relationship, however, between our prayers and God's actions has always given me reason to pause.

When the boys were little, I remember making special treats for them but patiently waiting to deliver until the boys politely asked. I fully expected them to ask but felt compelled to teach them a lesson in the process. They needed to learn about being well-mannered, discovering the finer points of offering requests to parents and others. It was not appropriate for them to be demanding or to stipulate any conditions on the offering. Rather, it was simply their privilege to solicit the treat. It was up to me whether or not to fulfill their desire.

I do not claim to be a deep theologian—or even a shallow one. However, perhaps we only need to offer God our request before he chooses to provide our treat. Just don't forget to say, "Thank you."

"Until now you have not asked for anything in my name. Ask and you
will receive, and your joy will be complete." (John 16:24)

Daily challenge:
The simple rule for the day: "Remember to say please and thank you."

Reap What You Sow

The last day of summer school. One by one, the kids entered the classroom. Some appeared relaxed, others anxious. They were about to embark on the final exam of the course and each had a different goal. Several students wanted to earn that perfect score, so unfamiliar. One kid, a football player, just wanted to pass with a C. Otherwise, his playing days were over. Another girl needed to have a good report to present to the judge. She was destined for a return trip to juvenile detention and a transfer to women's prison if she did not fare well. One boy was on the bubble—a ninety-percent meant he passed, an eighty-nine percent yielded a failure.

As the exams were completed, the grades were the best ever. Perfect scores by two students resulted in outrageous laughter. It was a time of celebration for all the students, save one. The exertion by this kid in prior weeks did not budge the needle on the effort meter. Having been told several weeks ago what was needed to pass, he chose to ignore the warnings. Alas, it was too little, too late. He was the only one who failed and there was nothing I could do about it.

It is very easy to shake our heads and *tsk-tsk* this young man. "How foolish," we sigh, shaking our head and wagging our finger. And yet, this behavior may not be too far off from what we do routinely. We are told by the doctor to lose weight, but we never follow through. The financial advisor tells us to pay off credit cards, but it's just not fun to be that disciplined. Perhaps a trainer assigns us workouts that we blow off because it's too hot, too cold, too windy or too dark.

And then there is the Holy Spirit that chides us to pray; for family, friends, leaders, church, missionaries . . . the list goes on. He pulls on our heart strings, urging us to minister to others. He asks us to meditate on the things of God. But what do we do? So often, we do absolutely nothing. Just like the student, we volitionally choose disobedience, or at the least, apathy. Should we be surprised when we don't reap abundant blessings?

> *Do not be deceived: God cannot be mocked. A man reaps what he sows. (Galatians 6:7)*

Daily challenge:
Choose to do something you know you should do—and do it today.

Cloud-gazing

It was nearly half-past eight when I turned down our long driveway on the final stretch of my evening run. The Peaks, with their bluish hue common in the Blue Ridge Mountains, stood tall against the sky. Fluffy cumulus clouds, backlit with pink and purple rays from the setting sun, billowed in contrast against the blue sky. I was startled to suddenly see a mouse, then a Jabba-the-Hutt type character. They were as clear to me as the sky in which they floated—distinct ears and a pointy little nose on the mouse and all the common features of the big fat guy in a cross-legged sit.

It took me back to when I was a little girl. I loved to dole away summer afternoons in the hammock. Sometimes I napped or read, but most often I watched the clouds as they floated by. I spent hours seeing how many identifiable shapes I could find. I played this game in long intervals for with each gentle breeze the shapes slowly drifted apart, preserved only in my memory banks. It was an entertaining venture, fleeting as it was.

On this first day of August, I'm wondering if this year has disappeared just like those clouds. Where has the time gone? The circumstances of my daily living have certainly changed from what they were on January 1. Job opportunities have come and gone and come again, a son has returned home to live and numerous learning scenarios have changed my way of thinking. Little remains the same, just like those drifting clouds. It makes life interesting. But it also makes me appreciate what is constant in my life—the love we have as a family and the care and protection of a Heavenly Father.

Nevertheless, we do well when we celebrate the uniqueness of each moment and embrace the changes. For in life, we get only one chance to seize the day. We have no idea what God has for us in tomorrow's sky.

Man is like a breath; his days are like a fleeting shadow. (Psalm 144:4)

Daily challenge:
Go lie in the yard and do some cloud-gazing. Take someone you love with you. Bask in the gift of imagination and thank God for the beauty of His creation.

Impending Death

12:08. 1:35. 2:02. The red numbers on the clock glared at me, taunting me, daring me to fall asleep. But alas. I could not. I got up and ran a hot bath, something I find calming when I'm restless and sleep is scarce. I could not get my mother-in-law off my mind. I felt compelled to pray for her, sure that Gary's father was going to call in the morning telling us she had died. I wondered whether her Alzheimer-inflicted mind was capable of knowing how close she was to death. A rapid pulse and weak, shallow breathing indicated the body's final attempt to prevent total system failure. I asked God to calm any remaining consciousness as He ushered her into eternity.

The call never came. She continues to cling to a slender thread of life. She cannot eat or drink. Surely, she will not last much longer. *God, be merciful and call her home. Don't let her suffer any more.* Dad seems to have made an emotional transition that will help him accept the inevitable. Arrangements have been made for when she passes. Now, we simply watch and wait.

Her death will not be surprise. We knew her disease state was going to lead to this point. And yet, it's sad to think that her life, once vibrant, giving and loving, will no longer be. I feel tears running down my cheeks when I think about the coming void. I have known her for thirty-three years. She has been a wonderful mother-in-law to me and grandmother to my children. I love her and she will be missed.

But our sorrow is not without hope. Death cannot rob her of eternal life with the Father. Death cannot hold captive her regenerated soul. When she passes into Glory, she will be in the presence of the Almighty, the Maker of heaven and earth. Angel song will greet her and she will have no more sorrow, no more pain.

> *When the perishable has been clothed with the imperishable, and the mortal with immortality, then the saying that is written will come true: "Death has been swallowed up in victory." "Where, O death, is your victory? Where, O death, is your sting?"*
> *(I Corinthians 15:54, 55)*

Daily challenge:
Are you prepared to die?

Family Fun

"Seth. Let me go!" I gasped, half-laughing, half-annoyed and embarrassed. Caleb followed behind, snickering. I had taken the boys shopping for a few necessities—jeans and T-shirts. Seth, breaking into some accent from outer space and babbling like a wild man, took hold of my shoulders, dragging me along the store aisles at a blistering pace. The more I protested, the crazier he got. He refused to let go. Customers far and near looked on—some breaking into bewildered grins, some not very amused. When he finally relented, I caught my breath and slinked over to the checkout, hoping we wouldn't get thrown out of the store.

Families should have fun together, even if it does mean periods of momentary insanity. I recall playing with my dad and brothers on the living-room floor. Milk cartons fashioned into miniature goals and magazines rolled into lethal weapons allowed us to play floor hockey. The play was furious as we whacked the ping-pong ball—and each other—toward the goal. After crawling, diving and fighting for possession of the ball, we all collapsed in a big heap. Though hot, sweaty and exhausted, our hearts warmed with feelings of love, family and belonging.

When our kids have kids of their own, what will they remember? What memories will they be able to voice to their children? Will they think their growing-up days as bland and boring, unworthy of recall? I hope not.

Let the good times roll. Make a memory.

Our mouths were filled with laughter, our tongues with songs of joy. Then it was said among the nations, "The LORD has done great things for them." (Psalm 126:2)

Daily challenge:
Laugh loud. Laugh often. Laugh together.

Safely Home

She just stopped breathing. Then she was gone. No fanfare. No choir's anthem. No sobbing and wailing. No visible opening of Heaven's gates. Sometime in the moments when her husband left her side to relax in the tub, she quietly slipped away from human life into eternal life.

It was not unexpected that we received the call late last night from Gary's father. Her mind and body, overtaken by Alzheimer's disease, refused to eat and drink for two weeks. In a near coma, she wasted away until her heart refused to pump and her lungs could not draw another breath. When we arrived at Dad's home this morning, we listened to the story of Mom's last moments before plunging into cleaning the house, anticipating visiting friends and relatives. Several friends came bearing lunch and dinner, a welcome break from our task. The last to arrive were gentlemen from Dad's Sunday-school class, one of whom had been widowed six months prior. As we stood in a circle of prayer before they left, Jim prayed, "Thank you, Father, that Pat made it safely home." *Safely home,* I mused. I felt my eyes blur with tears.

As a mother, I can relate to that concept. I lay in bed waiting for my sons to arrive home. When the door opens and they return my greeting, I relax. They are safely home. So many things could have happened on their travels. And yet, God was gracious to grant them traveling mercy despite the potential hazards.

God never promised a way home devoid of difficulty. Clearly, Mom's path was long and arduous. She never would have picked this path for herself—a slow and ugly loss of memory and function. But again, God's numbering of her days led her—and us—to this day. God's way is perfect and beyond understanding.

> *The Lord will rescue me from every evil attack and will bring me safely to his heavenly kingdom. To him be glory for ever and ever. Amen. (II Timothy 4:18)*

Daily challenge:
We're never guaranteed another day. Don't neglect saying "I love you,"
"I'm sorry," and "Please forgive me."

Deal with It

Purring like a well-oiled machine, the kitty in my lap was more than content. Curled into a little furry ball, the cat barely moved save the stretch of a paw. The more I rubbed my hand over his body, the louder his purr. Unfortunately, as my fingers ran through his coat, I felt a tiny bump, then another. *Not again*, I muttered. I hate ticks. Sure enough, there under his fur and embedded into the skin were several blood-suckers. I tightly held the kitty's head, pinched the tick and pulled. Each time, the stowaway was removed and the kitten settled back into his position of rest. He seemed not to have minded the momentary discomfort.

The story was different when I found a rather large spot on his ear. I wasn't quite sure if it was a well-buried tick or a scab from a minor accident. I donned my glasses to take a closer look. But this time, the cat was not so keen on further investigation. His head turned side to side, his paws batted at me and his tail whipped about. He was not happy. I relented for the night and he went his merry way.

The cat's behavior reminds me of my own. Mom and Dad used to point out some action of mine that needed attention. It might have been as simple as, "Please put those toys where they belong." No big deal. Do as they say and the world was good. However, if the offense was more a matter of attitude or selfishness, my response was a little more wild cat-like. I bristled at being told I was wrong. In fact, when told that the boy I was dating was less than honorable and I was unwise for going out with him, I wanted to fight and claw to have it my way. Big problem.

It's often easier to ignore a problem than to deal with it. At the moment, the cat is quite content to leave the tick alone. But if the tick remains, it will only cause bigger problems. It would be better for everyone to accept the relatively short period of pain to ensure a brighter, pure future.

How much more should we be willing to rid our lives of hindrances and spiritual blights, large or small? If we fail to take care of a problem at the onset, we set our-selves up for a much bigger problem further down the road.

If we confess our sins, he is faithful and just and will forgive us our
sins and purify us from all unrighteousness. (I John 1:9)

Daily challenge:
Have any buried ticks in your life? Get rid of them and save yourself some pain.

Difficult Conversations

Some conversations flow as easily as flood waters over a broken dam. Other times the dam poses a barrier that is difficult to breach. The conversation falters, each person struggling to communicate without offending. It's a tough situation to be in. I should know; I was in the river today, headed for the dam and I'm not sure I successfully made it to shore.

A dear friend came with her brood of kids to enjoy an afternoon by the pool. We chatted about this and that, eventually arriving at the subject of church, music and modes of worship. As we shared our ideas, it became obvious that we looked at the topics from different perspectives. Neither was wrong, just different. Tears came to her eyes. She was pained because she felt her husband, one of the lay elders, was being criticized despite his purest intentions and hours of preparation. I was just as pained. I feared she misunderstood my position.

Our friendship remains intact. We came away from that difficult situation better understanding both perspectives. However, part of me wishes the topic never had come up. It's often easier to remain silent with the idea that we are "letting love cover." But there are times when it is appropriate to discuss hard things.

The key to preventing the discussion from turning into an ugly argument is to listen carefully and honestly. It sounds easy enough. However, it seems like our natural tendency is to strike back with a lot of "But you . . . " and "Get a grip . . .." If only we could remember that God gave us the ability to *"come now, let us reason together"* (Isaiah 1:18). Each party is required to consider the claims of the other and make sound judgments. Though difficult, the sound discussion can produce a beneficial outcome.

As iron sharpens iron, so one man sharpens another. (Proverbs 27:17)

Daily challenge:
There's a difference between vicious confrontation and conversation
that confronts issues. Use an eager ear and gracious, controlled language
to encourage and challenge each other for the glory of God.

Mayday!

"Mayday!" That was the subject line of an email I received this afternoon. Having moved cross country last year to begin a new career, my friend was desperate to have meaningful human contact. Addressing the email to just eight people, she wrote of her downward spiral. "I'm on a slippery slope, sliding toward a life of days spent smiling, laughing and acting like I'm okay and nights of crying myself to sleep wondering why I even bother getting out of bed, why I even bother trying at this thing called *life*."

So what am I supposed to do from 2500 miles away? My note back to her sounded surface and trite. Depressed and discouraged people find it impossible to will themselves to do anything. Me telling her to get involved, volunteer and pour her life into someone else's is sure to fall flat.

It was not due to a lack of friends that I found myself feeling like "Brenda." It was during a horribly stressful period of life as we endured an unjust lawsuit. Some days I could barely breathe. My body felt weak and crippled. Even my face seemed to grow longer and sadder with each day. My sleep and eating patterns changed, my stomach revolted and I cried for no good reason. But, I emerged from that time a stronger, more spiritually mature woman.

Thinking back, I can identify the most valuable activity that helped me deal with my less-than-perfect life. When my Bible opened, it was to the book of Psalms. For nearly two years, I couldn't bear to involve myself in deep theological treatises. My soul desired only the words of the Psalmists, particularly David. There he wrote of utter despair, feelings of abandonment and relentless pursuit by his enemies. And yet, David testified of the Lord's salvation. He spoke of redemption and justice. When he cried to know more of God's mercy he was not disappointed.

God was faithful then and continues to be faithful now. Our mourning will be turned to gladness and our sadness turned to song.

But let all who take refuge in you be glad; let them ever sing for joy.
Spread your protection over them that those who love your name
may rejoice in you. (Psalm 5:11)

Daily challenge:
Make Psalm-reading a part of your day. See if it doesn't change your perspective.

Blood-suckers

I hate ticks. Their flat little bodies and eight scrawny legs are repulsive. These arachnids—yes, they are spiders—have a harpoon-like structure in their mouth, used for latching onto the host and sucking blood just like a vampire. Once bloated with volumes of the red stuff, they take leave of their host, content to live off the accumulated blood pool for a few days.

At the moment, I'm obsessed with these creatures. Our two kittens unknowingly bring them into our house. Every time one of the cats assumes a position on my white-topped desk, a small army of engorged ticks roam freely. These are seed ticks, visible only because the tiny black specks move against the contrast of the surface. Wanting to rid the world of a few more, I use my fingernail to cut them in two. The process is disgusting, as the blood squirts in all directions. I can only imagine how many ticks are hiding on the dark blue chairs. Ah, I think I feel something on my leg.

Besides their ability to suck blood and transmit disease, ticks are talented travelers. Changes in temperature and the length of days signal them to find a host. Since they can't jump or fly, they must have direct contact with the host. That's why they lay wait on blades of grass, hoping for a passerby. Sometimes they fall onto an animal, but more impressively, they actually stalk their victim. They are desperate to pursue a host because their life depends on it. Can you imagine that? How many steps does the tiny tick have to take to catch a deer?

Can we learn a lesson from these blood-suckers? If we were as persistent and bold in the pursuit of righteousness, peace, faith and love, I wonder what would happen. Would the world take notice? Would the name of Christ be magnified? I think so.

Flee the evil desires of youth, and pursue righteousness, faith, love and peace, along with those who call on the Lord out of a pure heart. (II Timothy 2:22)

Daily challenge:
Pursue righteousness, faith, love and peace. Pursue them as if your life—or the life of another—depends on it.

Go for the Gold

Can you hear it? Does the majestic tune ring in your ears? For weeks, I've seen announcements of the coming Olympics scroll across the bottom of the TV screen. The Games have now begun and I'm captivated by the coverage. I thrive on the stories of dedication, relentless training, overcoming adversity and the pursuit of excellence. Vicariously, I live through those performances, hoping to overcome mediocrity and regain my passion for competition.

In my elementary school days, my gym teacher believed in me. Whatever task he gave me, I excelled. I ran faster, jumped higher and hit a softball further than anyone—even the boys. More than once, he told me that he was going to watch me compete in the Olympics one day. I was inspired.

I recollect watching women's gymnastics one evening, motivated to start practicing. The back of our sofa seemed a good place to start. Running the length of our dining room, I catapulted myself through the air onto the back of the sofa, handspringing my way into the middle of the living room. It went pretty well. So well, in fact, that my brother joined me. Unaware of the shock we gave to the floor, our fun crashed to a halt—literally. We managed to knock the basement light fixture right off the beams, exploding into a zillion pieces onto my mother who stood there ironing. That was the end of our sofa handsprings. It was not the end of my dreams.

I never made it to the Olympics. I had offers to run in college but didn't accept. I wasn't good enough in gymnastics to compete at that level and my varsity play at a small college in several other sports failed to get anyone's attention. But I still had dreams and goals and loved the process of optimizing what potential I had.

To my shame, I have been less enthusiastic about training my spiritual life. I find I get lax, easily setting aside an edifying activity if it becomes inconvenient. Why is that? Often, I am simply weak or lazy—or both.

Perhaps these Summer Olympics will remind me of the importance of daily spiritual training and the need for perseverance.

Do you not know that in a race all the runners run, but only one gets the prize? Run in such a way as to get the prize. (I Corinthians 9:24)

Daily challenge:
Set a goal of performing an edifying act. Do it today.

Hope Springs Eternal

We were riding in the car on the way to my mother-in-law's funeral. Just for fun I asked my family, "What do you hope for?" Seth, the seventeen-year old, hoped he will win two-hundred-seventy-million dollars. Gary hoped that the big granddaddy deer that roams our property at night will show his antlered head during shooting hours. Caleb simply stated, "I hope for peace and quiet so I can read my book."

Hope. We all use this word in many different ways. Often, we may as well equate its meaning to wishful thinking. It's like jumping out from a perfectly good airplane hoping that we'll frolic on the fluffy clouds on the way down. Somehow, I don't think that will happen. Or, little children are good ones for hoping that Santa will bring them a special present.

Hope can, however, represent something far greater than frivolous musing. Hope is what happens when faith is well-placed. Let's say I go to the airport to board a plane. I have faith that the airplane will meet all the requirements of physics to take off and become airborne. Thus, I can have hope of arriving at my destination because the thing in which I have placed my faith is reliable.

In a spiritual sense, our hope of eternal life is borne out of saving faith. Our hope for a mature Christian walk is because we have faith that *"my grace is sufficient"* (II Corinthians 12:9). We have hope of running and not tiring, walking and not fainting (Isaiah 40:31) because we have faith that Christ strengthens us to do all things (Philippians 4:8). And we have hope that we will one day see Gary's mother again, because we have faith that Christ said, *"And if I go and prepare a place for you, I will come back and take you to be with me that you also may be where I am"* (John 14:3).

When faith is well-placed, hope becomes a reality. It is not something to be wished for; it is something to anticipate.

But as for me, I will always have hope; I will praise you more and more. (Psalm 71:14)

Daily challenge:
Could you use some hope? List three things about your faith that gives you hope.

Ashes to Ashes

"Be sure not to take Grandma with you," Dad Trittipoe lightly joked.

What is he talking about? We had been wandering around the house gathering up our things. Mom Trittipoe's memorial service was held earlier and we needed to be heading home. Then it occurred to me. There on the side table was a nondescript white paper gift bag. Inside was a black cardboard box, the edges sealed tightly. On the end of the box was a label that read: "Temporary urn for the remains of Patricia Trittipoe."

Whoa. What a strange feeling. For some reason, I almost laughed out loud. None of us had been aware that "she" was there in the house with us for a couple of days. *Hmm.* This was a first for me. Wondering about the weight, I picked it up. It was heavier than I thought but then again, how much of a weight reduction does cremation provide? How do you know it was her ashes and not the residue from someone's fire pit? Did all her ashes make it into the box or just a portion of them? All I knew was that it was not as light as the ashes I scoop from our wood stove. Questions unanswered, I placed the box back into the bag and left it there.

The earlier service was a wonderful tribute to Mom T and her role of wife, mother and Christian warrior. It was a relief not to have a casket there as a reminder of her mortality. Though tears rolled down cheeks as memories were rehearsed, it was a celebration of life rather than a mourning of death. That's the way it should be.

Dad is planning on taking Mom's earthly remains to rest in a cemetery next to her deceased sister. A week before her sister died, Mom had the opportunity to see her trust Christ as Savior. Though that spot in the cemetery will serve as a memory-marker for these lives, they are not there; they are with their Lord.

And so we will be with the Lord forever. Therefore encourage each other with these words. (I Thessalonians 4:17b, 18)

Daily challenge:
What will be said at your own funeral? Will a box of ashes be all that remains? Or, will your spiritual legacy be evident to all?

Warped

Today was a perfect summer day—sunny, blue skies, temps in the eighties and low humidity. I was working hard in my office and had about all I could stand. Gathering up my lunch, I headed for the hammock chairs hanging in the shade of a huge tree near the pool's edge. *Ah.* With wind chimes ding-donging in the breeze, it was a setting to be cherished. Cherished, that is, until I looked over at the table and benches that I made a few months ago.

I had been proud of my work. All was straight and plumb. The design was my own and everything stood solidly anchored in concrete. But over the past weeks, I have noticed the profiles of the furniture to be changing. No longer are the benches level or the edging on the table straight. Looking at it now, most would conclude this was not the job of a professional. In reality, I'm not a professional but . . . this was ridiculous.

The boards were heavy with the treatment chemicals when I bought them. What happened is that the boards have twisted and warped as the wood has gradually dried out. The process has been slow and the distortion measured. Though this process had been happening for weeks, it was only today that I noticed how bad everything looked.

This process reminds me of how we can become blind to spiritual warping. I know there have been periods when I thought I was doing okay. But all of a sudden, I took a look in the mirror and wondered what went wrong. How did I get so warped and off-track from where I wanted to be?

The answer is that I had not been paying attention to daily staying on course. The changes, the falters, the variances were so small that I could not see the effect. But after a while, the accumulated changes took on the shape of a volcano ready to explode.

Warped Christians are not what this world needs. Let's be vigilant in all we do, performing daily inspections and corrections when there's a potential for becoming twisted.

Only be careful, and watch yourselves closely so that you do not forget the things your eyes have seen or let them slip from your heart as long as you live. Teach them to your children and to their children after them. (Deuteronomy 4:9)

Daily challenge:
Look in the mirror of introspection. Straight or warped? Fix it before it gets worse.

Rocks

I could tell from the look on Seth's face that he was not happy. With a week before school begins again, he was less than thrilled with his wake-up call. But to have his dad describe the job for the day—well, it didn't go over too well.

His assigned task was to go out to the fifteen-acre field and pick up rocks. Yep, rocks. Big ones. Little ones. Medium-size ones. My husband was tearing up his bush hog and disc whenever he worked the rock-strewn land. Since the boys needed to be busy, they were asked—no, told—to fill the tractor's bucket with rocks and dump them into an out-of-the-way pile. But, hey, it wasn't all bad. His big brother was going to help. Caleb was equally thrilled.

Rocks certainly are the bane of a farmer's existence. It takes hard work to get rid of those hidden, and not-so-hidden, obstacles. But as aggravating as they are in a field, rocks are essential. We recently paid good money for truck loads of rock to dump on our driveway. And now, we have to buy additional loads of smaller rock to fill in between the bigger rocks. However, it is all necessary if we are going to have a solid foundation to drive on.

Does that remind you of the Bible story about the two builders? One guy built his house on sand. His house, of course, fell flat with the first stiff breeze. Contrast that to the other fella who built his house on the rock. Even in the midst of ravaging storms, his house stood firmly anchored.

To be secured to The Rock is a perfect strategy for survival. Rocks provide shelter in a time of need. They provide safety from the storm. They provide a saving fortress that no enemy can overtake. King David recognized this when he cried out, *Be my rock of refuge, to which I can always go; give the command to save me, for you are my rock and my fortress* (Psalm 71:3).

Run—don't walk—to the Rock and be safe and secure.

> *He is the Rock, his works are perfect, and all his ways are just. A faithful God who does no wrong, upright and just is he. (Deuteronomy 32:4)*

Daily challenge:
Feeling insecure? Affix yourself to the Rock and see if you don't stand firm.

Oops, I've Done It Again

I almost hate to admit I know the pop song so incredibly in vogue a few years ago. In the music video, the young starlet flitted about the screen, glibly recalling her pattern of bad behavior. Though it is a disturbing portrayal of disregard for good behavior, it is, unfortunately, a statement about our propensity to make the same mistakes over and over.

My own behavior reminded me of this today. I had gotten notice that a fee was being charged for my credit card. When I signed up for the card, I knew there was a fee but considered the benefits to outweigh the cost. I was wrong. I called last week to find out how to close the account and have the fee refunded. I followed up today, having verified the balance was zero and assuming it was going to be an easy process. Wrong again.

On this phone call I got another story about how all this works. What started as a very pleasant conversation changed as I became more frustrated. I was annoyed that this bank was going to keep my $90. I didn't want to get sassy. I tried not to sound riled . . . but I did. I felt bad for the gentleman on the other end. He ended by saying quite sincerely, "Well, I hope this disappointment won't keep you from having a good day."

Whamo. What a jerk I was to let this matter of a refund turn my disposition so far south. Had I written down the fellow's name and extension, I would have called to apologize and ask forgiveness. Regardless of the situation, I should not have reacted like I did. So, oops, I've done it again—but I really am sorry.

Thank God He is a God of forgiveness. This isn't the first time I've had to ask forgiveness for this kind of offense and it will likely not be the last. But God is so good to extend grace and forgiveness over and over again.

"Lord, how many times shall I forgive my brother when he sins against me? Up to seven times?" Jesus answered, "I tell you, not seven times, but seventy-seven times." (Matthew 18:21b, 22)

Daily challenge:
How was your tone today? Did you speak kindly and with patience?
If not, an apology and plea for forgiveness is in order—both from God
and the one you offended.

Enemies Turned Teammates

Earlier today I was watching a beach volleyball match. The Olympics have provided countless hours of motivational stories. This match was no exception. The two women on the Brazilian team had only been playing together for a week or two. An injury forced a substitution and this new team formed. The players had always been fierce competitors and yet they had to learn to be team players. Though there was first an element of distrust, the athletes warmed to the idea; they became comrades on the same side and no longer competitors across the net.

The situation reminded me of New Testament times. Think of the transformation of Saul of Tarsus into Paul, the apostle of Jesus Christ. Saul was known to be a persecutor of Christians, seeking to kill them. All of a sudden, he becomes a follower of Christ. Is it any surprise there were questions whether his conversion was real or fake? But the genuineness of Paul's new life was a convincing display. Though Paul was once an enemy of Christ, his conversion made him a friend of believers.

Sometimes we think that differences disqualify us from becoming team members. No greater example of this is that of a man and woman—purposely different by God's design but capable of making two become one. Once joined, the two can become an invincible force.

The beauty of the Body is that God makes it up with so many different people. Sure, we know the analogy of some being the hands and some the feet. But what we often forget are the many obvious differences—skin color, education, social standing, economic status, personality, likes, dislikes, interests, intellect and so on—that may seem to be a deal-breaker. How could we be joined with someone so different than ourselves? Christ's unity of purpose is the answer. Only He can make a functional team out of a bunch of intrinsically dysfunctional people.

Now you are the body of Christ, and each one of you is a part of it.
(I Corinthians 12:27)

Daily challenge:
Have you excluded someone from "The Team" because that person is different?

Come and Rest

I almost felt guilty. I spent a blissful hour in the pool, floating on my $1.98 raft and reading the latest edition of a favorite magazine. It's not that I hadn't done any work. I spent the morning chopping, pruning and digging in rock-hard dirt on a mission to transplant yucca plants from one spot to another. It was difficult, back-breaking work. Still, it felt a little odd to be relaxing when Gary and Caleb were sweating to replace a water heater that had sprung a major leak overnight.

Eventually, I dried off and made it to my office. A little work there and then back downstairs to clean and prepare a simple dinner. Afterwards, I grabbed a book, anxious to steal away a few more minutes. Nestled in my hammock chair out by the pool, I could not have felt more content. A kitty hopped into my lap, his loud purrs pacing the quick turning of the pages. I felt refreshed but wistful that these times did not come more often.

As God so often does, He provided just what I needed when I needed it. The book is all about restoring your soul, finding again the joy of knowing God. Up until a few months ago, I had been living under immense pressure, feeling some days unable to draw another breath. I felt no rest, no sigh of blessed relief. But with each passing day, I am becoming more cognizant of how those hard times have opened my eyes to God's faithfulness.

The process of restoration—and, no, it is not yet complete—is leading me into new opportunities for service. When others wept with me or shared their stories, I was encouraged beyond measure. Now it's my time to stretch out my hand and offer hope because of what God is doing in me.

When Christ says come and rest, He means it. It's essential to our spiritual—and physical—lives.

"Come to me, all you who are weary and burdened, and I will give you rest." (Mark 6:31b)

Daily challenge:
Feeling stressed? Uptight? Pull over from your hectic life. Take fifteen minutes to quiet yourself. Talk to God, read the Scripture, listen to edifying music.
Be encouraged.

Ah, I See Now!

"I can't see it! I can't see it!" There she was, nose plastered to one of those hidden picture things. As Kathy repeatedly struggled to find the focal length that allowed her to see the illusive image, we nearly doubled over in laughter. Time after time, she moved her head closer, then further away, eyes crossing and glazing over.

"Relax, Kathy. Don't try so hard. Just let the eyes do their thing." Most of the rest of us had no problem gaining focus but Kathy—not so much. "Can't you see it? There it is. I can see a big lion in the tall grass. Are you sure you don't see it?" Nope. She never saw the pictures. But she did provide hours of entertainment for the rest of us.

Spiritually, we can be just as blind. It's not that we intend to be blind; it just comes naturally. But thankfully, our blindness is not always permanent.

Starting in 2003, I had several dark years. Assaults on our lives plunged me into an oppressive time of suffering. No matter how hard I tried to focus, I couldn't see anything clearly. My vision was blurred. I wasn't sure why God had chosen me to be in this situation. What was His purpose? What would happen to our family? What would life look like on the other side of this?

Johnny Nash wrote and recorded a hit song in 1972. The first stanza, though not intended to be a theological treatise, does have some application to a Believer's perspective.

> *I can see clearly now, the rain is gone,*
> *I can see all obstacles in my way*
> *Gone are the dark clouds that had me blind*
> *It's gonna be a bright, bright, bright Sun-Shiny day.*

By God's grace, I'm beginning to see clearly. The Son reveals that those hard times built my character and matured my faith. Had I not been under the dark clouds that blinded me, I could never appreciate the Son-shiny days.

> *Now we see but a poor reflection as in a mirror; then we shall see*
> *face to face. Now I know in part; then I shall know fully, even as I*
> *am fully known. (I Corinthians 13:12)*

Daily challenge:
When you can't see clearly, step into the Sonlight.

Merely a Suggestion

That's how I view most recipes—they are mere suggestions. If it calls for two cups of semi-sweet chocolate chips, I make them dark chocolate and throw in a couple extra handfuls. One tablespoon of soy sauce might end up as a two-second shake from the bottle. It's not that I'm an excellent cook; I've just learned what the critical elements are and are not. If I'm baking cookies, the amount of flour is fairly important. If the recipe says to dust the pan with two tablespoons of flour, I ignore that and use the dump method instead. Now, I don't guarantee that everything turns out perfectly, but normally it's edible.

We can laugh about less-than-optimal cooking methods and get away with it. But, success sometimes requires a strict adherence to the "recipe." Take, for instance, the compulsory routines in a gymnastics event. Every turn of the hand, direction of pointed toes and rotation of a turn is prescribed for the gymnast. There's no room for individual interpretation or personalization. And, as I tell my sons, speed limits are not suggestions. They are, in fact, very precise rules. Obey them and you will never get a ticket for speeding.

Likewise, God gives us some rules for living that are not open for discussion. We are told in Proverbs 22:23 that if we train a child properly, he won't turn from that teaching when he is old. The converse is that if we don't train a kid according to God's principles, all bets are off. In chapter 19 (v. 20) the writer tells us that wisdom is sure to follow if we *listen to advice and accept instruction.* A sure-fire way to live stupidly is to close your ears and disregard sound counsel.

We need to begin to read our Bibles more as an instruction manual than optional suggestions dropped into a comment box.

Commit to the LORD whatever you do, and your plans will succeed.
(Proverbs 16:3)

Daily challenge:
Is there something that you chose to "do it your way" rather than by the Book?
Make a commitment to precisely obey.

Word Play

I'm still laughing. I suppose you had to be there to understand. Earlier today, I was having an email exchange with author and speaker, Virelle Kidder. She asked me to do something, to which I responded, "Onkey-donkey . . . a talking donkey's way of saying 'okey-dokey' . . . since I hear donkeys still talk." A rather lame joke playing off the title of one of her books, I was proud for the attempt at humor. But, her response back was stupendous. She simply wrote, "Braying for you." My husband thought I lost my mind when my laughter erupted at regular intervals whenever I thought about her punch line.

The English language allows for word play. I remember us kids chanting, "I scream for ice cream," a good example of an oronym (or homophone). And, consider this example of homonyms: "Know Jesus. Know peace. No Jesus. No peace."

Then, there are many instances when the light of the sun gets compared to Sonlight—but not in the same sense as Pepsi-Light; there is nothing missing from Sonlight. Actually, Sonlight makes sense since Jesus is the light of the world. I thought about these word plays when I read I John 5:12: *He who has the Son has life; he who does not have the Son of God does not have life.*

I understand this better in the context of Biology. There would be no life on earth without the sun. The rays hit the chloroplasts in the chlorophyll pigment contained within plants. From there, a chemical reaction takes place—photosynthesis—that in turn produces energy and oxygen. The oxygen is taken in by animals and people in a process called *cellular respiration* that produces the carbon dioxide required of the plants to continue the photosynthesis cycle. Therefore, it is true that without the sun, there can be no life.

Without the Son, Christ Jesus, there can be no life.

"I am the way, the truth and the life. No one comes to the Father except through me." (John 14:6)

Daily challenge:
Do you live in the Sonlight or in the shadows?

Did You Get My Message?

I'm about ready to spit nails. For three days, I've been trying to send a simple introductory letter to my online high-school students. The software used by the on-line school has been newly created and more than a few problems exist. No one seems to have a reason why my messages don't launch into cyberspace. Finally, after count-less attempts and painstaking entry of each student's address, I was able to send a message and ask my students, "Can anyone hear me? Did you get my message?"

It's frustrating not to be heard. I think of many times when my boys had selective hearing. If they liked what I had to say, they acknowledged me. But if my words told them to clean their rooms—well, somehow they never got the message. If however, I then shouted, "Dinner's ready," their hearing turned on again and they came running.

I think we must be awfully frustrating to God. How many times does He have to tell us how to live? How many times does He tell us how not to live? And yet, we act as though we don't hear Him. He must be on the throne looking down and saying, "Helllloooo. Anyone there? I'm trying to tell you something."

Jonah didn't like what God was telling him. "Go to Nineveh and tell those people to repent." But that was the last thing on earth he wanted to do. So, what did he do? Yep. We all know the story. He jumped on a boat and headed in the opposite direc-tion. A raging storm finally got Jonah's attention—and the attention of the sailors. Over the side Jonah went, because everyone but Jonah knew God was trying to get his attention. He finally got it all right, right down into the belly of the great fish. When he miraculously crawled onto the shore after being spit out, I think he was listening.

Let's stop making the same mistake. Listen when God speaks. Don't call down a storm just so He can get our attention.

I will listen to what God the LORD will say; he promises peace to his
people, his saints—but let them not return to folly. (Psalm 85:8)

Daily challenge:
God's talking. Are we listening?

Water Me—Now!

I heard their silent screams. The dreadfully dry weeks of summer had taken their toll. I knew the odds stacked against me in transplanting anything into the bone-dry ground, but I did it anyway. Surely, I could remember to water them. *Oops.*

Five days ago I dug up some yucca plants. They were pretty, producing a stately stalk full of flowers. But they surrounded an ugly, gnarled tree destined for a mercy killing. Out they came and around the pool fence they went. Eventually, I got them all settled in and watered them down. Sometime after that, I gave them another good soaking—once. But taking a break just now from my desk work, I went outside to water my vegetables and found the carnage. In particular, I had forgotten two of the yuccas planted away from the rest. They were limp and the once lush foliage had turned an unsightly hepatitis-like yellow.

This scenario is certainly the antithesis of the tree that is planted by the water *which yields its fruit in season and whose leaf does not wither* (Psalm 1:3b). The passage paints a picture of a clear running stream cascading over flow-smoothed rocks, birds chirping, a deer drinking to quench his thirst, the sun filtering down through leaves so healthy and full of life. It must be nice to be in a situation that naturally lends itself to life—rich soil, plenty of water and just the right amount of sun.

But what happens if we find ourselves dry? David felt like that when he was in the Judean desert. *O God, you are my God, earnestly I seek you; my soul thirsts for you, my body longs for you, in a dry and weary land where there is no water* (Psalm 63:1). Did he like it? Would he rather have been dipping his toes in the cool water? Sure. But God had other plans. He has a way of bringing water to the desert. He meets us where we are with what we need just when we need it.

> *They did not thirst when he led them through the deserts; he made water flow for them from the rock; he split the rock and water gushed out (Isaiah 48:21) . . . They will neither hunger nor thirst, nor will the desert heat or the sun beat upon them. He who has compassion on them will guide them and lead them beside springs of water. (Isaiah 49:10)*

Daily challenge:
Are you wilting? Look for God to water you.

It's Dark Out There

The butterfly flapping in my gut is unsettling. In the last several years, I haven't had a problem with nervousness before a race—probably because I haven't been competitive enough to worry about it. But now, just an hour or two from driving to West Virginia, I feel tingly and anxious. Nothing has changed about the lack of competitiveness but still, I am on edge. The race will begin at nine o'clock tonight, winding through, up, and over the rugged mountains. I like nighttime running. So why do I feel like this?

Opening my Bible, I had to laugh—at least for a moment. Reading references to darkness, I found this ominous piece of truth: *You bring darkness, it becomes night, and all the beasts of the forest prowl* (Psalm 104:20). Maybe I have a subconscious fear of mountain lions hungry for a midnight snack. But, nah, I don't think that's it. I'm probably uptight because I haven't raced since April and I am not at the peak of fitness.

This race will be interesting in that we'll be running toward the light; the darkness can last only so long before the sun starts to shine on another day. No matter how difficult the path, how tired I get, how puny my headlight might seem compared to the dark curtain through which I run, the morning will come—guaranteed.

Physical darkness has always been a great analogy for spiritual darkness. The prophet Isaiah wrote in the famous chapter predicting Christ's birth that *The people walking in darkness have seen a great light* (Isaiah 9:2a). The *great light* to which Isaiah referred is none other than Jesus Christ. Christ himself declared, "*I am the light of the world. Whoever follows me will never walk in darkness, but will have the light of life*" (John 8:12b).

With the light comes responsibility. No more stumbling and fumbling, groping in the darkness. No more using the darkness to disguise our bad behavior. No more fear of what lurks behind a rock or tree.

If you find yourself in the dark, keep walking. The Son will soon shine.

For you were once darkness, but now you are light in the Lord. Live as children of light. (Ephesians 5:8)

Daily challenge:
If you are constantly living in the dark, perhaps you have never known the source of all light.

235

It Hurts, but Run Anyway

"Look. I think that's a woman in front of us."

"Oh, no," I groaned. I knew what Sophie wanted to do. With five miles left in a very tough fifty-mile trail race, she wanted to hunt her down, leaving her to choke on our dust. In actuality, overtaking her—a much younger runner—also appealed to me on some warped level. "Ah, this is gonna hurt."

We had been running all night. The race started last night at 9:00 p.m., having traveled along gnarly single track trail and undulating dirt roads for the last nine and a half hours. We ran together until mile nineteen, when Sophie lived out a burst of energy from the music playing in her ears. At mile thirty two, I caught and passed her, expecting her to catch up. She did. But with thirteen miles of a predominately downhill assault off the mountain, we joined forces and decided to leisurely run it in together . . . until we saw "her."

We made a decisive move and blasted past, hoping to break her will. Her breathing was labored. She was struggling. With each turn in the curvy road we looked back. She was not there. Still, we kept the ferocious pace. I was on the edge of exhaustion. Now my breathing was labored. Still, we pressed on, arriving at the finish line several minutes before her. Relieved, we headed to the showers.

I knew that committing to the challenge was going to be difficult. I understood that my body and mind would vehemently protest. And yet, it was important to see it through.

There are similar decisions in our spiritual and personal lives that require comparable commitment. When societal pressure calls for us to deny Christ, we may suffer contempt. When we decide to take a stand on an ethical issue, it can be very unpopular. If we decide to be firm in disciplining our children, they may not appreciate it very much. Still, we do what we know is right even if it hurts.

For the grace of God that brings salvation has appeared to all men. It teaches us to say "No" to ungodliness and worldly passions, and to live self-controlled, upright and godly lives in this present age, while we wait for the blessed hope—the glorious appearing of our great God and Savior, Jesus Christ . . . . (Titus 2:11-13)

Daily challenge:
Facing an intimidating challenge? Write down the action you must take,
pray over it and begin today to do it.

Going Nowhere Fast

"For passengers awaiting Flight 4236 to White Plains, New York, we regret to inform you that this flight has been canceled. Please proceed to customer service."

Great. Another travel disaster. This is why I quit my job in the first place. With little recourse, I gathered my belongings and like a sheep being led to the slaughter, followed the herd. *Baaaaaa.* Filled to capacity, the serpentine rope corridors left me with little hope. I watched as person after person got the bad news. No more flights until tomorrow. No possibilities of getting into an alternate airport. I was stuck in Charlotte for the night and there was nothing I could do about it.

In my non-descript hotel room eating a non-descript meal, I flipped channels on the TV sitting on the non-descript dresser. A news story caught my eye, one of a mature Florida couple whose home had flooded. "What are you going to do?" they were asked.

"I don't know. I'm not in charge. God is."

That is a profound statement. Do I believe that on an everyday basis? Is God only in control if the plane I was supposed to be on crashed to the earth killing everyone? Or maybe the anything-but-non-descript hotel I was originally scheduled to stay in will burn down tonight.

We like to tell stories of incredible Divine intervention—and I have some I could share. But I think we miss the point all too often. We want something grand, something incredible rather than accepting the "routine" work of God in our lives. There doesn't have to be an obvious reason why I'm spending the night in a lousy hotel. God is still in charge. When I get to my job assignment later than planned tomorrow morning, I should not fret. For some reason, whether known to me or not, God wants me in this situation.

If only I could remember this principle, I would have less sleep-deprived nights. I would not waste time fretting over how or when or why or where. Rather, I would simply accept the way God has chosen.

I'm not in charge. God is. Profound, huh?

" . . . Great and marvelous are your deeds, Lord God Almighty. Just and true are your ways, King of the ages." (Revelation 15:3)

Daily challenge:
Fretting? That's sort of dumb. We're not in control.

Well Done

It was not my favorite way to start the day. The wake-up call never came and the alarm went off way too soon. With the fiasco of my plane breaking down last night, I only managed to get about two hours of sleep. *Ugh.* How will I ever survive the day?

Despite the odds, I made it to my destination and my worksite. My task was to assess how well a provider of autotransfusion services complied with standards. Plunging into my work like a diver into the depths, I asked unending questions and reviewed mounds of paperwork. The more I investigated, the more I became convinced that this organization was exemplary in the conduct of services. *Well done.*

Those two words have become commonplace. Just go to any soccer game. Well-meaning coaches shout out "Well done" when a kid serves a well-placed ball to a teammate. Teachers write the words in red at the top of strong assignments. And music teachers offer the encouragement in the aftermath of a piano recital. But despite the almost cliché nature of the phrase, its utterance can be powerful.

As a gymnast, I lived for my coach to convey that I had done well after dismounting the beam or after the last pass of my floor routine. Compliments never came easily from her lips. She pulled no punches. If I screwed up, she let me know—which made the occasional kudos even more valuable and motivating.

Can you imagine how the servants in the Matthew parable felt when the Master uttered those famous words to them? The guys given the two and the five talents invested them wisely, doubling the money on the master's behalf. "Well done." But on the other hand, how devastating it must have been to think you had done well by burying your money only to be chastised for being wicked and lazy.

The lesson here is clear. An honest assessment of "well done" is to be as sought after as it is to be given. Do you want a sure way to discourage your child? Fail to give him the thumbs-up when he does well. Don't devalue the phrase by frivolous use, but be generous in delivering the message that says, "You did great. Keep it up!"

"Well done, good and faithful servant! You have been faithful with a few things; I will put you in charge of many things." (Matthew 5:23)

Daily challenge:
Deliver a well-deserved "well done" today.

The Stench

I have to admit it. If I have to travel on business, I enjoy staying in nice hotels—especially if I'm not paying for it. Such was the case today. This time, the accommodation was a high-end suite hotel with a resort feel. I couldn't wait to get in my room and relax. With plastic key card in hand, I walked down the hallway, entered the elevator and pushed the button for the top floor. *Great.* I like the top floor. With a smile on my face, I stepped off the elevator and sniffed the air. *Uh-oh.* Sliding the key into the lock, the door opened in front of me and a revelation came to me. *Yuk.* This is a smoking room on a smoking floor. It was putrid and my anticipation of a perfect stay turned sour.

Of course, I tried to change rooms with no success. "No more room in the inn," or so they said. Everything reeked—the carpet, the drapery, the bedding, the towels. The obnoxious stench even permeated my clothes just by hanging in the closet. It was amazing how one bad habit could completely ruin the ambience of an otherwise beautiful suite.

This phenomenon is not rare. I've run along a lovely country road when I suddenly noticed a rancid odor. There, out in the wide-open spaces, the carcass of a mangled deer in the ditch completely overwhelmed the senses. And, just the other week we noticed a putrid smell in the laundry room. Try as we might, we could not locate the source, the smell becoming stronger with each passing day. The whole house paid the price until we finally realized it was spoiled potatoes that created the problem. With that discovery, we finally got the relief we sought for weeks.

Likewise, it's amazing how pervasive and overpowering the stench of wrongdoing can be. Whether it be flagrant sin, a bad attitude, selfishness or simple stupidity, these things mask what is honorable and true. An explosive fit of anger destroys an otherwise sound reputation. A pattern of lying makes it difficult for a parent to trust the offending child. And a selfish wife destroys a previously fine marriage.

Fling open the windows. Clear the air. Get rid of the stench and become *the aroma of Christ among those who are being saved and those who are perishing* (II Corinthians 2:15).

As dead flies give perfume a bad smell, so a little folly outweighs wisdom and honor. (Ecclesiastes 10:1)

Daily challenge:
Does your life "stink?" Find the source and get rid of it.

Judge Not

Goodness me. Look at that family. I felt a wave of ugly criticism sweep over me, seemingly powerless to stop the tsunami of emotion.

Traveling back from a business trip, I watched the scene unfold. At the ticket desk was a morbidly obese young black woman with two kids in tow, her name tattooed onto her arm. *What? She can't remember her own name?* The two children were soon joined by four more and a husband. Their belongings, packed into garbage bags, were strewn about and in the path of passersby. A teenage girl, a daughter, carried her own tiny baby. They struggled to make it down the hallway and through security. *I sure hope they aren't on my flight.*

I was aware of making judgments based on their color, size, clothes and "baggage." Shame on me. But what was this low-socioeconomic family trying to prove? Besides, they were going to Disney World. Shouldn't they stay home and pay the rent instead? Shouldn't both Mom and Dad shed about one-hundred pounds each? Shouldn't they keep better control over their daughter who had already become a mother? *Tsk. Tsk.*

Wouldn't you know it? Not only were they on my flight, I was completely surrounded by them. In the same row, behind me, in front of me. The tiniest babe was in the arms of the very large woman across the aisle from me. I looked into the eyes of that child and fell in love. Then, I heard the three-year-old boy repeatedly ask, "Mama, are we flying yet?" The rest of the children sat obediently in their seats. As the plane's engines roared, the little boy's laughter was contagious. It crescendoed as we accelerated and broke into a fit of uncontrollable glee as the plane soared upward. "Mama. We're flying! We're flying!"

At that moment, I began to overcome my critical spirit and see this family through the eyes of an adoring, precious little boy. Despite the differences, that mother and I were more similar than not. We had hopes and dreams, good days and bad, children who can be so sweet and our share of frustrations and challenges. I spoke with her for a few moments and heard these things in her soft and humble voice. Silently, I asked God for forgiveness for being such a foolish, critical observer.

I hope this family has a great time on vacation.

But Jesus called the children to him and said, "Let the little children come to me, and do not hinder them, for the kingdom of God belongs to such as these." (Luke 18:16)

Daily challenge:
When an opportunity to judge presents itself,
fight it off with a genuine encounter.

Payback

Having returned from a business trip last night, my day has been filled with the mundane duties of playing catch-up. Catch up on correspondence, catch up with my on-line students, catch up filing paperwork and catch up sweeping up the cat hair and dust bunnies that accumulated in my four-day absence.

But the most important activity was gathering my receipts from the trip and getting my expense report in order. I have to pay the costs up front and then submit them for reimbursement, carefully transcribing them onto the proper form. I never feel too bad laying down my credit card because I know I will get paid back—even if the hotel is ridiculously expensive.

In my mind, there are two negative types of payback—the "tit-for-tat" payback and the "payback-is-hell" variation. In the first case, it is much like the principle in physics that states that for every action, there is an equal but opposite reaction. *You do me wrong, I'll do you wrong back.* The second is darker and more intense. *You do something to me, I'll come after you with a vengeance.* We see this at the movies all the time.

On the other hand, there are positive forms of payback. "Every good turn deserves another." The action and reaction are equivalent in scope and degree. My reimbursement is an example of this. I get back exactly what I spent—nothing more, nothing less.

But the one type of payback that is less familiar is the type where bigger and better is returned. Does a store ever give you more goods than you pay for? Does your boss give you more time off than you have earned? Rarely. However, there is One who gives back abundantly and without reserve. Our actions have nothing to do with what comes back to us.

God has promised an abundant life. Through the ages, Jehovah promised His people health and healing, letting them *"enjoy abundant peace and security"* (Jeremiah 33:6). But the generosity did not stop there. It is not by our work that we are saved but by His grace (Titus 3:5). It is not just enough grace to get by; it is *God's abundant provision of grace and of the gift of righteousness reign in life through the one man, Jesus Christ* (Romans 5:17).

Don't be greedy and selfish. Pay back more than is deserved.

The grace of our Lord was poured out on me abundantly, along with the faith and love that are in Christ Jesus. (I Timothy 1:14)

Daily challenge:
Surprise someone with an abundant payback.

Energy

Sometimes you got it. Sometimes you don't. Energy, that is. As I was watching Seth's soccer game today, you could see energy levels wax and wane. Energy was high at the opening whistle. But in the hot and humid afternoon, it became obvious that maintaining that level of output became progressively more difficult. Understandably so. I was getting tired just sitting on the sidelines.

I don't know about you, but sometimes I wonder how I'll get through the day. I wake up tired. Coffee doesn't have much of an effect and if I sit in one position too long, my eyes droop and my head does that awkward bobbing thing.

Women living in the United States—and elsewhere—wear many hats: wife, mother, housekeeper, chauffeur, financial analyst, economic advisor, counselor, teacher, administrator, nutritionist and cook, waitress, daycare provider and nurse, among other things. Everywhere we turn, we have responsibilities. Somebody somewhere needs us. It's exhausting.

Sometimes it's not so much a physical exhaustion; it's mental. My mind just won't shut off. But worse, sometimes it will hardly turn on. What a sad state of affairs. So what are we to do? From where are we to draw our strength?

Isaiah knew we get tired—men and women both. In a well-known passage he writes, *Even youths grow tired and weary, and young men stumble and fall; but those who hope in the LORD will renew their strength. They will soar on wings like eagles; they will run and not grow weary, they will walk and not be faint* (Isaiah 40:30, 31).

Until tonight, however, I never realized the connection between the need for renewed energy and the reason for the renewal. We are granted energy so that we may continue in the work of the Lord—teaching, edifying, encouraging and admonishing each other. But lest we think of these activities on a grand scale, it is not. We are called to be energized right where we are—in our homes, at work and in our communities.

We proclaim him, admonishing and teaching everyone with all wisdom, so that we may present everyone perfect in Christ. To this end I labor, struggling with all his energy, which so powerfully works in me. (Colossians 1:28, 29)

Daily challenge:
Trust God to grant you the daily energy you need.

BYOB

Bring your own beer. Bring your own beverage. But, bring your own bucket? Sure—if you will be meeting at a well.

The Samaritan woman did just that. She came to the well because she was tired and thirsty. In her day, it was the woman's job to fetch water. And much like the water coolers in the modern office, it was as good as any place to socialize and catch up with friends. But she was hardly prepared to find a Jew hanging around the well. Jews didn't have anything to do with the half-breed Samaritans. So when this man asked her for a drink, she was taken aback; His identity hidden from her eyes.

The conversation continued when Jesus spoke in analogies about drawing living water. *"If you knew the gift of God and who it is that asks you for a drink, you would have asked him and he would have given you living water"* (John 4:10).

"Duh," and I'm paraphrasing here. "Didn't you forget your bucket? Sort of important if you plan on getting any water out of this deep well."

The Savior responds, *"Everyone who drinks this water will be thirsty again, but whoever drinks the water I give him will never thirst. Indeed, the water I give him will become in him a spring of water welling up to eternal life"* (John 4:13, 14).

We know how the rest of the conversation went. Jesus called her out on the carpet with the factoid about her five husbands and the current boyfriend. She was shocked. Up to this point, Jesus was virtually incognito; the woman had no clue who He was. But somewhere between "I'm thirsty" and *"I who speak to you am he* [Messiah]," the woman understood that only this man could fill her bucket to overflowing. She had come to the well and found satisfaction.

Isn't that they way our lives should be? We need to go to the desert well. But do we leave our buckets at home in case we can't find the well? Of course not. We tote our buckets in expectation of being filled. The walk to the well may be hot and dry, but we continue because we have the promise of a quenched thirst.

We have the answer to the question posed by the Psalmist. *My soul thirsts for God, for the living God. When can I go and meet with God?* (Psalm 42:2). Answer: Go to the well and bring your bucket.

> *. . . Whoever is thirsty, let him come; and whoever wishes, let him take the free gift of the water of life. (Revelation 22:17)*

Daily challenge:
Thirsty? Go to the well.

Here We Go Again

The weather reports look ominous. Most channels are dedicating reporters and air time to the impending storm. Nearly three years to the day from when Hurricane Katrina roared onto the Gulf Coast, her brother, Hurricane Gustav, is gearing up to begin his own rampage. Gustav has already been merciless, claiming the lives of over one-hundred islanders. But now as the killer storm advances north, New Orleans is once again bracing for a direct hit. What must be going through the minds of those people living in that below-sea-level city?

There is an obvious difference, however, between the preparation for the 2005 storm and this one, expected to hit by morning. Three years ago, the call went out. "Leave now. Run for your lives." Some left. Most did not. Rather, they must have thought themselves stronger than the wind and waves. But as we all know, the unthinkable happened. The hurricane hit, the storm surge was enormous, levies broke around the city and 1,600 Gulf Coasters lost their lives. Rioting and looting prevailed. Chaos reigned. Countless numbers lost all they had. Some have yet to return, 65,000 homes waiting to be rebuilt.

This time around, the monster storm is nearly identical, but the difference in attitude is obvious. Plans three years in the making are being forced into action. Folks are heeding the mandatory evacuations, rendering the streets eerily vacant. In fact, nearly two-million people have headed for higher ground. "Don't stay or you'll be on your own. Loot and you go directly to jail."

By lunch time tomorrow, we'll likely know the storm's damage. But one thing is for sure. The loss of life will not range in the thousands because men, women and children took the warning seriously.

As a parent, I have warned my children: "Don't do that," "Don't go there," "Don't talk back to me," "Put that away or I'll . . .." The list is long. God has done likewise by warning His children over and over again. It's the only way we learn. God's rules are never obscure and the line in the sand is clear.

We are wise to be careful with our warnings and consistent in delivering the consequences. Our children need to understand obedience the first time and accept responsibility for ignoring the admonition.

I am not writing this to shame you, but to warn you, as my dear children. (I Corinthians 4:14)

Daily challenge:
Warn when you must. Follow through accordingly.

Labor Day

Labor Day. On the surface it sounds as if we should all be shouldering our shovels or toiling in the noonday heat. Quite the opposite. In 1882 the Central Labor Union of New York City first promoted a day off from work. A dozen years later, Congress enacted the first Monday in September as a federal holiday, one intended to honor the working class. Today, it seems to be the "official" end of summer.

As I was growing up, every Labor Day signified the last day of freedom for us kids. My parents organized a big neighborhood picnic, complete with the world's largest wiffle-ball game, with at least twenty-five small, medium and large contestants per side. But once the chairs were folded and the tables put in their place, we had only the approach of the big yellow school bus the next morning to look forward to. *Ugh.* No more staying up late. No more homework-less days. No more napping in the hammock. We just knew it was going to be a whole lot of work.

Work is not a bad thing—at least that's what we tell our kids. Sure, we all enjoy a respite from the normal routine. But without work, nothing would ever get done, leaving piles of uncompleted tasks begging for attention.

The origin of work was in the Garden of Eden. *The LORD God took the man and put him in the Garden of Eden to work it and take care of it* (Genesis 2:15). But it was not arduous and unpleasant. It was only after the original sin that God's curse extended to sweat and toil in the newly imperfect world. The reality of labor can also be seen when the ancient ruler of Egypt used the Israelites as slave labor, turning out brick after brick in conditions unacceptable to any union.

Then, we have the Proverbial-type admonition that you must work in order to eat (II Thessalonians 3:10). Now, that hurts. Can't we ever get a break?

Work is good. It is expected. It is commanded. But there must be rest as well. Glorify God with your work and your rest by honoring His plan.

God said, "Six days you shall labor, but on the seventh day you shall rest; even during the plowing season and harvest you must rest."
(Exodus 34:21)

Daily challenge:
Don't sacrifice family time for that dirty floor or weedy garden.
It can wait. They cannot.

Visualization

I was working hard. Sweat poured off, the salt stinging my eyes, water dripping from my chin. My breathing was labored, my legs heavy. I thought about the night ahead of me and wondered if I could deal with the extreme fatigue and lack of sleep. Up one mountain and down another. When will this climb ever end? And, who knows what the weather will do. But then, snapping back into reality I reached for the TV clicker. So much for thinking about my next race. My workout on the Nordic Track was serving a purpose, but I wasn't getting anywhere.

I like these workouts. They are specific for uphill conditioning and allow me to put myself into a race situation, both mentally and physically. I never even have to leave the house. Is it realistic to train like this all the time? Of course not. But it's good to have a low impact workout that ultimately helps me negotiate those mountains. And, it helps me anticipate some of the difficulties I might encounter along the way.

As goofy as it may sound, mental preparation is nearly as important as physical preparation. Back in my gymnast days, I spent hours visualizing every routine. Not only did I think about the sequence of the tricks, I tried to anticipate how I might feel. How nervous would I be? Would my legs feel like mush? Would my heart beat wildly enough that my chest explodes? Would I be so terrified of doing a back walkover on the balance beam that I chicken out and fall on my head? Or, would I achieve such precision on my floor routine that my coach would become ecstatic? As each moment of panic or pleasure came into my mind, I tried to direct my thoughts to optimize my chance of success.

There's a time and a place to use visualization in the Christian life. Sometimes it might be the only way to see past the here and now. I think the Apostle Paul might have done this as he looked forward to heaven. He had to keep his eternal life in focus, or the constant beatings and persecution would have surely done him in. So too, keeping in mind the promise of a great future makes it easier to deal with a difficult now.

Let us fix our eyes on Jesus, the author and perfecter of our faith,
who for the joy set before him endured the cross, scorning its shame,
and sat down at the right hand of the throne of God. (Hebrews 12:2)

Daily challenge:
Facing a challenge today? Anticipate how it will look and feel
on the other side.

Hot or Cold

If it wasn't so annoying, it would be hilarious. Any woman of peri-menopausal age will likely relate. For several years I was constantly tormented by wild temperature swings capable of producing ice cubes at one end and boiling water at the other. Before I knew what was happening, the sweat poured off like rivulets. I could wring the water out of my clothes. It was particularly dreadful at night. I often awoke feeling frog-like sleeping in a puddle. Off went the covers and the clothes in search of a respite from the intense heat.

I don't care much for being hot under any circumstances. This morning I was able to get in a run before the sun turned up the thermostat to unbearable. Even so, a dive into the swimming pool did wonders for freeing me from the torment.

I suppose that in a few weeks, I'll be complaining about being too cold. I hate going out to run on a day that is freezing, wet and gray. The drawer holding my running clothes seems to stick and the door to the outside just won't open. Funny how that works.

We are finicky people. We complain about the heat and then the cold. We are never satisfied. But God actually prefers that we are one way or the other. Not that God literally want us to have a heat stroke or frostbite. Rather, He wants us anything but lukewarm in the way we live out our lives.

It's easy to take a middle-of-the-road approach; not taking a firm position on anything—especially in a society that expects political correctness. But compromise is not always appropriate. James 5:12 instructs, *but let your yea be yea; and your nay, nay.*

Don't be wishy-washy on issues that matter. Say what you mean and mean what you say. Be either black or white. Hot or cold.

> *"I know your deeds, that you are neither cold nor hot. I wish you were either one or the other! So, because you are lukewarm—neither hot nor cold—I am about to spit you out of my mouth."*
> *(Revelation 3:15, 16)*

Daily challenge:
Don't sit down if you should be taking a stand.

Drill, Drill, Drill

What in the world are you doing? Drilling to China? My mouth forced open by some tortuous spreader, I cringed as the *whirr* of the drill continued for what seemed like four days and twenty-nine minutes. *How in the world could one little tooth deserve such treatment? Surely the oil crisis could be averted with such a commitment to drilling.* The dentist nearly had to stand on her head to reach the culprit tooth, taking captive my tongue in the process. She pushed it down and out of the way, bringing on disgusting gag reflexes. I was not comfortable. My back muscles tightened, my hands clasping each other, knuckles white. *Please. Please. Be finished five-minutes ago.*

Of course, that dental visit finally came to an end and I survived—with the help of some ibuprofen. And as most often happens, I soon forgot the pain and went about my daily activities. I was content to know that the disease had been cut out and the tooth was salvaged.

When I was giving birth to my first son without an epidural, I had much the same thoughts; it hurt and I didn't like it. But when that child was placed in my arms, the pain suddenly became secondary. I could endure the pain because I knew my son was worth the required suffering.

I've had similar conversations with myself during races. It's always at the point when legs burn with fatigue and breathing is labored. I want so much to stop; to give into the weakness of the flesh. But then I think, *Come on. You worked so hard to get here. Don't quit. If you do, all will be lost.* The effort in preparation will be wasted.

I listened to John McCain speak tonight of the suffering he endured in the Vietnamese prisoner of war camps. The only reason he chose to endure was because he saw the cause as greater than himself. I think the Apostle Paul understood. He was in and out of prisons, beaten, left for dead, shipwrecked, cold, dirty and hungry—all because he, too, understood that his calling was for an eternal purpose.

For our light and momentary troubles are achieving for us an eternal glory that far outweighs them all. (II Corinthians 4:17)

Daily challenge:
Pain is only a means to see what lies beyond.

Guard Your Heart

All I wanted to do was make a quick stop at the house of a business acquaintance. In and out. Lickety-split. Instead, an unanticipated conversation began on the steps of the front porch.

"My husband had a total mental, spiritual and physical breakdown. I haven't seen him for weeks. I think he is deep in sin."

Whoa. That caught me off guard. This man was a prominent member of the Christian community, engaged in ministry. She didn't see this coming. Caroline did not understand nor did she know all the details. He was being less than truthful. Now she was selling the house, setting divorce proceedings in motion and figuring out where to go from there. Her tears revealed deep hurt. I felt utterly incapable of saying anything substantive or encouraging.

As I listened, I got the feeling there were a number of issues. His lying was troublesome because it indicted a desire to cover up wrongdoing. It is self-preservation at its worse. But sin is like that. We like to keep our deep dark secrets and sins hidden from others, not willing to admit when we are wrong.

Also troubling was that the powerful internet had lured another victim, much like the mythological sirens bidding men to venture near. I personally know at least a handful of men who have chosen to open their minds to cyberworld perversions. Whether it be pornography, illicit communications, fantasy or the addictions of gaming, each drag the participant by the earlobes further into this illusion of acceptable behavior. Some have disappeared into the darkness, their lives destroyed.

Most surface actions are rooted in a much deeper problem. Anchored in the remnants of the sin nature, these men have not been guardians of their hearts and minds. It is so easy to be, as James states (4:8), *double-minded.* The Psalmist understood this by saying *the mind and heart of man are cunning* (Psalm 64:6).

There is no simple answer, but there is a simple principle:

Above all else, guard your heart. (Proverbs 4:23a)

Daily challenge:
How is the security around your heart?

Patience

I'm normally a patient person. But today was one of those times when I did not accept my circumstances. Spending all day at a soccer tournament, I enjoyed watching Seth earn the MVP of the tournament, the team going undefeated. A good day by anyone's account. But time was fleeting and it was questionable if I could make it back in time to meet friends for dinner.

I'm not an aggressive driver. In fact, I am fairly cautious, cognizant of speed limits. I had about forty miles to drive and planned on driving as fast as I could without forcing my guardian angels out of the car if I exceeded the limits of the law. Wouldn't you know it? I got behind drivers even more cautious than me. They were obviously enjoying what had turned out to be a beautiful day, windows down and elbows resting on the frame. Since the road was narrow and twisting, passing was out of the question. I had no option but to bide my time, trying very hard not to be annoyed or ride their bumper.

I eventually got to my friend's house for dinner, howbeit late. But even then, I was rushing like crazy and unsettled by being behind schedule. It wasn't until I walked in the door that I relaxed and freed my mind.

Lack of patience produces a state of discontent. For whatever reason, we want something to be better, happen more quickly, produce results faster or offer us something we want. In reality, it is yet another display of selfishness, because it centers around me, myself and I. Not exactly the pinnacle of godly attitudes.

Patience is not something that comes naturally. Impatience, on the other hand, is easy and a display of the old nature. But patience can be achieved as a result of the Spirit's working in our lives. *But the fruit of the Spirit is love, joy, peace, patience, kindness, goodness, faithfulness, gentleness and self-control* (Galatians 5:22, 23). I see a direct relationship between the level of Spirit-control and the ability to accommodate things happening at a slower pace than we desire.

Therefore, as God's chosen people, holy and dearly loved, clothe yourselves with compassion, kindness, humility, gentleness and patience. (Colossians 3:12)

Daily challenge:
When you feel the angst of impatience, make sure it's not from being selfish.

Down by the Riverside

Well, maybe not the riverside, but we were all down by the murky little lake. The entire church was meeting at a farm pond. The day dawned sunny and bright, a contrast from the day before when the outer bands of a hurricane brought torrential rains. The water level, thanks to those rains, rose about two feet.

We did not meet for a picnic, although we enjoyed an outdoor meal. No. The reason we met was to witness the baptism of four individuals. There on the bank of the still-muddy pond, we sang together and heard testimony. Then, those choosing to identify with Christ waded out to waist deep. "I baptize you, my sister, in the name of the Lord Jesus Christ," the elder proclaimed. Down into the water each one went, raised again "to the newness of life."

Ever since the Lord himself was baptized by John, baptism has been used through the ages as a demonstration of being a Christ-follower. His death and burial are symbolized by submersion; His resurrection by being raised up out of the water. Baptism in the New Testament appears to have been the immediate consequence of believing. Phillip baptized the believing eunuch along a dusty road. Simon believed and was baptized. A three-thousand strong crowd heard the message, believed and were baptized. Even the jailer who believed at the midnight hour, the quaking jail loosening Paul and Silas from their bonds, went beneath the water before the sun rose. Belief and action went hand in hand.

Even today, we are joined together with those saints from centuries ago when we are obedient. We are one in Spirit, one in love, one in service. Baptism should always be a gentle reminder of the price that was paid and our call to serve.

At that hour of the night the jailer took them and washed their wounds; then immediately he and all his family were baptized. (Acts 16:33)

Daily challenge:
Don't hesitate to act out your belief as a testimony to Christ.

Sick and Tired

My head feels like it's going to explode. Fever and chills play games chasing each other, much like a kitten chases her tail. My eyes are watering, my nose is stopped up and my body feels like I am in the final stages of a hundred-mile race. I feel lousy and I don't like it.

Being sick is annoying. I don't get sick very often, but when I do, it's usually a doozie. Being reduced to a weak and powerless individual is not something I enjoy. Plans go by the wayside and what does get done requires maximum effort.

No. I don't think my present infirmity is life-threatening, but it makes me appreciate my normal state of health. I think we all have a tendency to take our health and fitness for granted. Perhaps it is when we are thrown off-course by something like illness that we look more closely at where we are and where we are going.

At times like this I wonder how I would respond if I got sick, deathly sick. Perhaps I might have cancer, a heart attack or maybe some strange and rare disease. Would I be able to trust God with my literal life? Would I be like Jeremiah, Mr. Tough guy himself? *Woe to me because of my injury! My wound is incurable! Yet I said to myself, "This is my sickness, and I must endure it"* (Jeremiah 10:19).

Maybe I would claim the promise that the Psalmist described: *The LORD will sustain him on his sickbed and restore him from his bed of illness* (Psalm 41:3). Or perhaps I would count on the effective prayers of the elders on my behalf. *And the prayer offered in faith will make the sick person well; the Lord will raise him up* (James 5:15).

I hope I don't have to be desperately sick for God to capture my undivided attention. I want to give him the attention He deserves. But if that's what it takes for me to turn my heart fully to Him, then I suppose being sick could be the best thing that ever happened to me.

Until then, I'll take a few more decongestants and try to get some sleep.

Dear friend, I pray that you may enjoy good health and that all may go well with you, even as your soul is getting along well. (III John 1:2)

Daily challenge:
Thank You, Lord, for being with me in sickness and in health.

Connectivity

Connectivity. That's an important word in today's society. TV commercials have strange-looking men in faraway places saying, "I've found it. I've found the internet." Cell-phone providers urge us to join them and have the "network" travel with us. Just stand by the side of the road and see how many drivers are connecting while driving. It seems like every other person in the mall is multi-tasking—talking and texting while they shop. How did we ever stay connected without these modern conveniences?

Being connected is a very good thing. I currently teach science in an online high school and depend on being connected daily with my students. Being connected allows me to offer help and encouragement to the kids. They also have the ability to converse with me. It's a two-way street that keeps traffic moving in both directions.

The problem comes when something interrupts the line of connection. That has been my story the last several days. A number of simultaneous technical difficulties have made it difficult for me to connect to the educational software. Countless frustrations over "Connection to the server lost" messages have almost made me lose my Christianity. I have fretted over all those hours that I've been trying, unsuccessfully, to contact my students. I don't want them to think that I am a terrible, lazy teacher. And, trouble on the students' end has made the situation even bleaker. The severed communication standstills any positive gains in learning or teaching.

Come to think about it, the results are much the same when we interrupt the line of communication between us and God. Unlike my online education example where the interruption could have been from either end, we have only ourselves to blame when we can't hear God. He hasn't moved. He hasn't stopped talking. He isn't deaf. We are.

For there is one God and one mediator between God and men, the
man Christ Jesus. (I Timothy 2:5)

Daily challenge:
When you pray, don't say "amen." Leave it open-ended. Carry on a running
conversation all day to stay connected.

The Great Cover-Up

Goodness. I'm a mess today and I want to whine about it. Every bone in my body is aching. My muscles feel like they are ninety-two miles into a race. My neck is creaking and cracking, bringing on a monster headache. And, I'm having a hard time mustering up enough energy to walk across the room. Even my fingers are sore. But to make things even worse, the gray in my hair's part is showing again. Will it ever end?

My genetic makeup has destined me to be gray. From the time I was seventeen, a few isolated grays morphed into clumps of drab color. If I pulled my hair back during my college years, I looked skunk-like, a band of white running right down the middle. It wasn't pretty. But it wasn't until I went as Miss Scarlett to a "Clue" party that I dyed my hair dark and liked it. So for the last twenty-some years, I've had to play the game of covering up those roots whenever they became too obvious.

Sometimes I feel like I do that in life. I don't want the real me to be seen, so I cover it up. I smile when I think ugly thoughts. I use a different vocabulary depending on the situation. Or, I feign an interest in "spiritual" things when I really don't give a rip.

Should I stop covering up those roots of dishonesty and let the truth be exposed? I am currently in a situation where I'm torn about holding my tongue to keep the peace or risk an unpleasant confrontation by speaking my mind. What makes this difficult is that we are responsible, at different times, to do both. We must be respectful but also speak the truth in love. It's a hard task to walk that line with integrity.

I trust I will properly understand how to proceed. But I have confidence that God will make the way clear, gray hair or not.

"Even to your old age and gray hairs I am he, I am he who will sustain you. I have made you and I will carry you; I will sustain you and I will rescue you." (Isaiah 46:4)

Daily challenge:
What are you covering up? Is it time to be honest with yourself and others?

Remember When

911. Chances are that two thoughts just come into your mind. It's either a number you call when there's trouble or it's a date forever emblazed in our memories—or maybe it's both.

On a warm fall day with skies bright and blue, the New York City skyline turned black with smoke. Two jet liners crashed into the Twin Towers of the World Trade Center, ultimately ending the lives of three-thousand people. In Washington DC, the Pentagon and its occupants were attacked by another plane flown purposely into its walls. And in a Pennsylvania field, a plane fell from the sky and claimed the lives of all onboard. The terrorists involved in all three attacks heightened our patriotism but also changed the definition of *normal* in the United States.

Today I had the opportunity to substitute teach. As the class period progressed, the second graders busily chatted amongst themselves as they worked on their Monet-inspired paintings. I don't really recall what prompted me to ask, but I asked them to tell me the significance of 911. "That's the day the terrorists attacked us."

They were right. But what I found most interesting were the hands that flew into the air so they could say, "I was only one-year old." It had not occurred to me that so much time had passed since that day. Those kids were only babies. There is no way they would have remembered. And yet they knew. They knew exactly what happened.

How is important information passed on? Is it important for the youngsters to know these things? Of course. Recalling from one generation to another is how we remember. It is how we learn.

How many times was it said to the Israelites, "Remember when . .. ?" "*Remember how the Lord your God led you all the way . . .*" (Deuteronomy 8:2). "*Remember well what the Lord your God did . . .* " (Deuteronomy 7:18). "*Remember that you were slaves . . .* "(Deuteronomy 5:15). The examples are endless.

But isn't remembering just living in the past? Isn't that counterproductive? Not when remembering puts everything into perspective. When remembering serves to remind us of our own weaknesses and failures, it's a good thing. But even better is when remembering our weaknesses and failures reminds us of God's unlimited faithfulness.

We need to remember.

I will remember the deeds of the LORD; yes, I will remember your miracles of long ago. (Psalm 77:11)

Daily challenge:
Remind yourself of what God has done in your life. Pass it on.

What's Your Story?

A kindergarten teacher asked me to speak to thirty-six of the school's youngest students. I was asked to chat with them about being an author. These children listened attentively, but when it came to asking questions—well, that's where it got interesting. This early in the school year, they didn't understand that a raised hand to ask a question did not give them free rein to tell stories.

As we worked through my fifteen-minute talk, I told them that authors write because they have a story to tell. Some authors tell a story of insects, or science, or fantasy. Other authors write a story about people or jobs or history or interesting places. But regardless of the story, there is always a purpose in telling it.

The purpose of storytelling can be purely for education—biology, physics, chemistry, literature, grammar. Sometimes a story is told to make people laugh. But a story can also open a spigot of empathetic tears. Some stories chronicle an adventure that serves to motivate and inspire. And many stories are written to uplift and encourage those who read the words.

As a child I remember singing an old hymn: "Tell me the story of Jesus, write on my heart every word; Tell me the story most precious, Sweetest that ever was heard." That song by Fanny Crosby, a story in its own right, outlines how Christ came as a babe, grew into a young man, was tempted in the desert, betrayed, crucified and rose again. And by the end, the singer understands: "Love in that story so tender, Clearer than ever I see; Stay, let me weep while you whisper, 'Love paid the ransom for me.'"

Christ's life told a wonderful story. But our lives tell a story as well. Our story did not have a divine start. And yet, it should include a chapter of our encounter with the Divine.

Experience His story.

Let us fix our eyes on Jesus, the author and perfecter of our faith,
who for the joy set before him endured the cross, scorning its shame,
and sat down at the right hand of the throne of God. (Hebrews 12:2)

Daily challenge:
What's the next chapter in your story? Will it be worth reading?

Wind and Waves

The last week has been filled with images of coastal areas ravaged by hurricanes. First it was Gustav coming in near New Orleans. Now, in the wee hours of this morning, Hurricane Ike hit near Galveston, TX. The waves crashed over the seventeen-foot sea wall, claiming houses and businesses in its wake. As the storm overtook Houston, nearly every window in downtown blew out, allowing even the furniture within to be sucked out and hurled into neighboring buildings. For many, clean-up will take a long time. For others, hardly anything remains to be cleaned.

Amidst all the storm stories, one in particular caught my attention. Reportedly, a group of Galveston Island residents chose to watch the storm's approach from their box seats at a local bar. Mind you, all had been ordered to evacuate or face "certain death." The band of thrill-seekers eventually went their way, deciding that leaving might be the best option after all. So they left—all but one man, that is. He went to his home to await his promised ride off the island. But that ride never came. Just a block or two from the sea wall, this man rode out the storm, sleeping through most of it under the oppressive influence of the alcohol. When he woke, water surrounded him. But he had survived.

I wonder what that felt like to be alone in the middle of a raging storm. There was no hope of rescue. No hope for companionship. Just the realization that the crashing waves made the house groan and tremble. Had it not been for the alcohol, I don't think anyone could have slept through the gale.

Sleep is reserved for those who are at peace. Remember how the Lord was in the boat when a vicious storm arose on the Sea of Galilee? Waves washed over the sides, nearly swamping it. The disciples were frightened senseless. And yet the Lord slumbered, the disciples thinking Him oblivious to their peril. Finally awakening Him they said, *"Teacher, don't you care if we drown?"* (Mark 4:38b). I can see it now. Jesus probably gave them that "give-me-a-break" kind of look, drew in an exasperated breath and then told the wind and waves to cease.

Silence and calm. That's what happens when the Lord is in control. But we err if we think God was not in control when the seas churned and the wind blew. The only difference is our ability—or willingness—to believe that God is as much God in the storm as in calm.

The LORD is slow to anger and great in power; the LORD will not leave the guilty unpunished. His way is in the whirlwind and the storm, and clouds are the dust of his feet. (Nahum 1:3)

Daily challenge:
In the midst of a storm, you can still rest.

257

The Least You Can Do Is

"Come on now. The least you can do is say 'I'm sorry.'"

I said that to my sons on more than one occasion. Most of the time it was when one fouled the other—stole a favorite truck, hit the other in the head with a flying object or sent his brother catapulting through the air with a well-timed trip.

We can also adapt the phrase by saying, "The least you can do is say 'thank you.'"

I said this to my brother long ago. My brothers and I were in the car with Grandma coming home from church. She made it a habit to carry small pieces of candy in her purse, just waiting for us to ask for some. We popped the question, already knowing the answer. True to form, Grandma opened her pocketbook and distributed the candy. "Thank you, Grandma," was the general response. But my one brother, Mr. Grumpy on this particular occasion, was not happy. He didn't like that kind of candy and resorted to ugly pouting. Of course, I felt compelled to act as the older, wiser sister and let him have it with "the-least-you-can-do" line. I'm not sure I got much of a response except for more of that surly scowl.

This kind of sentiment is often used as an appeal for humanitarian efforts. Telethons reach out by pleading, "Just a few pennies a day can feed a homeless child. The least you can do is to give up a cup of coffee for the sake of these little ones." Even in the midst of the latest round of hurricane devastation, similar appeals abound.

But the Apostle Paul used this reasoning back in the early church. He had just finished describing to the church how his imprisonment was advancing the Gospel. He tells them, *Whatever happens, conduct yourselves in a manner worthy of the gospel of Christ* (Philippians 1:27).

Then Paul opens the next chapter of his letter with the equivalent of "the least you can do is . . .." In essence he says: If you value your relationship with Christ, if you desire love and compassion, then the least you can do is to work together toward the common goal. A worthy challenge indeed.

> *If you have any encouragement from being united with Christ, if any comfort from his love, if any fellowship with the Spirit, if any tenderness and compassion, then make my joy complete by being likeminded, having the same love, being one in spirit and purpose.* (Philippians 2:1, 2)

Daily challenge:
The least I can do is _____. You fill in the blank.

Bumps and Bruises

Like any responsible soccer mom, I set my schedule around the 4:00 p.m. game. It was being played at the competition's home field. The field was small and if you wanted to, you could play two other sports at the same time. At one end was the scruffy dirt infield of the baseball diamond; at the other, the overgrown outfield of the softball field. In between America's favorite pastimes was not much better. Clumps and bumps prevailed. And for a team like ours that relies on a controlled passing game, the venue did not promise optimal play.

Optimal play we did not get. In addition to the field, the Monday-afternoon doldrums down-shifted all the kids into slow motion. The ball went every which way other than where it was supposed to go. On one play Seth ended up flying through the air, colliding with the goalie and falling hard. He slowly managed to find his feet, picking grass and dirt out of his mouth. Our team scored twice but in the final moments had to settle for a tie. It was just one of those games good for only pointless bumps and bruises.

Pointless bumps and bruises? It's easy to see adversity like that. Sometimes I cause my own bumpy playing field. When I manufacture the bumps, I cause my own pain. If I only learned not to create those situations, I might be able to put away the plastic bandage strips.

But what happens when there's no way around an uneven playing surface where I am destined to meet my opponent? I muster up all my strength and courage and take to the field. I know there is a coach who measures out the assignments and referees who enforce the rules of the game. But it's only when I truly believe they have my best interest in mind that I can continue to play through the difficulties.

In this you greatly rejoice, though now for a little while you may have had to suffer grief in all kinds of trials. These have come so that your faith—of greater worth than gold, which perishes even though refined by fire—may be proved genuine and may result in praise, glory and honor when Jesus Christ is revealed. (I Peter 1:6, 7)

Daily challenge:
Are you beat up and bruised? Know that God will level the playing field
at just the right moment.

Grass Is Greener

What a difference a few inches of rain makes. Several weeks ago the grass was brown and crunchy. Grass isn't supposed to make noise when you walk on it—but it was nearly deafening (to the ants). The only good thing about the ugly yard was that it required no mowing, a fact both my sons embraced with open arms.

That same yard looks completely different today. With several good rains in the last week or two, new life has come back to the once desiccated landscape. Now you can almost see the green blades grow right before your eyes. The lawn mover has been oiled up and put into service several times already. The colorful picture outside my window is currently much prettier than the boys' attitude about the renewed mowing responsibilities.

I'm not an expert on grass. I just know what I see. My husband, on the other hand, is a grass expert. It's part of his job as the facilities manager at a school. "Yeah, I get paid to make the grass grow," he snidely comments. He tells me that rye turns brown at the onset of hot weather and is accelerated by drought. I guess that explains our yard. In this brown state the grass is not dead; it's just not very pretty. But come the refreshing rains, the rye responds by plumping up and flipping on its vivid technicolor.

Seeing the transformation of dry grass to green to dry and back again reminds me of my spiritual life. I'm not particularly proud of the dry periods but I've had them. I wasn't totally dead, but it sure wasn't pretty. I wonder what others thought as they saw a non-vibrant, unfruitful life. But thank God, the rain came and I began to thrive again. Roots grew deeper and the blades of life greener. Existing in a drought sucks. Living under the influence of rain is magnificent!

"Let my teaching fall like rain and my words descend like dew, like showers on new grass, like abundant rain on tender plants."
(Deuteronomy 32:2)

Daily challenge:
Are you feeling brown and crunchy? Let God fall like rain and make you green and growing once more.

Holes in the Bucket

I wanted the ladies to "get it." Setting aside my dignity, I enlisted a friend to be Liza and I played the role of Henry. She wore a long prairie skirt and bonnet and I donned a construction paper beard, Elmer Fudd hat and an old red-checked hunting jacket. Together we sang through the story of the hole in the bucket as told by two dim-witted individuals. In short, the series of suggested repairs to the hole in the bucket were for naught. Despite their efforts, the hole remained, the bucket unfit for carrying water.

But how can we fill our buckets with the Living Water, renewing our souls in the process? You see, when we became Believers, a bucket was handed to us with the means to fill it. But there are two types of buckets: holy ones and holey ones. Unfortunately, if our bucket is the holey type, it's not God's doing; it's ours.

Just like the morons in the silly song who tried to fix the holes, "we" cannot plug the holes in our own buckets; only God can make the fix. In fact, the reason the holes got there in the first place was our own fault. We strive so hard to be everything to everyone. We summon strength based on our muscle power. We figure that more is better and seeking rest is only a sign of weakness. As we desperately try to keep the bucket full, that bucket becomes more sieve-like, dribbling water from the holes. The harder we try to "feel" full, the quicker the water drains out. We feel incomplete and dissatisfied.

We must recognize that the bucket Provider is also the one who can fix it. When we step back and stop trying so hard, the inflow of the new water refreshes and renews. It gives us time for reflection, a recharge on our batteries and the ability to respond to others as we should. I picture this akin to when I fill my birdbath. I put the hose in the bowl and let the water flow. In fact, I continue to flood the bowl until the old, nasty water is replaced by the new. The result is a vessel that is brimming over with healthy, sparkling water.

If you find your bucket full of holes, quit trying to plug them yourself. Allow God to cork the holes and fill you to overflowing once again.

> *"Come away with me by yourselves to a quiet place and get some rest." (Mark 6:31)*

Daily challenge:
Can you pinpoint the cause of your holey bucket? It is when we rest
that the holes are sealed.

Contamination

Chicken has always been a staple in our house. It's plentiful, cheap and can be fixed in a zillion different ways. When the boys were little, they preferred to have what they called "chicken on the bone." They loved those drumsticks because utensils were optional.

I prepared another chicken dinner tonight. I suppose it was "on the bone", because I roasted the whole bird. I had mashed potatoes and gravy, salad, green beans and biscuits waiting on the table for the boys when they came through the door. It was a nice dinner if I say so myself.

While I was preparing the chicken, however, I was faced with the unenviable task of touching it. It's slimy and I don't care for the smell. But with no one else to do it, I dutifully got the olive oil from the cabinet and slathered that hunk of poultry. Problem was this: Once I touched that chicken, everything else I touched was contaminated with whatever horrible bacteria existed on the bird. Every cabinet door, seasoning bottle, oil flask, sponge . . . everything was guilty by association. When I finally tucked the chicken in the oven to bake, I had to backtrack and clean up the messy sequence.

God was pretty smart to provide food-preparation rules for the Jews way back when. Before anyone knew about bacteria and cross-contamination, God had it all figured out. Keep the meat from the vegetables. Clean from the unclean. Even today, a kosher kitchen has specific sinks and food prep areas, strictly adhering to set rules. It's more than rules for rules sake—the rules were ordained for the safety and health of the people.

It seems to me that cross-contamination in the kitchen is not the only place that it's a problem. I think of the contamination of my language—even if unspoken—once I started spending time in operating rooms. It didn't take very long to start thinking in vulgar terms when it became part of my environment. I also have to consider my reaction to sex as portrayed on TV or in the movies. Years ago, I closed my eyes, or at least cringed, at immorality. But now it's so pervasive, it almost seems normal.

If we were as careful about cross-contamination in our lives as in our kitchens, I suspect we would be much more pleasing to the Lord.

"You must distinguish between the holy and the common, between the unclean and the clean." (Leviticus 10:10)

Daily challenge:
Where are you most suspect to contamination? Decide how to protect and keep yourself clean.

Work, Work, Work

You just can't get around it. There's a lot of work to be done every day, every night. But unfortunately, not everyone feels the same compulsion to put a shoulder to the grindstone. I have always heard the 20/80 rule: twenty percent of the people do eighty percent of the work. Robert Frost must have had that in mind when he wrote, "The world is full of willing people, some willing to work, the rest willing to let them."

I admit there are many times when I wish I had less work to muck up my days. Today was one of those days. Frustrated by slow internet connections at home, I rode into town and settled into a cozy coffee-shop corner determined to catch up on my online teaching. I sat there for hours clicking until I thought I could click no more. The time went by quickly for me—and apparently for the women at the table beside me.

They were doing anything but working. They chatted about kids and college and drinking and date rape and a myriad of other topics as they sipped away. I wasn't trying to eavesdrop. It was just hard not to overhear since they were mere feet from me. I wondered how much longer they would dawdle the day away. *Don't they have any work to do? Must be nice to just sit there and socialize.*

Suddenly, one woman glanced at her watch. She visibly gasped. It was after one in the afternoon and she was supposed to be at work hours ago. *Oops.* They blasted out of there in a flash, nearly leaving a jet stream in their wake. I guess they had to work after all.

It's easy to complain about our appointed tasks. But maybe we ought to remind ourselves that being able to work—at anything and anywhere—indicates vitality. For goodness sake, even God worked for six days before deciding to rest. Maybe work would not seem so much like work if we consider the alternative: a lack of vitality equals death.

Proverbs is full of wise sayings about work. Things like work hard, eat well (28:19). Be a sluggard, then you die (21:25). Work hard, live in prosperity (14:3). Be slack and be destroyed (18:9). It doesn't hurt to remind ourselves that working is a good thing.

> *May the favor of the Lord our God rest upon us; establish the work of our hands for us—yes, establish the work of our hands. (Psalm 90:17)*

Daily challenge:
Let's be careful about talking down work. Our kids might get the wrong idea.

I Will Always Have Hope

My run today was a great reminder of my new favorite verse. With a scary hun-dred-mile footrace looming in two short weeks, I knew I had to spend some time out on those trails. But I decided to sleep in with my husband instead of heading out before first light. In my mind, this plan still gave me some afternoon hours to be pro-ductive. Boy, was I wrong.

I thought my course was twenty miles. I remembered tricky footing with lots of rocks and a return trip with tons of elevation gain. So much for a fifty-one-year-old memory. It was twenty miles—plus several more. And those rocks and climb? Much worse than I recalled. I was tentative on the rocks and started bonking (a low-blood-sugar phenomena) on the way back. My pedestrian pace was slower than normal and I was forced to heavily ration my remaining food and water. I was not particularly encouraged by this outing that took two hours longer than anticipated. How will I ever run this distance plus seventy-six more miles on race day?

But discouragement, fear and disappointment are not reserved for trail runners. These same sentiments creep into my thinking other times. How can I be the "always-available" online teacher to my students? How can I make money go further? As soon as I think the income/outgo is in control, someone breaks another tooth and signs up for a costly crown. And how can I possibly be the spiritually mature, Proverbs 31 woman to my husband and kids? I fail on so many levels.

But God is a God of hope. *It is God who arms me with strength and makes my way perfect* (Psalm 18:32). He will always provide a way when there seems to be no way. Having that knowledge—that expectation—that things will work out (Romans 8:28) lifts the spirit and refreshes our purpose.

Don't despair. There is always hope.

But as for me, I will always have hope; I will praise you more and more. (Psalm 71:14)

Daily challenge:
Make a short list of what is stressing you. Now, say with me:
I will always have hope; I will praise you more and more.

Fur Balls

I'm beginning to understand why older folks love their pets. I've heard of programs that introduce nursing-home residents to visiting animals. I suppose these furry friends enjoy the petting and cuddling as much as the ones offering the love. Dogs are normally the animals of choice, but I think our two kitties could hold their own.

A lot of people don't like cats because they can be haughty and independent. Not ours. Within minutes of their being born, my niece began stroking and loving those little fur balls. Never before has a litter of kittens gotten so much attention. I guess we should not be surprised when the two we have, now about six-months old, act like they are starving for attention. *Meow, meow,* they whine, begging us to open the laundry room door first thing every morning to let them in. They follow you everywhere and come when you call. They follow you around the yard and even watch poolside as you swim. And once they jump in your lap, you better be ready to give them your undivided attention. Their purr boxes start in as they force their heads into your hands for more attention. Pick them up and hold them in arms like a baby and they throw back their chins, spread out their legs and expect a belly massage.

Their desire for attention can be a bother—like when I'm at my computer and they position themselves on the desk between me and the keyboard. But, there is something very soothing about having an animal love you no matter what. Ra and Juno don't care if I'm having a bad hair day. They don't care if I burn dinner. They don't even seem to mind if I accidentally step on their tails. Their memory is short and they quickly come back for more love.

Like the kitties who love me, I wish I was better at loving people no matter what. It seems to me that I allow personal preferences and pet peeves to get in the way. And honestly, I sometimes find it inconvenient to take the time to love someone in practical terms. How selfish is that?

Note the lesson: love earnestly and unconditionally.

> *Above all, love each other deeply, because love covers over a multitude of sins. (I Peter 4:8)*

Daily challenge:
Be eager to love so others will know where to come back for more.

Change

Change sure is a popular word these days. In this political season, nearly every candidate proclaims to be the agent for change. The clear implication is that whatever has been the status quo is not good enough. "I have the answer," they exclaim. "I can bring the change you need." But change from what to what? That is the question.

Change can be a good thing—especially when it refers to a poopy baby diaper! But change can also alter a lifestyle. Eat less, exercise more. Or, change can come to your closet or living room depending on color and style. It's common for college kids to change majors and majors to change medals. World travelers change money by day and socks by night. Yes, change is good.

On the other hand, change can go the other way—from good to bad. For example, a beautiful new car meets Mack truck head on. Or, a teenager's room demonstrates the Second Law of Thermodynamics going from a state of order to disorder. Both are not particularly great changes.

I found a great story of change in I Samuel 10. The scene is this: Samuel had been searching for the first king of Israel and found him in the man called Saul. He instructs Saul to do some very odd things that seem more like a story line in a spy thriller. Go here, stop by the big tree, say this, take the bread, hand them that, yada, yada, yada. But the interesting thing is what Samuel says next: *"The Spirit of the LORD will come upon you in power, and you will prophesy with them; and you will be changed into a different person. Once these signs are fulfilled, do whatever your hand finds to do, for God is with you"* (vs. 6, 7).

How exciting to be so changed by God that you obey even when not fully understanding. And the outstanding consequence of that obedience is freedom to serve. The person you become equips you to do whatever God ordains.

So go ahead. Let God change you into a new person.

> *"The Spirit of the LORD will come upon you in power . . . you will be changed into a different person . . . do whatever your hand finds to do, for God is with you." (I Samuel 10:6, 7)*

Daily challenge:
Ask God to change what you have not been able to alter on your own.

I Can See Clearly Now

My son Seth is a great photographer. The shutter is continuously clicking away—except when he takes to the soccer field. He handed me his camera this afternoon and said, "Go for it." Great. I wasn't even sure how you turned it on. It is a heavy, complicated piece of technology with a foot-long lens. He adjusted this and that and left me to capture action images. It was fun.

After the game he loaded the pictures onto his laptop. "235 shots!" he marveled. Many of the images were blurred. Some were too far away. Some were pretty good, but the lighting wasn't optimal. Most pictures ended up in the electronic trash bin but in the end, Seth viewed thirty-five shots as worthy to be saved on his hard drive.

Why did those pictures made the cut? I think it was because the story in the picture was clear. Sometimes, the important thing was action. In others, it was facial expression. Still others were valued for the height of the jump or the battle between the players.

I clearly remember, no pun intended, a piece on Wide World of Sports back when I was in high school. As video of Hawaiian sun and surf flashed across the screen, the popular song, "I can see clearly now the rain is gone . . . " accompanied the surfers riding those big waves. It was a great pairing of music and movies that made the intent of the story clear to all who watched.

Clarity can be in what we see, how we speak and to what level we understand. Abimelech and company understood Isaac's relationship with God. "*We saw clearly that the LORD was with you*" (Genesis 26:28). Moses postponed the fate of a blasphemer *until the will of the LORD should be made clear to them* (Leviticus 24:12). And the Levites *read from the Book of the Law of God, making it clear and giving the meaning so that the people could understand what was being read* (Nehemiah 8:8).

The lens through which we view our lives should not be clouded by ungodliness and poor judgment. *All of us who are mature should take such a view of things. And if on some point you think differently, that too God will make clear to you* (Philippians 3:15).

> *For since the creation of the world God's invisible qualities—his eternal power and divine nature—have been clearly seen, being understood from what has been made, so that men are without excuse.*
> *(Romans 1:20)*

Daily challenge:
Is our spiritual vision clouded by a faulty lens? Perhaps we need
to wipe it clean so we can more clearly see God.

Provision

I don't know about you, but I tire of finding "pass-this-on-and-get-blessed" emails in my in-box. They normally get trashed without opening. But I did open one such email and am glad I did.

I found a story written by an unnamed missionary doctor working in Africa. The abridged version goes like this. The doctor delivered a premature baby but was unable to save the life of the mother. Left behind was a two-year-old sibling and this needy infant. No incubator was available, but it would not have mattered—no electricity to power it. Instead, the only hope for the babe was to be kept warm in a cardboard box, heated only by a hot water bottle. Unfortunately, the only rubberized vessel burst when filled.

Somehow, the baby survived the night. Come morning, the doctor gathered the orphans living on the compound to pray, as was her custom. Explaining the critical situation, ten-year-old Ruth prayed, "Send us a hot water bottle today. It'll be no good tomorrow, God, as the baby will be dead, so please send it this afternoon. And while You are about it, would You please send a dolly for the little girl so she'll know You really love her?"

The missionary gulped. Intellectually, she knew God could do anything. But still, she found it impossible that a hot water bottle and dolly would show up before the sun set in that remote village. Besides, never once in four years on the field had she received any package from home. Why would today be different?

But it was different. Very different. A car pulled up and delivered a package. Eyes glistening, she anticipated a miracle in the making. She called the children to help open the twenty-two-pound box. New clothes, bandages and some treats. When the good doctor returned her hand to the box, she felt something hard. *Could it be?* Yes! A hot water bottle. Ruth saw this and blurted out, "God has sent the bottle, He must have sent the dolly, too!" You guessed it. The last thing in the box was a doll baby.

The box had been sent by her Sunday-school class, beginning the transcontinental journey five-months prior. God knew the need and used that class to answer it before it was ever realized. God is ever faithful.

"Before they call, I will answer." (Isaiah 65:24)

Daily challenge:
Don't sell God short to provide your needs. And never sell-short how God
can use you to provide someone else's need.

September
❦ 25

Survivor

I guess I have "Survivor" on the brain. A new season of the popular reality show began tonight. Our house has always been a fan and I even applied to be a participant one year. Seeing the new cast of characters was fun, trying to predict who could go the distance. The game is one that requires wit, strength, cunning and perseverance. But the reward is surviving—with a million bucks.

I wonder about my ability to survive eight days from now. On my docket is a one-hundred mile race and I'm petrified. I can't get my arms around how my body will be able to survive the rigors of the challenge. And, I can't stop thinking about how much worse it will be if it is cold, wet and blustery for all those hours.

Just for fun, I searched my online Bible for the word *survive*, hoping to find some magical formula to get me through that race. I didn't find what I was looking for, but I did run across an interesting story long-ago forgotten.

As a prisoner, Paul was being transported via boat from Adramyttium to Italy. They had been sailing for about two weeks and having a difficult time of it. Ports of call and change of ships did not improve the situation. A northeaster of epic proportions blew the ship all over the Adriatic Sea as the crew worked feverishly to save the boat and all aboard. Just before dawn after another frightful night, Paul's practicality revealed itself: "*Now I urge you to take some food. You need it to survive. Not one of you will lose a single hair from his head*" (Acts 27:34). After that he took a bite, the others following suit. The Scripture says that *They were all encouraged and ate some food themselves* (v. 36). The storm did not halt, the ship ran aground and broke apart, but as promised, all of the 276 sailors, passengers and prisoners made it onto dry ground.

So what's the moral of this story? The way I see it, we cannot afford to be dumb—even in the middle of a storm. Sometimes we have to remember the practical stuff. We need to pause and take care of ourselves. We need to eat and drink, maintaining our strength. But most of all, we have to lay claim that when God promises survival, nothing can interfere—not waves, wind and broken ships.

> *"For the last fourteen days," he said, "you have been in constant suspense and have gone without food—you haven't eaten anything. Now I urge you to take some food. You need it to survive." (Acts 27:33b, 34)*

Daily challenge:
Take care of your physical needs. You're no good to anyone if you're too weak.

Sleepytime

Do fish sleep? That's what I asked myself just a few minutes ago. I was lying on my bed looking over at the aquarium in the corner of the room. The seven or eight fish—don't ask me what kind—are all several years old, as hard as that might be to believe. They are most often neglected but seem to do all right, even so.

The biggest fish is white and about four-inches long. Most of the time he spends his time motionless in the left front corner of the aquarium. He seems to float near the surface of the water, tail down, looking quite dead. But throw a little food his way and he comes to life. After the flakes are consumed or fall to the bottom, he once again returns to his slightly askew, mouth-up position in the corner.

I did some reading and found out that all fish "sleep." It's hard to tell by looking at them, because they have no eyelids to close and not many scientists conduct EEG's of the fish's brainwaves. Nevertheless, it has been observed that nearly all fish have periods of quiescence. Catfish swim into a crevice or underneath a submerged log to rest during the night. Minnows reportedly take respite from the frolicking, daytime group swims, separating at nightfall to become motionless until light of day. Other fish, like the flesh-eating piranhas, sleep during the day to prowl at night. Clown fish choose to rest by lying on the bottom and sleep on their sides. But regardless of how or when, all gilled swimmers, big or little, take measures to assure their rest.

From the time that God put Adam asleep to make Eve, sleep has been critical to mankind. Without proper sleep we lose our health and can even become neurotic and psychotic. Sure, Proverbs warns of loving sleep too much. That's just plain laziness. But on the other hand, sleep is restorative. We need our rest to be returned to service the next day.

When I was a kid, I never imagined being delighted to get to bed early. Staying up late was a sign of being grown up—a symbol of maturity. Who could have predicted that slumber could be so cherished?

God is a sensible God who understands our weakness and creates a practical solution.

I will lie down and sleep in peace, for you alone, O LORD, make me dwell in safety. (Psalm 4:8)

Daily challenge:
Take care of yourself by getting enough rest. It's not selfish. It's crucial.

It's a Team Thing

As the kids gathered on the steps of the old school, they demonstrated a wide range of emotions. Some of them were lighthearted and laughing. Others had a vacant look on their faces as if to say, "And why are we doing this?" Still others bemoaned the early hour and lack of sleep. One girl anxiously awaited the arrival of her father. She had forgotten her race number. But despite the variety of attitudes, they were united in purpose.

At the beginning of the soccer season the coach announced that all team members were to run the well-known Virginia Ten-Miler. In its heyday, the Lynchburg race drew upward of ten-thousand runners. Though not as popular in recent years, it is still a race with over thirteen-hundred runners; these soccer players were an integral part of it. Coach instructed them to push themselves to levels unknown. Just a handful of the kids had ever run the distance. But to make it even more interesting, several of the faculty members also entered. In fact, the headmaster had made it a fundraising opportunity. Pick a teacher and pledge an amount for every student they can manage to beat. That provided some incentive for the teachers as well as bragging rights for the kids.

The gun sounded and off they went. Seventy-two minutes later, Seth completed the very hilly and challenging course, first for the New Covenant contingent. Over the next thirty minutes, kids and coaches alike crossed the line, most of them paired up for moral support. The spirit among these soccer players was one of camaraderie and accomplishment. Each went home knowing that he or she had met the challenge head-on and won.

Working together toward a common goal can be exhilarating. I remember volleyball matches that were won only because we rallied behind each other and played each ball as if it were our last. We bumped, set, spiked and scrambled not as individuals but as a team.

When we recognize fellow Believers as teammates rather than competitors, we can work together for the Kingdom's good.

Consequently, you are no longer foreigners and aliens, but fellow citizens with God's people and members of God's household, built on the foundation of the apostles and prophets, with Christ Jesus himself as the chief cornerstone. (Ephesians 2:19, 20)

Daily challenge:
What are you doing to strengthen your team?

It's Only Money, Honey

I grew up in a home where money was handled very conservatively. My dad was a dentist by trade but never made the kind of money people assumed he did. He didn't have the heart to charge standard fees and often provided gratis services for those in need. Still, we always had enough.

My parents used an envelope system for budgeting—a grocery, clothing and gas envelope, along with a few others. Each week my dad handed over the proper amount to my mother and into the envelope it went. Only on occasion did she ever "rob Peter to pay Paul." But even then, the amount was always repaid to the penny. Seldom was a check written and never were credit cards used. It was a cash-only system that taught me how to handle money.

My view of money was fashioned by what I learned as a child. My mom and dad always gave first to the Lord, then to savings and lastly to budgetary items. Even as a young girl, I had a similar system—one piggy bank for my tithe, another for spending and a little cardboard jewelry box for savings. I had a handwritten accounting system to track the money. Loans didn't exist. No money? No spending.

From my reading in I Timothy 6, it looks like we are not the only generation to have problems with money. Paul passionately teaches that money is not to be at the center of our universe. That attitude alone can tempt us into destructive living (v. 9) and distract us from faith (v. 10). Rather, we are to *pursue righteousness, godliness, faith, love, endurance, and gentleness* (v. 11).

The hot news item this week has been the financial collapse and potential government rescue of some of the biggest organizations on Wall Street. I certainly don't like the fact that our retirement savings have plummeted. However, I can be content in knowing that God will provide.

Command those who are rich in this present world not to be arrogant nor to put their hope in wealth, which is so uncertain, but to put their hope in God, who richly provides us with everything for our enjoyment. (I Timothy 6:17)

Daily challenge:
Wisely use the money God lends you.
. . . be generous and willing to share. (I Timothy 6:18b)

Slow as a Turtle

"Mrs. Trittipoe," the cheerful voice queried. "How would you like to be judge for the ninth-grade poetry contest?" It was the English teacher on the other end of the phone. She needed to fill the final spot on her judging panel. An annual fall event, the dramatic (and not so dramatic) renderings by the students are embraced by some and loathed by even more. Nevertheless, the show was on and I was going to be part of it.

Some of the kids gave winning performances complete with costuming, props and lines uttered with great precision. Unfortunately, a few of the less-enthusiastic pupils stumbled through their lines. Nevertheless, I was entertained by most and impressed with the students' ability to commit to memory such lengthy poems.

But one poem in particular captured my attention. The Victorian poet, Guy Wetmore Carryl, wrote *The Persevering Tortoise and the Pretentious Hare*. The lines of this literary masterpiece (and I jest) share the conversation and facts about a foot race between a slow-moving terrapin and a flippant, arrogant bunny. Without even knowing the poem, I'm quite sure you can predict the outcome. The slow and plodding turtle soundly beats the cocky, loud-mouthed rabbit. I laughed out loud as I listened intently to the story. That turtle's my hero.

The timing was perfect for this poem. With my hundred-mile race just days away, I wanted a glimmer of hope—the hope that perseverance, patience and a slow steady pace could carry me to the finish line.

Sometimes being slow is a wise thing to do. After an emotional reunion, the brothers Jacob and Esau decided to migrate with their huge clans, complete with wives, children, cattle and sheep. Jacob says in Genesis 13:13, 14, "*If they are driven hard just one day, all the animals will die. So let my lord go . . . while I move along slowly at the pace of the droves before me and that of the children . . . ..*" And guess what? They arrived safe and sound.

We don't always have to rush. Not everything has to be done at full speed lest we break down and fold under the pressure. Just slow down.

> *After Jacob came from Paddan Aram, he arrived safely . . . .. (Genesis 13:18)*

Daily challenge:
When you feel the need to rush, ask yourself if it will do more harm than good.

Sudden Death

Sudden death. I wish I was talking about what happens at the end of regulation play when the score is tied. But I'm not. I'm taking about the kind of death that comes out of nowhere, as biting as the cold north wind on a wintry day. We expect grannies and grandpas to die. We expect a patient in the last stages of cancer to die. We even expect the cheetah to bring down the impala. What we don't expect is for a seventeen-year old boy to die on a Saturday night.

Seth got word on Sunday that a friend had been killed. A car accident on a winding road ended this young man's life and badly injured the driver and two passengers. Henry was not a best friend but a friend nonetheless. It seemed to affect Seth deeply. He made a trip to the crash site and captured digital images of the spontaneously erected memorial. He requested to leave school early to attend the funeral. He even seemed to be driving with more caution than normal. Something about the fragility of life had left its mark on Seth.

Sudden deaths like this one leave a mark on me as well. As a mom, I cannot imagine the parents' depth of grief. Tears well up just thinking about my reaction had Caleb or Seth been the victim. Neither can I comprehend the angst of the responsible driver and his parents. The anguish, the devastation, the heartbreak must be crushing.

Though God has written the calendar of events for our lives, we are not privy to that information. Somehow, it seems the younger we are, the less we consider that next Tuesday may be our last—or our child's. So, "How should we then live?", to quote Christian thinker Francis Schaeffer. Certainly, we need to live today as if it was our last day to live Christianly. But how do we do that? I think Paul knew the secret:

> *Do not conform any longer to the pattern of this world, but be transformed by the renewing of your mind. Then you will be able to test and approve what God's will is—his good, pleasing and perfect will. (Romans 12:2)*

Daily challenge:
We need not live in fear of dying. But we need to live as if we were dying.

Black Marks

"Ugh. I sure wish someone would have asked me about those shoes before making them mandatory," my husband, the facility manager of the school, remarked. Shaking his head, he peered down the long hallway. The tile floors could have been mistaken for a hit-and-run zebra accident for all the black stripes. No matter how hard the janitors worked each evening, their task had to be repeated the next night after the school kids spent seven hours in the building. It was a never-ending battle.

The dress code calls for certain shoes to be worn. The advantage is uniformity and eliminates shoes that blink. The problem this year is that they make horrible black marks that are resistant to standard mopping. By some stroke of genius, someone figured out that rubbing a tennis ball across the marred floor removes the skid mark. Gary, in concert with the Headmaster, combines that cleaning technique with discipline. Kids who act up are seen wielding the tennis ball sticks all over the school. The kids learn a lesson and the marks get erased.

Just as those black marks on the tiled floor, there are all kinds of "black marks" in the Scriptures. The mark of a tattoo was a nod to paganism, a black mark in Israel's community (Leviticus 19:28). Practiced sins and evil thoughts made black marks and ushered in destruction (Isaiah 59:7). Zechariah tells of a prophecy that marked a flock of sheep (aka *evildoers*) for slaughter (11:7). And, there is the infamous mark of the Beast in Revelation (16:2).

On the other hand, positive marks can be made. Nature marks off the seasons by the moon (Psalm 104:19) and the horizon when God set the heavens in place (Proverbs 8:27). Think about the mark of blood on the door posts when the Israelites were Egyptian captives. When the Death Angel saw the mark he passed over the household (Exodus 12:23). Ezekiel marked the foreheads of the righteous in Jerusalem, sparing them from annihilation (9:4). And marks are also used to describe certain characteristics: *The things that mark an apostle—signs, wonders and miracles—were done among you with great perseverance* (II Corinthians 12:12).

When we disobey God, we scuff our shoe and make a black mark that mars His reputation. But when our lives are marked by righteousness and good works, much fruit and well doing, we present a clean floor to the world.

> *"I know your deeds, your love and faith, your service and perseverance, and that you are now doing more than you did at first."*
> *(Revelation 2:19)*

Daily challenge:
What kind of marks are you leaving in your community?

The Great Debate

Tonight will be an historic event. For just the second time in the history of the United States, a woman will be debating in the Vice-Presidential war of words. There is a mounting excitement as the nation watches to see how Sarah Palin, the hockey-mom turned governor turned VP candidate, holds up against Washington insider Senator Joseph Biden. Questions will be asked, answers given and ideologies compared and contrasted. This is a high-stakes contest, each vying for a win at the polls in November.

As intriguing as that debate promises to be, the whole idea of knowing how to articulate a position is an important component of classical education, one that our children have been privileged to undertake. A premise of the dialectic phase of training involves teaching the students the fine art of logic, reasoning and arguing well. An emphasis is placed on being able to synthesize facts and construct logical arguments that stand up to an opponent's challenge. At stake is the ability to intellectually defend yourself—and in this case, earn good grades.

Arguing for the sense of arguing, however, has little merit. Other than making you feel intellectually superior, a "win" doesn't really mean a lot. It won't end wars or usher in world peace. It will simply make you feel better.

But is there an instance when it becomes expedient to debate? Is there a time to answer the tough questions? You bet there is. As I was reading in I Peter 3, I noticed that following a discussion on husbands and wives, Peter tackles the hard subject of suffering for doing good. And incidentally, I don't think that he was tying together marriage and suffering. However, a key to endure suffering seems to rest on being able to defend the faith. Peter says this: *But even if you should suffer for what is right, you are blessed. Do not fear what they fear; do not be frightened. But in your hearts set apart Christ as Lord. Always be prepared to give an answer to everyone who asks you to give the reason for the hope that you have* (vs. 14, 15a).

Prepare yourself for debate. But . . .

. . . do this with gentleness and respect, keeping a clear conscience, so that those who speak maliciously against your good behavior in Christ may be ashamed of their slander. (I Peter 3:15b, 16)

Daily challenge:
There's a fine line between defending your faith and being obnoxious.
Be bold but careful.

On the Mountaintop

In a little over an hour, I will head off to run the inaugural Grindstone 100 race. It's difficult to think that at six o'clock this evening, Friday, I will begin my journey and assuming all goes moderately well, should stop running at about two or three Sunday morning.

These endeavors morph into introspective journeys. With plenty of time for heavy thinking, my mind will mull over all kinds of things. For this race, my mind has started churning way before the starting gun sounds.

My biggest concern is how my body will hold up under the stress. How will my quads fare on all the downhills? They took such a thrashing on a short training run a few weeks back. How will I be able to make it up the relentless climbs without keeling over? And how will I be able to get up and go again if I stop for a twenty-minute nap?

The answers lay in the fact that I will have provisions along the way. Between the race-sponsored aid stations and my own crew, they will have all the food and fluids that I could possibly need. That is not in question. What is not as clear is whether or not my stomach will allow me to take advantage of those provisions. A nice ham sandwich on the go will only do me good if I eat it—not carry it in my hand for miles on end.

The idea of provision makes me think back to the story of Abraham and his son Isaac. God instructed Abraham to go to the mountaintop to offer a sacrifice to his God. But Isaac did not understand. *"The fire and wood are here," Isaac said, "but where is the lamb for the burnt offering?"* (Genesis 22:7).

Abraham responded, *"God himself will provide the lamb for the burnt offering, my son." And the two of them went on together* (Genesis 22:8). Content for the time being, they journeyed on and upon arriving at the top, built the altar. But can you imagine how pained Abraham must have been to bind his only son, knife raised? Even more, imagine Isaac's panic, fear and incomprehension that his own Father was going to kill him.

But, and blessed be this *but,* God provided the lamb and Abraham gladly received the provision.

So Abraham called that place The LORD Will Provide. And to this day it is said, "On the mountain of the LORD it will be provided." (Genesis 22:14)

Daily challenge:
It's ludicrous to ignore the provisions God offers.

And Miles to Go Before I Sleep

"And miles to go before I sleep." That classic Robert Frost line lurked in between my brain wrinkles. It was in the wee hours of the morning and I had already been running for nine hours with twenty-some more to go. I tried not to think about that. Rather, I had to reduce the race into manageable pieces. Just get to the next aid station . . ..

During races, I prefer to be alone. That way, no one slows me down or pressures me to speed up. I had been with a group for a while, enjoying their company. But now alone, I renewed my focus. My solitude was short-lived. Approaching a turn in the trail, I heard voices behind me. *Shoot. I need to get away. Vicki is in my age group!*

I turned my attention back up the hill and saw the headlight of the person ahead turn left. Arriving at the same spot, I turned left, stealing another glance at the three headlights climbing the hill. I took off.

The course was marked by reflective ribbons and followed a double-white blazed trail. I noted the blazes on the trees but saw no streamers. *Maybe someone took them down.* Though uneasy, I continued on. After a mile or two of downhill running, I arrived at a gate. *Oh, no!* I was just a few feet from a double blaze and noticed that rather than white, it was yellow. I screamed into the night, frantic. Not because I was lost, but because I knew I had to go all the way back up that mountain. *So much lost time and effort.* I wanted to cry but could not. I didn't have an ounce of energy to waste.

It's no fun to wander off-course. In this case, I knew something wasn't quite right but rationalized enough to keep going in the wrong direction. I think we have a tendency to do that in life. Watching that much TV doesn't really seem like the best thing to do but . . .. Or maybe we offer more information about someone than we should. Something whispers for us to stop and we almost do. But regrettably, we find ourselves at the bottom of a hill with our only recourse to turn heel and admit we were wrong. Wouldn't it have been easier to listen to the "still small voice" in the first place?

" . . . and that you may love the LORD your God, listen to his voice, and hold fast to him. For the LORD is your life . . .." (Deuteronomy 30:20)

Daily challenge:
When your heart is pricked, stop and listen. It may be the Spirit
throwing darts to get your attention.

On the Mountaintop and Down in the Valley

I'm alive, praise God! The Grindstone 100 is now history. The 6 p.m. Friday-night start culminated for me at 4:26 Sunday morning, nearly fourteen hours after the winner crossed the line. There were periods of highs, lows and in-betweens. But in those thirty-four hours of forward motion, I had time to examine life and draw conclusions.

First of all, the need for pacing was never so clear. It was easy to get swept along as the starting gong sounded. But for most of us mere mortals, a pace based on uncontrolled emotion is a harbinger of pain and agony. This race was brutal in every way—terrain, footing, endless trudges and quad-pounding descents on rocky mountain trails. The ability to be patient and focused was critical.

I was also reminded of how vital support staff can be. Friends Jordan and Deb consented to spend the weekend in the woods, enduring two chilly nights and one day of sitting, waiting and sleeping in the car. Without fail, they had everything I wanted laid out in preparation. One word from my mouth, "Cheetos," for example, made them spring into action. They looked out for my best interest even when my thinking became too clouded to know what I needed. We all need friends like that.

We also need those who will go the distance with us, leaving the warmth of the fire behind. Both Deb and my son Seth took turns running the last twenty miles with me. Though the hour was late and the darkness cold and lonely, they followed my feeble efforts. They didn't have to expose themselves to my whimpering when toenails lifted off or my quivering quads rebelled. They loved me enough to see me through.

And lastly, the idea of perseverance and determination was personified in my friend Jenny. She is a talented runner with a heart for God, family and excellence. For three weeks, an injury forced her from running a single step. And to make matters worse, a flu wreaked havoc, starting just a day before the race. Nevertheless, she carried on through eighty miles until her body betrayed her all together. Her willingness to persist against all odds was powerful.

You don't have to run one-hundred miles to learn these things. But, it doesn't hurt to have a reminder every so often.

Therefore, since we are surrounded by such a great cloud of witnesses, let us throw off everything that hinders and the sin that so easily entangles, and let us run with perseverance the race marked out for us. (Hebrews 12:1)

Daily challenge:
Let friends help you persevere through challenges.

Beautiful Feet

It was a crazy scene as I struggled to extricate myself from the car. On the day of Caleb's twenty-first birthday, we decided to meet up at his favorite restaurant. But just a day after completing my hundred-mile race, I was not in pristine shape. Overall, my body didn't feel too bad. In fact, I was sorer after a short twenty-two miler a couple of weeks ago. What was curious was that I could no longer rise from a sitting position. It's as if my brain had forgotten how. That's what Caleb was laughing at—me trying to find something to grab in order to stand. Without hands, it was impossible. My quads were on strike.

The other malady was my feet; my poor, poor feet. They were ugly to begin with, but after this last thrashing, they are really grotesque. Not one, not two, not three, but four toenails have left this world and now reside elsewhere. The cavernous dents left in my toes where the nails used to be are deep, red and inflamed. People at the soccer game today were aghast at the sight. I just hope my toes don't get infected.

In general, my feet feel like they've been the victims of a meat-grinding accident. The blisters under my calluses burn and throb. And my feet feel puffy, hot and tighter than a tick. Beautiful feet? Not really.

I am reminded, however, of the antithesis of my own feet. Isaiah proclaims, *"How beautiful on the mountains are the feet of those who bring good news, who proclaim peace, who bring good tidings, who proclaim salvation, who say to Zion 'Your God reigns!'"* (52:7).

So I wonder. . . When my feet were going up and over those mountains, did they bring good news to anyone? Did they give hope to the hopeless or peace to the restless? Maybe I expected someone else to do it. I know how selfish I can be—especially when I'm suffering.

I'm not implying that we literally have to be in the mountains in order to have "beautiful feet." We can have pedicure-perfect feet anywhere by having an ever-present sense of sharing the wonders and benefits of our God.

And how can they preach unless they are sent? As it is written, "How beautiful are the feet of those who bring good news!" (Romans 10:15)

Daily challenge:
How are your feet looking? Have you used them to take good news
to anyone lately?

An Example

I did not ask for the pedestal. I had no desire to be at the epicenter of attention. But I was and it was all David Horton's fault. Horton, an ultrarunning guru and long-time professor at Liberty University, had invited me to speak and run with his running class before my race. Then I was to return to his class two days after the race. "Well, I hope you're gonna sell tickets. I want a cut of the action," I offered.

The real life show-and-tell was scheduled for today. The fatigue from the weekend had suddenly hit me and I was dog-tired. The soles of my feet still protested when I walked and I was unable—still—to rise without the use of my hands. My face looked drawn and weary. Great example I'll be.

As I sat among the college students, they eagerly asked questions and listened intently as I answered. They were genuinely intrigued with the challenge I had embraced. When the time was gone, however, Horton questioned the students about their own running. Many of the kids reported less than acceptable mileages, far from the expectations of class requirements. The professor compared my toughness to theirs. It was humbling to hear him speak in such glowing terms. As I prepared to leave, he walked me to the door and said, "Thanks for coming. They're a bunch of wee-nies and they needed to see some real toughness. They need an example."

Though I was thrilled he thought me capable, I was intimidated by that responsibility. If he—and those kids—only knew how many times I failed, they might not be so impressed.

I often read the words of Paul, *Follow my example, as I follow the example of Christ* (I Corinthians 11:1). *Whoa.* That takes courage to say that. Almost sounds a little arrogant. But is it? Probably not. He was confident of his position in Christ and the lifestyle it produced. He was actually reiterating what His Lord said in John 13:14-15. *"Now that I, your Lord and Teacher, have washed your feet, you also should wash one another's feet. I have set you an example that you should do as I have done for you."*
So go ahead. Be an example. It's your right and responsibility.

> In everything set them an example by doing what is good. In your teaching show integrity, seriousness and soundness of speech that cannot be condemned, so that those who oppose you may be ashamed because they have nothing bad to say about us." (Titus 2:7, 8)

Daily challenge:
What kind of example are you?

281

Poetry in Motion

I really didn't want to get up this morning. It was dark and chilly and I craved more time for snoozing. But that wasn't in the cards. Having promised the grammar-school principal to help, I was to be one of two judges for the seventh-grade poetry contest. Now you have to understand something about New Covenant Schools and poetry: they go hand in hand. Since the opening day, every kid, every year, has been assigned the task of delivering a poem from memory. From the kindergartners to the seniors, no one is exempt. The poems just get harder and longer with the older grades.

This particular group of middle schoolers gathered in the Commons, parents taking the chairs in the back. I seated myself at the judges' table and looked over the sheet. I was to score them for diction and pace, stage presence and creativity. All of the kids knew their lines—impressive. One young man rushed through as if in a time trial. And admittedly, a couple left me yawning. Drama was not their thing. But for five of the children, the contest's stage allowed them to step outside themselves and take on another personality. I sat enthralled, wishing for them to go on longer.

I have never considered myself to be particularly fond of poetry, much to the chagrin of my English teachers. But I will have to admit that certain poems convey much in emotion and expression, my first poem not included. "I know a little bee that comes to play with me . . .."

The Scriptures are a rich collection of fine literature. Moses' song in Deuteronomy 32 was a didactic poem, teaching the masses. Songs of Moses and Miriam and Judge Deborah are recorded in Deuteronomy, Exodus and Judges. Well-organized acrostic poems are found throughout the Psalms. Elegies of fallen heroes can be found in II Samuel. And poems in the form of lyrical songs have been sung by Hannah, Elizabeth and Mother Mary.

God loved us so much that he gave us literature—and truth—in the form of brilliant writing, Spirit-breathed. We are wise to spend time reading the Word for pleasure's sake—and not out of obligation.

Your word is a lamp to my feet and a light for my path. (Psalm 119:105)

Daily challenge:
Grab a cup of coffee, put your feet up and spend some time in the Word.
It's good reading.

Whatsoever Is Lovely

I arrived home from yet another soccer game and looked at the pile of mail on the counter. Most of it was destined to the trash, but a few required attention. One bill in particular caught my eye and immediately irritated me. It was not a large amount but was unnecessary. I probably had some moments of sanctimonious deliberations. *Ugh.* I was annoyed.

Being the mature person that I am (I jest), I tried to put my less-than-honorable thoughts aside. I grabbed a snack and sat down to watch a favorite show, making small talk with whoever wandered through the room. But my relaxing was short-lived when I remembered that Seth's uniform had to be washed for tomorrow's game. The clothes had been piled by the washer and like always, I checked the pockets for pens, pencils and money. I found none of that but pulled out a piece of paper folded into a small wad. Once the door of the washer closed and the cycle began, I unfolded the note to see if it was a keeper. The handwriting was small and tidy, but the words were anything but. It was a joke of sorts but crude and inappropriate. Seth had been the recipient. I was so disappointed.

Purity and wholesomeness are often ridiculed. Modesty is scoffed as old-fashioned. Just flip the TV channels and see if I'm right. Depicted on the screen is the obsession for sex, lust, money, beauty, drugs, alcohol and anything that can produce a sense of "coolness." Hedonism is at historic highs, driven by images on the big screen, small screen, across the airways and in print.

I'm not so naïve to think that our society bears this problem alone. Sodom and Gomorrah, Nineveh and Corinth represent cities with reputations for unrighteousness. All were warned to repent, but few regarded the admonition worthy enough to solicit a behavioral change. What was the difference in those who turned from debauchery and those who continued to wallow in the filth? It was a regenerated mind—a God-induced desire for righteousness.

Pure thinking is not natural. It takes the power of the Spirit to turn our minds to what is upright and holy. It takes practice. It takes prayer. And it takes making wise decisions about what we see and hear and speak.

Finally, brothers, whatever is true, whatever is noble, whatever is right, whatever is pure, whatever is lovely, whatever is admirable— if anything is excellent or praiseworthy—think about such things. (Philippians 4:8)

Daily challenge:
You can't be swimming in the gutter and expect to stay clean.

Our Universal Lord

"I greet you in the name of our Lord and Savior, Jesus Christ." If you think I was reading one of the Apostle Paul's greetings, you're wrong. What I read flowed from the pen of a seventeen-year old girl.

Lavanya lives in an impoverished Indian province. When the opportunity came to select a child for sponsorship, there were plenty of young children to choose from. But when I saw her picture, a dark-skinned girl with long braids, she beckoned me with her deep brown eyes. The deal was sealed when I saw she was within a week of the same age as Seth. Perfect. Lavanya was ours. The boys had a "sister."

Over the months the letters have come with regularity. She always opens her notes in the name of the Lord and closes them with love and prayers. She told me of her intercession for Seth when he had his motorcycle accident. She asked if Caleb had found a job. She wanted to know if Gary was OK and let me know that she was praying for him as he works. She also solicited our prayers as she entered her twelfth year complete with compulsory exams. She affectionately calls us *Aunti* and *Uncle* and refers to the boys as *Brother*. Though we have never met, we have become extended family.

Why was this bond formed? Was it the magic of humanitarian effort? Was the plight of a desperate, poor girl and the sponsor's generosity what brought the two together, much like magnets of opposite charges? No. I propose that it was solely the Lord.

Throughout the ages, Believers of all stripes and nationalities have been joined together through the work of the Spirit. Have you ever been standing in line at the store and just known that the cashier was a Christian? Or have you been on vacation, drawn to another family, only to find out that you share a common faith? Each time it happens to me, I'm amazed at the common ground we share.

> *There is one body and one Spirit—just as you were called to one hope when you were called—one Lord, one faith, one baptism; one God and Father of all, who is over all and through all and in all. (Ephesians 4:4-6)*

Daily challenge:
What kind of "vibes" do you send out? Would another Believer feel drawn to you?

Signs of the Season

It seemed more like May than October. The sun was shining, a breeze tussled my hair and the temperature was the shorts and T-shirt kind. There was plenty of work to keep everyone happy—or not. By the time we met up for lunch, no one was smiling.

Caleb had just gotten dumped off the back of the four-wheeler, wild man Seth at the helm, of course. His forearm was scraped and bleeding. Seth took exception to the accusation that he was driving too aggressively. Then Seth informed us that he had lost his class ring last weekend during the race. *Great. Another chunk of money down the drain.* I got perturbed just thinking about it. We decided it best to split up the forces for the afternoon. Caleb could help me and Gary would take Seth. The tension eased.

Our task was to close the pool. On such a wonderful summer-like day, it seemed unnecessary—until I looked at the thermometer and realized the water temperature was a chilly sixty-eight degrees. I begrudgingly dumped in the recommended chemicals. As we pulled out the ladders and dragged the cover over yet-sparkling water, we busied ourselves with filling the water tubes used to hold down the cover. The time it took to fill them gave us ample opportunity to watch the grass grow another inch. But finally, we finished tucking in the pool for another winter, the pump and filter silenced once more. It was sad.

I love the summers because of the pool. We entertain our friends and have long conversations in the hammock. It's a perfect place for frolic. It's also a retreat—an after-dinner escape, cup of coffee in hand. It's a place to idly float on a Sunday afternoon. And on a hot and humid night, a refreshing dip lit by moonbeams is the best. But it's over. Now, a new season approaches.

Sometimes I get frustrated with the seasons of life. When I was younger, I wanted to be older. Now that I am older, I want to be—or at least act—younger. But I think God was very wise to create seasons for us, each with an express purpose. Periods of drought make us to appreciate the rainy seasons. The cold and dark of winter help us welcome periods of exhilarating growth as the freeze eases.

Be content knowing that God is preparing us for the next season. Embrace the process.

There is a time for everything, and a season for every activity under heaven. (Ecclesiastes 3:1)

Daily challenge:
Make the best of each season. Moping about it won't make a bad season go away any faster.

Raise the Banner

The sunny skies and warm fall glow drew me outside. It had been a week since I ran, my quads still sore from my hundred-miler last weekend. As I sauntered down the country road, I heard the sound of a vehicle in the field beside me. At first, I could not see the noise maker but laughed as I spied a ragged Confederate flag moving above the weed tops. Within a few moments, a decrepit-looking dune buggy occupied by two "tween" girls rolled along beside the road. There was no doubt we were in the south-land.

I guess the confederate flag—or any flag, for that matter—is a sign of allegiance. Think back to all those Olympic opening ceremonies that you've watched. As each of the nations take to the stadium floor, the front-runner is always the flag-bearer. But the competitors who follow in the flag's wake also bear symbols of their country on uniforms or carry small versions of the flag. Throughout the Games, athletes and fans alike sing anthems, hold signs and in a frenzy, shout out things like "U-S-A! U-S-A!"

I remember my high-school days when I was so proud to wear our green-and-white colors and gather by the banner leading the band and cheerleaders onto the football field. Pennridge Senior High School was the best school in the world as far as I was concerned. On game days, all of us on athletic teams wore our warm-up jackets to show unity. We were proud to be "Rams."

Even today, I love to be associated with the boys' school. I hear myself saying "we" when I refer to the soccer team or school philosophy. I also take pride in wearing the products and logo of the company, INOV-8, who graciously allows me to represent them. I guess some things never change. If they had a flag, I'd wave it.

Flags are to rally around. Men on the battlefield looked to the flag bearer to see how the battle raged. Each of the tribes of Israel and the families within camped under their own banners, symbols of strength and unity. Ancient troops, described in Song of Solomon carried banners. Jeremiah cried, *"Announce and proclaim among the nations, lift up a banner and proclaim it"* (Jeremiah 50:2).

But banners are more than adorned cloth. A banner proclaims power. A banner asserts victory. A banner shows solidarity. God's banner loves, protects and embraces. We are safe when we cling to His banner.

We will shout for joy when you are victorious and will lift up our banners in the name of our God. May the LORD grant all your requests. (Psalm 20:5)

Daily challenge:
Under whose banner do you find your identity?

My Plans

In light of an interesting job offer, I'm wondering if I should pursue it. Seth's time at home is reduced to months and it could help make up a financial shortfall. Ironically, or maybe not, the "verse of the day" on my computer screen was taken from Jeremiah 29. He wrote of God's plan . . . not his own. Maybe this applied to me as well.

To put things into perspective, the prophet wrote this letter to *the surviving elders among the exiles and to the priests, the prophets and all the other people Nebuchadnezzar had carried into exile from Jerusalem to Babylon. (This was after King Jehoiachin and the queen mother, the court officials and the leaders of Judah and Jerusalem, the craftsmen and the artisans had gone into exile from Jerusalem)* (29:1b, 2). The situation was dismal and the people were exhausted emotionally, spiritually and physically. They had been jerked away from Jerusalem and ended up in a strange land. I would have wanted to crawl in a hole and die. But God had different plans.

He told them to build houses, plant gardens, eat what they grew, marry and most importantly, have lots of kids. Their numbers were to increase, not decrease. But why did God require them to put down roots and live contentedly? I think it was because of the next step.

The exile was going to last a mere seventy years—just one generation. But after that God declared, *"I will come to you and fulfill my gracious promise to bring you back to this place"* (29:10). And why would He do that? Because *"I know the plans I have for you," declares the LORD, "plans to prosper you and not to harm you, plans to give you hope and a future. Then you will call upon me and come and pray to me, and I will listen to you. You will seek me and find me when you seek me with all your heart. I will be found by you"* (29:11-13).

Think about it. God has a fully formed plan and keeps our best interest in mind. Each circumstance, each hardship, each blessing, is designed to turn our hearts toward God.

> *And we know that in all things God works for the good of those who love him, who have been called according to his purpose. (Romans 8:28)*

Daily challenge:
God has *"plans to give you hope and a future."* That should make you seek Him.

Hold Fast

The boys were starving when they moseyed in from soccer practice. Pleased with myself, I pulled a hot dinner from the oven. Together we enjoyed the meal, chatting about teams, homework, senior thesis progress and other disjointed bits of conversation. But as dinner drew to a close, Seth got up to retrieve a soccer cleat. "Look, Mama," as he likes to call me, "Want a project?" The heel of his left shoe had come disjointed from the sole. *Oops.* Just a few weeks of the season remained and I did not want to buy new cleats.

Gary took on the job of cementing it back together with epoxy. I wondered if the repair would hold fast or if the heel would go winging from his foot on his first ball strike. The claims of the epoxy makers were impressive but promises can be as empty as a dry well.

Maybe it was the glue fumes—I hear they can be wicked—but my mind started thinking about this concept of holding fast. The phrase rung a bell. With a little digging, I found two different situations. In the first, we do the active holding. In the second, someone else has the death grip.

When I picture *hold fast,* I see someone who has slipped off a high cliff and is clinging onto a slender branch, knuckles white and fear stricken. To let go would be disastrous. In the same manner, we are to hold fast *"to the LORD your God"* (Joshua 23:8) and to the statues of the Lord (Psalm 119:31). Over and over we are told, *hold fast.* Yes, *hold fast* as if your life depended on it—because it does.

But what if we are incapable of holding fast? What happens when our grip slips? God has that one covered as well. In the beautiful 139th Psalm, David makes his case. *If I go up to the heavens, you are there; if I make my bed in the depths, you are there. If I rise on the wings of the dawn, if I settle on the far side of the sea . . .* (vs. 7-10). What then? Listen to this: *even there your hand will guide me, your right hand will hold me fast.*

How wonderful to know that when we can no longer hold on, God reaches down with that big, strong right hand of His and snatches us from catastrophe. He pulls us from that cliff to a solid place where we can wrap our arms around the Savior and hold on for dear life.

"But be very careful . . . to love the LORD your God, to walk in all his ways, to obey his commands, to hold fast to him and to serve him with all your heart and all your soul." (Joshua 22:5)

Daily challenge:
Make sure that you are holding fast to the Lord . . . not a flimsy branch that can't be trusted.

Checkups

I finally did it. I was motivated by the month-long push for breast cancer awareness. I marched my little behind right off to the mammography center at the local hospital. "Good luck," I told the technician as she wrangled my not-so-voluptuous breasts, one at a time, of course, between the plastic plates. *Squish. Crinkle. Splat. Flat.* All that and more as the machine inflicted about four tons of pressure onto the delicate tissue. "Take a deep breath and hold," she said. That wasn't hard. The pain had sucked the breath right out of me.

The exam was over quickly and I walked into the parking lot relatively unscathed. I am not expecting a bad report, but neither was my mom about eight years back when she was told the news. I will wait to hear the radiologist's reading and then likely go on with life. But there is always that chance that I could have a potentially fatal disease.

So I speculate. What would I do if I was called into the doctor's office diagnosed with an aggressive cancer? I'm not sure. I've read about the reactions of others. I've listened as people spoke of dealing with the mental and physical aftermath. Some sobbed, some whimpered, some fell silent, some became depressed, some gave up, some fought, some lived and some died. I hope I would fight and live. I also hope I don't have to find out.

A song written and popularized by Tim McGraw tells of a man who is told he has a serious illness. He responds by doing extraordinary things. And his advice? "Live like you were dying." In this song that meant jumping out of perfectly good airplanes, climbing rock faces and going for a ride on a bucking bull. But more than that, it changed behavior: "and I loved deeper and I spoke sweeter and I gave forgiveness I'd been denying and he said someday I hope you get the chance to live like you were dying."

The country star has a point. If we knew our time was limited, would our behavior change? Would we be more serious about the depth of our sincerity and practicality of service? Probably. But I submit that if we truly grasp the importance of living fully and above reproach, we will wake up every morning and "live like we were dying"— because we are—some just more quickly than others.

> *He replied, "Go tell that fox [Herod], 'I will drive out demons and heal people today and tomorrow, and on the third day I will reach my goal.' In any case, I must keep going today and tomorrow and the next day . . .." (Luke 13:32, 33a)*

Daily challenge:
Do something today that you would normally put off until tomorrow.

Fence Me In

Fences serve two purposes—keep something out or keep something in. Lots of families like fences to keep the little kiddies from running into the street. But gardeners are not concerned with kids. They build impressive fences to keep the four-legged rodents—deer—out of the vegetable patch.

I remember hearing Mom and Dad speak of their time living on the Fort Peck Indian reservation in northeast Montana. It was the mid-1950s. Their quaint little house was fenced and they soon found out why. One night the gate was left open. By dawn, a whole herd of wild horses were grazing in the yard. And what goes in must come out, if you know what I mean. What a mess!

When we first moved into this house, there was a fence around the pool, if you call the hog wire strung between forsythia bushes a fence. We decided on a more substantial fence. We coughed up the money and purchased one that met all the standards for safety and insurance carriers. It not only looks better than hog wire, it is substantial, sturdy and does its job of keeping out small, feral children who wander from the forest in the cover of darkness. (I jest about the children.)

My current occupation with fences came about when Gary told me of a new "fence" he installed at school. It is merely a chain strung across portions of the access road. It should keep cars out of the restricted areas. However, what if he just drew a line in the road and wrote "Keep out"? What if he used wimpy string instead of chain? Do you think such feeble fences could withstand the challenge of a car? Probably not.

There's an interesting analogy to a fence in Psalm 62. David begins the chapter with *My soul finds rest in God alone; my salvation comes from him* (62:1). He continues claiming that God is his rock, his salvation and his fortress. *I will never be shaken*, David states. But when he begins to talk of those who assault him, he refers to his own vulnerability as *this leaning wall, this tottering fence* (62:3).

But praise God—the one who instills hope and protects the righteous also mends broken-down fences. Whether we need protection from those outside the fence or from within, God is the ultimate fence-builder.

> *My salvation and my honor depend on God; he is my mighty rock, my refuge. Trust in him at all times, O people; pour out your hearts to him, for God is our refuge. Selah. (Psalm 62:7, 8)*

Daily challenge:
The only fence surrounding you should be the one God put there.

Restraint

After weeks of Indian summer, temps in the forties and steady drizzle made the bones ache and innards shiver. But there I sat—a loyal soccer mom watching her senior boy in the regional playoffs. With only a single loss to mar a perfect season, today's opponent was the team who had been the spoiler. Our team was missing a key player but our defense seemed to be missing their minds. It was not pretty. To make matters worse, the other team had one particularly dirty player. Late hits, trips and cleats up marked his play, all the while decrying to the officials supposed ills against him.

It was late in the first half when Seth apparently had enough. Being a high-impact striker, Seth drew the majority of the foul play from this defender. As a ball rolled toward the sideline, Seth was in a footrace with this kid. I could see it in his eyes. *Oh, no! He's gonna do it. He's gonna take him out!* And take him out he did. He didn't even try to disguise the attack. His shoulder dropped and boom—the kid flew through the air like a spineless ragdoll, landing hard. I knew it would be a card for Seth. It was just a matter of what color.

Fortunately, the card was yellow and resulted in just a short interlude in his play. However, had it been a red, he would have been ejected for the rest of the game, the team would have been forced to play one man short, and Seth would be prevented in playing tomorrow's game. Hardly worth the short-lived pleasure in delivering a blow to a bothersome opponent. I'm sure the rest of the team would have been very upset—and rightly so—had they been forced to suffer for my son's impulsive actions.

If I'm honest, I have acted on an itch only to later regret it. Loose words flying from the mouth come to mind. Wife to husband, mom to kid, friend to friend . . . the list goes on. Had I only kept my big mouth shut, I could have preempted a serious problem. But no, I just had to let 'em fly and wreak havoc with those I love the most. *Dumb. Really, really dumb.*

A little restraint, a little self-control goes a long way.

> *Therefore, prepare your minds for action; be self-controlled; set your hope fully on the grace to be given you when Jesus Christ is revealed. (I Peter 1:13)*

Daily challenge:
Think before you act. Seal the lips before you let them flap.

Never-Ending Questions

As I opened the computer program, I hoped to see a blank screen—no messages and no assignments to be graded. But as the page emerged, I felt like a little hamster on that stupid wheel. *Will it ever end? Do I not have a moment's reprieve?*

Teaching online high school science is a challenge. It's a part-time job that requires time and a half to do. My students, nearly one-hundred-forty strong, work all hours of the day and night. There is no gong to mark the day's beginning and no closing bell to designate the end. My students spread across the country and around the world. They might have defined start and stop times, but I can never take a break and still meet their needs. "Please Mrs. Trittipoe. I'm trying to catch up. I'd appreciate it if you could answer my questions quickly so I can move on." *Ugh.*

However, the thing I find most rewarding is the exchange I have with these kids in a virtual world. I work hard to recognize and encourage solid work. After receiving kudos for a well-done quiz, one girl wrote, "I called my mother strait away and she was so happy for me :). Thanks for your support!" Some of my students seek advice before asking how to calculate the specific gravity of gold. With each week, I feel more attached to my classroom of kids on the other end of the Ethernet cable. I have a responsibility to teach them science. But I must also instruct them to become discerning learners, thirsty for knowledge.

I find it most interesting that wisdom combined with prudence results in *knowledge and discretion* (Proverbs 8:12). The Merriam-Webster online dictionary defines *prudence* as "1 : the ability to govern and discipline oneself by the use of reason 2 : sagacity or shrewdness in the management of affairs 3 : skill and good judgment in the use of resources 4 : caution or circumspection as to danger or risk ." In mathematical terms, wisdom + prudence = knowledge + discernment. *Goodness. If my kids could understand this profound equation, they could set the world on fire. Come to think of it, if I understood, I might set the world aglow myself.*

"I, wisdom, dwell together with prudence; I possess knowledge and discretion." (Proverbs 8:12)

Daily challenge:
How prudent are your actions and thoughts?

Ready for Winter

For as much as I like the seasons, there are still times that are hard to take. I don't like to be cold . . . and neither do my plants. With scattered frost forecasted tonight, I have to make sure my potted plants are comfortable.

I've had a few of my geraniums and begonias for years. During the cold months, they reside in the coziness of the sunroom, growing vigorously in the controlled environment. But come spring, out they go. Today, however, I worked in reverse. I dug up some of the annuals and transplanted them into pots. After removing the dead leaves and pinching off spent flowers, I had Caleb carry them into the house. Now when I go to bed, I won't have to wonder if the plants will survive the cold.

I'm proud that I thought about this when the sun was shining. Last year I forgot. I was watching the late night news when the word *frost* caught my attention. In my pajamas and sandals, I spent the next half hour prowling around in the dark to save my potted plants. By the time I finished, I was cold, wet and dirty. The floor was covered with plant refuse. A little foresight on my part could have spared me.

It wasn't that I didn't know it was going to get cold. Some things just don't change. *"As long as the earth endures, seedtime and harvest, cold and heat, summer and winter, day and night will never cease"* (Genesis 8:22). But my knowledge wasn't sufficient. I needed action on top of the knowledge in order to avoid the inconvenient late night recognizance.

It's so easy to get lazy and complacent. "Yeah, yeah. I'll do it." That seems to be the motto of one of our sons who shall remain nameless. He has good intentions—I think—but more times than not, his intentions are not equivalent to action. Chalk it up to immaturity. A mature person anticipates and performs. An immature one rarely even anticipates.

We do not want you to become lazy, but to imitate those who through faith and patience inherit what has been promised. (Hebrews 6:12)

Daily challenge:
Anticipate. Plan. Do.

Connections

I can't believe it! I made a trip into town to spend an hour or two at a popular eatery offering free high-speed internet. Like always, I flipped open my computer and clicked on my browser. I sat back to wait and took a bite of my salad. "Unable to connect." I checked the settings and tried again. It told me I was connected, but my browser begged to differ. I tried another browser. No go. I checked my security settings and all seemed to be in order. So why was I still dangling in the foyer of cyberspace? I looked around and watched people at six different computers click away. Not fair.

It's amazing how dependent we have become on this nebulous thing called *the World Wide Web*. It is a complex tool we use in our work, research and recreation. We establish relationships with people on the other side of the world, sight unseen. Communication is nearly instantaneous. Libraries have been put on the endangered species list and email is the contact mode of choice. Shopping is fast and all too easy. Even banking and mortgage loans can be obtained in the virtual world.

Our constant state of connectedness through the internet is both a blessing and a curse. Our productivity is enhanced over the pencil-and-paper world of yesteryear. But on the other hand, the Web can beckon and beseech the user to spend way too much time engaging with microchips rather than fellow man.

I wonder what would happen if we valued our personal relationships as much as our electronic ties. I suspect that if we shut down our computers and turned off our cell phones and Blackberries, we might have time to look directly into the eyes of another. After all, Jesus Christ is a bond much stronger than anything electronic.

In 1792, a London preacher loaded his family's belongings onto a cart, preparing for a move to pastor a larger church. But the emotion and love between the parishioners and Dr. and Mrs. John Fawcett were too strong. Not able to bear the thought of separation, the wagon was unpacked and Dr. Fawcett penned the now-famous hymn:

> *Blest be the tie that binds*
> *Our hearts in Christian love . . .*
> *We share each other's woes,*
> *Our mutual burdens bear;*
> *And often for each other flows*
> *The sympathizing tear . . ..*

We proclaim . . . so that you also may have fellowship with us. And our fellowship is with the Father and with his Son, Jesus Christ. (I John 1:3)

Daily challenge:
Unplug and reconnect.

Losing Sight of the Goal

With the soccer state quarter-finals as reward, today's soccer game was a must-win. Played on a neutral field, it required a long drive. We finally pulled up and groaned. The field was tiny and scruffy, a baseball dirt infield occupying the middle third. The style of our team required a larger field where Seth's speed could be capitalized on as the most forward striker. But we had no such luxury today.

The other school scored first, then us. 1-1. Then we scored. 2-1. Then they scored 2-2. Then they scored again. 3-2. And when we thought all hope was gone, we scored with 45 seconds to go. 3-3 and a double overtime to follow. The score remained at 3-3 during the first overtime. Our kids controlled the play and it looked like they might pull it out.

But with the starting whistle of the second overtime, our kids fell asleep. They walked to balls kicked out of bounds and lollygagged at a pedestrian pace. Only once did they take the ball down to our end. With thirty seconds to go, a competitor dribbled the ball between two of our defenders and scored the winning goal. Any thoughts of a glorious outcome at state championships were dashed.

Why did they shut down and surrender? I suppose there are two possibilities. 1) They got so tired their bodies disobeyed their brains, or 2) they lost sight of the goal. The mental and physical pain of exertion superseded the desire to leave the field victorious. Sometimes it's just easier to give up and face the consequences later.

The twelfth chapter of Hebrews speaks so well to this phenomenon. Verse 2 begs us to *fix our eyes on Jesus, the author and perfecter of our faith . . . .* The author continues the discussion by telling us to *endure hardship as discipline* (v. 7), because it is an integral part of growth.

Will it always feel good? Certainly not. *No discipline seems pleasant at the time, but painful. Later on, however, it produces a harvest of righteousness and peace for those who have been trained by it* (v. 11).

And what are we to do? In colloquial language, *suck it up. Therefore, strengthen your feeble arms and weak knees. "Make level paths for your feet," so that the lame may not be disabled, but rather healed* (vs. 12, 13).

Let us not become weary in doing good, for at the proper time we will reap a harvest if we do not give up. (Galatians 6:9)

Daily challenge:
Simple. Don't give up.

Plans

Don't you wish God was in the crystal-ball business? Not that He doesn't know what's going on. It's just that we don't.

Planning for the future is in high gear with Seth solidly into his last year of high school. He's on track to be a professional photographer. But there are two- and four-year degrees in photography, professional certificate programs, internships, apprenticeships and the very pricey art institutes that can set you back $165,000. He also has to decide where to live. Programs near ski resorts top his list while huge metropolises beckon as well.

I can't say that I spent that much time contemplating my future when I was eighteen. I applied to one college and got in. I had big plans to major in Biology, take lots of chemistry and go off to medical school. I didn't plan on staring into the eyes of my future husband just two months into my freshman year. Within a week of our first date, we assumed we would marry and did—a year-and-a-half later. I accelerated my college pace, added in teaching credentials, taught and coached, went back to school for perfusion training and here I am today, sitting at my kitchen counter, content to be out of the operating room. What happened? I never could have predicted this back in 1975.

I think God showed his sense of humor by inventing plans. His plans are all laid out, but how He must laugh—or maybe cry—at how well we follow them. If we had a blueprint, a map, it would be much easier. Think about David and Solomon. David spent a long time envisioning what the temple in Jerusalem was supposed to look like. In fact, he gave Solomon *the plans of all that the Spirit had put in his mind for the courts of the temple of the LORD and all the surrounding rooms . . .* (I Chronicles 28:12). Must be nice to have it laid out so perfectly. How hard could it be to get it right?

But we fool ourselves. We have a way of messing up even when the plan is set in stone. Sometimes God simply says *do this* or *do that.* There is no need for analysis. But do we follow directions? No. Now, that's just plain stupid.

I don't expect handwriting on the wall or a message written in the clouds in terms of Seth's plans. What I do expect is that we will pray a lot while we explore options. But I rest assured that God has it all figured out.

Many are the plans in a man's heart, but it is the LORD's purpose that prevails. (Proverbs 19:21)

Daily challenge:
Believe it. God's plans are to *"prosper you and not to harm you and plans to give you hope and a future."* (Jeremiah 29:11)

Burdens to Bear

We can't fix all the problems in the world, right? I don't think too many people will disagree. But do we have a responsibility to fix at least some of them?

If you consider all the solicitations we get in the mail and by phone, it becomes easy to say, "Sorry. I gave at the office." Many are legitimate causes, but there is only so much money to go around. But it's even tougher when there's no question about their authenticity: feed the starving children, support missionaries and send relief to disaster areas.

Years ago, a friend of mine told me that when faced with a valid request, he tried never to say *no*. He did what he could at the moment. That is an admirable approach and many have benefitted as a result. However, I have to think that addressing needs is greater than giving money, as important as that is. The Apostle Paul needed money from the churches to support him in his missionary efforts. He also needed practical offerings such as food to eat and a warm coat for winter. But he yearned for what money could not buy—encouragement, prayer and loving concern. What is the lesson for us?

Sometimes we "can't see the forest for the trees," as the saying goes. We are blind to the need we see out the window or driving down the street or sitting in the pew beside us. There are people all around us who are burdened by grief, illness, family issues, job difficulties and deep financial trouble. While we cannot be the answer to every need, we can reach out and lift some of the weight their shoulders bear.

I've been impressed by that spirit of help within our own church. I've never seen a body of Believers respond to needs in such practical ways. One young wife and mother has been left alone as her husband was called to war. Weekly meals, childcare and companionship have been planned for the duration of his absence. A mother of seven had surgery today. The ladies of the church rallied to prepare meals for a week. New mothers receive meals for several weeks to help ease the transition in caring for a new baby. The list goes on.

I don't have to reach across the ocean to help. I need only cross the street where I live.

Carry each other's burdens, and in this way you will fulfill the law of Christ. (Galatians 6:2)

Daily challenge:
Find a practical way—today—to help someone bear his or her burden.

Trophies Up for Grabs

I had enough. The upstairs landing was full of dead creatures—literally. They were all over the floor. To make matters worse, two huge and scary things were in my bedroom.

You need to understand. We are a hunting family and evidence of success can be found all over the house. I doubt that the fine folks at HGTV would be impressed with our wall decorations. Nevertheless, the number of deer and turkey mounts has increased over the years. Wall space is at a premium. To make matters worse, three of the deer and one turkey mount that graced Seth's room did not make his last room redo. That's why I found the deer mounts on the floor of the landing. Two of the turkey mounts ended up in our bedroom—hardly the epitome of romantic décor.

With hammer in hand, I took matters into my own hand. *Bang, bang, bang.* After eyeballing the available wall space in the hallway and stairwell, the turkeys vacated my bedroom and found a new home—along with all the deer mounts. Although we might frighten small children with the display of wildlife-gone-dead, that area in our house pays tribute to the trophies earned over the years.

I have always had a love-hate relationship with trophies of another sort. To win a trophy has been satisfying. But what good are they? The boys used to love getting their little plastic trophies. And I've had my own share through the years, boxes of which now sit in the attic. But trophies hold little value other than as a reminder of the past. Perhaps the most valuable part of trophy-getting is the process it takes to attain them.

We're familiar with the inspiring verses about pressing on to the goal (Philippians 3:14) and running to obtain the prize (I Corinthians 9:24). But I was most impressed with what motivated Moses. *He chose to be mistreated along with the people of God rather than to enjoy the pleasures of sin for a short time. He regarded disgrace for the sake of Christ as of greater value than the treasures of Egypt, because he was looking ahead to his reward. By faith he left Egypt, not fearing the king's anger; he persevered because he saw him who is invisible* (Hebrews 11:25-27).

He persevered because he saw him who was invisible . . .. Wow. That's incredibly mature. Seeing a big hunk of a trophy is one thing. Persevering in pursuit of an invisible motivator is quite another.

"The LORD rewards every man for his righteousness and faithfulness." (I Samuel 26:23a)

Daily challenge:
What kind of trophies are you pursuing?

Rain, Rain

With prediction of cold and constant rain, I looked forward to sleeping in on this Saturday morning. There's just something cozy about drawing the covers up around my neck, content to steal away a few extra minutes. When I did rise, a nice cup of coffee awaited me as I listened to the steady rain falling against the glass roof of the sunroom. I didn't mind the rain; I had no plans for the day. But Gary, on the other hand, had been eagerly anticipating the drenching.

Farmers and facility managers have a vested interest in the rain. Gary and his crew had worked hard and long this week redoing a soccer field at the school. Finally, they got the last of the grass seed sewn yesterday. Now, they just needed the predicted rain. And rain they got.

Rain is an interesting phenomena. Can you imagine the folks living in Noah's time? Never before had it rained but when it started, boy, were they in for a surprise. Forty days and nights of rain have a way of ruining most plans. Even in the context of modern times, torrential rains flood cities, drown livestock, ruin crops and knock houses right off their foundations. In this case, more is not better.

But what about no rain? The lack of fluid precipitation can be just as devastating. Reading through the Old Testament, God often withheld rain as punishment for disobedience. All life is dependent on rain and without it comes death.

God has used lots of rain—or lack of it—to bring judgment. However, one of the reasons why God is God is that He knows exactly what we need when we need it. In His mercy, "*The LORD will open the heavens, the storehouse of his bounty, to send rain on your land in season and to bless all the work of your hands*" (Deuteronomy 28:12).

Too often we fail to understand that rain in any amount is the express work of God, sent to point us to the Rainmaker. In times of drought we are forced to look to God for provision. In times of flood, we cry out for salvation. And when the rain is "just right," we rejoice in His goodness.

"Let my teaching fall like rain and my words descend like dew, like showers on new grass, like abundant rain on tender plants." (Deuteronomy 32:2)

Daily challenge:
Run through the rain and soak in His love.

What Good Is It Anyway?

"Mrs. T. I'm not good at math and science and no matter what I do, I can't get it. Besides, why do I need to know about specific gravity? It's worthless information!"

A student, frustrated by a difficult unit in his science class, scribed this note. He made it clear that he saw no need for learning something he considered rubbish. How does a teacher respond? Well, this one went through the routine of "God expects you to do your best no matter what and I expect you to fulfill your responsibility to be disciplined in your studies." I'm not convinced it changed his mind about those density calculations, but the reluctant student managed to slither his way through the unit.

As much as we hate to admit it, we adults are pretty good at copping the same attitude. Why clean the house if it's just gonna get dirty again? What good is it to exercise if I won't lose any weight? Or maybe this one sounds familiar: I'm tired of saying "no" to Jimmy. He won't listen and I don't want to deal with it.

We can laugh—or cry—at these circumstances. But it's an advanced form of adult whining cultivated by years and years of practice. And the thing is, we not only whine out loud, we whine on the inside in a scrutiny-free zone. "It doesn't matter if I don't read my Bible today. I went to church on Sunday. And, I don't have to pray. God will do whatever He wants anyway."

Some things are worthwhile even when we don't fully understand. When we encounter difficulties and wonder why, do we consider it *pure joy* (James 1:2)? When we were children, we understood as children. But with time we will be able to say, *Now I know in part; then I shall know fully, even as I am fully known* (I Corinthians 13:12).

A prerequisite for living is not possessing full understanding. The required commitment is fully living.

All Scripture is God-breathed and is useful for teaching, rebuking, correcting and training in righteousness, so that the man of God may be thoroughly equipped for every good work. (II Timothy 3:16-17)

Daily challenge:
Never let not knowing keep you from moving forward.

Fox-like

As I walked through the sunroom, movement out by the persimmon tree captured my attention. I picked up the binoculars from the table nearby. They always stand poised for action lest a deer's antlers need to be inspected more closely. But it was not a deer that I beheld. Rather, it was a large gray fox, its bushy tail and red neck and nose giving it a unique appearance. It appeared to be enjoying the fruit fallen from the tree. He was a pretty specimen, but I hoped he would be content with eating the persimmons, leaving my kitty-cats intact.

I began to think about Aesop's fable about the fox and the grapes. Remember? A fox unsuccessfully tried to get the grapes at the top of the vine. Creeping away defeated and still hungry, he grumbled how the grapes were sour anyway. The moral? "It is easy to despise what you cannot get."

I went to my computer to check my recall's accuracy and somehow ended up pleasantly lost in Aesop's writings. I discovered that no less than sixty-five fables were written about a fox. As I flipped through one after another, I laughed out loud at some of them. *That's a good one!* I thought. *I'll have to tell the guys at supper.*

The fable that roped me in like a rodeo cowboy was entitled—get this—"The Ass's Brains." Laughter erupted. Though you will have to Google the story yourself, it reminded me of an answer a slick lawyer might give. But the next story, "The Ass, the Fox, and the Lion", is the one I want to share. It seems like Ass and Fox made a pact to enter the woods to hunt. Before long, they came face to face with Lion. Since Fox understood imminent danger, he told Lion he could help him catch Ass if Lion agreed not to harm Fox. Lion consented. Hence, Fox led Ass to a deep pit into which Ass fell. However, Lion immediately seized the fox and attacked Ass at his leisure.

Isn't that just what we do? We think we can outsmart the Evil one—or at least make him leave us alone. We decide to be buddies only to find we are destroyed by that decision. And sometimes, this kind of thing happens before we even realize it.

We must be vigilant. We must not conspire with the enemy lest we be consumed ourselves.

Be self-controlled and alert. Your enemy the devil prowls around like a roaring lion looking for someone to devour. (I Peter 5:8)

Daily challenge:
Stand guard of your mind, soul and body.

Something's Wrong

We drove up to the house and parked. Going through the normal routine, I gathered up my things from around the car before walking up the sidewalk. Absentmindedly, I glanced up and did a double take. Curtains in the sunroom windows had been pulled down. Seeing them strewn about made me wonder if someone had ransacked the house. When I opened the door, I began to understand. *Feathers. Lots and lots of feathers.* I tiptoed through the mess in the sunroom and saw more feathers in the kitchen and piles and piles in the laundry room. Blood splatters—and more feathers—were on the kitchen counter. The crime scene was coming together. The criminals? Two cats.

Over in the corner, both of the kitties soundly slept. So exhausted were they that nary an eyelid budged. The feline siblings had previously brought other treasures into the house: grasshoppers, crickets, tiny moles, baby mice and even a bat. But never, ever a bird. It must have been quite a scene—cats chasing a panicked bird from room to room, feathers flying, curtains downed, until the final and fatal assault near the cutting board and knives . . . how fitting. We can only assume the cats ate the bird. We found no remnants other than dried blood on the male's face. No wonder they were sleeping off the big meal.

As I swept up the carnage, I laughed out loud imagining the massacre. I bet that bird was surprised at the cats' ferociousness. I wonder if it was on the ground when overcome. Perhaps it was perched upon a branch. And there is a possibility that it was snatched from the sky. I've seen the cats leap into the air and catch butterflies. Why not a bird? Whatever the circumstance, I guarantee that bird would have changed his behavior had he known two marauding hunters were hot on his tailfeathers.

We act like that naïve little bird. We are content to flit about, blinded by the status quo and oblivious to dangers that lurk behind the next bush or around the corner. Seems to me the writer of Proverbs warned about this kind of thing. I paraphrase. Play with fire . . . get burned (6:27). Don't be cruising the street where wild women lure (7:7-10). Keep your distance from foolish people (14:7). Don't shirk discipline (15:32). And don't get drunk and do something stupid (20:1).

I think you get the idea. There must be a conscious effort to avoid perils and traps. Take off the blinders and make good decisions before you get caught in a heap of trouble.

I applied my heart to what I observed and learned a lesson from what I saw. (Proverbs 24:32)

Daily challenge:
To be wise we must learn to remove ourselves from danger.

Lost and Found

My phone rang and a cheerful voice greeted me. "Hi there," said Deb. "I have some good news."

"Really? Did Jordan get accepted into another school?" I inquired.

"No. But I found Seth's ring!"

Ever since my hundred-miler at the beginning of the month, I've been praying specifically for that school ring. I felt sick when I heard it was lost. Seth actually wore his ring, unlike his older brother whose ring sits dormant since its purchase. I prayed that someone would find it and trace it back to my boy. It seemed a far-fetched scenario but still, I could not shake the impulse to pray for that stupid hunk of metal.

I had no idea God was going to answer otherwise. Sorting clothes to give away, Deb placed a jacket in the pile. As an afterthought, she unzipped the pockets to check for that forgotten twenty-dollar bill we always hope to find. Instead, her fingers felt something hard. Out came the ring. She gasped, having no earthly idea how it got into that zippered pocket. There is no recollection of being handed a ring for safekeeping and Seth did not place it there. I am convinced that God somehow, someway chose to answer my prayer. I rejoice.

There are other stories of lost and found. In Luke 15, The Lord and the Pharisees are having a discussion. They must have been slow learners; he had to tell three different versions of the same parable.

In the first, he spoke of the farmer who had lost BaBa Black sheep. He scoured the hillside and after finally finding it, carried it home. All rejoiced.

A woman lost a silver coin. She searched high and low, sweeping the floors and illuminating dark corners. She and her neighbors rejoiced when the coin was spied and placed back in the purse.

And then we have the parable of the prodigal. After years of raucous living, a broken and repentant son returns to his Father. A huge party ensues. When the older son protests over such treatment the father proclaims, *"'My son . . . we had to celebrate and be glad, because this brother of yours was dead and is alive again; he was lost and is found'"* (vs. 31 and 32).

The point is clear. The Father rejoices when one of His own repents and is found.

> *"'Rejoice with me; I have found my lost sheep.' I tell you that in the same way there will be more rejoicing in heaven over one sinner who repents than over ninety-nine righteous persons who do not need to repent." (Luke 15:6b, 7)*

Daily challenge:
Have you been found? Have the heavens rejoiced on your behalf?

Vision

You know how a tiny cut on your finger makes you think of nothing else? Well, for the last week, I can think of nothing but my vision. The aging presbyope that I am, my brain has been trying to get used to new contact lenses. I wear one for distance and one for reading. My poor gray matter is supposed to figure out which eye to use when. "It took me about thirty minutes to adjust," said my optometrist of his own experience. That gave me hope. But after a week, I still can't see. When I went in for a follow-up today, I reported my adaptive failure.

First we did testing. From his perspective, I had 20-20. But from my point of view, my left eye was still blurry. We tried bifocal lenses. While I could read, I was struggling too hard. And signs in the distance became fuzzy. Then we tried a different power for my left eye. *Ahh.* Much better. But after hours on the computer, I find that I'm straining. Maybe I should stick with glasses.

Since my mind was stuck on vision issues, I recalled a verse that said, *Where there is no vision, the people perish* (KJV, Proverbs 29:18). I had always heard it in the framework of missionary motivation. That is, if we don't understand the natives' need for the Lord, they will perish when we fail to introduce Christ. While that may be true, I was surprised when I read it in context. It really had nothing to do with that. It's all about knowledge of God and obedience.

The Message translation renders it this way: *If people can't see what God is doing, they stumble all over themselves; But when they attend to what he reveals, they are most blessed.* The NIV reads: *Where there is no revelation, the people cast off restraint; but blessed is he who keeps the law.*

A lack of vision results when we pay little attention to the written Word. A lackadaisical attitude keeps us from understanding God's will and ways. It's like the kid who gets in trouble with the law and lamely offers the excuse, "Well, no one told me it was wrong." In fact, the law had been written and was available to him. The offender simply chose to ignore it and must now bear the consequences.

See then that ye walk circumspectly, not as fools, but as wise,
Redeeming the time, because the days are evil. (Ephesians 5:15, 16)

Daily challenge:
If you keep your eyes open to see God, you won't get tripped up nearly as often.

Discouragement and Disappointment

The school soccer team left earlier this week for a national soccer tournament in Tennessee. Two of the moms went along for moral support—and to be the designated laundry persons. They also served as the line of communication to those of us back home. Our phones rang every time our team scored a goal. But it also rang every time the other team scored. You never knew which way it would go.

The team had a record of two wins and two losses coming into today's final game. The losses were poorly played games when either the defense or midfield struggled. The last game would determine either fifth or sixth place out of eight. "Good news or bad?" I inquired when the phone rang only a minute after the game began.

"Bad. The other team just scored."

"Well, thanks. Keep me posted." I could almost feel Seth's pain from here. He took yesterday morning's loss hard. After leaving it all on the field, he was disappointed at a perceived lack of competitiveness from some of his teammates—that and a fair share of novice-type mistakes that gave away goals. I longed for the next report to be a good one. But alas, the phone fell silent as the final whistle drew the contest to a close. There were no glory goals, no defining moments when the team "stepped up." There was only an "L" in the win-loss column.

As a senior, Seth is beginning to realize that opportunities and friendships unique to high school can now be measured in months—not years. The reality is that when the final graduate walks across the stage and caps are thrown into the air, the end of an era is sealed. No more "top-dog" status, no more soccer games, no more spirit days, no more ties and blazers on dress days.

While it is true that graduation begins a new era as much as it ends one, there is a certain sadness attached to the final chapter. I'm sure the senior players recognized that game as their last chance to take the field together.

I trust those kids will not be discouraged. I pray they will learn a life lesson about disappointment, perseverance and camaraderie. I hope they'll hold their heads high and look to the future.

"Have I not commanded you? Be strong and courageous. Do not be terrified; do not be discouraged, for the LORD your God will be with you wherever you go." (Joshua 1:9)

Daily challenge:
Discouraged? Take the first step of a new journey.

Fifty Miles Closer

Fifty miles closer to what? Good question. But to be honest, the answer might be a little hard for non-ultrarunners to understand.

I set a goal this year—a goal to complete six ultramarathons to tackle a new series called "The Beast." This meant doing three 50k races in February, March and April followed by a horrendously difficult hundred-miler in October, a tough fifty-mile race in November and sixty-seven challenging miles in December. This was the first year for the series and I was drawn by it. I love doing what few dare attempt. But to earn the impressive bear trophy, the designated prize, I had to run my fifty miles today.

My goal for the day was simple: run without hurting myself and cross the finish line. The day was unseasonably warm, the leaves at peak color. It was perfect. I felt good and enjoyed the times of solitude as well as periods of chatting with other runners. What I discovered in those conversations was that everyone had a story.

One young runner ran with a hand brace. Diagnosed with juvenile rheumatoid arthritis, all the joints in her left hand had just been replaced. An ultrarunner for just ten months, she had run seven ultras and four marathons in that short time. She ran despite her doctors advising against it. To her, overcoming challenges outweighed the increased pain from extreme running.

Another guy, a soldier, ran with a picture of a warrior who died in service to his country. Every race he entered raised money for an organization providing counseling to the families.

One fella ran because his friend wanted him to in celebration of his fiftieth birthday. A good friend of mine ran simply because she loves these events. A college student decided last night to run because a spot opened up due to another withdrawing. A mother of three ran despite an extruded disc in her neck that caused her much pain. She had committed to the race and wanted to carry through.

Just as each runner has a reason for enduring the hardships of training and racing, each of us have reasons for choosing the way we live our lives. Some of those reasons may be foolhardy. Some pure and sweet. And others may be altogether selfish. If a runner enters a race knowing that substantial injury will likely occur, it's kind of stupid to do it anyway. But just as stupid is our decision to choose a course of action that will damage the reputation of Christ.

Who is wise and understanding among you? Let him show it by his good life, by deeds done in the humility that comes from wisdom. (James 3:13)

Daily challenge:
Examine your motives. Act only on those that are pure and wise.

Exhausting, Worthless Work

I'm sick of political ads. In fact, I'm to the point that the mute button on the remote is my best friend whenever I see one queue up on the screen. I just don't want to hear the spin anymore. Thankfully, it will be all over in two days. So much effort and money has been put into the process. Has it been worth it? Did it make a difference?

I must admit that I am concerned about the results of the elections. Yeah, I know God is not a Republican—or Democrat—but I can't help wonder about the changes that are likely to occur no matter which candidates are elected. And yet, I must remember that God is still God no matter what. Nothing that happens is outside of His plan for the blessing or punishment of a nation.

We were privileged this morning to have a missionary share his work with our congregation. He works with Wycliffe Bible translators, lives in Europe and is integral in providing the technical support necessary to get the Word into nations closed to the Gospel. His perspective was interesting in light of what prophet Habakkuk said: *"Has not the LORD almighty determined that the people's labor is only fuel for the fire, that the nations exhaust themselves for nothing?"* (2:13).

Some nations exhaust themselves to suppress the Truth. In these places it's illegal to mention the name of Christ or proselytize in any fashion. Loss of property, imprisonment and even death comes to one who offends the law. But their efforts are for naught, because the Kingdom of God can not be squashed.

Are we not also guilty on a personal level? We exhaust ourselves with work, with hobbies, with school, with community projects or volunteerism. And yet, all our best efforts are of little consequence if not powered by the Almighty.

We can be confident, however, that when God is in it, He will be glorified and the earth will have opportunity to know Him.

> *"For the earth will be filled with the knowledge of the glory of the LORD . . .." (Habakkuk 2:14a)*

Daily challenge:
Take inventory. Are you exhausting yourself for nothing?

Fathers and Sons

Instead of four people living under one roof, *five* is the magic number for this week. My father-in-law made the four-hour drive yesterday, just in time for the first week of muzzleloader deer season. Having been recently widowed, the logistics seemed easy compared to when Mom T was still alive. He gathered a few things, got in the car and headed west.

Dad is a wonderful man, eighty-three years young, strong in his faith and robust in lifestyle. He still works hours a day in his garage and prefers riding his motorcycle over a car. He spends at least one day a week doing repair and construction work at his church and lives for going to local auctions to find the next project car.

Despite his relative good health, signs of aging are apparent. His vision is faltering and he can't climb easily into a deer stand. In deference to his dad, Gary sites in his bow and guns, makes provision for easier access to hunting spots and offers Dad all the help he needs to enjoy some time in the woods. He checks the weather forecast for wind direction and makes sure he hunts the right places at the right time.

Gary's mom often told me, as we awaited the guys to come in from hunting, how she respected the way Gary treated his father. "Gary sure does take care of Jack. I just hope the boys will learn from his example and take care of Gary when he is old."

There's something to be said for being a good example. King Amaziah followed the example of his father Josiah (II Kings 14:3). Paul boldly proclaimed, *Follow my example, as I follow the example of Christ* (I Corinthians 11:1). And in John 13, Christ set an example for His disciples by washing their feet. "*I have set you an example that you should do as I have done for you. I tell you the truth, no servant is greater than his master, nor is a messenger greater than the one who sent him*" (vs. 15, 16).

Kids watch parents. Friends watch friends. Teachers watch students. Employees watch bosses. The unchurched watch the churched.

Who is watching you?

> *In everything set them an example by doing what is good. In your teaching show integrity, seriousness and soundness of speech that cannot be condemned, so that those who oppose you may be ashamed because they have nothing bad to say about us. (Titus 2:7, 8)*

Daily challenge:
Make sure the example you set needs no apology.

Pundits

On this Election Day, I look forward to the end of a long and protracted political season. For two years, one of the candidates virtually ignored his job in the Senate to campaign, spending in excess of five-hundred-million dollars. The other spent less money but made an equal effort. Every time we turned on the TV, there they were, spinning the merits of their platforms. But that wasn't the worst.

The worst was the preponderance of pundits. I suppose the media thinks the public is stupid, not able to decipher the validity of the message. As a result, the pundits engaged in loud and verbose battle, trying to out scream their opponent. Each held a strong party line and spoke as if he had all the answers. In most cases, it was a revolting exchange in the pundit pit.

But what is a *pundit* anyway? The Merriam-Webster online dictionary gives several definitions: 1) a wise or learned man in India—often used as an honorary title 2) a learned man and 3) a person who gives opinions in an authoritative manner usually through the mass media. I think option three matches what I have observed: folks who love to tell everyone else what they think.

It reminds me of those three friends of Job: Eliphaz the Temanite, Bildad the Shuhite and Zophar the Naamathite. They sure thought they had the corner on the spiritual-insight market. They were pretentious and haughty. And they apparently felt compelled to tell Job why such calamity had befallen him.

And advice? Boy, did they have some advice. *"Call if you will, but who will answer you?"* (Job 5:1). *"But if you look to God and plead with the Almighty . . .."* (8:6). *"When will you end these speeches? Be sensible . . .."* (18:2). Had these ancient pundits lived about 3,500 years later, they would undoubtedly be booked on all the morning news shows.

As inane as pundits can be, we can be just as guilty by choosing to listen to them. Lack of discernment shows an inability to decipher right from wrong, truth from error. And, it can be a waste of precious time. Rather, to filter all we hear and say through God's wisdom is the only guaranteed path to prudent living.

> *Listen, my sons, to a father's instruction; pay attention and gain understanding. I give you sound learning, so do not forsake my teaching. (Proverbs 4:1, 2)*

Daily challenge:
"Oh, be careful little ears what you hear . . .. "

Purr, Kitty, Purr

As Caleb sank into the couch, he picked up Ra, one of our quickly growing kittens. He placed this cat on his chest and within seconds, I could hear the distinct rumble of purring all the way across the room. The more he—Ra, not Caleb—was stroked, the louder he got. The cat, eyes closed in blissful respite, stretched out and turned his head to allow for better petting. It was a picture of complete contentment. He was happy and let everyone know so.

Ever wondered why cats purr? I did. When I searched for the reason, several explanations were offered. From a mechanical aspect, the actual noise is produced when air flows across the vocal cords, the diaphragm moving the air in and out, much like a piston. Kittens purr on the second day after birth, even before they can meow. And, they can also purr and nurse at the same time. *Who knew?* But it is thought the kittens do this to communicate with mama: "Hey, I'm OK and this milk tastes good."

But is it automatic or intentional? Most authorities believe this verbal expression is highly intentional. Cats purr only when they want to. Chemically, endorphins are produced in the brain and lead to the nervous-system stimulation, innervating the mechanical actions that produce the melodic hum. Ironically, cats also purr under periods of great stress. Just like we might hum or sing to ourselves when we're scared of the boogy-man, the cat will purr to reassure himself and/or offer solace to other cats nearby.

Cats have no difficulty in expressing their bliss. Both of ours purr often and loudly; there is no mistaking when they are happy. Wouldn't it be nice if people could be just as expressive? But no. We are loudest when we are angry or discontent. We whine, complain and protest. We make our displeasure known to everyone around us, often in rude or unkind ways.

"Can't you ever keep your room clean?" we bark in a gruff voice to a child. But on that one occasion when little Billy puts his toys away without being asked, does that child hear the equivalent of a happy purr? It's a fact that people are calmed by stroking a purring kitten. Our children will also benefit from having a parent frequently show contentment and pleasure.

Maybe we should all strive to "purr" more often.

A happy heart makes the face cheerful, but heartache crushes the spirit. (Proverbs 15:13)

Daily challenge:
Encourage others with a conscious expression of contentment and gratitude.

The Secret

Some years ago when the boys were young, Gary and I planned a short vacation. I packed for everyone and then crammed it all into the hatch of the oddly shaped Ford Festiva. Off we went. Excitement was higher than normal. Why? Because the boys had absolutely no idea where we were headed.

As the hours in the car increased, the excitement levels nearly lifted the roof from the car that looked like a high-top tennis shoe. Guesses flew out of their mouths faster than the miles whizzed by. Gary and I just kept nodding and said, "You'll see." It was funny to read huge roadside billboards drawing visitors to our location—but the boys never caught on. It wasn't until we exited from the highway and approached the hotel that we unveiled the secret: we were going to visit the Dollywood amusement park, ride lots of roller coasters and have several days of family fun. The secret was out. The boys were happy.

Secrets, by their very nature, deliver an element of mystery and intrigue. Eager anticipation occurs when we suspect the secret is a good one. But conversely, dread and trepidation creep in if we fear the worst.

As I read the Scriptures, I'm impressed with the number of mysteries described between the covers of the Good Book. Flip through Daniel and see how often mysteries were solved. Daniel became the master of mystery-solving and everyone knew it: the king, the court, the people. But mysteries were not reserved for the prophets of old.

The coming of Christ, the Messiah and salvation for both the Jew and the Gentile had a lot of people puzzled. They couldn't grasp how a kid from Nazareth could possibly be the world's Savior. But He was. He was the mystery revealed in flesh.

Though the Mystery has been revealed, discovering the reality lends excitement and newness to our everyday living.

This mystery is that through the gospel the Gentiles are heirs together with Israel, members together of one body, and sharers together in the promise in Christ Jesus. (Ephesians 3:6)

Daily challenge:
Can others see the mystery of the Gospel revealed in you?
Or, is Christ just as much a mystery because of you?

First of All

Goodness. If I had a nickel for each time I've said "first of all," I'd likely have a stash of cash. It's a common expression used when we have a whole list of things to say. Young writers have a habit of using the "first of all," "second of all," and "third of all" approach when listing their arguments. Likewise, debaters use a similar strategy when trying to convince their opponent of all the reasons why their stance is correct. And parents use it on their kids when lists of demands are communicated.

I used the phrase just the other day when I wrote a note to one of my students. He had expressed an unmistakable air of disrespect, demanding his questions be answered immediately. "I don't like to be held up!" *Whoa.* My head spun all the way around, my eyes bulged out of my head and every muscle in my body stiffened. Imagine. A ninth-grader speaking to a teacher like that. Good thing he wasn't in front of me. But my fingers lit on the keyboard and started flying. "First of all . . .." You can imagine the rest.

When we use that term, the implication is that there are multiple things to say. However, the one that gets top billing is the one at the list's leading edge. The information coming behind the "first of all" phrase is the cornerstone of the entire conversation. If you don't get it, you won't get the rest of the discussion either.

When the Apostle Paul wrote to Timothy, he used this same phrase as he tackled the subject of worship. If our premise is correct, then we can assume that the point directly following the phrase is paramount to everything else. So, what did he write? *I urge, then, first of all, that requests, prayers, intercession and thanksgiving be made for everyone . . ..* (II Timothy 2:1).

OK. Requests, prayers, intercession and thanksgiving all sound like lovely spiritual activities. "Lord, bless the missionaries and take care of Nana and Grandpa." Nice, but a little general. But, what comes next is truly significant. Who is the first group of people to be prayed for?

> *. . . for kings and all those in authority, that we may live peaceful and quiet lives in all godliness and holiness. (2:2-3)*

In the aftermath of a national election, it's a good reminder.

> *This is good, and pleases God our Savior, who wants all men to be saved and to come to a knowledge of the truth. (2:4)*

Daily challenge:
Pray often and specifically for those in authority. It's not optional.
It's a spiritual requirement.

Country Girl, Big City

I've felt like a little country bumpkin all weekend. From the time Seth and I made it onto Washington DC's Metro last night until we landed back at my niece's apartment, I have been walking the street in wide-eyed wonder. I'm not accustomed to seeing such a variety of nationalities, languages, dress and attitudes. And concrete? I think I walked miles and miles of it. Unlike home, there wasn't a cow in sight and no deer were seen crossing Pennsylvania Avenue.

The lights and sounds of a city are far-removed from my world. People are everywhere. They line the streets, fill the buses and stampede the Metro. Fail to stand to the right on an escalator ascending from the underground rails and you might not live to regret it. Sirens scream and cars speed along, many vying for the few available parking spots. The city does not sleep.

Besides the noise and the concrete, tall buildings and an imposing labyrinth of public transit, the most impressionable thing were the faces—the empty, dejected, pitiful faces. I saw a young man riding the Metro last night. He sat alone wearing a blank expression, his body jostled by the rhythmic movement of the train. I wondered if he really had a place to go. Perhaps he was riding until he could ride no more. Perhaps he was putting off the inevitable night on the street as long as possible.

Another fella, dirty and smelly, sat close to where I stood on this morning's Metro ride. He looked rough but managed to intertwine head-nodding cat naps with verbal encounters with seatmates for the purpose of seeking spare change. He made one young lady obviously uncomfortable by suggesting he follow her to meet her family.

I didn't know how to deal with the street beggars. Do I drop in change or hand over a dollar? If I give to one guy, can I not give to another? I found that I looked away, not wanting to chance a moment of eye-lock. Instead, I fixed my eyes on something else, feigning interest in a storefront just to avoid the situation. *If I give him money, he'll probably just spend it on booze.* I felt guilty, uncharitable and calloused.

I've pondered this kind of situation before and have yet to come to a conclusion. But one thing I know—these people need hope. They need to know the Author of Hope. How can I communicate a spiritual hope if I don't give them some moment, however brief, of physical hope?

All they asked was that we should continue to remember the poor,
the very thing I was eager to do. (Galatians 2:10)

Daily challenge:
How can you meet the needs of someone in want? Even if it's just to one person,
minister both spiritually and physically.

Sound Judgment

I just arrived home from my first college visit with Seth. We spent yesterday morning looking at a professional photography school and the rest of the time stomping around DC. I watched as Seth worked his magic capturing images of people, places and things. He drew the attention of curious onlookers as he wielded the camera with the huge lens.

While I'm excited at Seth's professional prospects, as a mom I can't help thinking about how he will fare on his own. Will he remember the things he was taught to value? Will he be able to handle the freedom? Will he be able to manage money? Will he exhibit good judgment?

The concept of judgment was illustrated for me on this trip. Seth is a capable driver—perhaps too capable. Since he was a little guy, no matter the mode of transportation, he excelled at maneuvering the vehicle: a two-wheeled bike at age two and a small motorcycle at age four that he rode as fast as he could while he stood on the seat. Now the toys are bigger and more powerful, but one thing remains. He likes speed. He likes power. He likes both at the same time.

Seth wanted to drive on the way to the big city and I was glad to let him. But I have to admit that once we got into traffic on I-95, my nerves got plucked. It's not that he was necessarily dangerous. It's just that, in my humble opinion, he was driving—well—ambitiously. He wasn't just going with the flow of the traffic; he set the pace. And, when brake lights in front of us suddenly glowed, I preferred our car to brake rather than accelerate. I bit my tongue as much as I could—and prayed a lot.

Seth drove part of the way home as well. He is a good driver, but his youth can cloud his own sense of safety. We got off the freeway and headed down a busy commercial street. I saw the line of cars in front of us stop for a red light. Unfortunately, Seth's foot was not on our brake. As the back end of the car in front of us got bigger and bigger, I yelled out. "Seth. Stop!" I couldn't help it. Though he did not relish my admonition, he backed down his driving. I think he got the message.

All of us, young or old, have lapses in judgment. How come? We have solid knowledge on how we should act. We can quote Bible verses and favorite authors. But the thing we forget is that it takes a concerted effort to exhibit sound judgment.

My son, preserve sound judgment and discernment, do not let them out of your sight . . .. (Proverbs 3:21)

Daily challenge:
Discern. Think well. Act even better.

Here, Little Kitty . . .

Our two kittens have grown into cats, but they remain sweet and cuddly. So, I was in a panic last night when Ra, the male, was nowhere to be found. I called for him inside and out, but he did not appear. I was worried that the fox we saw on the farm had a cat-snack. Boy, was I relieved when I heard his distinctive *meow* this morning.

But sometime when I was calling for him in last night's darkness, I was startled to see something small and furry approach me. There at my feet was a dark gray kitten. He shivered from the cold and emitted a squeaky little *meow*. His coat was matted and his tail stood straight up, as if at attention. *Where did he come from?* Having pity for the kitty, I sneaked out some food and water for the little guy.

When I awoke this morning, there he was. He rushed to my feet, tail still quivering. He seemed more comfortable, allowing me to pick him up. I even combed some of the knots from his fur, rendering his coat soft and smooth. I arranged a box and a blanket for shelter. But still, as the other cats freely migrated in and out the kitty door, the little rascal looked all alone. He wasn't included in the family. He had not been offered the comfort of a warm house and the last licks on the ice cream bowls. No amount of crying by the front door or hopelessly trying to push open the kitty door earned him entry. Even the other cats looked warily upon him, making soft but firm noises as if to say, "You don't belong here, Fur Ball. Take it down the road." If the kitty had feelings, I bet they were hurt.

It's no wonder that God had to give us clear instructions about our interactions with those that are "different." Remember that James 2 passage? I paraphrase: A dirty, ugly, poor guy came into church at the same time as a fabulously rich dude, dressed out in the finest fashion. The rich guy was offered the best seat in the house; the poor guy was relegated to floor space. James made clear the ills of favoritism. *Have you not discriminated among yourselves and become judges with evil thoughts?* (v. 4).

Good question. Do we?

If you really keep the royal law found in Scripture, "Love your neigh-
bor as yourself," you are doing right. But if you show favoritism, you
sin and are convicted by the law as lawbreakers. (James 2:8, 9)

Daily challenge:
Be careful how you treat others.

Missing the Mark

Kaboom! I looked out the kitchen window and saw the telltale smoke drifting out from the tree. There is never any doubt when a black powder gun is fired. These old-time guns are still loaded from the end of the barrel, some form of powder and bullet rammed down with a stiff rod. Our friend was hunting the last few hours of light and let a shot fly at a deer that dared pass by the stand.

Chris climbed out of the tree, sure the deer was mortally wounded. When the bullet hit, the deer went down hard. However, in the next moment, it jumped to its feet and bolted across the yard and into the woods. Seth and Gary helped track the deer, finding only a few tufts of white hair but no blood. That's always a bad sign. After dinner, they decided to take one more look and spotted the wounded deer on the other side of the creek. It was still alive, but a final shot finished it. The first bullet missed the mark. The second did not.

It was interesting watching the Olympics this past summer and the coverage of the shooting events. One thing was clear: the guy or gal who ended up with a gold medal did not miss the mark. In fact, many of the contests were decided by mere millimeters. It was only those who could hit the center of the bull's eye consistently who won. Being close was not enough.

Many people in our society believe that getting close will get the job done. "I try to live a good life. I'm kind and generous and I don't mess around with someone else's husband. I even go to church every Sunday and put money in the plate. Certainly, God has to be impressed. He'll let me into His heaven."

Unfortunately, it doesn't work that way. Our sin makes it impossible to hit the mark no matter how hard we try. The only way to make the shot is to depend on the Perfect One to draw the bow. It was Christ's sacrifice that makes the arrow fly straight toward the target of salvation. In fact, the arrow of Christ's work is drawn to the target by the mercy and grace of the Father; it is irresistible. If God had not willed the arrow to be aimed and launched, the goal would never be attained.

> *For all have sinned and fall short of the glory of God, and are justified freely by his grace through the redemption that came by Christ Jesus. (Romans 3:23)*

Daily challenge:
Don't play with salvation like a game of horseshoes. Being close won't cut it.
Only faith will hit God's target.

Countdowns

Pushing my cart between the rows of shelves, I tried to remember what was on the list left on the counter. My pondering was interrupted, however, by the intrusion of music. *What is that tune? Ah. Christmas carols.* The holiday decorations had been adorning the store since the time the ghosts and goblins flew in. But the music was a new touch. "It's beginning to look a lot like Christmas . . .. "

We all look forward to key events in our lives: birthdays, a vacation, weddings, the birth of a child. I remember making "countdown" helps. As a child I made a construction paper chain of red and green loops and tore one off each day. When the last one was gone, I knew that Christmas Day had arrived. And, of course, I always counted down the days to June—school's out for summer. What a wonderful feeling!

But what if you were Abraham? He was asked to pick up and go live in a foreign land. He made his home in tents, put up with blowing sand and harsh conditions. Why? *For he was looking forward to the city with foundations, whose architect and builder is God* (Hebrews 11:10). He never saw what he hoped for.

Moses chose to suffer with his own people rather than capitalize on his position in Egypt. He left Egypt despite the anger of the ruler. Moses observed the Passover so that the firstborn would be saved. Why? . . . *because he was looking ahead to his reward* (Hebrews 22:26b).

Noah, Abraham, Sarah, Moses, Isaac, Jacob, Joseph, Rahab, Gideon, Barak, Samson, Jephthah, David, Samuel, the prophets and more. All of them had their countdown techniques in place. They were looking forward to fulfilled promises. It was the only way to get through the persecution, testing and suffering. And yet, none ever got to rip off that last paper loop. Why? *All these people were still living by faith when they died. They did not receive the things promised; they only saw them and welcomed them from a distance* (Hebrews 11:13).

There is something to be said for counting down. But we dare not think that looking forward is only beneficial if we realize the prize in our lifetime.

These were all commended for their faith, yet none of them received what had been promised. God had planned something better for us so that only together with us would they be made perfect. (Hebrews 11:39-40)

Daily challenge:
As we enter the "look-forward-to" holiday seasons, let's not forget that
*faith is being sure of what we hope for and certain
of what we do not see* (Hebrews 11:1).

Put Up or Shut Up

"Put up or shut up," he said to another runner. This runner was bragging about his ability but refused to enter the race's fray. "If you're so great, prove it. Otherwise, quit flapping your jaw about it."

Think about other times it might be used. A young man keeps talking about asking Ms. Perfect out on a date but never gets around to it. It turns out to be a lot of talk and not a lot of action. Or maybe a friend keeps talking about being overweight. However, the diet and exercise program never begins. The talk, however, continues. Makes you sort of crazy, doesn't it?

There is a similar idiom: "Put your money where your mouth is." We wish politicians could understand this concept. They all talk a good game—especially standing atop the campaign stump. Unfortunately, what happens most often is that those lofty promises for lower taxes and less spending never become a reality. The only thing accomplished is reinforcing the idea that politicians can not be trusted.

As Christians, we need to get this right. Certainly, we must be bold in what we say, and more importantly, do. But for centuries, Believers have gotten a bad rap. We are accused of being hypocritical—and sometimes we are. We say "love your neighbor", but we don't even know his name. We shrug off community responsibility and leave good-doing for established organizations. We are proud of being a member of Church XYZ on Sunday but act like the devil on Monday. Sure, I know we're not perfect—and never will be—but it's no excuse for sloppy living. The sloppy living is just more food for fodder.

Why should we do good? Is it because it will make us feel better? Not really—although it might give us a warm and fuzzy buzz. Is it because we have to earn our way into heaven? Nope. We know we get there by grace and that works has nothing to do with it. We do good because our "putting up" will "shut up" those who oppose us.

So, go ahead. Don't shut up. Put up.

For it is God's will that by doing good you should silence the ignorant talk of foolish men. (I Peter 2:15)

Daily challenge:
Be sure to back up with action what you talk about doing.

Forecasts

I downloaded a nifty tool for my computer. Every time I boot it up, a window sponsored by The Weather Channel appears. I have an instant purview of the temperature and chance of precipitation. It tells me when sunrise will be and what I can expect this evening, tomorrow morning, thirty-six hours and three days from now. At the click of the mouse, I can toggle between Celsius and Fahrenheit and can even see a radar weather map depicting cloud movement. It provides wind speed and direction, gives driving conditions and links to points of interest and weather news.

I'm finding the site helpful in planning the activities of the day. But most curious is another feature: "Exercise and Fitness." Beneath the boxes listing the temperature, wind and chance of precipitation are pictures of the clothes you should wear. Along with this is the "comfort index"—a one-to-ten rating system accompanied by an adjective. For example, this morning's 55 degrees and 30% chance of rain produced a picture of long pants and a comfort index of "6 moderate." However, tonight's forecast for 60 degrees and torrential rain yields a jacket and "2 uncomfortable." This idea of predicting our level of impending discomfort is intriguing.

When the Apostle Peter wrote his first book, he was writing to Christians who were *strangers in the world, scattered throughout Pontus, Galatia, Cappadocia, Asia and Bithynia* (I Peter 1:1). It is a book of sweet encouragement and instruction in how to live in a hostile spiritual environment. Sounds like it might have some application to today, doesn't it?

By the time we arrive at Chapter 4, it is understood that for the Believer, there is a forecast of "1 uncomfortable." In fact, verse 12 makes this clear. *Dear friends, do not be surprised at the painful trial you are suffering, as though something strange were happening to you.*

Suffering for the name of Christ is inevitable. But inevitable suffering is not equivalent to pointless suffering. In fact, suffering is a reason to *rejoice that you participate in the sufferings of Christ, so that you may be overjoyed when his glory is revealed* (v. 13).

> *However, if you suffer as a Christian, do not be ashamed, but praise God that you bear that name. (I Peter 4:16)*

Daily challenge:
Embrace the forecast for suffering. Prepare by putting on the *full armor of God*: *the belt of truth, breastplate of righteousness, feet fitted with the readiness, shield of faith, helmet of salvation* and *sword of the Spirit.* (Ephesians 6:13-17)

It Just So Happened

I admit it. I stole the title of this devotional from my mom. For several years my mother has been compiling her life's stories. This memoir is meant to be a testimony of God's work and a way to pass life lessons on to her children. She wants to call the collection this very title. She wants everyone to understand that "It just so happened" could be more appropriately termed, "And God so arranged."

Just today, it "just so happened" that I was desperate to find L.K. a permanent home. "Little Kitty," as we have come to call her, showed up at our back door earlier this week, her *meow* thin and fragile. We've been feeding the gray tiger kitten outside and made a dry place for her to eat and sleep. Still, she looks longingly at the door the two resident cats use to come and go. One person in our house, who shall remain nameless, has insisted we find her a home—or else. I know what the *or else* entails and I'm sure the kitten much prefers adoption.

I decided to make one phone call to our friends, the Devoses. They have a new home on many acres and are filling it up farm-style—cats, goats and chickens. "Ron, how do you feel about adding an adorable little kitty to your menagerie?" To my surprise, Ron told me that both of their cats had recently fallen victim to untimely deaths. In response, "it just so happened" that Ron had been checking the papers to find a free kitty. Then I called.

Did all this just so happen? Was it coincidence? Or was it God?

Do we really believe God is interested in placing small furry pets into loving homes? Some cynics might say that God could care less about the details. After all, doesn't the God of the universe have bigger things to worry about: wars, crime, poverty? Besides, people control their own destinies. They are responsible for seeing opportunities and kitty redistribution happen.

I can't buy the cynic's rationale. I believe that our God is big enough to care. He takes delight in the little things. He gives the birds a nest. He grows grass for the cattle. He provides springs of water to quench the thirst. He gives plants for us to cultivate. He provides prey for the lions. (See Psalm 104.) He does care . . . even about kitties.

The LORD is good, a refuge in times of trouble. He cares for those who trust in him . . .. (Nahum 1:7)

Daily challenge:
Make it a practice to thank God for all the "little things" He does.

Open Your Eyes

When Seth was in second grade, he ventured out to the playground. With his sweatshirt worn backward so that the hood covered his face, he listened to the commands of his girl friends: "Turn right. Turn left. Go straight." Seth did exactly as instructed. The only problem was that he was running at full speed. Not surprisingly, the girls became distracted. Seth ran directly into the wall with his face. The impact was so great that for several days his forehead bore the imprint of the brick.

Because his mouth and gums shredded from the blow, we sat in front of the pediatrician seeking treatment. The doctor questioned Seth. He spoke carefully and intentionally to ascertain the context of this accident. However, one question deeply puzzled Seth. "Were your eyes opened or closed when you hit the wall?" *Hmm.* You could see Seth's little mind working hard. What would it matter? His face was completely covered by his hood. He was effectively running blind.

Seth wasn't the only one to run blind. Balaam the prophet also had a problem with obscured vision. Balak, a Midianite king, was terrified that Israel would wipe his people from the face of the earth. The king sent messengers to fetch Balaam, hoping to convince him to place a curse on the would-be conquerors. But God had other plans. "Don't you dare go," he was told. But did he listen? Nope. He mounted his donkey and started on the journey.

All of a sudden the donkey veered off. Balaam beat the animal. A little further down the road the donkey faltered again, this time crushing Balaam's leg into a wall. The donkey paid for that one as well. Third time's a charm. They rode through a narrow passage in which the donkey stopped dead in his tracks and lay down. Balaam was really ticked. As he thrashed the donkey the third time, God opened the mouth of the donkey. *"What have I done to you to make you beat me these three times?"* (Numbers 22:28b). Imagine his surprise at a talking donkey—and yet he answered that ass!

Finally, Balaam saw what the donkey had seen the whole time: the Angel of the Lord with sword drawn. God captured the prophet's attention when he opened his eyes and clearly saw God.

How many times do we run blind? The answers are right there in the Word, but we keep our eyes sealed shut. Whether it be out of ignorance, rebellion or selfishness, we miss truth.

Open my eyes that I may see wonderful things in your law. (Psalm 119:18)

Daily challenge:
Take off your blinders and see truth.

Do You Believe Me Now?

"What? I'm not late. Look. My watch says 11:55." As an eighteen-year-old high school senior, I voiced those words to my parents, pointing like Vanna White at my wristwatch. It was worth a try. I knew I was in big trouble for being late. I took the only reasonable course of action: I turned my watch back five minutes before I walked into the house. *They'll believe me. I've earned their trust.*

Guess what? They didn't. They weren't as naïve as I thought. Maybe it was the look on my face. Maybe it's because I've always been a lousy liar. Maybe it's because I was feeling especially guilty since I was out with a guy my parents didn't trust. *Shame on me.*

"Liar, liar. Pants on fire." I used that phrase as a kid. It's an odd thing to say and I'm not sure where it originated. But it's hardly true. If it was, all the politicians in Washington would have third-degree burns! Nevertheless, what is true is that lying comes way too easily.

"Sammy. Did you take the cookie from the jar?"

"No, Mama. No," he counters as crumbs hang from his lip. Busted.

Lies roll from the tongue before our brain even registers the offense. But our actions lie as loudly as our words. John knew that when he wrote the first Epistle. Claiming to have fellowship with Christ while living in darkness is nothing more than a big fat lie (I John 1:6). If we claim to be free from sin, we lie again (I John 1:8). And in a practical sense, don't even think about claiming love for God if you can't love a brother (I John 4:20).

I learned a lesson about lying on that night long ago; it does no good, you are sure to get caught and the consequences aren't worth it. I wonder why we find it so difficult to learn the equivalent spiritual lesson.

But if we walk in the light, as he is in the light, we have fellowship with one another, and the blood of Jesus, his Son, purifies us from all sin. (I John 1:7)

Daily challenge:
Identify one area where you are less than honest. Confess it.
Ask God to help you fix it.

Beside, Before and Behind

"Dear God, please give us a safe trip. Amen."

As a child, I said or heard this simple prayer thousands of times. My parents took nothing for granted. Before the key was slid into the ignition, the appeal was offered heavenward. While it may have seemed redundant and superficial, it served the purpose. And to this day, I understand—at least intellectually—the importance of seeking God's protection.

Caleb left today for a trip to Ohio. I worked hard to keep my mouth shut with reminders: "Have your toothbrush? Don't speed. Be careful. Stop if you get sleepy." A twenty-one-year-old may not appreciate such mothering. I gave him a hug and kiss before watching him pull away, trying to suppress an element of trepidation.

Hmm. How is it that my brother prays? Something about angels . . ..

A few years ago, a younger brother started praying for journey's mercy in a different way. In trying to find the Biblical basis for his prayer, I came across instances when God appointed angels to lead the charge. When Abraham sent his servant in search of Isaac's future wife, an angel was sent with [beside] him to *"make your journey a success"* (Genesis 24:40).

At the onset of the Exodus from Egypt, the angel went ahead of the burgeoning nation to lead the way and protect from enemies. And after the golden calf incident, built by Aaron while Moses was writing down the Ten Commandments, God gave Moses marching orders again. But Moses was not the one first in line: *"Now go, lead the people to the place I spoke of, and my angel will go before you"* (Exodus 32:34).

Can a case also be made for protection from behind? I think so. After Moses and company left Egypt, the angel traveling in front of the army left to stand guard at the rear, preventing the pursuing Egyptian army from overcoming the escapees. So yes. Angels also protect from behind. *Then the angel of God, who had been traveling in front of Israel's army, withdrew and went behind them* (Exodus 14:19).

I just called my mom to ask her if she remembered Dan's prayers. She said, "I pray that the angels will go beside, before and behind you." I guess his prayer is right-on. I'll have to remember that next time I watch the boys drive away.

"For it is written: 'He will command his angels concerning you to guard you carefully . . . '" (Luke 4:10)

Daily challenge:
Bless someone by praying that "the angels go beside, before and behind."

Write This One-Hundred Times

When I was in second grade and trying to learn cursive writing, my teacher used repetition to help us get the hang of it. As instructed, I wrote, "My name is Rebecca Eleanor DeLancey", one-hundred times. There was only one problem. My name was Rebekah . . .. In all my youthful wisdom, I decided that the more popular "Rebecca" was a superior name than the one I had been given. My teacher sided with my mom and dad. I spent the next evening writing that sentence using the proper spelling. I never spelled it incorrectly again.

Just this evening as I was chatting with friends, the mother of an effervescent child related another story. Ethel (name changed to protect the not-so-innocent) is full of life, her antics even humoring adults who try to dish out deserved discipline. After Ethel got in trouble at school, her dad gave her a spanking and relegation to her room. Her assignment was to write many times, "I will not lie. I will not say shut up." Unfortunately, it turned out "I will not lie. I will not s_ut up." An "l" stood in place of the "h". *Oops.* Oh, the difference a single letter makes. But for Ethel, she'll probably remember not to lie or say shut up.

Something happens when we write it down. I always do better studying for a test if I write notes, highlighting the most important items. That process forces my brain to organize the material and gives me a mental picture to recall. Is it any wonder that God has used that method of teaching from the beginning?

The Lord told Moses to write down the story of Amelek's defeat so Israel could remember it (Exodus 17:14). Parents were instructed to write the commandments on the doorposts of homes to reinforce learning (Deuteronomy 6:9). Moses and the elders coached the nation to write all the commandments on large stones upon crossing the Jordan (Deuteronomy 27:8). Jeremiah had to write God's instructions on scrolls so the message could be remembered (Jeremiah 36:2). Even Habakkuk was told to write down the revelation on plain tablets (Habakkuk 2:2).

The moral of the story? If you want to remember, write it down. Maybe we should be writing over and over again, "I will not gossip" or "I will not lose my temper." The possibilities are endless.

Let love and faithfulness never leave you; bind them around your neck, write them on the tablet of your heart. (Proverbs 3:3)

Daily challenge:
Need to remember? Write it down and post it on your mirror. Pray over it.
Work on it.

Fragrance

On this cold and windy day, I enjoyed being home alone to work. *Ah, peace and quiet.* As the clock rhythmically ticked away the seconds, I gave into my stomach and headed downstairs for lunch. But lunch was not all that I was hungry for. I wanted a batch of the Cowboy cookies my mom used to make: an oats-and-chocolate-chip combination. As a schoolgirl, I loved walking into a house where the smell of baking permeated every room. I decided to treat Seth to the same simple pleasure.

Sure enough, as soon as he walked in the door, a cookie was in his mouth and a smile on his face. I knew he was pleased. I also suspect that he might even admit to a "warm and fuzzy" feeling knowing his "mama" had milk and cookies waiting for his return from school.

Fragrances are very powerful. When I used to run along Rivermont Avenue in the dead of winter, the smell of fresh bread baking at a nearby factory offset the frigid temperature. It was a wonderful fragrance. I liked to breathe in deeply to optimize its effect on my senses.

Conversely, I've experienced other fragrances that were anything but wonderful. The stench of a decaying deer alongside the road. A dumpster full of garbage. Bourbon Street in New Orleans after revelers fail to hold their liquor. There is no warm and fuzzy feeling then.

Solomon sure knew something about fragrances. In his Song, he gushed on and on about the pleasures of a woman's perfume, the deliciousness of her breath and the allure of the flowering vine. Certainly, all things wonderful and lovely were enhanced by the fragrance. Do you think he would have had the same praise if his beautiful woman had a bad case of halitosis? I don't think so. Beauty and an awful odor just don't go together; it's not like peas and carrots.

Do you realize that as Believers, we carry a fragrance? The question then becomes: What kind of fragrance? Are we like those about whom Isaiah prophesied? *"Instead of fragrance there will be a stench . . ."* (Isaiah 3:24). Or are we like Mary, who poured out the expensive perfume to wash the feet of her Lord? Her humble act filled the house with the beautiful fragrance of sacrificial love.

Our fragrance is not based on the deodorant we wear. It is based on the aroma that our lifestyle produces.

But thanks be to God, who always leads us in triumphal procession in Christ and through us spreads everywhere the fragrance of the knowledge of him. (II Corinthians 2:14)

Daily challenge:
Do a quick sniff test. Do you stink?

Value

Unlike the times my mom made me interrupt my play to take a bath, I now love my nightly bath time. I run the water hot and steamy into the old claw-foot tub and gather my magazines. *Ah . . . what luxury.*

Tonight I paged through a decorating journal. Nary one advertisement for Walmart or IKEA. As I turned the pages, I was flabbergasted by the prices. A waste basket for $500. $1,350 for a small, handheld magnifying glass held in place by a lollipop-shaped twig. And a floor lamp that looked like it was made out of an old iron pipe for $3,575. Who buys this stuff?

What we value is very telling of our priorities. If we value a big house, we mortgage ourselves to the hilt. If we value a perfectly sculpted body, we spend time, money and energy to produce one. If we value an impressive resume, incredible sums of money are spent to go to the best schools. But what if we value things that are a little more . . . well, eternal?

I found Leviticus 27 to be fascinating. The entire value-filled chapter contains redemption instructions. It went something like this. You chose the things you valued. Then you offered them back to the Lord via the priests. For example, if you wanted to dedicate your house to the Lord (v. 14), the priest assigned a value. You could redeem it back by adding on an additional fifth of the assigned value. The same redemption scheme applied to family land (v. 16), animals (v. 9), non-family land (v. 22) and crops (v. 20). But it didn't stop there. People were also dedicated to the Lord at an assigned value—fifty shekels of silver for a male aged twenty to sixty (v. 3). In fact, there were redemption values placed on a male and female of every age. If you were too poor to pay the price, the priest would set the price according to what was possible. It was an interesting system. But at least it demonstrated what was truly valued.

Solomon reminds us that *the tongue of the righteous is choice silver* (Proverbs 10:20) and that *ill-gotten treasures are of no value* (Proverbs 10:2). A man is valued if he *speaks the truth* (Proverbs 16:13). And, *a wife of noble character* (Proverbs 31:10) is to be highly esteemed by her husband.

The things of greatest value cannot be bought or sold.

For in Christ Jesus neither circumcision nor uncircumcision has any value. The only thing that counts is faith expressing itself through love. (Galatians 5:6)

Daily challenge:
If you value the price Christ paid, your life will tell the story.

The Warming Fire

I really didn't want to get out of bed. I was perfectly content to pull the covers up around my neck and keep my eyes sealed shut. But alas, I had promised my friend Deb that I would join her for a run. With the temperature outside a frosty seventeen degrees, I pulled on my tights, layered two tops, grabbed my coffee and headed off to meet her.

The ground crunched under our feet as we started down the trail, but we both warmed up quickly. The wind was behind our backs and the early sun in our faces. Several deer crossed our path, undeterred by our presence. We followed the trail by the creek as long as we could before we ran the macadam bike path. It led us to the old downtown, a work in progress. As we passed one of the vacant brick buildings, a mere shadow of its former glory, we noticed a door standing ajar. It was spooky to think that homeless people had taken refuge within. Our pace picked up as our imaginations raced.

How awful it must be to have nowhere to get relief from the elements. That building might have protected from the wind, but it did little to provide warmth. It must be a lonely, miserable existence to wonder if you'll even wake up after a night in freezing temperatures. I bet a homeless person would give about anything for some warmth.

The Apostle Paul knew the feeling. He was having a really bad day when, being transported as a prisoner, he washed up on Malta's shore as a shipwreck victim (Acts 28). It is reported that the islanders showed extraordinary kindness by building a roaring fire to warm the wet, shivering men. What relief, what hope to go from the depths of despair to the promise of a better day due solely to a vibrant fire.

Earlier I mentioned a song from my youth: "It only takes a spark to get a fire going. And soon all those around will warm up to its glowing. That's how it is with God's love . . .." It was usually sung, appropriately so, around a campfire. But there is truth in the message. When others are in our presence, do they feel the warmth of love or the chill of insincerity and apathy?

When we arrived at Jerusalem, the brothers received us warmly.
(Acts 21:17)

Daily challenge:
Do your part to contribute to "global warming"—as long as it means
spreading the hope and warmth of Christ's love.

Spice Up My Life

A popular television show is called "Spice Up My Kitchen." The premise of the show is to take drab and dreary kitchens and morph them into elegant, organized work spaces. The predictable cast of characters—designer, carpenter, handyman and homeowners—are shown going through the arduous process. In the end, the newfound glory of each kitchen is spotlighted.

However, the way a kitchen looks has absolutely nothing to do with the way the food produced in that kitchen tastes. That job is left to the way ingredients are blended together: a complicated matrix of textures and seasonings. Cooking meat without the benefit of salt, pepper and other seasonings will provide required nutrition but minimal taste-bud satisfaction.

I guess I'm thinking about spices because I received a gift bag of the same. It was sent by my friend, Anita, who lives in France. Though I'm unsure what combination of spices is in that bag, its aroma begs to be used the next time I prepare a pasta dish or cook up some chicken.

Spices have long been treasured. From the beginning of written history, spices were a valuable commodity to be traded and sold. Merchants journeyed far to barter for cumin, mint, dill, cinnamon and myrrh. The spices were used in cooking as well as for the fragrance they produced. In fact, the most fragrant spices—gum resin, onycha, galbanum and pure frankincense—were used for offerings to the Lord (Exodus 30:34). And, from before the days of King Asa, spices were integral in the burial process. It signified love and respect. It also covered the stench of death.

Each spice carries a different flavor—a different aroma. Some are hot and spicy. Others are mild and deep. What is good in one situation may not suit another. Nevertheless, salt is the one seasoning that is nearly always appropriate. Even the grain offerings described in Leviticus 2:13 were to be seasoned with it. Salt preserves and makes the offering palatable. Is it any wonder that we are instructed to be the salt of the earth, preserving the name of Christ?

Go ahead. Flavor your world.

Let your conversation be always full of grace, seasoned with salt, so that you may know how to answer everyone. (Colossians 4:6)

Daily challenge:
What flavor are you? Are you too hot, too mild or just right?

Nature and Nurture

There is an ongoing debate over which is stronger: nature or nurture. Those who believe that nature is the victor assume a pre-determined position. Either fate or the force of nature determines how a person will be. A psychopathic killer can't help it. The person is simply wired that way. On the other hand, the nurturists think that if a person is put in the proper environment, any natural deficits can be overcome. That same psychopathic killer in the hands of a nurturist could be reformed into an upstanding citizen.

The debate is obviously more complicated than that. But there are elements of truth in both camps. From a Christian perspective, because of one man's sin, Adam's, sin and death entered into the world (Romans 5:12). It is this sin that separates us from God and it is sin that controls us (Romans 7:5). As a kid, I used to be "mad" at Adam and Eve for messing up the whole world. I would never have sinned like them. Optimistic albeit unrealistic. Nevertheless, our "nature" is indeed corrupt and there is nothing we can do to make ourselves acceptable to God.

But we are not without hope. The regenerating power of Christ's blood changes our nature from one of sin to one that has a disposition for righteousness. It empowers us to make subservient the sinful nature and allows our minds to be set on godly things. *Those who live according to the sinful nature have their minds set on what that nature desires; but those who live in accordance with the Spirit have their minds set on what the Spirit desires* (Romans 8:5).

As parents, we like to think we provide our children with an environment that nurtures the child—an atmosphere that allows for growth and maturity. When I was growing up, my mom turned on the old Hi-Fi radio and tuned into church music on Sunday mornings. She wanted to use that simple act to direct our thinking toward worship. My parents also knelt by our beds in prayer each evening to bring the day to a close. And, there was always a time for family devotions. In so many ways, Mom and Dad crafted our surroundings to help us grow in our spiritual walks. They were nurturing us in our faith.

Why did they do this? They were following the example of the Father. God did the rooting and they followed through with the watering in.

> *So then, just as you received Christ Jesus as Lord, continue to live in him, rooted and built up in him, strengthened in the faith as you were taught, and overflowing with thankfulness. (Colossians 2:6-7)*

Daily challenge:
List two definitive ways of nurturing another—then do it.

At a Moment's Notice

With an odd sense of anticipation, I arrived early at the doctor's office. Being a new patient, I knew there were pages of forms to complete. A five-year hiatus from having a woman's physical—shame on me—made me anxious to get back on track with some semblance of a health plan. In fact, I was feeling pretty good about my new-found commitment. Earlier that day, I had an ultrasound as a follow-up to a mammogram. Notwithstanding a few cysts, I received a passing grade on those body parts and wanted to move on to the next round.

Seconds after the nurse closed the door with instructions for me to shed my clothes, she rapped and said, "No, don't! The doctor just got a page about a baby in distress. She has to do a C-section. We'll reschedule." *Heavy sigh.*

To watch the doctor rush out the door brought back memories of my own unexpected pages. Emergency heart surgery is never convenient. It seemed like a case came up just at the wrong time: the middle of the night, just as I was starting a run, or when I had plans to attend a special program at the boys' school. Despite the inconvenience, I had accepted the responsibility to be ever-ready and I took that commitment seriously.

Though no one's life depended on it, when our house was for sale, I had to keep it clean. It's uncanny how potential buyers always wanted to come through just when the kids went wild, the bathtub overflowed and the kitchen was a wreck. Hardly the picture-perfect presentation.

Perhaps the most poignant example of being ready is this: *Now, brothers, about times and dates we do not need to write to you, for you know very well that the day of the Lord will come like a thief in the night* (I Thessalonians 5:1, 2). Have you ever thought about how comfortable you would be if the Lord came back and found you doing your normal routine? It's sort of like the kid who throws a wild party at the house. Little did he anticipate his parents flinging open the door in the middle of the shenanigans. Busted. The result? An embarrassed child and a disappointed parent.

So then, let us not be like others, who are asleep, but let us be alert and self-controlled . . . Therefore encourage one another and build each other up, just as in fact you are doing. (I Thessalonians 5:6, 11)

Daily challenge:
"Ready or not, here I come," Christ says.

Stay Warm in the Son

Sometimes I despise winter running. But today was one of those days I actually enjoyed myself. The sun was shining and the temperature was in the forties. Not bad for late November.

With my headphones stuck in my ears, I enjoyed the music, the scenery and rhythmic sound of crunchy gravel under my feet. I ran well, feeling strong and capable. I was even able to shed my gloves despite the chilly temperature.

However, when parts of my run led me along shaded roads, I noticed my fingers growing cold. In fact, I could even see my breath create a moisture cloud as I exhaled. What a difference from being exposed to the full rays of the sun. This contrast was made clearer when I finally reached a road meandering between open fields. *Ahh.* The sun felt so good and I once again was toasty warm.

This experience begs the question: Is the sun any less the fireball in the sky just because we happen to be running in a shadow? Of course not. Think about this. You climb aboard a jetliner. The rain is pelting and the winds howling. The plane takes off, shuddering against the gusts. But moments later at 30,000 feet, the plane pops through the clouds and into the bright sunshine. Was the sun absent when the plane was on the ground? No. You just weren't in a position to see it.

My spiritual life leads a similar course. I feel bright and cheery, encouraged when I am exposed full blast to heaven's light. It seems I have a direct connection (and I do) to the Father and delight in a "feeling" of wellness. I am confident that God sees me, loves me and guides me.

But what happens when I end up on a shady lane? Perhaps things don't "click." Maybe I feel stressed or oppressed. I may even believe God has abandoned me on this dreadful, lonely road.

Be encouraged. Without a light source, no shadow could be cast. It's just impossible. The mere presence of the shadow confirms a bright light on the other side. The Psalmist found refuge in the shadow of the Almighty's wings. He did not have to see the Son in order to find peace.

We must learn to embrace the shadows.

I will take refuge in the shadow of your wings until the disaster has passed. (Psalm 57:1b)

Daily challenge:
Whether you find yourself in the sun or the shadow, the Light is always on.

Thanksgiving

Today was the official day for giving thanks. The celebration goes back to 1777 when all thirteen colonies celebrated the perseverance of the original settlers. George Washington proclaimed a day for Thanksgiving eleven years later, though there was substantial disagreement about having a time of merriment in memory of so many lost lives. But in 1863, President Lincoln proclaimed the fourth Thursday in November as the National Day of Thanksgiving.

With this holiday, I'm sure we all have vivid memories of past celebrations. I remember dressing up like Pilgrims and Indians in grade school. I remember making construction-paper turkeys by tracing my hand. In high school, recollections of the big football game between the Pennridge Rams and the rival Quakertown Panthers are strong. And then, of course, there were all those feasts followed by TV football games, a crackling fire and an impromptu nap. Good stuff.

We have much to be thankful for. No matter how difficult a situation, it could always be worse. In comparison to many around the world—or even around the corner or over the mountain—we have more than we need: bigger houses, more "stuff," plenty of food, ample clothes and shoes and time and money left over for recreation and leisure.

But more than material things, we should be thankful for family, health, friends and fellowship. We should appreciate opportunities for education and self-improvement. We should be grateful for freedom to worship and speak our convictions. We can be satisfied with loving and being loved.

The concept of being thankful was not novel in 1777. There was an Old Testament offering of thanksgiving (Leviticus 7:13). God's name was to be praised in song and glorified by thanksgiving (Psalm 69:30). And thanksgiving was always used in approaching the King of the universe (Psalm 100:4).

But what happens when we are thankful? I was amazed to read that the ultimate reason is to worship God.

Therefore, since we are receiving a kingdom that cannot be shaken,
let us be thankful, and so worship God acceptably with reverence
and awe. (Hebrews 12:28)

Daily challenge:
Do you want to worship more fully? Try being more thankful.

Friends

The morning was chilly and overcast. The weather report was off by ten degrees. Instead of forty-seven it was thirty-seven. *Brrr.*

The high-school team gathered to take the field against a group of alumni players. Nearly everyone showed up. Some families had four siblings on the field at one time, good-natured shoving and ribbing taking place between them. But the fun did not stop there.

The kids in this small school practically grew up together and kinships, especially in the early years, were strongly forged. Together they survived embarrassing losses and glorious victories. School uniforms and clunky shoes were subject to their scrutiny. They commiserated together over Latin and Greek lessons, physics and calculus. They even traveled as a team to Europe. Those kids from past years were great friends—and remain so today.

Friends can make or break a person. Choose the wrong friends and you create an accident waiting for a place to happen. The writer of Proverbs reminds us that *A righteous man is cautious in friendship, but the way of the wicked leads them astray* (Proverbs 12:26). Think of all the stories from your own high-school days. I remember a preacher's kid who did not choose his friends wisely, precipitating a long string of trouble for himself and his family.

But on the other hand, choosing the right friends can be sweet. A true friend will cover an offense with love, not repeating it to others (Proverbs 17:9). A friend will love at all times, not just when it's convenient or socially expedient (Proverbs 17:17). And a friend is loyal, just as though he was of the same flesh and blood (Proverbs 18:24).

I'm sure that many of the young adults who took to the field learned lessons of enduring friendships while in school. Great life lessons, to be sure. However, I am just as grateful for a few very special friends of my own. Even as I sit in the home of a friend who may as well be a sister, I thank God for her unconditional love and advice, tears of both joy and sorrow—and yes, even for all those hair colorings, eyebrow tweezings, manicures, shopping trips and shared meals.

If one falls down, his friend can help him up. But pity the man who falls and has no one to help him up! (Ecclesiastes 4:10)

Daily challenge:
Practice being a good friend. Do something friendly today.

Noisy Kids

There's just something about a house full of kids that warms the heart.

I was invited to attend brunch at my friend's parents' house. Eight young boys and one little girl took over. The decibel level rose with sounds of laughter and all those other noises boys like to make. The lone girl tried unsuccessfully to find a quiet corner. The boys wrestled and chased each other before tromping through the woods in search of the perfect stick. Only then did adult conversations dominate. Before long and with huge piles of shoes, jackets, hats and mittens mounded by the garage door, the kids returned to the warmth of the indoors, the clamor escalating once again.

In this case, noise was a good thing. It indicated healthy interaction. Let's recall other instances of good noise. Remember when Ezra (chapter 3) wrote of the people watching the temple's foundation being built? It had been a long time coming and many wept for joy while others laughed. In fact, the Prophet said *No one could distinguish the sound of the shouts of joy from the sound of weeping, because the people made so much noise. And the sound was heard far away* (v. 13).

And can you summon up the famous story about the tumbling walls of Jericho? After rounding the city for a week, the priests sounded the trumpets, the masses shouted and those walls came crashing down.

Furthermore, who can forget the Psalm writer who told of praises offered *with songs and with harps, lyres, tambourines, cymbals and trumpets* (I Chronicles 13:8)? This was neither quiet nor serene. Psalm 150:5 instructed, *praise him with the clash of cymbals, praise him with resounding cymbals.* Hardly a hushed response.

But in some cases, noise can disguise an underlying problem. The Tower of Babel (Genesis 11) was constructed with the hopes of reaching God. But so profoundly arrogant were their actions that common language ended. Instead, a cacophony of mixed-up tongues ensued—a noise of confusion.

If you were an enemy of Israel, you would be terrified at the Lord's approach: *"the LORD Almighty will come with thunder and earthquake and great noise . . . "* (Isaiah 29:6). Destruction was imminent. And just as a distraught spouse might wail for her deceased husband, those separated out as unbelievers will be subject to a place *"where there will be weeping and gnashing of teeth"* (Matthew 25:30).

There is a time for noise. But we must be careful that the noise pleases God's ear.

In a loud voice they sang: "Worthy is the Lamb, who was slain, to receive power and wealth and wisdom and strength and honor and glory and praise!" (Revelation 5:12)

Daily challenge:
What kind of noise is produced in your home?

The Journey

The rain came down hard. I was not looking forward to the trip home. Caleb and I had been sent to Ohio to pick up a car Gary bought through eBay. The convertible top added appeal—but not today. We had a seven-hour trip ahead of us, each in separate cars. "Lord, go beside, before and behind. Protect us," I prayed.

With every mile, the weather deteriorated. The rain continued, fog moved in and the truck spray made me think I was underwater. I felt disoriented on the unmarked, lane-less highways. The suboptimal wiper blades failed to leave a clean-swept window. *Where's the dumb road? Am I even in a lane?* It was horrible. My back tensed and eyes strained. I felt slightly out of control as I pushed the accelerator pedal down to keep up with Caleb. *Please Lord. Stop the rain.*

Shortly, we pulled into a rest area. When we got out, we saw that one of the retractable headlights was stuck. One headlight would not do in this weather. But wait. I noticed the rain had stopped. *Yeah. Thank you, God. Now can you help us fix this thing?* I didn't notice when an old truck filled with firewood pulled up. When the driver asked if he could help, I knew God had intervened. After twenty minutes, the situation was resolved; off we went. The rain started again as soon as we pulled out.

Further down the road Caleb zoomed through a toll booth, leaving me to watch his taillights fade in the distance. *Caleb! Slow down!* I could not call him. Caleb's phone went dead back at the rest stop. I prayed he would be standing at a preappointed place where we discussed having dinner. Thirty minutes later, my prayer was answered when I saw him waiting at the door.

But the trip wasn't over yet. He was supposed to stay behind me. I kept checking for his headlights. Suddenly, they were not there. I slowed down. No sight of him. Then I pulled over and waited. Still no Caleb. *What happened to him? God, if you could just resurrect his phone for a minute . . . .* As I melted down to Gary on my phone, I heard another call come in. It was Caleb on his "dead" phone. He had gone around me and I didn't see him. Somewhere between relief and anger, I understood that God had intervened—again!

Why am I surprised when I ask God for something—even somewhat flippantly—and He answers? I guess I can be a slow learner. When God promises to guide and protect, he isn't joking. As the people declared to Joshua, "*He protected us on our entire journey . . .* " (Joshua 24:17).

> *. . . for he guards the course of the just and protects the way of his faithful ones.* (Proverbs 2:8)

Daily challenge:
Don't be afraid to ask God for anything.

That's Life

Oh my! One minute, Juno, our female cat, was sitting on my lap, licking my hand and purring softly. In a flash, the male cat, Ra, joined us momentarily before pushing her to the floor. Grrr . . . hiss . . . moan . . . deep, throaty moans. He got behind her, grabbing her neck with his mouth. Yep. You guessed it. Right there, smack-dab in the middle of my living room, I watched two cats do the wild thing. It was almost embarrassing. Seth bounded down the steps only to stop dead in his tracks at the sight. "Whoa!" he cried out, shaking his head in disbelief. He immediately pulled his phone from his pocket and texted his best friend.

"Want kitties?"

In the aftermath of that hormonally-induced fracas, both cats laid contented, eyes closed. They no longer hissed and swiped at one another. They did what came naturally. Assuming it "took," the newest kitties should arrive in about sixty-three days. I just hope we don't get mutant, two-headed cats. After all, Ra and Juno are siblings.

As Christians, we can be prudish about intimacy. God could have created another method of procreation had He chosen to. Perhaps touching together index fingers or bumping elbows. But He did not. He devised a scheme capable of evoking pleasure as well as offspring.

I can not say that the animal world emotionally enjoys sexual intercourse, although, looking at the exhausted felines lying close by, one could argue the fact. For them, I think it has more to do with submitting to natural impulses. However, God created humans as emotional and physical beings, capable of love and connectedness. Sexual desires are a natural part of human development. Nevertheless, the intimacy involved in sharing that relationship is unique.

Sexual intimacy was intended for husband and wife. It denotes faithfulness, self-lessness, wanting the best for the other, fulfilling desires and commitment. It's shameful to see the beauty of this holy union defiled by a flippant approach to the sexual act.

Perhaps it's time to remind ourselves of the privilege and responsibility of intimacy. For a woman it is a beautiful process of sharing yourself with your beloved and meeting his needs. It's a way to say "I love you." It's a way to encourage and build him up (vice-versa for the relationship of the husband toward his wife). And it's an activity meant to bring physical pleasure and emotional satisfaction to both parties.

Renew your commitment to your spouse. Offer yourself wholeheartedly. Enjoy fully.

I am my lover's and my lover is mine. (Song of Solomon 6:3)

Daily challenge:
Need inspiration? Read the Song of Solomon.

Pre-Plan 101

As the facilities manager at a school, Gary is responsible to make sure there is compliance to various regulations. Fire safety is among those requirements. And with unannounced visits, you have to be ready at all times.

Two fire marshals walked into school today. They made their way through each hallway and into every nook and cranny. The men checked to make sure each of the fire doors was kept closed at all times. Closet shelves had to be inspected to see if there was twenty-four inches of clearance to the ceiling. Exit signs were tested and they made sure that nothing blocked an outside door. By the time they left, the checklist had been completed and the school received just a few minor suggestions for improvement.

The school community can feel confident that the environment is safe for students, faculty and staff. That's a good thing. But in reality, most people have never given a thought to the details of fire safety other than in the midst of a fire. Why is that?

I've seen a similar situation within the medical community. As an analyzer of potential risks, it is my job to play the "what-if?" game. What if someone tripped and disconnected the power cord? What if the blood circuit suddenly sprung a leak? What if the pump console caught on fire? What if . . .?

Unfortunately, more times than not we fail to be proactive in planning for emergencies. When a beetle crawled inside Gary's head and started munching on his ear drum, I had no preconceived plan in place. A speedy trip to the emergency room ensued, as a very young Seth queried from the back seat, "Is that bug gonna eat Dad's brains?"

Had I known what to do in that situation, that hospital trip could have been avoided. Had operating room personnel thought out solutions to potential problems, fewer patients would have been harmed. And had a downtown family installed smoke detectors, perhaps they could have made it out alive.

If we took care to think through potential difficulties, a lot of heartache could be avoided. If you want to *make your paths straight*, trust God in all his ways (Proverbs 3:5, 6). If you want to die with hope, then live righteously (Proverbs 11:7). To keep from wounding with words, use the tongue to encourage (Proverbs 12:18). And if you want to keep the peace, don't start the quarrel (Proverbs 17:14).

Don't get caught wishing, "If only I had . . . ." Guard your mind and actions.

Be very careful, then, how you live—not as unwise but as wise.
(Ephesians 5:15)

Daily challenge:
"An ounce of prevention is worth a pound of cure."

Eat Up

I knew the words that I was sure to hear. The words strike fear. The words make one tremble. The words cause grown women to cry.

"Step on the scale," the nurse ordered.

Ugh. No matter how skinny or how fat, no one likes their weight to be measured, especially when the digital scale is in the middle of a busy hallway. At least a computerized voice did not announce the number for all to hear, like the scale at my in-laws' house. In that case, only the kids liked to jump on it to hear the tinny woman's voice call out the number. To them it was a game. To the rest of us, it was unnecessary truth-telling.

I realize that I'm not particularly overweight. Nonetheless, when the time came to be weighed, my first impulse was to kick off my shoes and take off any clothes not necessary for modesty. After all, that is Biblical. Didn't the writer of Hebrews say to *let us lay aside every weight*? (Hebrews 12:1 KJV). I jest.

My weight was taken last week at an appointment and I didn't like the number. Knowing that I would again be weighed this week, I paid more attention to what I ate. I wanted the number to be lower, not higher. And it was. A whole half a pound.

As a society, we're obsessed with weight—by some accounts, for good reason. We have become an overindulgent society. By day we sit behind desks and by night become couch blobs. Our diets have too much fat that produces, well . . . too much fat. We don't eat balanced meals and food resembling fruits or vegetables aren't on the menu. Plus, the models, actors and actresses—the "beautiful people"—are slim-jims that we idolize. Hence, the food fetishes and constant weight struggles.

Truly, we need to maintain a healthy weight, eating a well balanced diet and getting good exercise. Gorging ourselves is never good. Or is it?

If there is ever a time to have a ravenous appetite, it should be in wanting to know God more fully. In the Book of Matthew, Jesus said, "*Blessed are those who hunger and thirst for righteousness, for they may be filled*" (Matthew 5:6). The food source is none other than Jesus Christ, the Bread of Life who removes hunger and the drink that quenches thirst.

Go ahead. Get filled up. Get fat.

May the God of hope fill you with all joy and peace as you trust in him, so that you may overflow with hope by the power of the Holy Spirit. (Romans 15:13)

Daily challenge:
Being spiritually fat all by yourself is selfish.
Help others gain spiritual weight

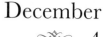

Don't Be a Drip

Drip. Drip. Drip. That's what I must have been to my husband today.

For some odd reason, Gary has never cultivated the habit of wearing his seat belt. It's not that he never wears it, but nine times out of ten, it hangs limp from the door. I admit it. That really irritates me. Does he think the law of the land does not apply to him? Does he actually believe compliance is optional? Does he let our kids decide what rules to obey and which to ignore? Of course not. So why can he take this liberty of civil disobedience?

I've been known to softly utter—more than once—"seat belt" as the car begins to roll. It's my duty as his wife to set him straight, isn't it? I am merely interested in his safety and aiding him in becoming a law-abiding citizen. In response, Gary normally reaches over his shoulder to grab the belt, inserting it into the buckle with an exasperated grunt.

As we ran errands and got into the car for the last time today, those two words slipped from my lips—"Seat belt." I couldn't help it. He had not worn the belt all morning. He needed reminding . . . or maybe not.

"Will you quit nagging me! I am a grown man. I know I'm probably safer with it on, but just let it go!" His words stung like the driving sleet against my cheek. I felt wounded. (Sob here.) But wait. Maybe I was the one who wounded him.

I sat silent on the drive home. He tried to talk and half laughed that I was giving him the silent treatment. "I have nothing to say," was all I could manage. My mind was racing back to what I read last night. In her book Virelle Kidder wrote of nagging her husband before he became a Believer (*The Best Life Ain't Easy, But It's Worth It*). It was undercover nagging: leaving books and articles lying open, having devotions in plain view and making a production of going to church. But as God softened her heart; she understood that she needed to love him into the Kingdom—not drag him kicking and screaming.

I need to learn to let some things go. I will stop making seat-belt comments. I will stop bugging Caleb about getting registered for next semester. And I will drop the "clean-your-room" routine—well, maybe not that one. No one's perfect.*

A quarrelsome wife is like a constant dripping on a rainy day. (Proverbs 27:15)

Daily challenge:
When you feel a nag coming on, ask God to shut your mouth
and open your heart.

(*Post-script: Since I've stopped nagging, my husband consistently wears his seat belt.)

But . . .

"But you have to understand. My family moved. Then Aunt Matilda got sick and my computer broke and we have a lousy connection . . . and the dog chewed the cord."

I spent the last two days sending each of my on-line high school students a progress report. Although some are working ahead of schedule and a few more are right on track, the majority are lagging behind. In three months, a handful of kids haven't even finished the first lesson. Hence, time to tell Mom and Dad.

Although this was an arduous task to gather the data and put together one-hundred-forty personalized emails, it was a necessary evil. The kids needed to know where they stood, as did their parents. Sometimes the truth hurts and sometimes it just produces the wackiest excuses.

Since I requested an "I read this message" back from the parents, my inbox filled as quickly as the outgoing messages left. All the parents thanked me for the information, some assuring me that "I'll get him moving!" But the messages back from the kids made me laugh. They used two approaches: 1) They either begged forgiveness and promised never to be complacent again, or 2) They presented intriguing reasons why they had failed to keep up. Just what I needed—a little comic relief.

Kids, school and excuses go hand-in-hand. Is it any wonder that after so many years of practice we as adults refine the art of excuse-making?

"I don't have enough time."

"I don't have enough money."

"She made me do it. I didn't have a choice."

"He made me so-o-o-o-o mad, I had to hit him."

To be sure, circumstances affect our decisions. But once it becomes an excuse, we must claim it for what it is: a choice.

Shouting back, in frustration, at a child is a choice—not an unavoidable circumstance. Not having enough time to read the Bible and good books is an excuse if I have the time to watch TV instead. And not supporting the Lord's work in deference to donating to the local library is a volitional decision.

Let's be careful in accepting responsibility rather than offering excuses.

You, therefore, have no excuse, you who pass judgment on someone else, for at whatever point you judge the other, you are condemning yourself, because you who pass judgment do the same things. (Romans 2:1)

Daily challenge:
When you begin a sentence with *But*, be careful that what follows is not just a bad choice.

Shine On

With guests expected tomorrow night, I decided today was a great time for much-neglected chores. Living in an old farm house, it seems we have more than our fair share of dirt, leaves and dust that get tracked in through the drafty doors. Coupled with the ever-shedding cat hair, our floors look tired and worn. The main room, the place we spend most of our time, bears the original 110-year-old floor, complete with worm holes and filled with lots of *character*. At least that's what we like to call it. But scuffed and dirty, that floor needed my undivided attention.

I hauled the furniture out of the room and prepared the floors for their mini-makeover. During that process, Caleb stumbled down the steps and opened the refrigerator door to stare into the chilly void. It's like he expects something new to have evolved overnight. Grabbing some soda to jump-start his morning, he inquired, "So, do we get to slide around on the shiny new floor when you're done?"

"Funny you should ask . . .."

I recall when my Mom tackled the kitchen floor. In those days, she scrubbed the floor on hands and knees, laying on a thick layer of wax. When we rushed through the door after school, Mom handed us a pair of heavy socks. It was our job to "skate" all over the floor, buffing the wax to a high gloss. It was the only time we didn't get in trouble for wearing holes in our stockings.

There's just something about shiny surfaces that makes us feel good. The gleam of polished granite counter tops. Stainless-steel appliances without fingerprints dulling the surface. Mirrors sans streaks or toothpaste splatters. And Christmas ornaments that catch the glimmer of the lights hidden within the fragrant tree branches.

Good and evil. Light and dark. Shiny and dull. I think God invented opposites so that we can better understand His character. Whatever God is, those without God are the contrary.

If we want to be a shining witness of the Light, we must come out of the darkness. Shine on, my friend. Shine on.

He will make your righteousness shine like the dawn, the justice of your cause like the noonday sun. (Psalm 37:6)

Daily challenge:
For God, who said, "Let light shine out of darkness," made his light shine in our hearts to give us the light of the knowledge of the glory of God in the face of Christ. (II Corinthians 4:6)

Lose It Again

I'm not sure about you, but I can get a little stressed when I feel pushed—or pulled. Admittedly, I'm the one to blame. No one makes me that way. I manage to work myself into a tizzy all by myself. It's not a trait I'm proud of.

I hosted a bridal shower tonight. All day yesterday, I directed my attention to preparing for this event. There were floors to be scrubbed, cakes to be baked and nuts to be roasted and glazed. Today the bathrooms, sinks and counters cried out for attention. The old toothbrush even came out to clean the nooks and crannies that are so good at harboring crud. Last-minute food preparations preceded running up to the home office to print off a devotional for the bride-to-be. I felt good about how things were going until nothing happened when I hit the "print" key.

Grrr. The new network Caleb set up had done something dastardly to my printer interface. I tried to no avail to fix it. "Caleb. Get in here!" I demanded. When he came without exhibiting as much concern as I thought he should, my angst increased.

I finally gave up and retreated downstairs only to find that the bulb lighting the little fiber-optic Christmas tree was burnt out. "Seth, please take this apart and find out what kind of bulb it takes." Believe it or not, he didn't seem all that concerned either. *Fine. I'll do it myself. Now where is that little screwdriver? Someone took it and didn't put it back. Grrr* again. I rummaged roughly through drawers, distraught that guests might come and not see the pretty tree. Wouldn't that be tragic?

My dear husband came to my aid, found a screwdriver and sent Seth to buy a replacement bulb. Caleb solved my printer problem and handed me the printed page. The candles flickered gently, the tree in the corner magically changed colors and the aroma of freshly prepared food wafted through the air. All was well.

All was well, that is, except for that twenty-minute period when I lost control. I allowed a few small details to distract me from my true purpose: to encourage a young woman as she prepared for an adventure of a lifetime.

I'm glad that momentarily veering off course did not ruin the evening. But I have room for improvement. It is my mind, so says the Apostle Peter, that must be tuned in and prepared before self-control can be realized. Self-control is a mental decision. Losing it is optional.

Therefore, prepare your minds for action; be self-controlled; set your
hope fully on the grace to be given you when Jesus Christ is revealed.
(I Peter 1:13)

Daily challenge:
Keep the big picture in focus. We will be less likely to lose control over minutia.

Hurry, Hurry!

In this Christmas season, everyone seems to be on super charge: the old hustle-and-bustle thing. For me, it's not so much Christmas but work and projects. When it rains, it pours. Last night I was slammed with entertaining. Today I'm assigned to take a meal to a family with a new baby. Of all times, I had orders pour in from my medical-education site on top of heavier-than-usual student questions. My brain screamed, "Hurry, hurry!"

Sometimes hurrying is a necessity. When I was carrying a pager for a living, its loud *beep, beep, beep* signaled an emergency. Often it was *slam-bam*. If I didn't hurry, a patient could die. I sped to the hospital, rushed to change clothes and pitched boxes and wrappings over my shoulder as fast as I could as I was preparing my equipment. It was organized but controlled panic.

Now imagine your response if you got a call and the person on the other end said, "Hurry. Get out of your house. It's going to be destroyed." Do you think you would listen? If the person had any credibility, you would.

Good old Lot got that call. In fact, he got a personal house call to deliver the message from two angels disguised as regular guys. Sodom and Gomorrah were beyond wicked. The men of the city caught wind and even came looking to defile the visiting angels. Didn't get far, though. The angels blinded them all so they could not find the door of the house. Well, by then, Lot knew they were serious when they said, *"Hurry! Take your wife and your two daughters who are here, or you will be swept away when the city is punished"* (Genesis 19:15).

The night before, Lot told his daughters and their husbands the same thing: *"Hurry and get out of this place, because the LORD is about to destroy the city!"* (Genesis 19:14). These foolish people thought he was joking. In God's mercy, the visitors took them all by the hand and led them away. But the messengers warned: *"Flee for your lives! Don't look back, and don't stop anywhere in the plain! Flee to the mountains or you will be swept away!"* (Genesis 19:17). We all know what happened then. Lot's wife couldn't resist. She looked back toward the city and turned into a salt lick.

Like Lot, sometimes we have to hurry away, but often, we should hurry toward something good. Aaron hurried to offer sacrifices (Numbers 16:46). Paul hurried toward ministry (Acts 20:16). David hurried to a place of safety and contentment.

So go ahead, hurry when you need to. It's okay.

I would hurry to my place of shelter, far from the tempest and storm.
(Psalm 55:8)

Daily challenge:
Make sure that when you hurry, you are rushing in the right direction.

Leaving

"Parting is such sweet sorrow." You'll recognize the line from Shakespeare. It is late and Juliet is standing on the balcony, Romeo gazing upward. The words slip gently from the lips of the young woman, anguished that her love had to part but holding onto the promise of his return. I wonder if she cried at the thought of separation.

I cried buckets—not at the drama nor atop a balcony but last night in the darkened stillness of my bed. I thought I was in control this morning, but my spontaneous tears defy that premise. I ache in my gut. I guess the sweetness will come later.

Our oldest son, having turned 21 in October, has been eager to get out on his own. I understand. He feels he's been on hold since returning from college in Ohio to live and study at home. Last night he asked for an audience. I clutched my coffee cup between my hands as I braced myself for the inevitable.

"Mom. Dad. What do you think about me moving to Columbus?"

Oh, my. It's really happening. This time he's leaving and never coming back. Get a grip. Don't cry in front of him. Just listen. I heard his plan and details of the promised job. I listened to his financial status. He spoke from his heart about needing to make this change. Although I'm concerned about the particulars, I know in my soul that it is time.

But it hurts. It's not like he's leaving for college, predictably returning on holidays and summer breaks. When he leaves this time, it's for good. He leaves not as a child but as a young man. That means my mothering is done. Over. Finished. No more.

I wonder if the last twenty-one years have prepared him. *Will all my own inadequacies haunt him? Will he be a good employee? Will he finish college before he's thirty? Will he prioritize Christian fellowship? Will he eat right and brush his teeth?* The questions in my brain rattle on.

My own angst must pale in comparison to the Father's. When his Son left home, the Father knew what was in store: a lowly birth, upbringing in a carpenter's home and hatefulness directed at Him. Then to hang His Son's sinless body on a tree must have ripped at the very heart of God. He darkened the sky so men could not see and turned His back on the one He adored. It had to be. There was no other way.

The parting was sorrowful. But the sweetness is in what happened because the Son left home.

But he was pierced for our transgressions, he was crushed for our iniquities; the punishment that brought us peace was upon him, and by his wounds we are healed. (Isaiah 53:5)

Daily challenge:
Our children are just rented from God. Place them in His care.

Flash Flood

The weather report doesn't look good. Rain was spotty today, but in the next thirty-six hours, we are supposed to get deluged with up to four inches of the wet stuff. Flash-flood warnings have been posted. By the morning after next, temperatures are predicted to drop into the thirties. Up in the mountains, you can guess what that means. Ice and snow. Great. Just in time for my race later that night—the race known for wicked weather and frigid temps.

The rain will raise creek levels, forcing us to wet our feet just three miles into a sixty-seven-mile race. But I better get used to the idea. Rain run-off in the mountains is a fact, swelling streams and creeks beyond the borders of their banks. I'll just have to deal with it.

The extreme run-off from monster rains causes flash flooding and in some cases, devastation beyond belief. In my own state of Virginia, the largest rainfall occurred in 1906, when 9.2 inches of rain fell in a slim forty minutes. But in August of 1969, the remnants of Hurricane Camille delivered 27 to 30 inches of rain to the Blue Ridge Mountains in Nelson County, not far from where we live. With no time for the ground to absorb the downpour, the waters ran into the gullies and raced downhill. Creeks normally inches deep morphed into fifty-foot raging walls of water. Houses took violent leave of their foundations, entire hillsides scourged of trees, hurling boulders downward. Survivors reported a night of terror, still haunted by the deafening roar of the catastrophic event. At least 117 people lost their lives.

I imagine the ancient prophet Habakkuk knew what those people experienced. In chapter 3 of the book that bears his name, he "sees" the force of God's power and exclaims, *I stand in awe of your deeds, O LORD* (v. 2). He continues, *Were you angry with the rivers, O LORD? Was your wrath against the streams?* (v. 8). The mountains *writhed* and *torrents of water swept by* (v. 10). And yet, as he watched God destroy those who opposed Him, Habakkuk cried out, *yet I will rejoice in the LORD, I will be joyful in God my Savior* (v. 18).

Sometimes it takes the deafening sound and power of a flash flood to grab our attention. But once God sends a remnant of a shattered house for us to grab onto, we are saved. And like Habakkuk , we can say:

> *The Sovereign LORD is my strength; he makes my feet like the feet of a deer, he enables me to go on the heights. (v. 19)*

Daily challenge:
Don't give up at the sound of a flood. Just hang on until God comes to the rescue.

Pictures Speak

A burgeoning photographer lives in my house. Seth's fascination was realized during spring break of his sophomore year. Seeing pictures shot by a friend, he was inspired by the images. They told a story. They captured emotion. They depicted parts of life that few outside the photographer's mind ever glimpsed.

Since that time, cameras and Seth are inseparable. He has talent—professionals say so. People hire him and pay good money for the images. He is headed to a professional photography school. And, he has an impressive portfolio. It was only logical that Seth take the photos for our family Christmas card.

With a rigged portrait studio in his bedroom, he shot Caleb's picture first. It was fantastic—rugged and mysterious, deep brown eyes staring from the page. Then, he gave me the camera with strict instructions. The lighting was perfect and Seth is photogenic—good combination. Gary's turn in front of the lens produced handsome pictures as well. But me . . . that was a far different story.

I fixed my hair and put on makeup. But after one session of sixty-eight pictures (no exaggeration), Seth found only five worthy to keep and edit. I hated them all. So, I changed my hair, refreshed my makeup and tried again. This time, thirty-six shutter clicks and only one keeper. *Heavy sigh . . . .*

I look old and harsh in the pictures. When I view them, I see something I don't feel. Could the pictures be lying? I don't think so. The pictures tell the real story—a few brown spots, skin that's starting to sag, eyes that look anything but fresh and vibrant.

The trouble with pictures is the same trouble we have in person. We may feel pretty good on the inside, but to anyone looking at us in true light, they see the flaws we fail to acknowledge. What they notice can be ugly—mean spirits, harsh words, selfishness, laziness and a host of other inadequacies. But there is hope. Touch-ups.

God is the king of touch-ups. He can take what is unsightly and cover our blemishes with His miraculous love and grace. In one stroke of genius, He paints us to reflect His own image, full of life and beauty. Who needs Photoshop?

Do not lie to each other, since you have taken off your old self with
its practices and have put on the new self, which is being renewed in
knowledge in the image of its Creator. (Colossians 3:9, 10)

Daily challenge:
What picture did people see today? Was it a keeper?

Preparation

I hate the coming of a race, especially this one: the Hellgate 100K. This devilish event is held no matter what the weather doles out. The action starts as the gun sounds at one minute after midnight, the second Friday night of December. From there the course entices runners up, over and through the Blue Ridge mountains, finally arriving at the finish—if all goes well—nearly sixty-seven miles later.

You have to be prepared for anything. Rain, snow, sleet, icy roads, missing aid stations and winds that threaten to blow everybody into the next county. Last year I had a crew meet me along the course. I could rely on them to give me what I wanted. But this year, I'm on my own. I have to anticipate my needs and prepare my drop bags, which will be carted to various locations along the course. I can put anything in there, but it's just like me to forget the one thing I need the most.

As I was packing my bags earlier today, the room looked as windswept as those mountaintops. Clothes everywhere. I repeatedly stripped and redressed, trying on various combinations. *Will I be too hot? Too cold? Just right?* Eventually, I settled on my attire but threw in a few extra pieces in case I changed my mind. Now all I had to do was take a catnap, pack it all in the car, drive to the race, fret about everything and then run into the blackness. If my preparation has been adequate, I'll be okay. If not, it could be a disaster.

Life is all about preparation; it's not an optional activity. The people of Israel prepared offerings and sacrifices. The preparation of the tabernacle was assigned to the priests. Often, individuals were charged with preparing "tasty food," wedding banquets, dressed stone for building construction, spices for burial, penalties for wrongdoing and arguments for court.

The most important preparation is, however, readying yourself for service. Why is that? The answer is found in Ephesians 4:12-13: *to prepare God's people for works of service, so that the body of Christ may be built up until we all reach unity in the faith and in the knowledge of the Son of God and become mature, attaining to the whole measure of the fullness of Christ.*

Knock yourself out. Prepare as if the Kingdom depended on it.

Preach the Word; be prepared in season and out of season; correct, rebuke and encourage—with great patience and careful instruction. (II Timothy 4:2)

Daily challenge:
Be sure that your preparation is pointed—not pointless.

It Is Finished

"It is finished." Before you accuse me of having a Jesus complex, I do not. Nor am I writing sacrilege. It is merely a comment I whispered with the greatest relief at precisely 5:13 p.m. this evening.

At one minute past midnight, I toed the line for the last race in The BEAST series. Six races must be completed by the successful entrant, the three shorter mountain races (34, 31 and 29 miles) in the spring and the remaining hellacious contests in October, November and December. The October race demanded 100 miles, then 54 in November and now nearly 67 miles to finish it off. This last race is known for its extreme difficulty, tight cut-offs and a midnight start. Freezing temps, howling wind and difficult footing are all par for the course. Of those who dare sign the application, relieving the race director for incurred injury or death (I'm not joking), a slim average of sixty percent cross the finish line. It is not a race for the timid.

My goal this year, being a BEAST entrant, was simply to finish. I was not concerned, or prepared, to break any land speed records. I just needed to be under the eighteen-hour time limit. The temperature and wind chill were worse than predicted. I was cold and my feet constantly wet from numerous stream crossings. My frozen shoestrings became impossible to adjust and my water tube iced up solid for ten miles. Nothing about this race was easy.

A lean twenty-five minute cushion on the cutoff at two of the aid stations escalated my fear of failure. And when my left outstep of my foot protested vehemently, I panicked. *Lord, help me stay calm and strong. Let me finish.* He answered that prayer. I crossed the line with forty-seven minutes to spare. So exhausted I could barely smile, I crawled into my sleeping bag, sweat, filth and all, and fell into a deep sleep.

Making a commitment to "finish" is not always easy. Often fraught with moments of regret, the required pain and hard work can take its toll. And yet, it is essential that we "suck it up." How else will our children learn that finishing—as opposed to quitting—requires commitment and dedication?

As Christians, we have the ultimate example of "finishing." Christ had to die on the cross to atone for our sins. There was no way around it. But it didn't just happen. It required a conscious decision and commitment to the will of His Father. Was it easy? Of course not. Was it worth it? Absolutely.

When he had received the drink, Jesus said, "It is finished." With that, he bowed his head and gave up his spirit. (John 19:30)

Daily challenge:
Choose your challenges carefully. Then make the commitment to finish.

It Takes a Village

Running along mountain trails for seventeen hours yesterday, one term kept floating through my mind. It was the phrase Hillary Clinton made popular by the book of similar title. I've never read the book, nor do I intend to. Nevertheless, those words were as stuck to my brain like a fly on honey.

Having hours to think, I contemplated the meaning of a village. I thought back to the villages I grew up with—Mayberry and Petticoat Junction of TV Land and the village square made popular in movies like "Back to the Future." Even my own home town, a small municipality in southeastern Pennsylvania, held memories of Santa's shed, candy canes and strings of Christmas lights strung across the roads. And everyone knew your name.

What does it take for a village to work? It takes people who bring a variety of skills to the town. Think how bloody the affair would be if only the butcher lived there without the baker and candlestick maker. A village provides a central place to come together and places of safety to return to at night.

As images reminiscent of Rockwell paintings came to life in my mind, I began to understand how the village concept applied to the women of our church. We essentially have a village of women. When we function as a village, we provide a place of safety, fellowship, accomplishment and encouragement. We cannot function on our own, nor should we try. Solitary confinement is a dreaded punishment for the worst criminals. It should not be a way of life.

As we ladies gathered tonight for a delectable cookie exchange, it became clear that God was working. He was planting seeds. How can we make a difference? How can we use everyday contacts as an opportunity to represent Christ? Is it the person sitting at the bus stop that needs our attention? Or how about the cashier at the grocery? Regardless, representing Christ through service, care and compassion should be an everyday, normal thing—not a scheduled event.

Yes, if our ladies' ministry is to be effective, we must come together as a village, looking out for the common good and making it a pleasant place to live. As the writer of Hebrews said, *Let us not give up meeting together . . . but let us encourage one another* (Hebrews 10:25).

My purpose is that they may be encouraged in heart and united in love, so that they may have the full riches of complete understanding, in order that they may know the mystery of God, namely, Christ . . .. (Colossians 2:2)

Daily challenge:
Sometimes you have to leave the village square to meet the people where they live. Encourage someone.

Pain

My deep, luscious sleep was rudely interrupted by, well, waking up. When I swung my feet to the ground, my weekend activities rudely reminded me of my mortality. The pain in my feet was palpable, especially my heels. I shuffled penguin-like into the bathroom. When I went to sit down, the pain in my quads screamed in opposition. It was just the start of the day and already, I was reminded that I probably deserved this. It was just reward for running sixty-seven miles.

Pain has a way of grabbing our attention. In my early years of ultrarunning, I had a string of five years of never-ending injuries, many of them stress fractures. Most provided no foreshadowing. One minute I was running footloose and fancy free and the next moment writhing from the pain. And that pain was persistent for weeks, a constant reminder of either too much training or being orthopedically impaired by bad foot anatomy. Either way, I didn't like the pain.

But as much as I don't enjoy pain, just the potential of pain can serve as a deterrent—which can be a good thing. If a child gets his molecules rearranged by sticking a wet and grungy finger into an electric socket, chances are he will not try that maneuver again. And, for as much as my husband enjoys soccer, having played in college, he is no longer willing to sign up for league play, because he knows pain in the aftermath is inevitable.

Pain can be so much more than physical. The prophet Jeremiah exclaimed, "*Oh, my anguish, my anguish! I writhe in pain. Oh, the agony of my heart!*" (Jeremiah 4:19). The mental torment can sometimes bring on unbearable, true-blue pain. That kind of pain is the hardest to fix.

We know that pain exists because of the curse of sin. And as I get older, there are days when I am feeling pretty well cursed! But isn't it wonderful that our God is big enough to use the pain to bring healing and maturity? God Himself said, "*See now that I myself am He! There is no god besides me. I put to death and I bring to life, I have wounded and I will heal . . .*" (Deuteronomy 32:39).

When pain comes—which it will—learn from it. May it remind us of what not to do. May it also encourage us to turn to God.

> "*For he wounds, but he also binds up; he injures, but his hands also heal.*" (Job 5:18)

Daily challenge:
Pain is like a string tied around our finger—a reminder of our weakness, a reminder of our strength.

Rejoice!

I'm living on a mountaintop today. For quite some time, I've been praying relentlessly about the struggle in someone's life. The addiction was not one of alcohol or drugs. It was an addiction to a virtual world of fantasy. No, not the pornographic kind but the kind that beckons one to enter a culture of power, presence, prestige and personalities. It was the kind that wooed the game player to disappear into the chasm, as if a giant hand had reached through the screen to stranglehold the player-turned-victim. It was the kind that was given more importance than real life. And it was the kind that put real life on hold.

This morning I heard the news that the bondage was ending. Virtual characters were destroyed and subscriptions cancelled. It is as if he has been set free. Duties long forsaken have already been addressed. He laughed. I cried.

There are countless reasons to rejoice. The father of the Prodigal Son rejoiced when he returned home. Though dirty and worn by a shameful life, the repentant was gathered into open arms. Forgiveness abounded and the young man's life was restored.

Think about how Hannah prayed for so long for a son. She prayed with such intensity that those in the temple thought her to be drunk. But nay. She prayed with fervor and faith and when God opened her womb she cried out, *"My heart rejoices in the LORD . . . There is no one holy like the LORD; there is no one besides you; there is no Rock like our God"* (I Samuel 2:1, 2).

And in this Christmas season, who can forget the uttering of Mary, the mother of the Christ child? She was carrying the very Son of God in her womb. "How could this be? Why was I chosen, a young girl, a common girl? And I'm not even married!" she must have thought. And yet she marveled and proclaimed for all who listened, *"My soul glorifies the Lord and my spirit rejoices in God my Savior, for the Mighty One has done great things for me—holy is his name"* (Luke 1:46-47, 49).

Rejoice often, then rest. God is so good.

Therefore my heart is glad and my tongue rejoices; my body also will rest secure . . .. (Psalm 16:9)

Daily challenge:
Want more rest? Rejoice more.

Study Hard

A lot of people thought I was crazy when I started a graduate program when I was in my late 40s. And when I was grinding away writing papers and spending hours fulfilling academic requirements, I had to agree. *What was I thinking?* It wasn't like my life was boring and empty. But I chose to place myself in a situation that further crowded my busy schedule. It was mind-stretching and frustrating. I had no time to relax or read a book. And yet when the final thesis project was submitted and diploma signed, it suddenly seemed worth it. I almost signed up for the doctorate program. *Almost. . ..*

This is the week of semester finals for both the boys. Today Caleb finished his semester by taking a college physics exam and Seth is hovering over his notes for two high-school exams tomorrow. I don't envy them. There is stress and pressure in preparing for an exam, especially if it's not a favorite topic. To excel, it takes effort and hard work. And just like physical work, mental gymnastics can claim just as much blood, sweat and tears.

Wouldn't it be nice if learning was easy? No doubt, some come by it more readily than others. But in the end, even the most brilliant are challenged at some point to test the synapses.

The wisest man on earth, King Solomon, realized this. As he opens the Book of Ecclesiastes, he speaks of enormous task given him. *"I devoted myself to study and to explore by wisdom all that is done under heaven. What a heavy burden God has laid on men!"* (1:13). He continued by saying: *"I thought to myself, 'Look, I have grown and increased in wisdom more than anyone who has ruled over Jerusalem before me; I have experienced much of wisdom and knowledge.' Then I applied myself to the understanding of wisdom, and also of madness and folly, but I learned that this, too, is a chasing after the wind"* (1:16,17).

Later on in his dissertation, Solomon speaks of the hard effort and the toll it takes. In fact, he admits that *"much study wearies the body"* (12:12b). Indeed! But study is good. It may not lead to a Ph.D., but it's good for the soul and the mind. Besides, you know what they say—"Use it or lose it."

Study to [show] thyself approved unto God, a workman that needeth not to be ashamed, rightly dividing the word of truth. (II Timothy 2:15, KJV)

Daily challenge:
What are you curious about? Start studying. Be a lifelong learner.

Bad Blood

When the phone rang, the voice on the other end stumbled over my name. *Oh, boy. The telemarketers are at it again!* But it was not someone wanting me to consolidate debt, cleanse my septic system, buy satellite TV or refinance my house. Rather, it was the belated call from my doctor with my lab results.

"Ms. Trittipoe, your thyroid levels are at the lowest range of normal, but your cholesterol levels are quite high."

Shoot. I hoped I could escape, but I guess not. I have a strong family history of high cholesterol and cardiac disease. Just a few months ago, one of my younger brothers found out his numbers were elevated as well. *What to do?*

My doctor suggested I have a six-month period of "lifestyle modification." "You could maybe add a little exercise and try a low-fat diet," she said.

"*Huh.* I think I get enough. I just ran 67 miles on Saturday."

"Oh." There was a long pause before she continued. "Well, in that case, maybe more exercise isn't what you need. How about your diet?"

I explained that I was careful but not obsessive. Indeed, there was room for improvement.

"OK. Try to watch the diet, but I think you need a referral to an internist. You may need to be put on medication. You just have bad genes."

Bad genes. Don't we all have bad genes on some level? We can't get away from the genetic makeup our parents gave us. But I can hardly be angry about it, blaming them for the ills befallen me. I just need to deal with it and optimize my own health.

As a child, I used to be "mad" at Adam and Eve for my sin nature. If they wouldn't have sinned, I wouldn't be in this pickle! My optimistic assessment was far from the truth. I would have screwed up, too. No doubt about it.

Technically, however, sin did enter the world because of them (Romans 5:12). Do I hold it against them? No. What I should do is be grateful for the "fix." Christ's shed blood was the cure for my bad blood.

Therefore, just as sin entered the world through one man, and death through sin, and in this way death came to all men, because all sinned—For if the many died by the trespass of the one man, how much more did God's grace and the gift that came by the grace of the one man, Jesus Christ, overflow to the many! (Romans 5:12, 15b)

Daily challenge:
What are you doing to improve your health—physical and spiritual?

What (Not) to Wear

"What Not to Wear," the small screen show with the huge fashion focus, has reached near-epic proportions. The co-hosts, Stacy and Clinton, have practically become household names. For anyone not familiar with the show, an unsuspecting, slovenly-dressed person is ambushed, their wardrobes confiscated and a credit card loaded with $5,000 handed over to purchase a new closet full of clothes. By the end of the show, the once-dowdy slob evolves into a well-dressed, beautifully adorned person, new hair and makeup becoming the finishing cherry on top.

I find the fashion tips and rules interesting and even catch myself thinking about them as I sift through clothing racks at the store. But what may be even more compelling is the person's obvious change of attitude by the time the credits roll by. Grown women break down and cry at the first glimpse of a new hairstyle and makeup. And the sight and feel of a perfectly coordinated outfit puts new bounce in their step. Does the change occur because of the designer clothes or because a high-dollar stylist did the hair? I don't think so . . . although those things don't hurt. I think the real change is happening on the inside.

That makes sense to me. When I put on a great dress or a cute ensemble, I feel different. I am empowered and confident. On the other hand, when I'm wearing my scruffy sweats and t-shirt and am in the middle of a bad hair day, I feel anything but self-assured.

Does this hold true in a spiritual sense? It should. Consider the apparel we are given as Believers: a breastplate of righteousness, good shoes ready for action, a protective shield, a saving helmet and good wide belt of truth and sharp sword of the Spirit for the ultimate accessories (Ephesians 6:14-17).

When we know we have on the right spiritual clothes, it should affect how we feel and conduct ourselves. We can exude confidence because the outfit was put together by the Designer of the Universe.

Go ahead. Walk tall in those duds. It's the ultimate in godly fashion.

Finally, be strong in the Lord and in his mighty power. Put on the full armor of God so that you can take your stand against the devil's schemes. (Ephesians 6:10, 11)

Daily challenge:
Don't go naked. Size yourself up for a favorite piece of spiritual clothing.
Try it on. Walk out the door more confidently.

Too Much

The day was productive and I loved it. There's nothing like organizing and getting rid of stuff to give make me tingly all over. With less than two weeks before Caleb moves up and out, we started with his closet and moved on to his drawers. Anything he did not love or had not worn in the last year ended up in a big heap, destined eventually for the Goodwill store. The pile grew larger and larger until I though it would surely bury us. Saving myself just in the nick of time, I slipped out to Seth's room.

The procedure was repeated. Again, another mound quickly formed. There were even a few items with the tags still attached. But Seth was adamant. "I'll never wear that stuff." So with that, onto the top of the heap they went.

Since I was on a roll, I emptied our drawers as well. A third pile started. By the time the purge was completed, I had four huge bags of stuff to donate. How did we end up with so much stuff?

We definitely live in a society that embraces the "more-is-better" philosophy. And granted, possessions have the ability to reproduce like rabbits. It's so easy to go from nothing to a lot in a nanosecond. I remember one Christmas when the boys and their cousins were quite young. Although the gifts were not expensive, the quantity was grand. They tired so much from opening the gifts on Christmas Eve that we had to postpone the remainder of the gift-opening for the next morning. How sad.

In some cases "less is more." I have a new rule that when I run out of hangers in my closet, nothing else comes in until something goes out. I love a great bargain, but . . . enough is enough.

God is gracious in providing grain and wine, but He warns that "stuff" can lead to greed (Genesis 27:28). *"Watch out! Be on your guard against all kinds of greed; a man's life does not consist in the abundance of his possessions"* (Luke 12:15).

The abundance that fills us to overflowing can not be held in hand or gift-wrapped with a big red bow. But it is palpable nonetheless. Be sure you have an abundance of what really counts.

Mercy, peace and love be yours in abundance. (Jude 1:2)

Daily challenge:
Get rid of what you don't need. Bless someone with your abundance.

The Key

Because Caleb was appointed to set up the sound system at church, we arrived an hour ahead of the first call to worship. Unfortunately, the key to the heavy equipment boxes did not arrive with us. With a few well-placed calls, a key was located and the set-up completed just in time. But the whole idea of keys started a domino-like stream of consciousness for me. I came across a story, partially forgotten.

Ever hear the one about the fat guy and the disappearing sword? It goes like this. Because the Israelites did evil in the sight of the Lord—again—He placed them under the thumb of the King of Moab, Eglon. Eventually, God's nation repented and begged for salvation. God gave them that in the form of a man named Ehud, a left-handed man. The plan was sneaky. Ehud fabricated a two-edged sword, about eighteen-inches long, strapping it to his right thigh under his clothes. He gained entrance to the King, bringing a tribute with him. Then, he left the court of the King.

The story would be boring if that was the end of it. But it's not. Ehud returned to the palace. "Oh, King," he enticed, "I forgot to tell you. I have a big surprise for you." And who doesn't like a surprise? Ordering his servants to be gone, the hefty king leaned forward in anticipation.

"So?" The King was hooked, just like a big ol' sucker fish on the line.

"*I have a message from God for you*" (Judges 3:20). As the King stood to his feet, Ehud reached to his side and plunged the sword into the King's belly. He did not remove it, for the fat closed in around it. Ehud beat feet and fled, the door locking behind him.

Meanwhile, the servants wondered why their King did not answer their knocking. Thinking that the King had to "relieve" himself, the Scripture says, "*They waited to the point of embarrassment, but when he did not open the doors of the room, they took a key and unlocked them*" (Judges 3:25). Only then did they see the fallen king dead on the floor. The Israelite army returned to kill 10,000 Moabites and usher in eighty years of peace.

God locks and unlocks doors at will. Had that door not been locked, Ehud would-n't have safely escaped. Sometimes God locks a door for our own protection and when it's safe, He opens it.

He will be the sure foundation for your times, a rich store of salva-tion and wisdom and knowledge; the fear of the LORD is the key to this treasure. (Isaiah 33:6)

Daily challenge:
Learn to respect the locks that God places and removes in our lives.

Blind Leading the Blind

"You have to give us more to go on." I heard the angst in Gary's voice but worked hard to suppress a giggle. "What do wonton wrappers look like and where are they?" Gary and Caleb were attempting to complete a shopping mission. With list in hand, my phone rang twice with them asking for help. At the debriefing upon their return, both looking somewhat bewildered, I learned they picked up the easy stuff first: soda, ham and cheese. But they had to ask for help when it came to picking potatoes. "Can you tell we don't know what we are doing?" Gary had queried the stock clerk.

"Yes," came the simple response. It was like the blind leading the blind.

Obviously, it's not like they were literally blind. They just didn't have enough knowledge or experience to guide them successfully up and down those isles. It happened to me in the Brazilian jungle. A group of us ran until the trail simply disappeared. Each in the group had an opinion about where to go. The loudest voices convinced the rest of us to take a trail we eventually found off to the left. Regrettably, we ended up circling back to the morning's starting line. Another unfortunate example of the blind leading the blind.

It's a phenomenon that happens often. It's kin to mob mentality. Someone with a "bright idea" convinces his neighbor of its validity—even if it's bogus. Before you know it, two believers turns into four, four into sixteen, sixteen into two hundred fifty-six and so on. Everyone buys in without honestly evaluating the truth of the original claim. Then weird things happen. As the message says on Seth's t-shirt, "Never underestimate the power of stupid people in large groups."

In a society that promotes political correctness and fads and trends of all kinds, it is essential that we live with eyes wide open. The great Healer promises to restore sight, just as he did for the beggar man in Bethsaida (Mark 8). No need to be blind or be led by those who are.

. . . the LORD gives sight to the blind, the LORD lifts up those who are bowed down, the LORD loves the righteous. (Psalm 146:8)

Daily challenge:
Are you blindly following something or someone? Be sure to evaluate everything in the light of God's Word before you take the first step.

Are You Ready?

"Are you ready? Ready for Christmas?" If I had a dime for every time I was asked that question . . . well, you know how that cliché goes. With a few errands still on the schedule, I was asked that question multiple times. Even the dentist inquired when she had four fingers and three instruments in my mouth.

My answer, muffled at best, was in the affirmative. Except for a few odds and ends, preparations have been smooth. We chose not to do much shopping and other than a few special treats, the kitchen chores are in check. The gifts that will be making the trip to relatives are standing ready at the door. So yes, I am ready.

But the question is not reserved for Christmas. "Are you ready for HDTV?" Over and over again, the public has been warned about the coming end of analog TV signals. "Get ready, get ready," is the cry of the broadcasters. "If you aren't ready by February 17th, you will not be able to view TV." *Hmm . . . might not be such a bad idea not to be ready.*

Let there be no doubt—getting ready is a critical and necessary part of life. We get ready for school, ready for work and ready for play. Rebekah and her maids got ready for travel by mounting their camels (Genesis 24:61), Joseph readied his chariot (Genesis 46:29), an altar was prepared by Joshua (Joshua 22:26), the Levites tuned up King David's instruments (II Chronicles 29:26), Jewish warriors prepared for battle (Jeremiah 1:17) and even the horses were readied for war (Proverbs 21:31). The disciples readied a boat for the Lord's use (Mark 3:9), Paul got ready and went up to Jerusalem (Acts 21:15) and even Mary hurried to get ready to visit Elizabeth (Luke 1:39).

I find, however, that there is a fine line between readiness and obsession. Sometimes I lose site of the goal, getting lost in minutia. So yes, get yourself ready, but don't be sidetracked from the true objective.

"You also must be ready, because the Son of Man will come at an hour when you do not expect him." (Luke 12:40)

Daily challenge:
Make a "get-ready" list. Create a step-by plan. Execute it well.

Follow that Star

Anticipating a cozy Christmas with family, we packed up the car and headed down the road. Gary drove twenty miles before he turned the wheel over to me. He was sick and feeling like death warmed over—and looked it, too. He quickly fell asleep in the passenger seat. With a broken radio, Caleb engrossed in a book and Seth plugged into his music, I guided the car in silence. I entertained myself by reading the signs that flashed by the window. On the marquee of a church, I read, "Follow Jesus and you'll never be lost."

Following the wrong person can be disastrous. Just ask an ultrarunner. In most cases, a solitary runner does not go off-course. Ironically, it's usually a pair of people who err. Chatting with each other, they get lost in their conversation and keep running on the path of least resistance. They forget to check for signs marking the true course. And sure enough, their off-course wandering becomes suddenly apparent, leaving them to wonder how they could have gone so wrong.

This happened to me at mile 95 of a 100-mile race. I was having a difficult time and wished for it to be over. In the wee hours of the morning and coming off the last mountain, I overtook another competitor. Our paces matched and we started talking to pass the time. We missed the last turn and ended up running several extra miles in the wrong direction. What a blow! We felt stupid as we retraced our steps. We had followed each other into a runner's nightmare.

Now, on Christmas Eve, the world falls silent as carols are sung and candles flicker in hushed sanctuaries. We think about Mary and Joseph trying to find a place to rest while the shepherds mind their flocks. And when we sing "We Three Kings," I wonder about their journey.

No Gazetteer maps. No GPS navigation. No lit roadways. So how did these Wise Men from the East find their way? They relentlessly followed the star. If the star was in front of them, they were on course. They could be confident that their way was true. They were destined to arrive at the house of the young child despite the long, long journey.

If we fail to follow the Star that still shines, we will be miserably lost. So take your bearings and set your course: fix your eyes on Jesus Christ alone.

After they had heard the king, they went on their way, and the star they had seen in the east went ahead of them until it stopped over the place where the child was. When they saw the star, they were overjoyed. (Matthew 2:9, 10)

Daily challenge:
Be sure that what you follow is a true course marking.

Christmas Clutter

Person by person, the house came to life, albeit it slowly. Long gone were the days of children rushing to rip open the gifts under the tree. Rather, the kids and cousins are now grown and appeared to be more interested in sleep than in an early morning gift exchange. So it was this morning. By the time we made coffee and cinnamon rolls and settled into our chairs, it was nearly 11:00 a.m.

It was a lovely time that concluded with a phone ringing inside a wrapped package. My niece, who had been begging for a fancy new phone seemed confused. Finally, after some teasing, she understood that the phone was hers—with one catch. She did not get to text the first word before her room was completely cleaned. Now, that was going to require a Christmas miracle!

Messy cannot begin to describe the room. The floor was not visible and the bed was piled high with clothes, books, papers . . . you name it. My niece was overwhelmed. In fact, I, the organization queen, was equally overwhelmed. But I promised her I would help. And help I did for the next eight hours. After six huge garbage bags filled to the brim with junk or giveaways left the tiny space, the room was returned to the land of the living. And my niece? She is happily texting her friends as I write.

Now that I'm finally sitting still and reflecting on the day, it certainly was productive. But what does all this have to do with such a sacred holiday?

God is a God of order. The entire universe is winding down. It proceeds from complex to simple—order to disorder . . . my niece's room a prime example. And why is that? Ultimately, it's because of sin. Left to our own devices, we can do nothing to restore order. And that's why Christ had to come.

Am I saying that Christ came so that we can have clean rooms? Not really. But the truth is, our lives are destined for as much disarray as that room unless we find focus and purpose in Christ.

Bring focus to a world in chaos.

> But everything should be done in a fitting and orderly way.
> (I Corinthians 14:40)

Daily challenge:
Are you living a chaotic life? Ask God to help you bring order into your life.
Merry Christmas!

Children

Like so many families, there was traveling to do and the traffic was flying—and we were not in an aircraft. Flying, that is, until a mile or two before a toll booth. Brake lights lit up like Christmas bulbs. It reminded us of how much we liked our country living. Nevertheless, we arrived safely, to the great joy of my mother.

One of my younger brothers had driven from South Carolina and his twin and family arrived shortly thereafter. Cousins home from college dropped in for supper. The condo quickly filled with suitcases, sleeping bags and wrapped packages. Dinner was noisy and wonderful, with multiple conversations going on at once. Had snow been gently falling outside, it could have been a Norman Rockwell moment.

As I looked around that room, I thought of my parents' rich heritage. I grew up in a house filled with love. My parents adored each other and their Lord. They demanded—and patterned—excellence and hard work. I am what I am today in large part due to them.

I wonder what family gatherings will look like in ten, fifteen or twenty years. Will the boys be bringing wives along? How many grandchildren will there be? What will their lives be like and where will they live? But, I wonder if they will remember their childhood with fondness. Will they have put into practice what we tried so hard to teach: perseverance, kindness, thankfulness and a heart set on the Lord?

Sometimes I fret. I want to preach at them—tell them again and again what I think they should know and how they should behave. But what I fail to realize is that no amount of reasoning on my part can effect change if God has not first opened their hearts. These imperfect but wonderful kids I look at across the table are not mine. They are rentals. In the end, my role is more and more becoming that of a support person—prayer support. Ultimately, it's God's problem to figure out what to do with them.

"Oh, that their hearts would be inclined to fear me and keep all my commands always, so that it might go well with them and their children forever!" (Deuteronomy 5:29)

Daily challenge:
If you get discouraged with your children, just think back to what your parents had to deal with. There is hope after all.

Good Value

Ah. Vacation feels so good! Though bodies were spread over every inch of the condo, we must have slept well. The clock said 8:30 when I finally pried open my eyes. After a run with my brother and family, we decided to hit the "Share and Care" thrift shop, a Mennonite ministry. The outing has reached near pilgrimage proportions. Without fail, we set apart time to shop whenever we get together.

This time, we were greeted by a newly organized store. New dressing rooms had been added and the endless racks of pre-owned clothing arranged into departments— men's, women's, children's, shoes and the like. A price-tag system had even been added. The improvements made it easier to shop. But one thing remained unchanged: the distinctive smell. It's not really objectionable, just predictably similar to your Grandmother's stuffy coat closet.

Milling around the store with other bargain-hunting shoppers, I perused the racks of previously-owned merchandise. Some were ugly and outdated. But with a little effort, discovering a respectable name-brand item made it all worthwhile.

Since I had just purged my closet, I was not looking for clothes. However, on the far wall, purses and handbags hung from hooks. There were at least a hundred, maybe double that. Big ones, little ones, green and blue ones, leather, cloth and plastic. But hanging behind a full row of bags, I spied a leather-and-cloth tote—a Liz Claiborne label. The inside was well compartmentalized to hold cell phones, wallets and make-up. It was absolutely perfect and had it not been for a tissue hiding in the corner, I would have thought it was new. At $6.50, this bag that normally sells for ten times that amount was a great value.

The value of anything is understandably subjective. Credit-card commercials like to tout value. I'm sure you've seen them. After rattling off the prices of this and that, the punch line always lists some intangible quality, finishing with "Priceless." In other words, the end result has sufficient "value" to offset the cost.

In a society that places so much value on material things, it's too easy to get our value system all mixed up. Let's not be shortsighted.

For in Christ Jesus neither circumcision nor uncircumcision has any
value. The only thing that counts is faith expressing itself through
love. (Galatians 5:6)

Daily challenge:
Be careful that our actions accurately reflect our true values.

The Amaryllis Lesson

In the corner of my mother's sun room sits an amaryllis plant. Half in the ground and half out, a strong, sturdy stem recently emerged from the orange-sized bulb, a necessary precursor to a beautiful flower. My brother, Dan, observed my curiosity and related the following lesson.

Shortly after a painful divorce, he had been given an amaryllis bulb. "The life cycle of that plant parallels the cycle of our lives," he began to explain. The bulb, in order to "live" again, had to "die." This period of dormancy was necessary to store up energy for the next phase of living.

Taking that lesson to heart, he planted the bulb and watched it sprout and produce a large and colorful flower. He appreciated this miracle and was disappointed, but not surprised, when it eventually faded away. Soon enough, as the cooler weather settled in, he forgot all about that solitary bulb. He forgot, that is, until the next spring when instead of one shoot, multiple stalks poked their way through the dirt. He had not counted on the fact that a healthy bulb could reproduce itself, offering not one but an attractive clump of flowers.

As he continued to think about his beloved amaryllis plants, Dan used alliteration to cement the spiritual lesson. He assigned the "G" to stand for the grind of life: it can beat you down and bury you. But the escape starts with "R" for "read." There is little growth if you fail to be a student of the Scriptures. "O" symbolizes "obey" and "W" for *Wow!*, an expression of joy at the end result of incredible growth.

But personal growth is not the only lesson learned. Once that bulb was involved in growing, the natural result was replication. The life of that one bulb gave rise to numerous others, each capable of producing the same kind of beauty.

Each time Dan sees an amaryllis, he is reminded how God's grace guides us through periods of darkness to raise us to become something beautiful. The next time you feel buried deep in grief or smothered by difficulties, just remember that God is strengthening you for a beautiful life.

But grow in the grace and knowledge of our Lord and Savior Jesus Christ. To him be glory both now and forever! Amen. (II Peter 3:18)

Daily challenge:
When all seems dark and dead, don't panic. God is developing in you the strength for a vibrant life.

A Brain Girdle

Just as Old Man Winter nips at our noses, resolution time is nipping at our heels. At two days and counting until the calendar flips the final page, weight loss and exercise top many lists. Year after year, we get excited about eating more fruits and veggies, cutting down on sugar and fat and nixing late-night snacking. We swear we'll develop "abs of steel" and do some flab firming. And sometimes we even write down our resolutions as if the ink bares some mystical power, enabling us to keep our freshly-made promises.

One thing's for sure: promises are a whole lot easier to make than to keep. In reality, most of our resolutions are admirable. On the long ride back from my mom's house Gary and I talked about our goals for the coming year. I want to take another stab at reading through the chronological Bible. My resolve failed me other years. I also desire to establish mentoring relationships with younger women. And, I want to serve in unique ways.

But what will it take to do this? It takes a *girding* (an old KJV term) of the mind. Our minds can run uncontrolled, just like a kid on a sugar rampage. But we must confine and manage our thoughts. I envision a girdle squishing my head. Not pretty. But, it would be like a compression bandage holding in the contents and providing protection, much like a dressing on a wound. John Gill, the theologian, makes commentary on I Peter 1:13: "do you apply your minds, and diligently attend unto them, in opposition to all loose and vagrant thoughts of the mind, about other things: give yourselves up wholly to them, meditate upon them, employ yourselves in them, and about them . . .." That's a tall order . . . but it doesn't end there.

We also need to be sober—self-controlled. Again, Gill explains it this way: "which is not only opposed to intemperance in eating and drinking, which greatly disqualifies for the above readiness and attention, but also to a being inebriated with the cares of this life, which choke the word, and make it unfruitful, and lead men into temptation, and many foolish and hurtful lusts, and from the faith of Christ . . .."

We have no idea what the new year may bring. But, we know that it will be rocky if we can't get the girdle around our heads.

Therefore, prepare your minds for action; be self-controlled; set your
hope fully on the grace to be given you when Jesus Christ is revealed
. . . "Be holy, because I am holy." (I Peter 1:13, 16b)

Daily challenge:
Resolve to have "mind-control" by limiting exposure time.

Peace in Trouble

As the sun rose higher, the day became unseasonably warm. The sky was a brilliant blue, a light breeze fluttered the tall grass and the resident birds sang a cheerful tune. It was a "peaceful, easy feeling," as The Eagles song goes. But as I worked around the house, catching snippets of the TV news, it was anything but.

The reports showed tanks lined up and jets screaming overhead. Dust from the bombings muddied the air as civilians rushed away hoping to find protection. Mothers lamented over their dead children as fathers pumped fists in anger. Certainly, *peace* was not the word of the day.

The conflict was occurring in Palestinian Gaza, Israel's retaliation for Hamas' cease-fire breach of launching thousands of rockets into Israel. Reportedly, more than 360 Palestinian lives had been lost, about twenty of them children. And although the death toll in Israel from the Hamas rockets is not as high, the toll is evident: constant terror from the relentless attacks.

Certainly, the absence of peace in the Middle East is as old as the times of Abraham and Moses, Joshua and the prophets. And there is likely no easy conflict resolution, no matter whose name is at the top of the political ladder. When I traveled to Gaza as a perfusionist in 2003, I saw first hand the mayhem and destruction that previous conflicts wrought on the area. But political peace is not the only peace that we need be concerned about.

Jesus himself ran into trouble. Such was the hatred against Him that He was crucified on that rugged cross at age thirty-three. He did no wrong and yet invited the anger of the mobs and the self-righteous religious leaders of the day. Should we be surprised when our world doesn't understand us, scoffing and ridiculing a Biblical world view? Probably not.

I wonder what trouble I might run into with the coming year. Perhaps there will be conflicts because of my faith. And maybe I will become afflicted with disease or a family catastrophe. It's possible we could lose all our earthy possessions in a fire or financial crisis. I pray not . . . but all these may be part of God's plan.

Regardless, I can have hope, because I know the One in whom all hope resides.

"I have told you these things, so that in me you may have peace. In this world you will have trouble. But take heart! I have overcome the world." (John 16:33)

Daily challenge:
Whether trouble comes or goes, turn your heart toward heaven.

The End . . . or Is It a Beginning?

It's hard to believe that this is my 366th devotional story—I would have to pick a Leap Year! When I began the project, I did so with much trepidation. Would the busyness of life impede my ability to write? It hasn't been easy. But if nothing else, it has been the most important project I've ever tackled.

I am not a spiritual giant. I've always struggled with maintaining devotional times and a structured prayer strategy. It's not that I didn't want to or failed to understand their importance; I just got diverted for one lousy reason or another. What made me think I could find spiritual truth every day of the year?

As I look back through the eyes of my writing, I'm impressed by God's faithfulness. There have been mountaintop highs and deep ravine lows. I wonder if I have been "too honest"—revealed too much. But then I think, "Anything else would not be true life."

The Christian walk is not a cookie-cutter activity. Sometimes we take a new day for granted—just another same old, same old. However, if there is one thing that I learned this past year, it is this: We cannot afford to see God and His truth as remote entities, only to be called into action in a time of crisis. We must purpose to set our minds on *whatever is true, whatever is noble, whatever is right, whatever is pure, whatever is lovely, whatever is admirable—if anything is excellent or praiseworthy— think about such things* (Philippians 4:8).

Many nights, the clock ticked closer and closer to my midnight deadline. I stared at my keyboard panicking that I had nothing to write. And then in the stillness, an idea stirred, prompting me to place fingers on keys. Sometimes I knew where the story was going. Sometimes it took a turn I did not anticipate. I wasn't always satisfied. At times, my stories seemed to be of little value. But more than once I was shocked to hear that what I thought to be dreadful met a need for an accountability partner. It proved that the Word of God, no matter how poorly conveyed, will not *"return void"* (Isaiah 55:11, KJV).

Thank you for sharing this year with me. I trust you have learned from my mistakes, been encouraged by God's faithfulness and been prompted to see truth even in life's mundane details. Carry on in the coming year.

This is what the LORD says—"Forget the former things; do not dwell on the past. See, I am doing a new thing!" (Isaiah 43:16a, 18, 19a)

Daily challenge:
Commit to keep a daily journal. Write down one truth that God brings
to your mind each day. Your worldview will change when you look
through God's eyes.